A GAMECOCK ODYSSEY

ALAN PIERCY

A
GAMECOCK
ODYSSEY

UNIVERSITY OF
SOUTH CAROLINA
SPORTS IN THE
INDEPENDENT ERA

THE UNIVERSITY OF
SOUTH CAROLINA PRESS

CONTENTS

11
A NEW WORLD ORDER

ILLUSTRATIONS

Are you kidding me? I was unavoidably, irretrievably hooked.

On those much-anticipated winter nights when there was a home basket-ball game, Dad would park somewhere along Main Street, south of the State House, in front of Sandy's Hotdogs with its ever-present chili fragrance or the South Carolina bookstore with its Gamecock-emblazoned sign. We would walk past the law school, down to the fluorescent-lit pedestrian tunnel that runs under Assembly Street, coming out at the north side of the Carolina Coliseum—the House that Frank Built. The grand structure was bathed in light and elegant and revealed itself by degree as we approached the end of the tunnel. The air was brisk on our faces, our hands stuffed in pockets against the cold.

We walked through the glass doors, handing our tickets to the genial doormen in garnet blazers, and were enveloped by the warmth and buzz of the place. The alluring buttered aroma of popcorn perfumed the air, and the spirited brass of the USC pep band washed over us as we stepped through the turnstiles to the notes of "Go Carolina" and "Step to the Rear." The sound of sneakers squeaking on the old tartan floor told us warm-ups were underway, and the retired jerseys of Roche and English and Joyce swayed from the mas-sive rafters overhead as we walked through the double doors separating the concourse from the arena proper. The exquisitely bearded Gene McKay's rich baritone rang over the loudspeaker, welcoming us to Carolina Coliseum and Frank McGuire Arena. We often arrived early, just to soak in the mystique of the place before tipoff, and I imagined what it must have been like to witness those powerhouse McGuire teams.

I hero-worshipped Rogers for his Heisman exploits and Fredrick for his high-flying dunks, but Jimmy Foster was the guy I wanted to be. The blue-collar hustler and battler, the whirling dervish of rebounds and trash buckets. Foster played with a wild abandon, once described by the *State*'s Bob Gillespie as "captain of the elbows-hustle-and-floor-burn brigade." I modeled my own game after his, wearing black sweatbands positioned on my scrawny forearms just so, looking to take charges and scrap for loose balls like he did. Though my lack of talent and size led to more flailing about than points and rebounds, I strived to emulate number 44, much as Protestant boys a decade earlier mimicked the great John Roche by performing the Catholic sign of the cross before free throws.

Foster was an undersized, six-foot-eight center as a freshman during the 1980–81 season under first-year coach Bill Foster (no relation) but moved to his natural position of power forward when seven-footer Mike Brittain arrived the following year. Foster's career at South Carolina was a brilliant one, finishing as the third-leading scorer in program history behind John Roche and Alex English. He was (and is) one of five Gamecocks (including Lee Collins, Alex English, Tom Owens, and Joe Smith) to reach both the thousand-point and thousand-rebound thresholds. He led his team in rebounding all four seasons—the only Gamecock player ever to do so before Michael Carrera equaled the feat decades later. He led the team in scoring as a sophomore, junior, and senior, second only to national scoring champion Fredrick as a freshman. The superlatives go on.

Foster off the court was another matter. Jimmy was a hot mess.

He would tell you the same. He was affable and popular and open to the illicit favors that often came to prominent players in the form of cash and free meals and comped hotel rooms at Myrtle Beach. And Jimmy was not bashful about milking it for all it was worth. It landed him, and the program, in hot water when he failed to return a borrowed coupe as agreed to a local Mercedes dealer. Legal troubles ensued. More about that later.

Jimmy played professional ball for a time in Australia but soon lost interest. Unable to return home because of an uncertain legal situation, he vanished, but not before revealing a number of violations within Bill Foster's program, which led to an NCAA investigation and, ultimately, sanctions against Gamecock basketball.

Foster resurfaced in a 1997 phone call to Gillespie of the *State*, wherein he professed a desire to return home, an eagerness to mend fences. His sincerity was compelling. He told of his wandering life since basketball. They were stories, as Gillespie put it then, worthy of a pulp fiction novel. Then, just as quickly, Foster vanished again.

I thought of him from time to time over the years, wondering where he ended up, what had become of that whirling dervish. Given his prominence in the USC record books, his name is conspicuously absent from the school's athletics hall of fame, in no small measure because of the trouble he left behind. I often thought his exploits, both on the court and off, would make for compelling reading. Maybe a novel.

The more I thought of Jimmy's story, the more I wanted to write about it. But as I began to revisit his time at Carolina, I uncovered other stories, other interesting tidbits, other characters. I soon realized that Foster was just part of a much larger story. The writing project expanded, eventually to include a period of two decades. It became a history of Gamecock athletics in the years between the ACC and the SEC, 1971 to 1991.

But really, the story goes beyond that. It is about, among other things, a southern college in the immediate post-desegregation years and the evolution of women's sports, from club level competition to varsity status in the wake of Title IX legislation. It is a story about the rise and influence of television money, of conference realignment, of the early arms race of facilities and coaches' salaries. In many ways it is the story of two decades of collegiate athletics and societal change, as seen through the lens of the University of South Carolina. Beyond that, any history of USC is by its very nature, a history of Columbia. The two are interwoven and inseparable.

But as much as all of those things, this book is a love letter to my school and my hometown. It covers what was often a difficult period in the history of Gamecock athletics—a period journalists and fans have often referred to as "the wilderness." It is a lost era in some ways, bookended by the incandescent rivalries that defined the Atlantic Coast Conference years and the lucrative stability of three decades in the Southeastern Conference.

There is a sizable segment of Gamecock fans who have no living memory of USC athletics outside of SEC membership. For them this is a story of what came before and how we got to where we are. For those of us who lived through it, it a chance to settle into the cozy confines of Frank McGuire Arena and Sarge Frye Field once more and to revisit the magnificent characters and world-class athletes who wore garnet and black and the coaches who led them along that long wilderness road.

1

Storms in the Southland

Why South Carolina Left the Atlantic Coast Conference

> The Atlantic Coast Conference was formed by the four North Carolina members for the benefit of the North Carolina members. They needed USC, Clemson, Maryland and Virginia (a late joiner) to fill out a decent conference. But the outsiders were supposed to be step-children, to be seen and not heard.
>
> —Editorial, *Columbia State,* March 17, 1971

I t was a Saturday evening, March 13, 1971. Temperatures were warm, in the upper sixties. Bradford pears, with their pungent, white blooms, were beginning to flower in Greensboro. Jessamine and honeysuckle, too, perfumed the early evening air as fans of both the North Carolina and South Carolina men's basketball teams made their way, tickets in hand, to the newly renovated Greensboro Coliseum. The air was peaceful, belying the coming storms both on and off the basketball court. Spring would officially arrive a week later, but winter had a score yet to settle.

South Carolina finished the 1970–71 regular season second in the ACC behind North Carolina, and as many had predicted, the two schools met in the conference tournament final. The Gamecocks had dispatched Maryland 71–63 in the tournament's opening round and dominated NC State 69–56 in the semifinal. Likewise the Tar Heels had taken care of business, eliminating Clemson and Virginia in rounds one and two.

After a game that saw the Gamecocks struggle mightily from the floor, UNC began to edge ahead late in the second half. With a 46–40 lead at the 4:34 mark, Tar Heel coach Dean Smith deployed his signature "Four Corners" offense, which was engineered not to produce points but to milk the clock and keep the ball out of the hands of the opposing team. It would be years before the shot clock was implemented in college basketball, and many teams used this strategy to slow down high-powered opposing offenses. Earlier in the season in a game at College Park, Maryland, the Terrapins used a similar strategy to neutralize John Roche and the Gamecocks, resulting in a 4–3 half-time score before things picked up in the second half.

With no shot clock, the Gamecocks were forced to foul. UNC needed only to hit free throws to preserve its lead and escape with a win, something Smith's Tar Heels had nearly perfected in those years. Remarkably, UNC missed the front end of five one-and-one opportunities down the stretch. The Gamecocks responded, pulling within a point, 49–48, with 1:04 remaining. The Tar Heels and Gamecocks exchanged free throws, and the game was still within a point, 50–49, with forty-five seconds left. After a steal by USC's Bob Carver, John Ribock was fouled on an attempted layup, making one of two free throws to knot it at 50 with thirty-nine seconds remaining. Over the next eighteen seconds, the Gamecocks missed from the floor and the Tar Heels' George Karl missed the front end of a one-and-one opportunity.

The Tar Heels went up by one, 51–50, on another Karl free throw, but he did not connect on the bonus shot, and USC's Rick Aydlett rebounded with twenty seconds remaining, passing the ball to guard Kevin Joyce. As Joyce drove the baseline for a shot, he was tied up by UNC's Dedmon, resulting in a jump ball.

Like the shot clock, the rule of alternating possessions was years away, so six-foot-three Joyce would have to vie for the tip versus six-foot-ten Dedmon. To compound the mismatch, Joyce was coming off a leg injury earlier in the season. With a one-point lead and Dedman sure to control the tip, Tar Heel fans were planning their postgame celebrations. McGuire claimed he saw a UNC assistant with a pair of scissors for the postgame net cutting.

Six seconds remained. McGuire called a timeout to talk through strategies for stealing the ball after UNC controlled the tip, which seemed a foregone conclusion given Dedmon's seven-inch height advantage. McGuire told Joyce, "Jump to the moon, kid."

During the timeout the atmosphere in Greensboro Coliseum roiled with dark malice and an intemperate energy. UNC and USC pep bands alternated fight songs, filling the air with the strains of brass and a drumming battle rhythm. Confident Tar Heel fans awaited another title. Gamecock fans agonized through the timeout, hoping for a miracle while bracing for the familiar gut punch of disappointment. Not a soul left the arena to get a head start on traffic. This was not one of those games. Fans had been standing most of the second half, living and dying with each shot and every frenzied loose-ball scramble, palms clammy, breathing shallow. The horn sounded, and officials summoned the teams to the floor.

Six seconds.

As the teams took their places for the jump, Joyce sensed a hint of complacency from Dedmon. He also noticed, perhaps assuming Dedmon would control the tip, no UNC players lined up between the Gamecocks' six-foot-ten Tom Owens and the UNC basket. As the official tossed the ball, Joyce jumped "like he had springs in his legs," as McGuire later said, managing to tip the ball to Owens, whose unopposed shot caromed off the glass and into the basket. The Gamecocks took a 52–51 lead, and as the final two seconds ticked away, a scrambling UNC squad failed to get off a shot.

Pandemonium ensued among the Gamecock faithful. Bob Fulton, the legendary Gamecock radio announcer, described the jubilation of the moment as the garnet-clad Gamecocks rushed the court in celebration: "The ballgame is all over—they're going wild on the court!" South Carolina partisans among the 15,170 inside Greensboro Coliseum were left jubilant, if emotionally drained, after the dramatic finish.

By virtue of winning the tournament, South Carolina represented the ACC in the NCAA tournament, which included only twenty-five teams at the time. USC was slotted in the East Regional Division, before a hostile and vocally anti-Gamecock crowd in Raleigh's Reynolds Coliseum. The Gamecocks matched up against a powerful University of Pennsylvania team, riding a twenty-seven-game winning streak, and ranked third in the nation. The partisan Tobacco Road crowd cheered not the ACC champion but Penn, illustrating the festering bitterness between USC and its ACC peers.

Further illustrating that bitterness was end-of-season voting for ACC coach of the year and player of the year among the North Carolina–dominated voting media. McGuire, despite winning the ACC championship and guiding his team to an ACC-leading sixth-place finish in national polls, did not factor into voting. UNC's Smith won out, with Virginia's Bill Gibson placing second.

John Roche, who won player-of-the-year honors after his sophomore and junior seasons, was denied the honor in '71 as media members voted overwhelmingly for Wake Forest's Charlie Davis. This despite South Carolina's twenty- and fifteen-point wins over Wake in the regular season. United Press International and *Basketball Weekly* selected Roche as a first-team All-American, and he received first-team votes from NBA coaches for the annual college all-star squad.

In a disappointing NCAA tournament showing, South Carolina went into halftime down just a point, but Penn dominated the second half to win going away, 79–64. The tournament hosted consolation games in those days, and USC came up short in that one as well, losing a high-scoring affair to Fordham, 100–90.[1] Just over three months later, the University of South Carolina relinquished its membership in the Atlantic Coast Conference.

How did it come to that? How did the University of South Carolina go from winning the ACC basketball championship to withdrawing from a conference it helped form eighteen years earlier? The story really begins in 1964, when USC lured Frank McGuire to Columbia. And it happened completely by chance.

The Irishman Comes South (Again)

McGuire had enjoyed highly successful stints at two schools prior to coming to Columbia: his alma mater, St. John's University, and the University of North Carolina. He had taken the Redmen to the national championship game in 1952, where they lost in the final to a high-powered Kansas Jayhawks team coached by legendary Phog Allen. Allen had played at Kansas, where he was mentored by James A. Naismith, the inventor of basketball. The '52 Kansas squad featured a senior guard who would have a close association with McGuire in future years, Dean Smith.

UNC lured McGuire to Chapel Hill following the 1952 season. The Tar Heels were not a recognized basketball power at the time and were attempting to match the success of rival NC State under coach Everett Case. Catch up McGuire did. By the 1956–57 season, his Tar Heels compiled a 32–0 record, achieving the first undefeated conference slate in ACC history and winning that season's national championship.

In winning the 1957 title, McGuire evened the score against Kansas, winning a thrilling triple-overtime championship game. Seven-foot-one Kansas sophomore Wilt Chamberlain scored twenty-three points and pulled down fourteen rebounds in a losing effort that day. Chamberlain was recognized as the most outstanding player of that year's Final Four despite the loss. He described the loss to McGuire's Tar Heels as the most painful of his life. Chamberlain and McGuire crossed paths again a few years later in the NBA.[2]

While at UNC, McGuire established his famed recruiting pipeline, bringing New York City talent to Chapel Hill and quickly establishing a basketball culture at the school. It was a strategy he successfully duplicated at South Carolina in the coming years.

McGuire enjoyed continued success at UNC until 1961, when the NCAA found his program guilty of recruiting violations. UNC chancellor William Aycock, who was concerned that sports had taken too prominent a role at the school, was determined to exert more control over the athletics department and particularly over McGuire's basketball program.

After the NCAA announced sanctions against UNC following their investigation, Aycock cautioned McGuire that he must bring his program under control. When two Tar Heel players were later caught up in a point-shaving scandal, McGuire saw the writing on the wall. Other points of conflict had developed between McGuire and Aycock and with UNC athletics director Chuck Erickson, including the school's failure to replace the outdated Woolen Gymnasium with a modern field house.

In May 1961 McGuire offered his resignation, which Aycock accepted. In parting McGuire recommended assistant Dean Smith for the top job. Aycock hired Smith, who went on to a brilliant career as Tar Heel coach.

During the 1961–62 season, McGuire moved to the NBA, where he coached the Philadelphia Warriors. The starting center on that team? Wilt Chamberlain. It was during this season that Chamberlain achieved his legendary 100-point game on March 2, 1962, versus the New York Knicks. Chamberlain averaged an unbelievable 50.4 points and 25.6 rebounds that season. The Warriors lost in the Eastern Conference finals to the dominant Boston Celtics on a last-second basket to end their season. When Warriors owner Eddie Gottlieb sold the franchise to a group of businessmen in San Francisco at season's end, McGuire opted not to move his family to the West Coast.

In three stops McGuire had established himself as a coaching blue blood. He was the only coach in NCAA history to take two schools to a basketball national championship game. Since that time both Rick Pitino (Kentucky and Louisville) and Dean Smith protégé Roy Williams (Kansas and UNC) have accomplished that feat.[3]

For the next two years, McGuire took a hiatus from coaching, working in a public relations job in New York City. It was a time he said was good for him, providing an opportunity to rest and mature. He also discovered that he still had a desire to coach. Now fifty, McGuire was ready for a new challenge.

The great Bob Fulton, "Voice of the Gamecocks" on radio for over forty years, detailed in his 1995 biography, *Frank McGuire: The Life and Times of a Basketball Legend,* the story of how McGuire ended up at South Carolina. As with many things in life, chance played a part.

Fulton related the story of Jeff Hunt, a Columbia businessman as well as an avid Gamecock fan and booster. One morning Hunt flew his private plane to Asheville, where he met friends for breakfast at Buck's Restaurant prior to a business meeting later that day. The group assembled for breakfast included restaurant owner John "Buck" Buchanan. Buchanan was a University of North Carolina supporter and had become a friend of McGuire's during his tenure at UNC. When Hunt walked into the restaurant that morning, McGuire was there for breakfast with the group.

Voice of South Carolina Gamecocks football Bob Fulton in announcer's booth at Williams-Brice Stadium, October 1972. Courtesy of the *State* Newspaper Archive, Richland County Public Library.

McGuire and Hunt struck up a conversation, during which McGuire asked what Hunt was doing in Asheville. Hunt, a heavy machinery dealer, told him that he had come to inspect a tractor he was considering for trade-in. A curious McGuire asked if he could ride along with Hunt to watch him inspect the tractor.

During the drive, Hunt said to McGuire, "Why don't you come and coach at the University of South Carolina?" Hunt was surprised by the reaction. He had expected McGuire to shrug off the question, but McGuire sounded vaguely interested, as if he would come if there were not already a coach in place. Hunt relayed the rest of the story:

> So, I pulled over to the side of the road, and I got serious with him. I said "Coach, I don't think we're gonna have a coach very long. I know for a fact that they're going to appoint an interim

coach." McGuire said, "If they're gonna let him go—and you're sure of that—I'm not out for someone else's job—let me hear from you." I said, "Give me your phone number. Can I have somebody call you?" He said, "Oh, no. I won't deal with anybody else but you."

Hunt was correct about the interim coach. Following the twelfth game of the 1963–64 season, USC appointed assistant coach Dwane Morrison as interim head coach. A USC letterman, Morrison replaced Chuck Noe, who had resigned during the season, citing "nervous exhaustion."

Following his conversation with McGuire, Hunt contacted Sol Blatt Jr. of the USC Board of Trustees. Blatt was the chairman of the board's athletic committee. He was also the son of Sol Blatt Sr., Speaker of House in the South Carolina General Assembly and arguably the most powerful politician in the state at the time. Together they wielded great influence over the affairs of the university.

The Blatts hailed from Barnwell, in the southwestern part of the state, as did Edgar A. Brown. Brown was a powerful state senator and served as senate majority leader for a period of time. Because of their power and influence across the Palmetto State, this group was known as the "Barnwell Ring." They were enthusiastic supporters of the university and its athletic teams but often employed heavy-handed tactics, as McGuire would discover in years to come.

Because McGuire refused to discuss the opening by telephone, a meeting was arranged at a New York City hotel between McGuire, Blatt, and USC president Tom Jones. The meeting went well, and a second meeting was planned to finalize details for USC's coaching offer. To McGuire's surprise, a subsequent meeting took place in Barnwell, not Columbia, giving him some insight as to why South Carolinians often referred to Barnwell as the de facto state capital.

During the Barnwell meeting, attended by Jones, Blatt, and several other board of trustee members, McGuire formally accepted the head coach position at the University of South Carolina. He was the university's third coach in five months. No contract was signed, and no specific salary was discussed. McGuire simply told Blatt to "just pay me what you pay Marvin." Marvin

USC football coach Marvin Bass (left) welcomes Frank McGuire
to campus in 1964. Courtesy of the *State* Newspaper Archive,
Richland County Public Library.

Bass was the head football coach at USC and McGuire's closest contact at
South Carolina, as he had been an assistant football coach at UNC during
McGuire's tenure there.

McGuire's lone demand beyond the vague mention of salary was that the
university construct a modern arena. At the time USC played in the antiquated Carolina Field House, which, along with Clemson's Fike Field House,
was among the venues most reviled by ACC coaches for its cramped and
inhospitable environs. Carolina Field House was built in 1927 and held only
3,200, which could not accommodate the student body (6,920 in 1964), much
less other area fans. The failure to build a modern arena had been one of the
main points of contention between McGuire and UNC. Blatt and the trustees
provided ample assurances of a new arena in Columbia.

The March 13, 1964, edition of the *State* declared in a banner headline that
McGuire had taken on dual roles at the university, that of associate athletics
director and "cage coach."[4]

McGuire, energized by a two-year hiatus and perhaps with a sizable chip on his shoulder, quickly set about building his new program. His first team (1964–65) took its lumps, finishing 6–17 (2–12 ACC). But he successfully reestablished his New York City recruiting pipeline, bringing in highly regarded recruits Skip Harlika, Jack Thompson, Skip Kickey, and Frank Standard. As freshmen were ineligible for varsity play at the time, the "Four Horsemen," as they would come to be called, were not an immediate help, but McGuire was building the foundation for future success.[5]

As the season drew to a close in the ACC tournament in Raleigh, USC achieved its best performance of the season, pushing ninth-ranked Duke to the final buzzer before coming just shy of the upset, 62–60. Meanwhile the freshmen team won fourteen of sixteen games, providing a tantalizing preview of what was to come. Gamecock fans were already looking forward to McGuire's second stanza.

To compound the excitement, that spring McGuire landed his highest-profile recruit since coming to Carolina in six-foot-eight center Mike Grosso of Raritan, New Jersey. Grosso averaged thirty points and thirty-one rebounds during his senior season at Bridgewater-Ruritan High School and received scholarship offers from more than forty colleges, including ACC blueblood Duke. Grosso's commitment to McGuire and the Gamecocks set in motion a chain of events that caused great acrimony between South Carolina and other ACC schools and would pave the road to USC's eventual conference exit.

The Dietzel Era Begins

"A New Era in USC Athletics Begins," proclaimed the headline of the *State* newspaper on the morning of April 7, 1966. At age forty-one Paul Dietzel came to Columbia from the US Military Academy, where he led his Army team to a 21–18–2 record in four seasons. He was the first nongraduate of the Military Academy to become its head football coach.

Prior to his post in West Point, Dietzel enjoyed a highly successful run of seven seasons in Baton Rouge, Louisiana, where he led the LSU Tigers to an overall 46–24–3 record and a national championship to conclude the 1958 season. The '58 championship team followed a rocky start for Dietzel in the Bayou during which his first three teams all had losing seasons and a three-year record of 11–17–2. Those teams finished no higher than seventh in the Southeastern Conference.

To address the fatigue of his players in an era when many played both offense and defense, Dietzel devised a platoon system prior to the '58 campaign, in which he substituted eleven players as a unit. The second platoon defense was known as the "Chinese Bandits," a rugged if less talented squad who played with great effort, becoming fan favorites and LSU legends.

The platoon system, unconventional though it was, worked. Dietzel's final four seasons at LSU were all winners, highlighted by the '58 championship team. The 1961 squad went 11–1, won a share of the SEC title, and brought home an Orange Bowl win over Colorado in Dietzel's final season at LSU.[6]

Tall and trim, with blue-gray eyes, wavy blond hair, and a boyish smile, Dietzel was movie star handsome. He possessed an infectious enthusiasm, a championship résumé, and represented another banner hire for the University of South Carolina.

It was the opportunity to take on the dual role of head football coach and athletics director that ultimately lured Dietzel to Carolina. In his opening press conference at the Rex Enright Athletic Center, affectionately known as the "Roundhouse" for its circular design, Dietzel fired a preemptive salvo at the South Carolina General Assembly. "I've worked in a state capital with a state university before, and I've learned that politicians are wonderful people. Those who aren't don't remain politicians very long. But I don't intend to tell them how to run their business." The implication was clear. Dietzel put everyone on notice that he would answer to one man and one man alone—the president of the university, Tom Jones.

Dietzel outlined a three-point plan to guide him in his new post. First, everything would be done by the rules. Second, Dietzel and Jones both wanted a winner. Third, the athletic department would operate in the black. It was a solid strategy. The first point, no doubt, addressed a controversy, which became Dietzel's first order of business upon stepping away from the press conference.

Just a few months later, the ACC concluded an investigation into recruiting improprieties within the football program under former head coach Marvin Bass. Dietzel, as directed by Jones, worked internally to cooperate with the conference during the later stages of the investigation, granting access to requested documents and interviews with former Bass players still with the program.

On July 30, 1966, the ACC released their report, which implicated USC for providing financial aid to three athletes who were ineligible to receive assistance because they did not meet the conference's minimum college board score to qualify for a scholarship (800 on the SAT). The players, two varsity and one freshman, were not named in the investigation by either USC or the ACC.

Reached for comment from his new post in Montreal, Bass took responsibility for the violations, going so far as to say that he had assisted the freshman player not with university scholarship money but out of his own pocket. Bass went on to speculate that Dietzel's role in the investigation and resulting penalties may have been of benefit to Dietzel himself. "If Coach Dietzel wanted to go in with a 1–9 record (rather than 5–5 before the forfeits) so he couldn't possibly do anything but improve it this season, I wish him luck. I hope he can live in good faith and look people in the eye. If I was going to conduct an investigation, I would have had the courtesy to contact the guy who was there before me." Bass later expressed regret over the remarks and shouldered all the blame for the violations.[7]

The ACC handed down stiff penalties, which included a $2,500 fine and, of greater consequence, voided wins over Wake Forest, NC State, Virginia, and Clemson. USC had won a share of the ACC title in 1965 along with Duke. The penalty cost the Gamecock program its first ever ACC title. NC State and Clemson, whose conference records improved to 5–2 by virtue of the forfeits, now claimed the ACC championship. For reasons that are unclear, Duke and South Carolina played one less conference game that season than did NC State and Clemson (USC did not play UNC, and Duke did not play Maryland, while the Wolfpack and Tigers played a full slate). Thus Duke, through no fault of its own, was robbed of a share of the title.

Even more consequential to Carolina's long-term affiliation with the ACC was the second of a four-part reprimand released by ACC commissioner Jim Weaver, on July 25, 1966, which read: "It is for this flagrant disregard for constitutional authority, that this office . . . declares that any student-athlete presently enrolled or incoming at the University of South Carolina whose eligibility is questioned be withheld from participation unless and until it is established to the complete satisfaction of the conference that there has been no violation in each individual case." It was tantamount to guilty until proven innocent. The mandate proved effective in ensnaring Frank McGuire's highest-rated recruit, Mike Grosso, as well as many of Dietzel's recruits in years to come. The restrictions outlined applied to the University of South Carolina and no other ACC institution.

Keeping the "Also-Rans" in Check: The Grosso Controversy

In his excellent 2011 volume, *ACC Basketball,* which chronicles the first two decades of the Atlantic Coast Conference, historian J. Samuel Walker manages to encapsulate the antipathy of the "Big Four" North Carolina programs, UNC, Duke, NC State, and Wake Forest, toward their conference step-siblings. The title of his sixth chapter, which documents the rise of Virginia, Maryland, Clemson, and, most notably, South Carolina, to competitiveness within the ACC, is titled "The Revolt of the Also-Rans."

Indeed South Carolina had not achieved particular distinction on the field or the court during its first thirteen years in the ACC. Between the conference's founding in 1953 and 1965, USC compiled conference records of 38–41–3 (.463) in football and, more dismally, 46–118 (.280) in basketball. Simply put, South Carolina was hungry for a winner and ready to ante up for the best coaches and, soon, the best facilities in the ACC. With McGuire and Dietzel now leading their respective programs, visions of championships took hold of coaches, players, and fans alike.

McGuire was firmly entrenched, one season under his belt with a fine sophomore class of Frank Standard, Jack Thompson, Skip Kickey, and Skip Harlicka ready to begin varsity play for the 1965–66 season. Three games into that season, he achieved the first of what would be many signature victories at USC in a thrilling 73–71 win against Duke at Carolina Field House. Although the Gamecocks finished with a losing tally of 11–13 on the season, the squad was competitive throughout and played with a toughness that was a hallmark of McGuire teams. It was McGuire's last losing season at South Carolina.

On the freshman team, meanwhile, Mike Grosso enjoyed a banner season, averaging 22.7 points and an unbelievable 26 rebounds per game. The

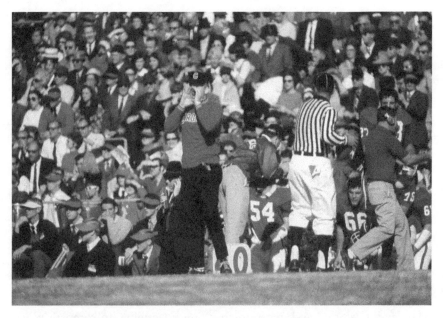

Football coach Paul Dietzel during the USC versus Clemson game in 1969. Courtesy of the *State* Newspaper Archive, Richland County Public Library.

freshman squad often enjoyed sellout crowds, unheard of before, and excitement continued to build around McGuire's program.

As Grosso led the freshman squad and Gamecock fans salivated over what was to come when he joined the varsity, a controversy unfolded over his eligibility. The ACC had adopted a rule in May 1964 that set a standard score of 800 on the SAT for incoming athletes to receive a scholarship. In Grosso's efforts to qualify for admission to South Carolina, his highest SAT score was a 789—high enough to earn admission into the school but not enough to earn a scholarship. Athletes scoring less than 800 on the SAT were permitted to play basketball or football, so long as they were not awarded a scholarship.

Grosso could have gone to any school of his choice outside of the ACC and qualified for a scholarship, but he wanted to play for McGuire. His family was of modest means, but his uncles owned a bar and grill in New Jersey where Grosso worked during the summers. The uncles agreed to pay Grosso's tuition until he could attain eligibility for a scholarship. Meanwhile Duke's athletics director, Eddie Cameron—who also chaired the conference basketball committee—maneuvered behind the scenes to encourage ACC commissioner Weaver to look deeper into Grosso's recruitment. Weaver had been uncomfortable with the Grosso situation but had no choice under the rules then in place but to allow Grosso to participate.

With Cameron's prompting, the ACC changed eligibility requirements to stipulate that a player must attain a minimum of 800 on the SAT to participate at all, not just to receive a scholarship. Although the action did not apply retroactively to Grosso, the controversy would not die. During Grosso's freshman season (1965–66), Cameron announced that Duke would refuse to play against South Carolina when Grosso moved up to varsity the following year, potentially forfeiting those two games to make a statement. Cameron's statement, according to him, was about upholding the spirit of the academic standards established by the conference. However, the personal acrimony between Cameron and McGuire, which intensified when Grosso spurned Duke for South Carolina, was obvious.

Meanwhile, as the investigation into violations within USC's football program unfolded, Weaver obtained the means he needed to head off Grosso's eligibility. In penning the sanctions levied against USC for the football team's violations, which would hold athletes "whose eligibility is questioned" by the conference ineligible for competition, Weaver cast a broad net, covering not just football but South Carolina's entire athletic program. Weaver's ruling was nebulous yet effective and clearly crafted with Grosso in mind.

Jones and McGuire, along with assistant athletics director George Terry, attended a meeting of the ACC executive committee at the Triangle Motel at Raleigh-Durham Airport on October 28, 1966, to appeal Weaver's decision on Grosso's eligibility. After meeting for four hours, executive committee head Ralph Fadum of NC State advised the USC contingent that the committee saw no cause to overrule Weaver's decision on Grosso. Neither Weaver nor Fadum provided an explanation regarding why Grosso was ruled ineligible. A November 7, 1966, article in *Sports Illustrated* titled "The Off-Court Uproar in Dixie" noted that McGuire had to be physically restrained by Jones following the ruling. McGuire saw the ruling as a personal vendetta against him by old

ACC enemies. Grosso, he believed, became an unfortunate pawn, with the start of his varsity career just weeks away.

In public appearances during the coming days, McGuire complained bitterly about the Grosso decision, calling ACC officials "skunks" on several occasions and adding that they "have forced me into the gutter with them." He insisted that the investigation and ruling arose from personal vendettas. His remarks drew sharp criticism and calls for a reprimand from coaches, athletics directors, and presidents of other ACC institutions. North Carolina State chancellor John Caldwell told Jones he had "some repair work" to do, adding that nothing short of an institutional apology could remedy the situation and insinuating that even that might not be enough.

Indeed the Grosso affair and McGuire's subsequent public disparagement of ACC officials had opened a deep chasm between South Carolina and the other member schools. Despite Jones's own misgivings about the ACC's handling of the Grosso affair, his mercurial basketball coach had become a loose cannon, putting USC's president in the awkward position of having to make amends on behalf of the university.

During a meeting of ACC presidents and athletics directors in early December 1966, Jones offered an apology for McGuire's comments, which he described as embarrassing both to the university and the conference. He went on to note that McGuire had been reprimanded, giving his personal guarantee that such behavior would not be repeated.

This mea culpa had the intended result of reducing tensions, but ACC officials did not reciprocate Jones's earnest attempts at reconciliation. Conference officials issued an unprecedented announcement that members could choose to cancel their basketball games with USC during the 1966–67 season without forfeit. Duke was the only school to take advantage of this option. Duke further opted not to play South Carolina during the 1966 football season. The two schools squared off on the baseball diamond during the spring of 1967, resulting in two wins by the Gamecocks.

The Grosso ruling prompted calls from university alumni to withdraw from the ACC. The clamor became boisterous enough that President Jones and McGuire issued a joint statement in which both supported continued membership in the ACC. This quelled a growing rebellion for the time being. But irreparable damage had been inflicted, both to the university's relations with its fellow conference members and to the perceived value of conference membership among South Carolina alumni and boosters.

USC fans saw the ruling as further evidence of political dominance by the North Carolina schools within the conference. The leaders involved, ACC commissioner Weaver of Wake Forest, ACC basketball committee chairman Cameron of Duke, and executive committee head Fadum of NC State, tended to bear that out. Indeed the power structure of the ACC remained firmly entrenched along Tobacco Road.

It would be naive to deny that politics were in play in the Grosso affair, given the Big Four's domination of the governing body and the bitter feuds between McGuire and those same conference leaders. Set against the backdrop of the Gamecocks' competitive emergence within the conference, elements of politics and spite among ACC leadership cannot be dismissed. However, it is helpful to set those elements aside and examine the facts surrounding Grosso's eligibility.

While Grosso was a high school senior in New Jersey, his SAT scores never reached 750, the minimum for competition in the ACC at the time of his recruitment. Upon his graduation he took the exams again, this time on the campus of the University of South Carolina. The Educational Testing Service (ETS) of Princeton, NJ, was the governing body that prepared and administered the board exam. ETS guidelines dictated that it would accept and recognize one institutionally administered college board exam. Grosso's first attempt at the SAT in Columbia resulted in a 706 score, still leaving him short of qualifying. This score was sent to the ACC offices and represented the only official score, according to ETS rules.

Grosso took the SAT once more in September 1965, again on the campus of the University of South Carolina. This time he scored 789, which would qualify him for competition in the ACC. Under the rules of the ETS, however, only one institutionally administered exam was recognized. Thus Grosso's second attempt was not recognized by the ETS and was not sent to the ACC offices. Therein lay the fly in the ointment for South Carolina. While the university contended that Grosso met their requirements for admission, the ACC maintained that he was ineligible for competition on the basis of his first and only official College Board score.

Would the Grosso affair have evolved as it did without the ill will between McGuire and Cameron, Weaver, et al.? Likely not. Did the ACC's Grosso decision hinge on an obscure technicality? Most certainly. But it was enough to keep Grosso out of the lineup for the opening game of his sophomore season versus Erskine on December 1, 1966. His varsity career at South Carolina now seemed tenuous at best, though he continued to practice with the Gamecocks while the university appealed his status.

The death knell to Grosso's tenure at USC came on January 8, 1967, when the NCAA announced the results of its own investigation into the football and basketball programs at USC. The investigation centered on the financial assistance that South Carolina had provided the three football players during Coach Bass's tenure, but the NCAA also voiced support for the ACC's position on Grosso's eligibility, citing the irregularities around his second board exam administered on the USC campus. Further, the NCAA determined that Grosso's expenses had been paid by "a corporation upon which the student-athlete was neither naturally or legally dependent." This was a reference to the bar owned by Grosso's uncles and the tuition assistance provided by them.

The penalties announced by the NCAA were harsh. The university's football and basketball teams were barred from postseason tournaments or bowl games and could not appear on NCAA-sanctioned television broadcasts for two years. Further, and most devastating, the NCAA made it clear that if USC did not get its house in order quickly, the university could be suspended from NCAA membership. It was a humiliating ruling and a black mark on USC's credibility. President Jones admonished McGuire that he was to refrain from comment on the investigation and was to follow the "letter and spirit" of the ACC and NCAA rulings.

In the aftermath of the NCAA's announcement, McGuire used his connections to help Grosso transfer to the University of Louisville, where he received a scholarship and played behind the great Wes Unseld during his first season before starting his final two seasons. Grosso averaged 16.2 points and 14.2 rebounds per game during his time at Louisville. The young man whose college career began with such promise never suited up for a varsity game at South Carolina. Rather than leading the Gamecocks to championships as McGuire had boldly predicted, Mike Grosso is a footnote, albeit a significant one, in the athletic history of the University of South Carolina.

In the wake of the Grosso controversy, South Carolina's new football coach and athletics director developed his own misgivings about the ACC's admission standards, which would ultimately determine the university's path toward major independent status.

Competing Standards Heighten Tensions

As the Grosso controversy unfolded, the NCAA instituted a new rule to address minimum academic standards for student-athletes, a new term coined by the governing body. In a 1965 study commissioned by the NCAA, a committee determined that it was possible to predict an athlete's first-year college grade point average on the basis of high school rank and scores on college entrance exams, either the SAT or the American College Testing Program (ACT). The NCAA set a bar of 1.6 out of a 4.0 system (equivalent to a C-minus) for an incoming student-athlete's projected GPA. Further, the student-athletes would need to maintain a minimum 1.6 GPA during their college career to maintain eligibility. This 1.6 minimum rule, effective January 1, 1966, was widely applauded by member institutions as a step in the right direction in addressing academic standards throughout college sports.

The 1.6 mandate created a sharp divide within the ACC regarding the need to maintain its own 800 standard in light of the NCAA's new rule. South Carolina's Paul Dietzel led the charge for those institutions wishing to scrap the 800 standard in lieu of the NCAA's less stringent 1.6 regulation. Clemson, Maryland, and NC State sided with South Carolina, while Duke, UNC, Wake Forest, and Virginia remained adamant about maintaining the 800 standard for the ACC.

Upon taking the South Carolina job, Dietzel was alarmed by the ACC's dismal record of futility against nonconference opponents in football. Indeed the ACC ranked last among all conferences in terms of nonconference victories. Against the SEC in particular, the ACC had compiled an embarrassing record of 19 wins against 105 losses since 1953.[8] This was particularly distressing to Dietzel, as South Carolina's recruiting footprint overlapped with SEC schools to a greater extent than the other ACC programs, with the exception of Clemson. In a case of politics making strange bedfellows, Clemson's football coach and athletics director, Frank Howard, became Dietzel's most vocal ally in the anti-800 argument.[9]

Dietzel sought to raise the profile and competitiveness of the Gamecock program in scheduling a strong nonconference slate, including likes of Georgia, Florida State, Alabama, and Tennessee, among others. All of those programs, which boasted well-established football traditions, were subject only to the NCAA's 1.6 rule. Dietzel saw a distinct disadvantage for his program and argued vigorously that the 800 standard hamstrung USC and other ACC programs.

As these matters were set against the backdrop of the civil rights movement and the integration of public schools and universities throughout the South, there was an important racial element to Dietzel's argument. Dietzel told USC president Tom Jones in 1970 that "it's going to be very difficult to explain to people around here, that of all the fine black athletes playing in our newly integrated high schools, we cannot find one of them who can attend his state university." Indeed Jones went so far as to refer to the 800 minimum as a "racist regulation" and questioned the morality of the conference.

Jones's sentiments were echoed by Clemson president Robert Edwards, who lamented that the standard created a major obstacle for Black athletes wishing to participate in sports at his school. Citing 1965 data, Edwards reported that 93.4 percent of Black high school seniors in the state of South Carolina who took the SAT that year scored below 800.

The irony of South Carolina's two major universities working as outspoken advocates for Black athletes was not lost on observers throughout the conference. South Carolina had, to a greater degree than other states within the ACC footprint, fought integration throughout its history.[10] As the only truly Deep South state in the ACC, South Carolina's racial and political identity was more reflective of that region than the Mid-Atlantic.

Though South Carolina did not experience the widespread violence that plagued the civil rights era in Alabama and Mississippi, it was not without incident. On February 8, 1968, approximately two hundred protesters gathered on the campus of South Carolina State University in Orangeburg to protest racial segregation at a local bowling alley. As police and firefighters attempted to extinguish a bonfire set by the protesters, an object thrown from the crowd injured a police officer. Within minutes officers from the State Highway Patrol began firing into the crowd, injuring twenty-seven and killing three.

Of the three killed, two were students at SC State and one was a student at local Wilkinson High School. The latter, Delano Middleton, had not been a participant in the protests but was sitting on the steps of the freshman dormitory, waiting for his mother to finish her work shift. Many of the injured were shot in the back as they attempted to flee the scene.

The incident, which predated the shootings at Kent State by two years, became known as the Orangeburg Massacre. In a press conference the following day, Governor Robert McNair called it "one of the saddest days in the history of South Carolina." He placed the blame for the incident on "outside agitators" from the Black Power movement. The federal government brought charges against nine members of the highway patrol, who claimed in their defense that they felt threatened by the protesters and had heard gunshots coming from the crowd. Though forensic evidence and witness testimony strongly contradicted those statements, the nine officers were acquitted.

Just two months later, on April 4, 1968, the moral and spiritual leader of the civil rights movement, Dr. Martin Luther King Jr., was assassinated in Memphis, Tennessee. Two months after that, US Senator and presumptive Democratic presidential nominee Robert F. Kennedy, who had aligned his campaign with the movement, was murdered following a speech in Los Angeles.

The University of South Carolina had only integrated five years earlier, when it admitted three Black students upon the order of a federal court. On the morning of September 11, 1963, Henrie Monteith, Robert Anderson, and James Solomon completed registration for fall classes at the Naval Armory on campus. It was 1969 before Carolina's athletic teams integrated. Casey Manning (basketball) and Jackie Brown (football) were the first African Americans to letter at USC, while Carlton Hayward was the first African American to be recruited to play football. Dietzel, realizing the need for a better connection with African American athletes, hired a Black assistant coach, Harold White, in 1971 to assist in recruiting and academics.[11]

From Simmer to Boil

By 1970 the situation between USC and the other ACC schools reached a boiling point. After South Carolina won the ACC title in 1969, Dietzel's in-state recruiting began to take off. But of the ten blue-chip in-state players he eyed, only two had managed the requisite score of 800 on the SAT. Beyond the 1970 recruiting class, Sumter wide receiver Freddie Solomon promised to be the most celebrated recruit of Dietzel's tenure, though the ACC's 800 standard remained a serious roadblock.[12] Dietzel vented his frustrations to President Jones, lamenting that he was tired of watching high school players from South Carolina go on to all-American careers at Big Ten and Big Eight schools, only because they were barred from competition within the ACC by the onerous 800 rule.

The NCAA expressed support for Dietzel's stance, noting that it was against the ACC's use of a minimum cutoff score. Further the 800 rule had caught the attention of the federal government, which was investigating colleges and universities across the South for prejudicial admissions standards.

On October 21, 1970, amid continuing acrimony between member institutions over the 800 rule, ACC presidents met to discuss the matter. They ultimately opted to pursue additional studies on the effects of dropping the rule in favor of another predictive model. Two days later the University of South Carolina Board of Trustees took the matter into their own hands, authorizing Gamecock coaches to recruit on the basis of the NCAA's 1.6 standard. While they pledged that the university would continue to work toward a solution with the ACC, it was a brazen act of institutional defiance.

With South Carolina forcing the issue, Clemson had to choose a course of action. Though Clemson's Edwards and Howard shared Carolina's stance on the 800 controversy, they were less inclined to bolt the ACC. Despite a popular misconception among Carolina faithful, there was never a pact between USC and Clemson officials to leave the conference together. Clemson ultimately chose to remain in the conference, while South Carolina charted its own course. On March 29, 1971, the board of trustees announced that the university would withdraw from the conference on August 15 of that year.[13]

Following a daylong meeting to discuss the matter, the board of trustees sounded an optimistic tone. Board chair T. Eston Marchant cited national legislation then under review, which would "remove the areas of disagreement which presently exist (between USC and the ACC)." The statement went on to express hopes that the separation would be of a temporary nature. Newly elected ACC commissioner Bob James attended a portion of the meeting and expressed similar optimism for reconciliation after returning to his home in Greensboro, North Carolina. "I was really impressed with the sincerity of the South Carolina people. I came away with the feeling that they want and would like to be in the ACC."

The measured optimism of USC's board and the ACC's new commissioner were balanced by comments from other officials who sounded a tone of resignation bordering on indifference. Maryland athletics director Jim Kehoe, in addressing the scheduling difficulties presented by South Carolina's withdrawal, noted that "it would seem to be more sensible to compete with teams 150 miles away than one 300 miles away." He added, "I'm sorry the matter couldn't be resolved, but realistically, South Carolina had gone too far down the road to remain in the conference."

And so, just over two weeks after that glorious day in Greensboro and only hours before the basketball team would meet for their annual postseason banquet to celebrate the school's first ACC basketball championship, the University of South Carolina officially announced a parting of the ways with the Atlantic Coast Conference.

The 800 rule controversy was resolved just over a year after USC's exit when two student-athletes at Clemson University filed suit in federal court against Clemson and the ACC. Their attorneys argued that the 800 rule deprived them of their constitutional rights to equal protection under the Fourteenth Amendment since the rule applied only to athletes. On August 7, 1972, U.S. District Court Judge Robert Hemphill agreed that the ACC's 800 standard was "arbitrary and capricious" and "not based on valid reasoning." On August 18, 1972, just over thirteen months after South Carolina's ACC exit, the ACC dropped the embattled 800 rule.

ACC football and basketball coaches would now recruit on equal footing with other NCAA programs. Reaction among ACC officials was generally positive. Maryland Sports Information Director Jack Zane, perhaps taking advantage of South Carolina's absence to claim an outsized role for his school in the SAT drama, told reporters, "Maryland was the one that made the proposal a couple of years ago to do away with it (the 800 rule)."

Moreover, with McGuire's Gamecocks removed from the equation, the Big Four North Carolina schools continued to dominate the ACC in basketball, collectively winning ten of the next eleven ACC championships between 1972 and 1983.[14]

The University of South Carolina, meanwhile, was now a major independent, joining the likes of Florida State, Notre Dame, Penn State, West Virginia, and Virginia Tech in that relatively small world of major universities unaffiliated with a conference. June 30, 1971, marked the beginning of a twenty-year journey—a winding wilderness road that ultimately ended on July 1, 1991, when South Carolina happily accepted an invitation to join the SEC. In the warm afterglow of over thirty years in the SEC, the events of South Carolina's two decades between membership in all-sports conferences are often overlooked by the sports world, sometimes even by Gamecock faithful.

But there are stories to tell.

2

Build It, and They Will Come

New Facilities Usher USC
into the Modern Era

He's quite the salesman. Before Paul came, we used to have to
beg money from the canteen and book shop for athletics.

—USC Board of Trustees chair T. Eston Marchant

O f the challenges Paul Dietzel took on upon accepting the job of head
football coach and athletics director in 1966, the most significant and
pressing was the need to upgrade facilities. The most glaring inadequacy
was the old field house—USC's basketball facility, with a capacity of thirty-
two hundred, providing only enough seating for around one third of the
student body and a few paying fans. By the time Dietzel took the helm, the
university had begun gathering bids for construction of what was initially
called "Memorial Coliseum" in conceptual drawings.

Built at a cost of $9.2 million, the coliseum more than answered the call for
an upgraded basketball facility. In an epic case of one-upmanship, McGuire
specified the seating capacity should be 12,401, exactly one more seat than
the 12,400-seat Reynolds Coliseum at NC State, then the largest arena in the
ACC and the entire Southeast. USC's new building would also house the university's journalism and general studies programs in underground classroom
space. It opened in grand fashion on November 30, 1968, with a thrilling

USC basketball coach Frank McGuire and football coach Paul Dietzel examine architect's model for Memorial Hall (later the Carolina Coliseum), 1966. Courtesy of the *State* Newspaper Archive, Richland County Public Library.

51–49 victory over Auburn in that season's first game. Sophomore John Roche drilled the deciding jumper in his first varsity game before a raucous capacity crowd.

The construction timeline of the coliseum advanced rapidly when two fires destroyed the Gamecocks' former home, Carolina Field House, in the spring of 1968, leaving the Gamecocks only one option for home games for the upcoming season. The cause of the fire was never determined, and stories have swirled over the years that Frank McGuire, sensing a lack of urgency in construction, may have had a hand in it.

On February 22, 1967, USC accepted a bid of $6.88 million from McDevitt and Street Co. of Charlotte. The scheduled opening date was December 1, 1968, which the contractor considered optimistic. The firm's contractual obligation was to have the facility completed by March 9, 1969, at the end of the 1968–69 basketball season.

Despite that, McGuire had recruited an outstanding 1967 signing class, which included Roche, Tom Owens, John Ribock, and Billy Walsh, promising them all that the new coliseum would be ready for the start of their sophomore season. After a season of playing on the freshman team in the old field house, McGuire's "super sophs" were eager to put the antiquated facility in the rearview mirror.

Carolina Field House was built in 1927 at the corner of Greene and Sumter Streets, across the street from Longstreet Theater, at a cost of $28,000 (around $470,000 in 2022 dollars). In addition to providing a home court for basketball, it housed coaches' offices and provided the university with a venue for concerts and dances. With a post–World War II enrollment boom, USC's student body surpassed the building's capacity by the early 1950s.[1]

The facility, obsolescent though it was, provided a compelling home court advantage for Gamecock basketball teams. The playing floor was sunken several feet below ground level, and the bleachers created a cantilevered effect, seeming to hang over top of the floor. A three-foot brick wall rimmed the court, topped by a metal railing that separated fans from players, coaches, and officials. Rowdy students would lean over the rails, shouting all manner of "encouragement," creating a deafening wall of noise. In a 2015 article in the *State,* columnist Ron Morris interviewed former Gamecock great Ronnie Collins about that home court advantage. Collins said that with a packed house, "it sounded like an atomic bomb going off, and it was always full, I don't care what our record was."

The conditions were less than pleasant for visiting teams. Opposing coaches characterized it as a "snake pit," among other less than glowing reviews. The pep band, which was always positioned directly behind the visitor's bench, wreaked havoc. Playing boisterously during time-outs, they often drowned out the instructions of the opposing coach. During a 1963 game between the Gamecocks and Duke, the trombone player kept moving his slide past the head of Duke's Jay Buckley, which the normally mild-mannered Buckley found so maddening that he grabbed the offending instrument and tossed it onto the playing floor. Duke coach Vic Bubas asked the officials if he could move his team to mid-court during timeouts, and when he did, USC cheerleaders surrounded the Blue Devils in a raucous "war dance."[2]

While demand for student tickets was always strong, the excitement generated by McGuire's arrival made it clear that the Field House had outlived its usefulness. McGuire's acceptance of the USC job was based upon a gentleman's agreement that the university would construct a modern arena, but there was the matter of fundraising and planning to navigate, which would take several years. The old field house had a few more seasons left, and it saw unprecedented excitement in those final campaigns.

In 1965 USC beat fifth-ranked Duke—McGuire's first signature win at Carolina. In 1967 South Carolina handed fourth-ranked UNC an upset. UNC went on to win the ACC and make it to the Final Four that year. It was evident that McGuire was building a program that would compete for ACC titles. As the basketball program rose to prominence, the cramped confines of the field house became more pronounced.

By the end of the 1967–68 season, the final one in Carolina Field House, it became evident that construction was running weeks behind at the new coliseum. Poor weather in January added significantly to the delays. McDevitt executives pointed to their contractual obligation of March 1969. McGuire chafed under the delays.

Just before midnight on Sunday, March 24, 1968, Columbia firefighters responded to a fire at the Field House, sending four pumpers and a ladder truck to battle the blaze. Hundreds of students rushed to work alongside firemen into the night, many of whom formed a human chain, salvaging trophies and furniture from the burning building. Columbia fire chief Edward F. Broome said that the fire "may have started around a breaker box" but could not comment conclusively as the investigation by arson experts with the State Law Enforcement Division was ongoing.

Chief Broome noted the next day that the fire destroyed everything but the roof and walls and estimated that the damage would approach $200,000. USC estimated that equipment and supply losses amounted to $15,900, including two scoreboards, eighteen Spalding basketballs, uniforms, and fourteen cartons of Camel cigarettes from the concession stand. University president Jones noted that despite a $375,000 insurance policy on the building, razing it might make the most sense rather than spending $200,000 to rebuild an already inadequate building.

A second, more extensive fire several weeks later put the matter to rest. That fire occurred on Saturday, April 13, 1968, and destroyed what remained of the field house. Fire officials announced that the second blaze was intentionally set but withheld further comment pending investigation. An unnamed man quoted by the *State* two days later said he had been walking by the field house that Saturday when he saw a "poof" explosion and then saw fire raging at the north end of the building.

Columbia was in the midst of a weeklong curfew, imposed in response to outbreaks of violence across the nation following the assassination of Martin Luther King just nine days prior. With the curfew in effect, National Guardsmen and state highway patrolmen on duty across the city descended upon the site of the fire to provide security. In contrast to the earlier fire, the campus was mostly deserted, with many away for Easter, and few onlookers showed to view the spectacle. Three Columbia firefighters were injured by falling debris while fighting the blaze.

While it is tempting to engage in speculation about McGuire's possible involvement in the field house fire as a means to advance construction time-lines at the new coliseum, that scenario is doubtful. A June 15, 1968, article in the *State* reported five suspicious fires at the university over four months. The latest, which fire officials said was intentionally set at the gymnasium behind Longstreet Theater, was the second at that that location within a period of days. Longstreet was just a stone's throw across Sumter Street from the ruins of Carolina Field House. In April of that year, a fire was set in a classroom near the USC Naval Armory, which caused $1,800 in damage.

Beyond the pattern of other campus fires, USC assistant and freshman team coach Buck Freeman had developed a well-known affection for the field house and had become its main caretaker.[3] Lastly, a vigorous arson investigation followed the field house fires, something a man of McGuire's intelligence would have foreseen.

Results of the arson investigations were inconclusive, which advanced the urban legend of McGuire's involvement. However, no credible evidence exists that the coach engaged in arson for hire. The arsons were crimes that resulted in the destruction of a university building, injured several firefighters, and, if the culprits had been discovered, would have resulted in criminal charges, public infamy, and possibly incarceration. Even granting McGuire's possible motives in the field house fires, he would have had no such motive in the other three campus fires.

With the field house in ruins, all attention turned to the construction of the new coliseum. McDevitt and Street stepped up its efforts, with crews working six days per week, ten hours per day, throughout the summer and early fall. USC made no contingency plans for the first game, adding additional motivation for all involved to ensure the building would be ready for basketball on November 30.

The House that Frank Built

Saturday, November 30, 1968, dawned with fair skies, temperatures in the low fifties, with a balmy sixty-five forecasted by late afternoon. Somnolent in the midst of a long Thanksgiving weekend, Columbia residents shuffled out to retrieve their morning papers. Meanwhile construction workers labored at a fevered pace to ready USC's new coliseum for its highly anticipated debut that evening.

Just five weeks earlier, things were very much still in doubt. An October 24, 1968, letter from Harold Brunton, USC's vice president for business affairs, to Jones, Dietzel, and McGuire updating the status of construction opened in a hopeful yet not altogether confident tone: "I am sure that if you have visited the Coliseum, you must have your fingers crossed (as I do) regarding getting the work done by November 30."

Brunton laid out a laundry list of challenges, from parking to laying of the rubberized tartan playing surface to a particularly vexing delay in delivery of arena seats from the manufacturer. Only twelve hundred seats had been installed, less than ten percent of arena capacity. "We should all remember that the official opening date of our contract is still March 9 (1969), and the fact that we are still hoping to open November 30 is somewhat of a miracle." In closing Brunton wrote in a tone that suggested both humor and disquiet: "Each of us might devote a little thinking in odd moments to what we would do if all the seats were not available."

A November 7 update by USC staff engineer G. T. Perry sounded a more optimistic tone while still noting challenges. A total of 3,750 seats had been installed, with enough received to keep crews busy through November 18. More were set to arrive from the factory within the next ten days. Perry advised that the team might be able to practice in the arena by November 23, so long as they kept to the arena floor, varsity dressing room, and Coach McGuire's office area.

Indeed McGuire's Gamecocks did tip off the 1968–69 season in their new home, though what greeted fans arriving before the 8 PM tipoff was still an active construction site. Fans walked blocks to get to the new building, as parking facilities had not been completed in time for the game. All energy and focus had gone into completion of the playing arena itself. The arena, in fact, was the only portion of the building anywhere near completion. Surrounding offices and classroom space would not be completed for months.

Fans navigated mounds of clay and kicked at wooden planks forming concrete walkways that had been poured just days before. They gawked at construction equipment still warm from use and stared inquisitively at blocked stairways. Exterior lights high above on the building's massive soffit worked on just two sides. One scoreboard was not installed; another did not work. Many of the large garnet double doors leading from the concourse to the arena leaned against walls unattached. Workers had finished installing the last of the 12,401 seats just hours before tipoff.

Yet, upon entering the playing arena, fans were amazed at the immensity and the luxury of the place. It felt massive, cavernous, in comparison to the more familiar 3,200-seat Carolina Field House. Fans in the upper rows marveled that they could see the ball bounce on the arena's tartan floor seconds before they could hear it. The 12,401 theater-style seats were lavishly upholstered in Gamecock garnet, with the exception of black seats on both sides of the arena arranged to spell USC. The aroma of popcorn and the new-car smell of freshly upholstered seats just days removed from the factory pervaded the arena.

Ushers were stationed throughout the arena, directing fans to their seats. Those with tickets in the higher rows encountered a vigorous workout as they climbed the steeply ascending steps. The precipitous incline of the seating was designed to keep fans as close to the action as possible. The space-frame roof of the building, held aloft by forty-four massive exterior columns, eliminated the need for interior columns and provided unobstructed views throughout the arena. It was the largest space-frame building in the world and the biggest arena in the Southeast.[4]

Herman Helms of the *State* wrote of that opening night that "the building was elegant, the crowd was big and noisy and had a gasser of a finish." Before the varsity debut, though, the first basketball game ever played at Carolina Coliseum was the freshman team's season-opening contest versus Spartanburg Junior College in a 6 PM undercard.[5] The "Biddies," as they were known, were coached by varsity assistant Donnie Walsh, and featured six-foot-ten consensus high school all-American Tom Riker from Rockville Centre, New York, and fellow newcomers Bob Carver, Bobby Grimes, and Rick Aydlett. USC's big man, Riker scored nineteen points, leading the freshmen to a 55–52 win.

The varsity tipped off versus Auburn of the Southeastern Conference at 8 PM in front of an announced crowd of 12,088 fans. Carolina started four sophomores in their first varsity contest: Roche, Owens, Ribock, and Walsh, along with the "old head" of the team, junior Bobby Cremins. The Gamecocks controlled the game early, leading by as many as twelve points in the first half and ten at the break.

With several players unavailable because of bouts of mononucleosis, McGuire's crew had a short bench. Fatigue set in, Gamecock shooting went cold as the second half wore on, and Auburn methodically chipped away at the USC lead. The Tigers' Wallace Tinker tied the game at 46 with a layup at the 4:39 mark, then tapped in another basket to put Auburn in front 48–46 a few moments later. Auburn's Ronnie Jackson hit a free throw to push their lead to 49–46 with 2:36 remaining. The arena was spring-loaded and nervous, the unspoken dread of an opening night loss creeping in like an unwanted guest.

After rebounding a missed Roche free throw at the 1:12 mark, Cremins was fouled and headed to the charity stripe for two shots. He hit the first, pulling Carolina to within two, 49–47. Cremins missed the second shot, but Owens managed a tip-in, knotting the game at 49. Carolina held Auburn on defense and regained possession with forty-nine seconds remaining. McGuire called a time-out, instructing his team to hold for a final shot. As the clock ticked below ten seconds, Roche made his move, rising for a jumper from the key with two seconds. Every eye in the building followed the ball's arcing path as it hit the rim and bounced off the glass before settling safely into the net, putting Carolina on top 51–49 as the horn sounded and pandemonium ensued.

The *State*'s Helms called the finish "nerve-tingling" and quoted a perspiring McGuire in the USC locker room moments after the thriller had ended: "What a way to open a new building," the coach said with a grin, "but I didn't plan it this way." He added, "I'm not that good a script writer." Of the new arena, McGuire said, "It's one of the most beautiful buildings I've ever seen for basketball"—pausing—"and that's a lot of buildings."

A jubilant Cremins said, "We needed the game and John won it for us, I love him. I think I'm going to kiss him."

One game into his varsity career, Roche had already entered into legend status in Columbia. It was a career that ended three years later with his name atop the program's all-time scoring list, and his number 11 jersey retired by the school. His late jumper also provided an apt beginning to the Coliseum's storied history. Setting off on a torrid start that last night of November 1968, the Gamecocks played their remaining three seasons as ACC members in the plush new digs, compiling a 29–3 home record, before rollicking sellout crowds.[6]

Tommy Moody, radio personality for Columbia's 107.5 *The Game*, former Gamecock baseball letterman, longtime analyst for USC baseball radio broadcasts, and a walking encyclopedia of Gamecock trivia, was a senior at Columbia's A.C. Flora High School during that 1968–69 season. He tells the story of attending a game that first season at the Coliseum.

"Carolina had upset #2 UNC 68-66 on the opening night of the North-South Doubleheader in Charlotte earlier in the season. The return game was in Columbia, and tickets were unbelievable. You didn't even *think* about going to the game.

"My dad was a highway engineer with the state, and he had a coworker who also worked as a doorman at the Coliseum in those days. I wanted to go to the game in the worst kind of way, so the coworker told my dad what door he would be working, and to have me wear my A.C. Flora letterman's jacket. He said he would act like he was taking my ticket as I walked through the gate. "And I walked through the gate and I was thinking to myself, 'my God, this place is fabulous.'" "But," Moody says laughing, "my next problem was, where am I gonna sit?" Moody ended up finding a small slab of concrete well up into the upper rows, near the television cameras. "I sat on that slab next to the TV crew the whole game."

Carolina unfortunately lost the game, 68–62, but Moody said, "I was just thrilled to be there."

Gamecock Baseball Finds a New Home at "the Roost"

As the basketball Gamecocks lavished in their posh new arena, construction crews were busy in other parts of campus as well. A new five-unit complex at the corner of Heyward and South Marion Streets, set to open in the spring of 1969, included dedicated athletic dorms, a cafeteria and lounge, a varsity tennis complex, and an upgraded baseball diamond. The thirty-acre complex was named for former football coach and athletics director Rex Enright. The dormitory, cafeteria, and lounge areas were affectionately dubbed "the Roost."[7]

Coach Dietzel, in his duties as athletics director, was the driving force behind the creation of this new home for Gamecock athletes, and it was a major priority from the outset of his tenure. Dietzel and university business manager Dean H. Brunton visited various athletic facilities at universities across the country, incorporating many of the ideas they gathered into the planning of the new Roost complex. Brunton, in an interview with the *State,* described the "total concept" philosophy of the complex. "The University is heading toward a total housing complex, including a study area, lounge, play and dining facility. Along with this we are trying to produce the home environment." Dietzel emphasized the importance of having a special facility designed with the college athlete in mind. "The college athlete is on a different schedule from most students. His time is taken up a great deal in the late afternoon with practice and training when other students can study. Academically, the greatest thing we can do is to give the athlete an opportunity to graduate, and we should do everything possible to help his study habits."

On March 17, 1969, the Gamecocks baseball team, under third-year coach Jack Powers, played the inaugural game at the new stadium. It was a disappointing start to a season that proved to be Powers's final one at Carolina. Virginia Tech's hurlers held Gamecock batters to an anemic five hits on the day en route to handing USC an opening day loss of 6–1. A sparse crowd of 250 spectators took in that first game at the facility. That opening loss set the tone for a frustrating season in which the Gamecocks compiled a 12–21–1 record and were outscored 111–148.[8]

The 1969 season came to an unceremonious ending with a 9–0 thumping at the hands of Virginia in Charlottesville on May 13. That game ushered in the "modern era" of Gamecock baseball, as Dietzel soon convinced Sumter, South Carolina, native and New York Yankee legend Bobby Richardson to accept the position of head baseball coach at USC.

Carolina Stadium Becomes Williams-Brice

On the afternoon of Monday, December 8, 1969, university president Jones and athletics director Dietzel held a press conference at the newly completed Capstone Building, an eighteen-story women's residence hall on Barnwell Street, in the expanding east side of campus. Jones outlined a proposed an ambitious $112 million expansion and construction program for the university. The proposals included a new library, a new college of business administration, a new school of nursing, two new residence halls, a parking garage, and a central administration building at 901 Sumter Street, across from the university's stately Horseshoe.

Also outlined in the plans was a multiphase expansion of Carolina Stadium. An article in that afternoon's *Columbia Record* included an artist's rendering of the proposed expansion, including a first phase addition of an upper-west deck and a second phase addition of a twin upper-east deck. The two phases expanded seating capacity at the stadium from 42,338 to a projected 70,000 seats. All of the proposed campus projects would be completed over the course of five years, requiring $97 million in state funds, with the stadium project costing $7.6 million.

Carolina Stadium, originally known as Columbia Municipal Stadium, was built as a project of the Works Progress Administration in 1934. The stadium replaced the wooden grandstands of Melton Field, where Gamecock teams played their home games since 1926.[9] The original structure, comprising east and west grandstands, sat 17,600. The stadium was officially dedicated on October 6, 1934, during a gray, drizzly afternoon that saw the Gamecocks defeat Virginia Military, 22–6. The City of Columbia deeded the stadium to USC in 1935, and the venue was officially renamed "Carolina Stadium" in 1941.

In 1948 seating was nearly doubled to 33,000 with the addition of south end zone seating, which formed a horseshoe. By 1959 another expansion in the north end zone completed a bowl and brought capacity to 43,212. In 1966 field-level seats were replaced by armchair-type seats, which reduced capacity to 42,338, where it remained on the eve of the 1969 expansion proposal.

State funding for the stadium project in particular faced tough sledding in 1969. Governor Robert E. McNair commented that the proposal was not number one on the university's building priority list. State senator Edgar A. Brown spoke in more definitive terms, stating that "any new building is out of the question." McNair and Brown, as well as other legislators, cited a tough budget year. President Nixon had recently asked state governments to place a hold on new building to combat inflation. McNair intended to honor the president's request. The university, meanwhile, pledged to fund the project through gate receipts and booster funding, a dubious proposal given its scale and cost. However, construction of the upper-west deck would soon begin thanks to a generous gift.

In January 1971 attorneys representing the estate of Mrs. Martha Williams Brice announced the intent outlined in Mrs. Brice's will to bequeath a $3.5 million gift to the University of South Carolina. The funds were to benefit various building projects on the Columbia campus and at Coastal Carolina, then a USC satellite campus in Conway, South Carolina. On the Columbia campus, funds would go to the College of Nursing as well as the ongoing building project at Carolina Stadium, with $2.75 million of the gift going to the USC Athletics Department. President Jones noted it was the single largest monetary gift to an institution of higher learning in the history of the state. The university announced plans to place the Williams Brice name on the new nursing building and the stadium in accordance with the directives outlined in Brice's will.[10]

By the 1970s the area surrounding USC's football stadium was a sprawling industrial district. Between Shop Road to the east and Bluff Road to the west, the stadium lay at the northern edge of a bustling corridor of machine shops and warehouses. To the north, across Stadium Road (now George Rogers

Boulevard) lay the State Fairgrounds, which provided row upon row of ample, if dusty, parking for Gamecock Club members.

Further north beyond the fairgrounds was Olympia Mill, the then still-functioning textile mill built in 1899, and the surrounding village. To the west across Bluff Road lay the State Farmers Market, an assemblage of low-slung cinderblock and corrugated metal buildings, housing produce vendors from the Midlands and beyond. Still further west flowed the slowly churning Congaree River. The stadium itself was ringed by asphalt parking areas reserved for well-heeled donors.

Carolina Stadium in those days was a spartan, utilitarian structure set against a gritty backdrop. It was the kind of rusty scrap-metal setting that made one ponder whether they might be due for a tetanus shot and lay in stark contrast to the stately and verdant USC Horseshoe at the heart of campus two miles north. But the off-campus location ensured ample parking, easy tailgating, and a carnival-like atmosphere, particularly when the State Fair visited town each October.

USC officially rededicated Williams-Brice Stadium in a brief ceremony on September 9, 1972, during halftime of that season's opening game versus Virginia. Attending the ceremony were USC president Jones, US senators Strom Thurmond and Ernest F. Hollings, and Bill and Tom Edwards, nephews of Martha Brice, among various other dignitaries. The game resulted in a 24–16 loss to the Cavaliers, putting a damper on the festivities.

Dietzel's Legacy

Though it would be 1981 before the matching east-upper deck was added, the newly christened Williams-Brice Stadium brought USC football into the modern age and continued an impressive effort to upgrade facilities across the Columbia campus. Williams-Brice, the Roost athletic dorms, the Rex Enright Spring Sports Complex, and the Carolina Coliseum had all been completed within a span of three years. The projects represented a quantum leap forward for USC and put Gamecock athletic facilities on par with the finest in the country.

Dietzel's impact as athletics director was extensive, his successes in that role notably greater than those he experienced in his dual role of head football coach. He resigned under pressure following an 0–2 start to the 1974 season, departing at the end of that campaign. In nine seasons Dietzel compiled a total record of 42–53–1 (.442). His 1969 team did provide USC with its first, and to this day only, outright conference football championship, no small accomplishment in the grand sweep of the program's history. But his influence and legacy go well beyond that: from leading the charge to exit the ACC and desegregating the athletic department to massive facility upgrades to penning the new fight song and directing the creation of a new Gamecock logo (both still in use today). The hiring of baseball coach Bobby Richardson also vaulted the Gamecock program into national prominence. The Dietzel era brought revolutionary change to Carolina athletics.

Dietzel, perhaps more than any single individual, is responsible for the look and feel of USC athletics over the course of several decades. In many respects his influence lingers today.

College Athletics Becomes Big Business

South Carolina's athletic department budget grew exponentially in the years leading to its ACC exit. As McGuire and Dietzel labored to build their respective programs, university leadership aspired to align USC with the nation's leading programs in terms of budget and facilities. The university had entered the modern arms race of ever-expanding budgets and building projects that came to define major college athletics over the decades that followed.

In 1961 the USC athletics budget was $563,000, with a profit of $12,000. By 1966, when Dietzel took over as athletics director, the budget had risen to $851,000, but the department struggled to remain in the black. By 1971 the budget had expanded to more than $2.2 million, with a profit of $10,900, representing a 400 percent increase in budget over the course of ten years.

Coaches' salaries and staff numbers increased as well. The national average for athletic department salary expenditures in 1965 was $120,000 for twenty coaches. By 1970 that average had risen to $184,000 for twenty-two coaches. By 1971 Dietzel was earning $31,000 (roughly $192,000 in 2021 dollars) in his dual role of football coach and athletics director. McGuire earned $25,000. Though these salaries pale in comparison to modern coaches' salaries in the

Power Five conferences, they were considered lavish sums at a time when the average wage in South Carolina was less than $7,000 annually.

Gamecock fans and boosters contributed impressively to this growth in revenue through the Gamecock Club. Founded in 1942 as the "Buck a Month (B.A.M.) Club," the Gamecock Club had expanded to include chapters in all forty-six South Carolina counties. By 1971 the club raised $550,000, which accounted for around 25 percent of total athletic department revenues. By comparison, booster club donations at USC outpaced Tennessee ($450,000), which had a similar total budget, and Florida ($407,000), where the budget was $2.7 million. Clemson's IPTAY Club ("I Pay Twenty a Year"—formerly *Ten*) raised $342,000.

In the 1960s university leadership committed to raising its profile and competitiveness, both within the ACC and nationally. The results were compelling. It started with the McGuire hire in 1964, followed by Dietzel in 1966. The two high-profile coaches brought USC national championship pedigree leadership. McGuire and Dietzel and later Richardson brought unprecedented interest to Gamecock athletics. Dietzel in particular, in his dual role of football coach and athletics director, changed the landscape and the culture of the university. New and upgraded facilities could be found across campus. Gamecock teams stepped out of the shadows of their Tobacco Road counterparts, competing for conference championships and winning ACC titles in football (1969) and basketball (1970 regular season and 1971 tournament).

The football team achieved another milestone in 1969 in a bid to Atlanta's Peach Bowl, only the second bowl game in program history.[11] And though that game ended in a 14–3 defeat to a Jim Carlen–coached West Virginia squad, the general optimism around the program was palpable. Meanwhile McGuire's program had become a legitimate national powerhouse.

Indeed, the Gamecocks had significantly raised the profile of their major athletic programs and now owned championship hardware to show for it. USC entered the post-ACC era riding a wave of momentum, accomplishment, and optimism. Sustaining that proved to be a monumental challenge.

3

Into the Wilderness

South Carolina Navigates a Post-ACC World

> Friends come and go, but enemies accumulate.
>
> —USC president Thomas Jones

Following South Carolina's March 29, 1971, announcement that it would leave the ACC effective August 15 of that year, life went on largely as usual for Gamecock spring sports athletes. The baseball team, under the direction of second-year coach Bobby Richardson, compiled a record of 18–12 overall and 7–7 in ACC play, finishing fifth in the conference. A two-game weekend homestand at the Rex Enright Athletic Center baseball diamond versus Virginia on May 8–9 resulted in two Gamecock wins.[1]

The second of those games was a Sunday noon contest. It was a typical early May afternoon in the Capital City. Shape-shifting puffs of cloud passed overhead against a cobalt sky, and the familiar Columbia mugginess settled into the park as a smattering of fans found their seats. Temperatures hovered around seventy-seven degrees at first pitch, and the forecast called for mid-eighties by late game. Blustery winds out of the northwest meant it would be a good day for sluggers in the small park. A cargo train shuffled laboriously along the Southern Railway tracks just beyond the right field fence, and the sounds of muffled clanking and baseballs popping into leather echoed as pregame warm-ups led to first pitch. Eddie Bolton got the nod for South Carolina, which entered the contest 6–7 in conference play, while

Steve Brindle took the mound for the Cavaliers, who sported a 7–6 conference ledger.

The subject of Sunday games had been fodder for an April 30 letter to the editor submitted to the *State* by one Rev. M. B. Anderson of Winnsboro. Of the scourge of Sunday contests, the reverend decried that "selling and yelling and gathering in large crowds for other than spiritual purposes . . . violates the will of the Almighty." He further predicted the end result of such foolishness might be the loss of eternal life itself.

Phriness E. Cox of Columbia took exception to the good reverend in his own letter ten days later, noting Richardson's unimpeachable credentials as a fine Christian gentleman. Richardson, the Sumter native and former Gold Glove New York Yankee second baseman was outspoken about his faith and had just the previous year spoken at the White House as a representative of the Fellowship of Christian Athletes.[2] Cox expanded, "If Bobby Richardson played a ballgame on Sunday, I am sure the good Lord above knew it was a necessity and smiled down on the good coach."

Indeed, just over four hundred fans descended upon the ballpark despite Reverend Anderson's admonitions and enjoyed a seesaw affair, including several lead changes. The Gamecocks built a 6–5 lead through seven innings before the Cavaliers took advantage of a tiring Bolton in the top of the eighth. The Gamecock starter threw six consecutive balls to open the inning, prompting Richardson to call on reliever Larry Erbaugh, who inherited a runner at first and a 2–0 count. Erbaugh put another runner on when his first two pitches missed the mark before settling in and retiring the next two batters. A two-out single by Virginia's Robin Marvin brought home the two baserunners, putting the Cavaliers on top 7–6 moving into the ninth inning after a quiet Carolina bottom of the eighth.

After Gamecock reliever Phil Houston stifled Virginia's bats in the top of the ninth, a one-out walk put Carolina's Butch Anderson on first, before Pete Carpenter, who had two hits on the afternoon, popped up to left field for out number two. Down to the final out, Buddy Caldwell, who had homered earlier, singled to left to keep the game alive, setting up freshman pitch-hitter Billy Gambrell. Gambrell gamely accepted the hero's role, roping a line drive to right field off Virginia reliever Mike Judkins to bring home Anderson and Caldwell, lifting the Gamecocks to an 8–7 win in dramatic, walk-off fashion. Virginia's Judkins took his first loss of the season, while Gamecock reliever Houston picked up the win.

So ended the final baseball contest as a member of the ACC for the University of South Carolina. Lost amid the finely detailed coverage of the game by the *State*'s Teddy Heffner was any mention of the historical significance of that final conference contest, as if sports columnists, like players and coaches and fans, had wearied of the drama surrounding Carolina's conference exit and were happy to focus on balls and strikes and box scores. It was another thirteen seasons before South Carolina played another conference game as a member of the Metropolitan Athletic Conference.

The following weekend South Carolina teams participated in the ACC track and field and tennis championship events. The Gamecock tracksters turned in a second-place finish behind powerhouse Maryland, which won its seventeenth of the eighteen ACC track and field championships in the history of the conference. The Gamecock relay team of Jim Small, Dickie Harris, Mike Haggard, and Keith Eidson captured the 440-yard event, while Harris, Bob Dempsey, Jim Schaper, and Bo Kaczka won the mile relay. South Carolina also won the high hurdles and 220-yard dash.

On Sunday, May 16, the Gamecock tennis team participated in the ACC championships, tying with NC State for last in the conference. It was the final conference event of the spring season and the last event for South Carolina as a member of the ACC. In another forty-four days, the University of South Carolina would officially relinquish membership in the Atlantic Coast Conference.

Independent Football Kicks Off in Upgraded Carolina Stadium

South Carolina rolled into independent status feeling good about where it stood in the landscape of college athletics. The school boasted ACC championships in football just two years prior and, in spite of their conference departure, were the reigning ACC champs in basketball. Sparkling new facilities dotted the campus, from the three-year-old Carolina Coliseum to the Roost athletic dorms and an upgraded baseball diamond. As important to

Installation of Astroturf playing surface at Carolina Stadium, 1971.
Courtesy of the *State* Newspaper Archive, Richland County Public Library.

fans, despite a disappointing 4–6–1 record in 1970, the football team boasted a three-game winning streak over archrival Clemson—a rarity in the history of that series. Moreover, work was just wrapping up on an ambitious upgrade to Carolina Stadium, including distinctive lighting atop the new upper-west deck and an Astroturf playing surface.[3]

The opening paragraph of the 1971 Gamecock football media guide noted that "a new addition to Carolina Stadium, a new Astroturf playing surface, an expanded home schedule, new independent status, and some unanswered questions face the Gamecocks as they look to the 1971 football season." The questions specifically pertained to an offensive line depleted by graduations and the departure of all-time passing leader Tommy Suggs, also lost to graduation in 1970.

But other questions must have lingered among Gamecock faithful. Was the ACC split to be temporary in nature? Would another conference, perhaps the SEC, come calling? What would this independent arrangement look and feel like after seventeen years of conference membership in the ACC and the Southern Conference before that? The University of South Carolina had charted an uncertain course and were about to take the first steps along that path.

Saturday, September 11, 1971, dawned ominously, with dark clouds and rain that lingered most of the day. South Carolina played host to seventeenth-ranked Georgia Tech for the season-opening game, slated for a 7:30 PM kick-off. The previous season it was the seventeenth-ranked Gamecocks who fell to Tech 23–20 in a season-opening contest at Grant Field in Atlanta, the first meeting between the two schools since 1950.

Intermittent rain could not dampen the enthusiasm of what was the largest crowd to ever witness a football contest in the state. The stadium was a kaleidoscope of rain ponchos, Gamecock-garnet and canary-yellow and generic shades of blue, and as kickoff approached, fans in the new upper-west deck gawked at newly elevated views of the State Fairgrounds and a rain-veiled capital city skyline beyond.

Late arriving fans with upper-west tickets ascended in serpentine fashion around and around the massive new concrete ramps at the northwest and southwest corners of the stadium. Some stopped along the way to catch a breath, taking in stadium views while leaning against ramp walls during the benediction and "The Star-Spangled Banner." The wafting aroma of cigarette smoke and Cromer's popcorn mingled in the early evening damp—both cigarettes and popcorn were available at concessions stands for forty cents a pack and twenty-five cents per red-and-white-striped box, respectively. It was the fragrance of football season in Columbia.

The big crowd witnessed a soggy gem by Dietzel's Gamecocks, in what the *State* sports editor Herman Helms ranked among the greatest wins in program history, right alongside Warren Giese's "smashing" of Georgia (a 30–14 win in 1959), his comeback victory over Darrell Royal's powerful Texas Longhorns in Austin two years earlier, and Rex Enright's "biggie" over a powerhouse Army squad in 1954.

Defense and special teams carried the night for the Gamecocks in a dominant 24–7 win over the Yellow Jackets. The Carolina defense, led by junior defensive tackle John LeHeup of Temple Terrace, Florida, and senior Dickie Harris, the defensive back and punt-return specialist of Point Pleasant, New Jersey, held the vaunted Tech rushing attack to an anemic 94 yards on forty-nine attempts and just 118 passing yards on thirty-one attempts.

Gamecock special teams were special indeed, as Harris blocked a Tech punt, which Jimmy Nash scooped up for an eleven-yard touchdown return just before halftime to give the Gamecocks an 11–7 lead at the break. Harris provided more fireworks on an electrifying seventy-seven-yard punt return for another score in the third period. When junior placekicker Tommy Bell's point after failed, the score stood 17–7 Gamecocks through three quarters. Punter Robby Reynolds averaged 42.8 yards on nine kicks and kept the Yellow Jackets pinned deep in their own territory for most of the night. Tech's special teams play, by comparison, was disastrous for the Yellow Jackets, giving up safeties in the first and third quarters when snapper Charley Cheney twice snapped the ball over the punter's head and through the back of the end zone—this in addition to the blocked punt and punt return for touchdown.

The Gamecock offense finally got on the board midway through the fourth quarter on a forty-seven-yard drive powered by tailback Carlton Haywood and ending with a one-yard Haywood touchdown and Bell point after, to provide the final 24–7 tally.

Dietzel was effusive after the game, declaring that for the first time since arriving in Columbia, he finally had the defense he had been trying to build. He tabbed his defense the "Carolina Bandits," a play on the "Chinese Bandits" made famous during his time at LSU. He singled out LeHeup as well as linebackers Dick Brown and Gregg Crabb for their stellar play and called Harris perhaps the best kick returner in the country. Despite an anemic offensive showing, which would spell trouble the following week, the independent era began in spectacular fashion. The Gamecocks appeared at number 19 in the next week's AP poll, ahead of a road contest at USC's old ACC nemesis Duke.

In the second game at Duke's Wallace Wade Stadium, the Gamecocks managed only thirty-seven yards rushing on ten attempts against Coach Mike McGee's Blue Devils, as Duke dominated time of possession to win 28–12.[4] Dietzel said his team "had almost no offense" on the day, and statistics proved

USC's Dickie Harris blocks a punt against Georgia Tech at Carolina Stadium (which was later renamed Williams-Brice Stadium) in 1972. Courtesy of the *State* Newspaper Archive, Richland County Public Library.

him right. Carolina drew to 1–1 on the season, their appearance in the AP poll a short one.

The Gamecocks got back on track at home the following week with a 24–6 win versus NC State, then won an ugly 7–3 defensive slugfest at Memphis of the Missouri Valley Conference, before consecutive home wins versus Virginia (34–14) and Maryland (35–6) in which the offense seemed to finally come alive.

Through six games South Carolina's record stood at an impressive 5–1, including wins over three former conference rivals. But stronger competition and injuries took their toll on the 1971 Gamecocks down the stretch. South Carolina lost three straight, starting with a strong Florida State team, which was 5–1 and unbeaten before a loss to rival Florida the week before.[5] Despite a promising start, in which the Gamecocks built a 10–0 first-quarter lead, the Seminoles dominated the final three periods, winning handily, 49–18. The

Gamecocks were blanked by number 7 Georgia the following week, 24–0, on another rainy Carolina Stadium evening, and next suffered a 35–6 drubbing at the hands of number 11 Tennessee in Knoxville.

South Carolina, reeling after three straight losses, returned home to face its fifth former conference rival of the season in 6–4 Wake Forest. The matchup in front of 43,285, the smallest home crowd of the season, proved good medicine for Dietzel's ailing crew. Following the opening kickoff, which South Carolina's Dickie Harris returned for 25 yards, Dietzel inserted Harris into an injury-plagued offensive backfield. It was a brilliant stroke, as the versatile Harris had a field day against the Demon Deacon defense, compiling 108 rushing yards, catching three passes, and scoring three touchdowns to power the Gamecocks to a much-needed 24–7 win.

November 27, 1971, dawned clear, with highs approaching 60 by the 1:30 kickoff for Carolina's season-ending contest versus archrival Clemson. The Gamecocks held a three-game winning streak headed into this contest and were looking to make it four. Clemson boasted a 38–27–3 advantage in the all-time series, which dated back to 1896, but the Gamecocks had won six of eleven since 1960, when the contest moved to an alternating home-and-home format.[6]

The Gamecocks' "surprise" running back addition of Dickie Harris, which worked so well versus Wake Forest, was no longer a surprise. Clemson's defense keyed on him, and an ankle sprain on his second carry further slowed him, despite valiant efforts throughout. The Carolina offense was plagued by turnovers, with quarterback Glenn Morris throwing six interceptions on the afternoon, which enabled Clemson to begin a number of drives with excellent field position. Clemson built a 17–0 lead by halftime, and that was enough. The Gamecocks added a third-period touchdown on a one-yard carry by Tommy Simmons, capping a fifty-nine-yard drive, and the Tommy Bell point after proved to be the final tally, Clemson 17, Carolina 7.

Despite a winning record of 6–5, losing four of the final five after a promising 5–1 start was a bitter pill. Injuries and inconsistent quarterback play, including twenty-five interceptions on the season—four of those returned for touchdowns—were too much to overcome against the strongest competition. However, the excitement of stadium improvements, the novelty of independent status, stellar defensive play, and the electric performances of all-American Dickie Harris, who returned three punts for touchdowns on the season, provided a lot to feel good about in 1971.

In many ways South Carolina's first season as an independent felt largely unchanged. The Gamecocks played six games versus ACC competition, missing only North Carolina from the rotation. Nineteen seventy-one marked the final contest versus Maryland, capping a spirited rivalry that dated to 1926, but the other ACC rivalries, particularly the North Carolina–based schools, frequented future schedules. It was not unusual for the Gamecocks to play three, four, or even five ACC schools per season throughout the 1970s and '80s. Clemson, naturally, remained on the schedule, and the NC State rivalry was a mainstay with yearly contests through the 1991 season. Fan interest and attendance received a substantive boost from the frequent renewal of those historically significant regional rivalries, and Gamecock football largely thrived as a result.

Frank McGuire's basketball program did not enjoy the same arrangement.

Early Excitement Belies the Start of a Long, Slow Decline

The cover of USC's 1971–72 basketball media guide featured an artistic rendering of Frank McGuire, set in hues of garnet. The pencil drawing reflects the fifty-seven-year-old coach, immaculately dressed and groomed in the McGuire way though graying around the temples, with deep wrinkles along the forehead and eyes, reflective of battles waged during two decades of ACC conflict at two different schools. His sidelong glance belies a deep weariness, as if the uncertain future of his basketball program in light of USC's conference exit had begun to settle, weighty and awkward.

While former ACC rivals were happy to continue lucrative home-and-home agreements versus South Carolina in football, other motivations prevailed in basketball. In the fallout of South Carolina's bitter ACC departure, the Gamecocks simply needed the ACC more than the ACC needed the Gamecocks. North Carolina, NC State, Duke, Wake Forest, Maryland, Virginia, and Clemson enjoyed continued fierce rivalries and rabid fan interest despite the loss of founding member South Carolina. Given the importance of win-loss records in qualifying for NCAA tournament slots, ACC teams had little incentive to play a powerful Gamecock squad who spent a good portion of the 1971–72 season in the Associated Press top five. Personal animosity toward McGuire certainly must have played a role as well.

In fact, Clemson was the only ACC program willing to play South Carolina, although they too disappeared from the schedule for a period of five years after the 1971–72 season. As Dan Klores wrote in *Roundball Culture,* his 1980 volume chronicling South Carolina basketball during the McGuire era, "He [McGuire] had to comprise a new schedule and convince fans of its worthiness. Unfortunately, the majority of South Carolina basketball supporters could not reach the same emotional level when watching DePaul, Niagara, Temple, etc." Still, the Irishman gamely devised an impressive schedule to open the independent era.

Calling in favors and leveraging his vast network of relationships and influence across the college basketball landscape, McGuire managed to put together what he touted as one of the most challenging schedules he had ever undertaken as a coach. Indeed, the Gamecocks would play from coast to coast, including matchups with national powers Marquette and Notre Dame, the University of California of the PAC-8, Iowa of the Big Ten, UNLV of the West Coast Athletic Conference, and independents Virginia Tech, Pittsburgh, DePaul, and Houston, in addition to Auburn of the SEC and Clemson of the ACC. The Gamecocks sported a preseason ranking of twelfth, and fan interest remained sky-high as they opened their first season as an independent at Auburn's Beard-Eaves Memorial Coliseum on December 1, 1971.

With stalwarts Roche, Owens, and Ribock lost to graduation, the Gamecocks were tasked with finding a new identity. McGuire looked to six-foot-three junior guard Kevin Joyce to provide leadership to the young team. Joyce, who was the hero of South Carolina's ACC championship win the prior season and averaged 12.1 points per game as a sophomore, was poised to provide that leadership both on and off the court. Six-ten senior Tom Riker from Hicksville, New York, finally had the opportunity to work out of the shadows of Owens and Ribock. Riker was a steady performer as a junior, averaging 14 points and eight rebounds. He and seven-foot junior Danny Traylor of Winston-Salem anchored the front court. Traylor appeared in twenty-four games as a sophomore, averaging 1.8 points per contest.

Starting alongside Joyce, Riker, and Traylor were the senior cocaptains: six-foot-seven Rick Aydlett of Blacksburg, Virginia, a versatile "shooting forward," and six-two senior guard Bob Carver of Forest Hills, New York. Both spent time as role players off the bench while also starting some games the previous season.

New to the varsity were a pair of six-foot-four sophomore guards, Ed Peterson of Silver Spring, Maryland, and Brian Winters of Rockaway Park, New York. Joining them in the sophomore class was six-six forward Rick "Moose" Mousa of Seymour, Indiana. Combined the trio averaged an impressive 70.2 points per game for the freshman team. The hot-shooting Peterson shot .521 from the field as a freshman and averaged a spectacular .933 on seventy of seventy-five shooting from the free throw line. Winters, whom McGuire described as a "complete player," was named to the 1970–71 all-ACC freshman squad and set a freshman record with sixty-nine assists. Rounding out the Gamecock roster was a trio of role-playing reserves, including diminutive junior guard Jimmy Powell of the Bronx, New York, six-five guard/forward combo Billy Grimes of Staten Island, New York, and six-two junior guard Casey Manning of Dillon, South Carolina, who made his varsity debut the previous season as the first African American player in program history.

After handily dispatching Auburn 84–63 in the season opener, the Gamecocks traveled to San Francisco for the prestigious Cable Car Classic. Now ranked eleventh in the AP poll, South Carolina improved to 2–0 with a 77–66 win over Santa Clara in the opening round, then took a 67–59 decision over California to win the tournament championship.

The 3–0 Gamecocks benefited from a wild week in which five teams in the AP top ten lost games, enabling a jump of eight poll spots to number 3, behind only second-place Marquette and top-ranked UCLA ahead of their home opener versus Virginia Tech on Saturday, December 18. South Carolina had narrowly escaped the upset-minded Hokies the previous season, managing to eke out a 78–76 win at Tech's rowdy Cassell Coliseum. The rematch would be even closer. A total of 12,516 fans jammed into the 12,401-seat Carolina Coliseum to welcome the top-five Gamecocks for an 8:30 PM tipoff, televised locally by WIS television.[7]

As in the previous season's contest, the taller, more talented Gamecock squad could never salt the Hokies away, and it was a seesaw battle throughout. Tech's Randy Minix hit the front end of a one-and-one opportunity with under a minute left, pulling the Hokies within one, 77–76, with a chance to tie on the bonus shot. He missed, preserving the slim Carolina lead. Traylor grabbed the rebound and was fouled on the play, giving the seven-footer a chance to secure the win with twenty-three seconds remaining. Traylor missed the front-end shot, but Joyce scrambled for the rebound, and as the Gamecocks set up their half-court offense, the game appeared all but over. When an errant cross-court pass from Riker to Bob Carver sailed out of bounds, the Hokies had the ball and new life with eleven seconds remaining.

The Hokies, still down one, set up for a final shot amid the cacophony of a raucous sellout crowd. As center Charles Lipscomb rose for a fifteen-footer with three seconds remaining, 12,516 fans rose in frozen anticipation, awaiting the shot's verdict like defendants in a high-stakes trial. As they followed the rotation of the ball in its arcing passage, the atmosphere of the arena was frenzied, electric. The ball caromed off the rim into the waiting arms of Traylor, who was fouled. That he missed another front-end charity shot mattered little, as time expired before Tech could get off another shot. The Gamecocks survived another Hokie upset bid and moved to 4–0 on the season, their number 3 ranking preserved.

The Gamecocks traveled to Pittsburgh, where they took a ten-point win over the Pitt Panthers, before moving east to Philadelphia for the Quaker City Classic holiday tournament. South Carolina dominated tiny Fairfield College in an eighteen-point opening-round win, then manhandled Boston College the following night, winning by twenty-two. That win set up a December 30 tournament championship matchup versus a strong Villanova team, which had started the season in the top twenty and would finish in March with an NCAA tournament appearance and a number 15 final ranking. The Gamecocks and Wildcats battled to a thriller, in which the Carolina erased a nine-point second-half deficit with a furious rally. With Villanova back up 77–76 in the final seconds, Joyce launched a pressured jumper from the deep corner, which was just off the mark, handing South Carolina its first loss of the season.

After a ten-day holiday break, the number 4 Gamecocks opened 1972 on January 9 in a top-five matchup on national television with second-ranked Marquette in Columbia. The high-powered Warriors were coached by McGuire protégé Al McGuire. Though the two McGuires were not related, Frank coached the younger McGuire, along with Al's brother Dick, at St. John's between 1947–51, and the two had remained close.

While at UNC, Frank had recommended Al for the coaching vacancy at tiny Belmont Abbey College, the Benedictine enclave just outside of Charlotte. "I thought he would leave me there forever to die in a monastery," Al quipped to Curry Kirkpatrick of *Sports Illustrated*, who covered the Gamecock-Warrior matchup for the magazine's January 17 issue. But Frank soon intervened on Al's behalf again.

In 1964 Marquette offered the elder McGuire its head coaching position, but Frank had already accepted the South Carolina job. He recommended his protégé, and Al began his career at Marquette the same season McGuire began at South Carolina. One of Frank's first calls following South Carolina's ACC exit was to Al, as he attempted to fill the vacuum left in the 1971–72 schedule when ACC schools refused to play his program.[8] In short order a home-and-home contract was finalized, beginning with the January 1972 matchup.

Kirkpatrick, in setting the scene for his *SI* article, wrote:

It was a game made not so much in heaven as in an emerald corner of hell. The coaches mean and hungry, the combatants bred on asphalt playgrounds and nurtured in the slinky, scar-tissue ways of the sport. All of the Irish gags were trotted out. The game should be played behind barbed wire somewhere in the shadows of Ulster. Sean O'Casey would throw up the first ball. Everyone would wear green, and how was the closed-circuit crowd in Belfast taking it anyway? But when the jokes and psychology were over, after the deception and the guile, it was time for the McGuires of college basketball to get right down there into the pit and slug it out in that fashion familiar only to alley fighters.

Reflecting on the game, Kirkpatrick told David Caraviello of the *Charleston Post and Courier* in 2017, "I had never been in the Coliseum with such suspense and tension and excitement." Caraviello noted that the whole event had the air of spectacle. Marquette debuted a new uniform, featuring alternate-colored striping down each side and what Kirkpatrick described as "a certain iridescent shade from which the color of blue may never recover." Al McGuire had designed the uniforms himself, tweaking them to shine under television lights.

Indeed, the game lived up to its bare-knuckled expectations, as just a few minutes into the second half, what had been highly physical play escalated when Marquette's Bob Lakey and USC's Riker tangled after grappling throughout the game. Lakey elbowed Riker in the throat, prompting a retaliatory Riker left cross to Lakey's "side-whiskers," as Kirkpatrick put it. Benches cleared, and several skirmishes ensued, with referees curiously standing aside in the manner of hockey fights, letting the players go at it. "It was ridiculous," Kirkpatrick told Caraviello. The pugilistic exploits continued for around three minutes—fittingly, the length of a round of boxing—before State Law Enforcement Division officers and coaches were able to restore order. Lakey, whose cut above his left eye required three stitches, and Riker, who suffered a sprained wrist, were both tossed. The remainder of the game unfolded without further incident, though plenty of drama awaited.

Al McGuire, with tongue planted firmly in cheek, called the lengthy brawl a "waltz," adding later, "A bar-hall bouncer wouldn't take off his coat for this one."

South Carolina found themselves down by twelve, 52–40, a few minutes after play resumed but mounted a furious comeback, fueled by the hot shooting of Ed Peterson. Competitive energy crackled like heat lightning among the Coliseum rafters, as two Rick Aydlett free throws propelled the Gamecocks into a slim 69–68 lead with 2:38 remaining. The lead was short-lived, as Marquette's big man, Jim Chones, drained a seventeen-footer thirteen seconds later, putting Marquette back on top. The teams traded buckets in the frenetic final two minutes, and Marquette clung to a 72–71 lead as the Gamecocks took their final possession with seconds remaining. Joyce, hustling downcourt against the clock, was forced to pull up for a twenty-two-footer with Chones in his face. The shot was well off mark, capping his worst night as a collegiate player in a 0–12 performance from the floor. The Gamecock all-American scored one point on a free throw, and the Warriors prevailed in one of the more memorable Carolina Coliseum contests of the independent era.

The Gamecocks maintained their number 4 ranking after the Marquette loss and went on to win nine of their next ten contests, the lone setback a 91–85 loss to Iowa of the Big Ten in a neutral-site game in Chicago on January 22. South Carolina fell to eleventh place following the Iowa loss but won the next seven games, including at home versus number 19 Northern Illinois and on the road versus Clemson and UNLV.

Predictably the Gamecocks received a rather unpleasant reception at Clemson's Littlejohn Coliseum on February 5. It was USC's only contest versus a former ACC opponent that season, but the Clemson partisans came armed with a full ACC slate worth of bad feelings on that evening. Tiger partisans behind the Carolina bench, unruly and contemptuous, did not dabble in half measures in displaying their well-honed disdain for McGuire and company. Gamecock supporter Rhett Jackson was compelled to write to Clemson president Robert Edwards two days after the game, describing the scene. "A few people behind our bench made some awful statements about a human being on our team who happens to be black. Also, a few had a dead chicken on a rope, bleeding, and passed it over our bench, players and coaches."

Carolina won the game, 62–58.

McGuire and company recovered to number 7 in the polls before a road trip to Houston on February 19, which resulted in the fourth loss of the season. The Gamecocks fell to ninth in the polls but hit another hot streak, winning the final five games of the regular season, including a rousing 109–83 win over Notre Dame and a thirteen-point win versus Clemson in the regular-season finale, both in Columbia.

USC finished with a regular-season record of 22–4 and were invited to the program's second ever NCAA tournament in the East Regional at Kaplan Arena on the campus of William and Mary in Williamsburg. There the Gamecocks took a low-scoring 53–51 decision over Temple, setting up a Sweet Sixteen matchup versus former ACC nemesis North Carolina (the tournament field included only twenty-five teams in 1972).

The Gamecocks and Tar Heels met on March 16, a year and three days after USC's ACC tournament championship win the prior season. South Carolina held a number 6 ranking, while UNC had risen to number 2. The Tar Heels proved too much, using a 19–5 run to close out the first half after Traylor and Joyce were forced to the bench with foul trouble. The Gamecocks never got back into it, and UNC won going away, 92–69. The Tar Heels went on to place third nationally, while UCLA defeated Florida State to secure their eighth NCAA championship in nine seasons.

Meanwhile South Carolina gained some measure of solace in the consolation game—a rematch from the early-season loss against Villanova in the Quaker City Classic. South Carolina rode a hot-shooting Riker, who poured in thirty-six points in a brilliant farewell performance. The Gamecocks overcame a nine-point deficit to win convincingly, 90–78, earning third place in the East Regional.

With that, the inaugural season as an independent came to a close for McGuire's Gamecock squad, which earned a 24–5 record, and a second-straight Sweet Sixteen appearance in the NCAA tournament. The program said goodbye to seniors Tom Riker, Bob Carver, and Rick Aydlett, program stalwarts, veterans of the ACC wars, and the first senior class to experience independent play.

McGuire's program still felt solid, even prominent on the national landscape. The 1971–72 team placed sixth in the final AP poll and were recognized by those in the college basketball world as a powerhouse, although a deep run in the NCAA tournament had eluded them thus far. Fan interest was still strong, reflected in an average attendance figure of 12,327 through twelve home contests—only 196 per game off the prior season's record of 12,523.

Thanks to an NCAA rule change, the upcoming 1972–73 season would mark the first year for freshmen eligibility on varsity rosters. The Gamecocks fielded a young team, led by senior captain Kevin Joyce, a veteran and starter on that summer's star-crossed US Olympic team, as well as fellow seniors Danny Traylor, the starting center, and guard Casey Manning, who looked for an expanded role in his senior season. The junior class included deadly accurate shooter Brian Winters and tough rebounding forward Rick Mousa.

Three sophomores moved up to varsity from the previous season's last-ever freshman squad in five-foot-eleven point guard Jimmy Walsh, younger brother of McGuire's top assistant, Donnie Walsh; South Carolina product six-seven Clyde Agnew of Greenville High School, and six-foot-six forward Tommy Cox of Washington, DC. Together the trio averaged sixty-two points for the 1971–72 freshman team. A new crop of talented freshmen, perhaps McGuire's last truly great class, was highlighted by a highly sought-after local product, six-foot-eight shooting forward Alex English of Dreher High School; six-seven rebound specialist Bob Mathias of New York City; six-two hot-shooting guard Mike Dunleavy of Brooklyn; and rugged six-six forward Mark Greiner of Charlotte.

McGuire and his Gamecocks entered the off-season cautiously optimistic about the future of the program.

Captain Kevin and His Kiddie Corps

Following the 1972–73 season, the USC athletic department released a twenty-five-minute video compilation of highlights from the 22–7 squad. Narrated by Joe Petty, the longtime sports director for Columbia NBC affiliate, WIS-TV, and the host of Frank McGuire's weekly television show, the film is a testament to the sustained level of culture and excitement that still defined Gamecock basketball.

In his crisp baritone, Petty tells the story of "Captain Kevin and his kiddie corps," a reference to senior captain Kevin Joyce and the talented freshmen who joined him in the starting lineup, Alex English and Mike Dunleavy. The theme music, Frank Sinatra's maudlin 1965 hit "It Was a Very Good Year," captures the sentiment, if not the style and soul, of that exciting team.

The Coliseum was still packed and provided a compelling home-court advantage—the Gamecocks were a perfect 13–0 at home in 1972–73, capping a five-year Coliseum record of 33–4 (.892). Though the average attendance dropped below 12,000 for the first time in three years to 11,770, McGuire's Gamecocks still enjoyed rabid support.

The freshmen, English and Dunleavy along with Mathias and Greiner, combined for 805 points and 460 rebounds, 35.7 percent and 34.5 percent of total team production, respectively. Dunleavy, "a hard-nosed Irish kid who plays the game with reckless abandon," as described by Petty, was all floppy brown hair and pumping fists—an injection of youthful zest and confidence that belied his eighteen years. Columbia's English, known as "Flick" for his release on short jumpers, chose to stay home to the delight of Gamecock faithful and became just the second African American basketball player in program history. He was a smooth shooter with a soft touch and played with an elegant, even artistic flair that belied his physicality. English compiled 422 points, second only to Joyce, and added 306 rebounds on the season.

Junior Brian Winters, the hard driver and downtown bomber, was a versatile, do-it-all performer, who made opponents pay dearly when they double- and triple-teamed Joyce. He struggled with mononucleosis during the season, missing three games, but still averaged 11.5 points per contest, good for fourth on the team. When healthy, he was a streak of wild black hair, diving, darting, driving, and filling the basket at will.

Senior captain Joyce engineered his finest season in garnet and black, pouring in 592 points for a 22.4 average. His 1,400 career points were good for the program's fifth best of all time. His number 43 was retired in a brief ceremony ahead of the final home contest, a 90–79 Gamecock win over Duquesne—only the third retired number in program history. Joyce's fellow seniors Traylor and Manning enjoyed their best seasons at Carolina as well. Traylor started all twenty-nine games, averaging 12.8 points on 52 percent shooting, and collected a team-high 308 rebounds. His hook shot, which he had developed into an accurate weapon over four seasons, could not be blocked. Manning was the team's sixth man, contributing 113 points and 58 rebounds.

The Gamecocks entered the season ranked number 16 but quickly fell out of the polls after an opening-game loss away to number 14 Tennessee. It was the program's first opening-game loss since McGuire arrived in Columbia in 1964. After getting back on track with three home wins versus UNLV, Michigan State, and Georgia Southern, the Gamecocks traveled to Salt Lake City for the Utah Classic holiday tournament. There McGuire's squad suffered a fifteen-point loss to number 14 Providence in the opening round before salvaging the second game versus host team Utah, coached by Bill Foster, a name Gamecock fans would get to know in future years. A nationally televised December 22 matchup with undefeated and ninth-ranked Indiana awaited the 4–2 Gamecock squad back in Columbia. The Bobby Knight–led Hoosiers were big, strong, and talented, featuring future NBA star guard Quinn Buckner, as well as undersized six-eight center Steve Downing, who would be a first-round draft pick of the Boston Celtics following that season.

The bruising Hoosiers dominated the first half and built a fourteen-point lead, but with just over fifteen minutes remaining in the game, Joyce found his range. His hot hand and an aggressive full-court press sparked a furious comeback, capped by an English three-point play, giving the Gamecocks a 78–77 lead at the 5:41 mark. As the Gamecocks came to life, so did the capacity crowd, which turned in a rafter-rattling performance of its own. After a series of lead changes, a Joyce baseline jumper gave USC an 86–85 lead at the 1:47 mark. The Gamecocks held their slim lead over the next ninety seconds, before two Brian Winters free throws at the nineteen-second mark salted the game away, 88–85, sending the crowd into a frenzy. Joyce turned in a career-best performance, scoring forty-one points, twenty-eight of them in the second half.

The 5–2 Gamecocks went 15–4 down the stretch, for a 19–6 regular-season finish and a third straight invitation to the NCAA tournament. This time the Gamecocks were slotted in the Mid-West Regional, where they faced Texas Tech of the Southwest Conference in an opening round game in Wichita. Joyce led a balanced Gamecock attack with twenty-one points, aided by sixteen from Traylor, fifteen from English, and eleven from Dunleavy. The game was a back-and-forth affair before a 26–13 USC run in the final eleven minutes put it out of reach for the Red Raiders. The Gamecocks won 78–70 to advance to their third Sweet Sixteen in as many seasons.

A hot-shooting Memphis State squad awaited South Carolina in the second-round matchup, played in Houston. The Tigers were too tough to tame, taking a 90–76 win and sending the disappointed Gamecocks to another consolation game, where they managed a 90–85 win over South-western Louisiana.[9] Memphis State, meanwhile, made it to the national finals, where they fell to perineal national champion UCLA. South Carolina finished the season unranked in the final AP poll for the first time since 1967–68.

✗   ✗   ✗

With Joyce, Traylor, and Manning lost to graduation, the 1973–74 Gamecocks were the first McGuire squad without a single veteran of the old ACC wars. The Gamecock coaching staff looked and felt different too. Gone was long-time fixture and McGuire confidant Buck Freeman, who retired due to health reasons in the summer of 1973. Assistant Bill Loving had departed as well, to pursue business opportunities. Top assistant Donnie Walsh was still on staff, but McGuire had to manage a substantive staff shake-up for the first time since coming to Columbia.

He lured South Carolina State coach Ben Jobe to take one of the open assistant jobs. Jobe, the program's first Black assistant coach, had compiled a 232–72 record of twelve seasons as head coach in three stops at Talladega College, Alabama State College, and, for five seasons, at SC State.

A native of Nashville, Jobe, like McGuire, was the youngest of thirteen children. He attended Fisk university in Nashville on an academic scholarship, attaining a bachelor of science degree in 1956 and later earning a master of arts degree from Tennessee State. He earned all-conference honors during his junior and senior seasons at Fisk. After a one-season coaching stop at Nashville's Cameron High School, Jobe began his collegiate coaching career in wildly successful, if unconventional, fashion, taking the reins of a junior college program in Sierra Leone, West Africa, where he also taught British history and art. He led the team to a 48–0 record in back-to-back undefeated seasons.

Rounding out the staff was program veteran Bobby Cremins, who McGuire promoted to full time after Cremins joined the staff as a graduate assistant the previous season.

The Gamecocks welcomed a deep, if not deeply talented, freshman class in 1973–74, highlighted by six-foot-four Columbia product Nate Davis, an excellent leaper and skilled rebounder who had led Eau Claire High School to the AAAA state championship the prior season. Another notable roster addition was six-three guard George Felton of Yonkers, New York. Felton had sat out the previous season but averaged 9.2 points per game on the freshman squad of two years prior. Felton hailed from All Hollows High School, the same school that produced former Gamecock captain and current assistant Cremins.

McGuire looked upon senior Brian Winters to provide leadership, picking up the role that had been so ably filled by Joyce the previous two seasons and Roche before that. English and Dunleavy hoped to maintain or improve their impressive play as freshmen, and Bob Mathias, along with Greiner and Davis, would be tasked with replacing Traylor by committee down low.

The '73–'74 squad started 4–2, with losses at seventh-ranked Indiana and a two-point setback to number 13 Alabama in a holiday tournament in Louisville, Kentucky. From there the young squad reeled off thirteen wins over the next fourteen games, highlighted by a two-point thriller over number 6 Marquette in early January before 12,460 fans in a rocking Carolina Coliseum. During a five-game stretch from late January through mid-February, McGuire fell ill with influenza and was unable to attend games. Top assistant Walsh capably filled in, leading the Gamecocks to five wins, the last of which was a February 13 contest at Dwane Morrison–coached Georgia Tech, which Carolina won 82–73.[10] The 17–3 Gamecocks rose to number 14 in the AP poll ahead of a matchup in mid-February with number 3 Notre Dame, coached by Digger Phelps. A total of 12,576 fans jammed into the Coliseum for the highly anticipated matchup.

Compounding a difficult stretch of illness for McGuire, his former assistant and closest confidant, Buck Freeman, died just days before the Notre Dame contest. The South Carolina program had lost its grandfather figure in Freeman, the tall, white-haired gentleman who had become a beloved figure at the university. The feeling had been mutual. Upon his resignation for health reasons in June 1973, he wrote, "I have grown to love Carolina, its faculty, student body, alumni, as well as the City of Columbia."

Despite thirty points from English and a late Gamecock rally, Phelps's Irish squad walked away from Columbia with a hard-fought 72–68 win, handing Carolina its fourth loss of the season. The Gamecocks held firm in the AP rankings, though, and reeled off five straight wins to conclude the regular season, including a seventeen-point humbling of number 11 Pittsburgh in Columbia and an eight-point win on the road versus number 19 Creighton.

The Gamecocks achieved their preseason goals, with a sixth straight twenty-win season and fourth straight invitation to the NCAA tournament. In an odd twist, USC was matched with Furman in the opening round of the East Regional in Philadelphia. The two Palmetto State–based schools, whose campuses were separated by only 112 miles, would have to travel 700 miles north for the matchup. Only 1,042 spectators filed into the 8,725-seat Palestra to witness an ice-cold Gamecock squad in a miserable 38.1 percent shooting performance from the field that got progressively worse, with 31.7 percent shooting in the second half. Despite a twenty-two-point performance by Winters in his final game, the Paladins prevailed 75–67, handing McGuire's program its first opening-round defeat in NCAA tournament play since 1971. The 22–5 Gamecocks finished nineteenth in the final AP poll.

Although those associated with the program could not begin to imagine it then, 1973–74 would mark McGuire's final twenty-win season in Columbia, and the program would not return to the NCAA tournament for another decade and a half. It would be twenty-three years before the Gamecocks would inhabit another season-ending AP poll. Fan interest, too, would begin a precipitous slide. The 11,107-attendance average for 1973–74 marked the final season above the 11,000 mark for Carolina Coliseum.

Slip-Slidin' Away

Despite still-talented teams, including English and Dunleavy for another two seasons, Nate Davis for another three, and other notable newcomers, such as a ball-handling whiz from New Jersey, Jackie Gilloon; sharp-shooting Buffalo, New York, guard Billy Truitt; SC State transfer center-forward Tommy Boswell; and forward Golie Augustus, a Columbia product, McGuire's program struggled to regain the success it had enjoyed over the prior six seasons.

An NCAA rule change for the 1974–75 season that allowed second-place conference teams into the NCAA tournament further crowded the field, leaving fewer at-large bids available for independent teams. This development had the additional impact of diminishing the prestige of the rival National Invitational Tournament (NIT), which had in years past been a highly desirable and competitive alternative to the NCAA tourney, particularly given the location of the NIT's final four, played at the mecca of college basketball, New York City's Madison Square Garden.

Indeed, the Gamecocks' 18–8 regular-season finish in 1974–75 might have been enough for an NCAA bid in prior years, but McGuire and company had to settle for the program's second-ever NIT bid. The Gamecocks beat the University of Connecticut in the opening round, 71–61, before losing 86–67 to eventual NIT champ Princeton. Carolina finished the season 19–9.

Besides the disappointment of missing the coveted twenty-win mark and a fifth straight NCAA tournament invitation, other factors converged to place pressure on McGuire's program. Recruiting was in decline and was becoming ever more difficult. The legendary Irishman, now sixty-two, was losing his grip on his vaunted New York City recruiting pipeline.

As Dan Klores noted in *Roundball Culture,* a number of McGuire's New York City contacts were dead. Age had weakened the judgment of others. Similar to his contemporaries John Wooden and Adolph Rupp, McGuire did not spend as much time on the recruiting trails as he once did. The highest-profile New York City recruits were increasingly committing to younger coaches like Lefty Driesell of Maryland, Al McGuire of Marquette, Dean Smith of UNC, and Digger Phelps of Notre Dame. With the rise and increasing dominance of elite Black players, those coaches all had the additional advantage of being located outside of the Deep South.

Diminished too, was the commonality between McGuire and his players, who had historically been almost uniformly Northeastern, White, and typically Catholic kids who grew up idolizing the coach. His young recruits strived to be tough, classy, and strong, like McGuire himself. They regarded him with unreserved respect bordering on awe. Increasingly, Klores notes, McGuire's new charges came from diverse backgrounds. They came from small southern towns and affluent suburbs, from the rural Midwest, and a lingering few from the big city. They all brought impressive credentials to McGuire's program, but they had differing ideas about the game and about life outside of the gym. The team no longer spent time together away from the court. There were rumors of dissension—no uniformity of purpose.

Four years removed from ACC membership, South Carolina was, by most measures, on the cusp of a sustained decline. Former ACC rivals, meanwhile, were thriving. NC State had just won the 1974 national championship—the ACC's first since McGuire's own championship with UNC in 1957. Driesell was building a powerhouse at Maryland. Dean Smith was churning out elite teams season after season. Virginia had hired a young Terry Holland away from Davidson, and he was building a highly competitive program. Duke, which had been stagnant in the post–Vic Bubas era, had lured program builder Bill Foster away from Utah, and Foster would have the Blue Devils playing for a national championship within just a few years. Even Clemson rose to competitiveness in the mid-to-late 1970s with another Bill Foster at the helm. ACC basketball was solidifying its reputation as the premier conference in all of college basketball, and within a few years it would have a lucrative new television package to show for it. Despite some hopeful talk of détente and ACC expansion, a suddenly struggling South Carolina program was on the outside looking in.

By 1975 the political scene within the university had turned in an unfavorable direction as well. Athletics director and head football coach Dietzel never realized the post-ACC nirvana he envisioned in leading USC out of the conference in 1971. After the 6–5 season that year, his program declined to 4–7 in 1972, his seventh season at the helm in Columbia, and pressure began to mount on the coach. G.R.O.D. (Get Rid of Dietzel) bumper stickers appeared around Columbia. An admirable rebound to 7–4 in 1973 raised hopes, and although the Gamecocks were left out of a bowl, expectations were high for the 1974 squad. But when the Gamecocks dropped that season's first two contests versus Georgia Tech and Duke, Dietzel tendered his resignation effective at the end of that season, which would end at 4–7.

Throughout the fall of 1974, speculation swirled in local media about who the Gamecocks would name to replace Dietzel. Mooney Player, the highly successful forty-two-year-old coach of Lower Richland High School just southeast of Columbia, lobbied openly for the job and gained broad-based support in Columbia, most notably from Frank McGuire. Player had won 80 percent of his games at the high school level and had served for a time as kicking coach under Lou Holtz at NC State before returning to the high school ranks. Player promised eight wins during his first season, or he would resign.

Meanwhile USC power brokers, including Sol Blatt Sr. and Jr., and board of trustees chair T. Eston Marchant supported Texas Tech head coach Jim Carlen, and McGuire's open backing of Player did not sit well. McGuire also pursued the open athletics director position. He had achieved an uneasy peace with Dietzel over the years and did not relish the idea of starting over with yet another football coach/AD arrangement. McGuire's advocacy for Player and his own AD aspirations soured relations between him and Blatt Sr., who still maintained an outsized influence over USC affairs in the position of Speaker Emeritus of the South Carolina House of Representatives.

The USC board hired Carlen on Friday, December 13, 1974, appointing him head football coach and associate athletics director for football. McGuire was named associate athletics director for basketball operations, while Bo Hagan, a Gamecock football letterman from the late 1940s, was given the nominal title of athletics director, though he had no influence over the school's two major sports. All three men were to report to the university's president, James Patterson. McGuire, who was in New York on a recruiting trip and unaware of the board's decision, discovered the news via press reports. Marchant claimed that both he and Patterson attempted to reach McGuire but were unable to do so.

Tension between McGuire and Carlen was evident almost from the outset and led to factions among the board of trustees, boosters, and fans. After a successful first season in Columbia, highlighted by a rousing 56–20 win over archrival Clemson and an appearance in the Tangerine Bowl, Carlen was named athletics director for all sports other than basketball in 1976, while McGuire maintained his title as associate AD for basketball.[11] Hagan, meanwhile, was reassigned within the department. By spring 1977 the university selected Jim Holderman as its twenty-fifth president. Additional political turmoil awaited McGuire as Holderman attempted to insert his influence over the state of athletics administration at the university.

An illustration of just how precarious McGuire's position had become by the mid-seventies was his hiring of assistant Gregg Blatt, the son of Sol Blatt Jr., to replace Bobby Cremins prior to the 1975–76 season after Cremins departed for a head coaching opportunity at Appalachian State. Blatt had served a brief stint as an assistant at College of Charleston and had been a member of USC's freshman team during his days as a student at South Carolina but did not possess the credentials of a typical McGuire assistant. The hire was a clear act of political expediency—an attempt to shore up his position with the university power brokers. The move failed to pay dividends, however, when McGuire kept the younger Blatt largely at arm's length, mostly away from active coaching and on the road scouting prospects. The elder Blatts were predictably unhappy with McGuire's treatment of young Gregg, and the coach's olive branch did not yield the desired results.

Another apparent political favor gone sideways involved a scholarship to six-foot-one guard Bill Gause for the 1975–76 season. The son of a prominent Columbia physician and well-heeled Gamecock booster, Gause had enjoyed a fine career at Columbia's private Hammond Academy, where he scored 2,277 points in leading Hammond to a 122–9 record during his high school career. But he did not possess the physical tools to compete at the Division I level, and when playing time did not materialize, McGuire lost favor with yet another influential figure.

During the 1976–77 season, McGuire reached a rare milestone with his five hundredth career win. The season had started poorly over the first fourteen games, with the Gamecocks compiling a 5–9 record. But there were glimmers of hope, including a spirited four-point loss at top-ranked Michigan on January 2, the Gamecocks' fourth top-five opponent in three weeks. By February 9 the Gamecocks were riding a five-game win streak, pushing their record above .500 ahead of a home matchup with the Citadel. South Carolina beat the Bulldogs handily, 85–66, pushing their win streak to six and providing McGuire the milestone win. It was an accomplishment that solidified his standing as a legendary figure in the college game and allowed his current squad to enjoy the reflected glory of teams past. The milestone also prompted a temporary thaw in relations between McGuire and his detractors, as the university looked for a proper way to recognize the coach.

When McGuire was inducted into the Naismith Memorial Basketball Hall of Fame soon after, the university feted him with a black-tie appreciation night and banquet at Carolina Coliseum on March 22, 1977. The event attracted a who's who of former players, fellow coaches, and celebrities from the sports, entertainment, and political worlds. Speakers included University of Texas coach Abe Lemons, the president of the National Association of Basketball Coaches; Martin O'Malley, McGuire's high school coach; Gamecock lettermen Bobby Carver and Bobby Cremins; Eddie Einhorn, a pioneer in college basketball broadcasting; Horace "Bones" McKinney, former Wake Forest coach; and Dean Smith of UNC. Other attendees included author James A. Michener; legendary former coach of the University of Kentucky Adolph Rupp; DePaul coach Ray Meyer; St. John's coach Lou Carnesecca; Claire Bee, an early innovator of the college game; ACC commissioner Robert James; and former South Carolina governor Robert E. McNair. The event also marked the twentieth anniversary of McGuire's 1957 championship at UNC, and many of his former Tar Heel players attended.

The splashy affair was designed to emulate *The Dean Martin Celebrity Roast,* a show then popular on television. Wake Forest's McKinney was a crowd favorite, bringing down the house with his humorous recollections of ACC battles and rivalries past. Pointing at the characteristically immaculate McGuire, particularly resplendent that night in tuxedo finery, a grinning McKinney quipped, "He looks so good in his game uniform."

In April USC trustees voted to name the arena portion of Carolina Coliseum for McGuire. In March the South Carolina legislature had voted overwhelmingly to rename the entire building "McGuire Coliseum," but Chairman Marchant, in his announcement to the press, clarified that the action related to the basketball portion of the Coliseum, not the entire complex, which included USC's School of Journalism among other classroom space. Under increasing pressure from the legislature and the public to properly honor McGuire, the board waived a self-imposed rule of not naming university buildings for present employees of the school. "There had been considerable feeling among the public and public officials that we honor McGuire now," Marchant explained, "and we felt it appropriate to do it now instead of waiting."

Prior to the 1977–78 season, longtime top assistant Donnie Walsh left McGuire's staff for an assistant coaching position with the Denver Nuggets under coach Larry Brown, a teammate of Walsh's at UNC in the early sixties. Walsh had served as McGuire's loyal right-hand man through twelve seasons, building a reputation as one of the bright young minds of the game. For many years Walsh appeared to be the heir apparent to McGuire at South Carolina. With the shifting political winds, however, Walsh ultimately decided the time was right to seek his fortunes elsewhere.[12] In the wake of Walsh's departure, McGuire named Jobe his top assistant. Former Gamecock great Kevin Joyce joined McGuire's staff as an assistant after his professional career was cut short due to a severe knee injury.

McGuire's final five squads at South Carolina would win eighteen, fourteen, sixteen, fifteen, and sixteen games, respectively. All were marginal winners, while only the sixteen-win 1977–78 squad reached the postseason—an NIT bid that resulted in a twelve-point first-round loss to former ACC rival NC State. Average attendance at the Coliseum continued to decline year after year, bottoming out in 1979–80, McGuire's final season, at 5,937 fans per game, less than half the arena's 12,401 capacity.[13]

The period was not without some success and a few bright spots, including the stellar career of Alex English, who performed with aristocratic elegance across a career that ended with him as the program's all-time scoring leader. His 1,972 career points would stand as a program-best for over two decades, and he remains in second place.[14] English's number, 22, was retired at season's end, the fourth player in program history to receive that distinction.

The 1977–78 Gamecocks defeated number 7 Notre Dame by a score of 65–60 on national television, the signature win of the latter McGuire years, marking the great coach's final victory over a ranked opponent. Six-foot-nine center Jimmy Graziano of Farmingdale, New York; six-eight power forward Cedric Hordges, a transfer from Auburn; and St. Matthews sharpshooting guard Zam Fredrick were among the notable players of McGuire's final few seasons. But the bright spots were fleeting, the talent not enough, the fan interest too far gone to revive by the late seventies.

Under increasing pressure, McGuire agreed to step away following the 1979–80 campaign after sixteen largely successful seasons that effectively changed the culture of an entire state. Dan Klores wrote eloquently of McGuire's legacy in *Roundball Culture:*

> Even the most diehard Clemson fans recognized, basketball had grown in South Carolina because Frank had popularized it. There were backboards in the driveways of private homes; television schedules with an abundance of hoop games; multimillion dollar coliseums; radical improvements on the junior high, prep school and small college level and competitive summer camps because in March, 1964 Frank McGuire moved to the Palmetto State and subsequently delivered. Moreover, in the process of doing so, Frank had always treated fans, listeners, country people, city folk and casual acquaintances with respect, not arrogance. He had never belittled his own players as an excuse for losing; he had never spoken negatively about the state; he had never talked down to his constituents, and he had brought more joy, laughter and pleasure to their hearts than almost any other individual.

A Forensic Accounting

ACC membership was not without vexing problems for South Carolina prior to its departure, but had cooler heads prevailed and the Gamecocks remained in the conference, that affiliation certainly would have insulated McGuire's program from the most debilitating reversals. Rivalries alone would have sold tickets. The opportunity for Gamecock fans to loathe UNC and Duke and Maryland in the flesh for forty minutes would have consistently drawn twelve thousand fans to the Coliseum year after year.

Continued ACC membership along with a more compelling home-court atmosphere would have solidified recruiting, keeping the Gamecocks competitive for years longer under McGuire and assuring the opportunity for more conference titles, more NCAA tournament appearances, and more national relevance as the television age unfolded. Those things, in turn, would have shielded McGuire from the toxic political elements within the university. Some of those elements may never have developed to begin with, given the stability of a prestigious conference home and sustained, high-level success in at least one of the major sports.

Perhaps given all that, a Donnie Walsh or a young Bobby Cremins might have stayed on to succeed McGuire, ensuring for the program an exciting young legacy replacement from the McGuire coaching tree and sustained ties to the program's storied past. As it was, an aging McGuire was cast adrift, largely alone and left to market a declining program to fans who had little interest in the likes of Duquesne, or Fordham, or St. Louis, or Canisius.

Fine programs though they might have been, there was just no draw, none of the dash and roar and roiling vitriol of the old Tobacco Road rivalries, which harkened back beyond the ACC to the sepia-toned Southern Conference days and the very origins of the program itself. Those echoes, though only faint whispers now, can still be heard on a quiet visit to the "House that Frank built" at the corner of Assembly and Blossom.

The forensic analysis shows McGuire's program died a death by a thousand cuts over the course of a decade. But South Carolina's ACC departure was the first and deepest, and it left the program vulnerable to the other cuts that followed.

4

Legends, Logos, Mascots, and Traditions

How the Independent Era
Changed Everything

South Carolina's twenty-year sojourn through independent status proved a font of vibrant Gamecock traditions. From the spine-tingling football entrance to Richard Strauss's *Also sprach Zarathustra* to the block *C* and Gamecock logo; from that much-heralded monument to tailgating, the Cockaboose Railroad, to Cocky, one of the nation's most beloved and recognizable mascots. The independent era changed the face of Gamecock athletics and launched the modern brand of South Carolina's flagship institution.

The era was bookended by the unpromising and the bizarre, starting with the introduction of a gangly, pre-Cocky mascot prototype in 1971 and ending with an exorcism just one day before the Gamecocks kicked off their first SEC football contest in 1992. Yes, an exorcism. But more about that later.

Early Birds

In a 2017 article for *NCAA Champion Magazine*, Jeff Vrabel explores the origin of the term *mascot*. The term seems to have come from 1880s France and an opera titled *Le Mascotte*, which loosely translates to The Lucky Charm." The work centers around a poor Italian farmer who, among other misfortunes, cannot get crops to grow. Enter Bettina, a mysterious and lovely stranger who visits the farmer, turning around his luck and fortunes. The term

Cocky walking with USC cheerleader and young fan in 1983.
Courtesy of the *State* Newspaper Archive, Richland County Public Library.

crossed the Atlantic in the 1900s and came to mean a talisman—a bringer of good fortune.

Live mascots have been around since at least the 1890s, when "Handsome Dan," a bulldog owned by a member of the student body, began appearing at Yale football games. By the 1970s, in part an outgrowth of the highly popular Muppets from television, costumed mascots increasingly became fixtures of both professional and college sports, most notably the San Diego Chicken in 1974 and the Philly Phanatic in 1977. They were dynamic, engaging, and inextricably tied to branding. "A mascot is the personification of a school's brand," according to Michael Lewis, a marketing professor at Emory University. "They work because they give something for the community to rally around, something for everyone to have in common. Everyone at the University of Florida knows about the Gators. Everyone at Texas A&M knows about the collie. It's a social point for the university and the community."

Indeed, Gamecock Nation has fully embraced Cocky, that lovably goofy and slightly rotund costumed chicken who has roamed the sidelines and courtsides of Gamecock sporting events since 1980. He has endeared himself to the broader community as well, appearing at charitable events, children's hospitals, celebrations, and private parties in Columbia and beyond. His likeness adorns stuffed toys, Christmas ornaments, and all manner of T-shirts and memorabilia.

Cocky has also won national acclaim, bringing home championships from National Cheerleaders Association competitions in 1986, 1994, and 2008. In 2004 he won the inaugural Capital One Mascot Challenge, and *Sports Illustrated* ranked him seventh on its list of the greatest mascots in college football history. Cocky has become such an iconic fixture at USC that in 2017 the university unveiled a six-foot-five, 773-pound bronze statue of the bird on Gibbes Green, in the heart of campus. There Cocky sits on a bench, whimsically inviting a steady stream of selfie takers and Instagram posters.

He hasn't always been so popular.

South Carolina experimented with various iterations of costumed Gamecocks over the decades. Perhaps the first known effort was the brainchild of Jerry Spann, a USC cheerleader in 1961. Spann worked with his girlfriend's mother to create a costume that featured a rubber glove attached to a beanie cap, vaguely resembling a cock's comb. Spann wore this in combination with a long-tailed coat, a feather duster on the rear for a tail, and yellow leggings. Spann gave his costume the no-nonsense if slightly unimaginative title "the Gamecock."

In an episode covering the evolution of Cocky on *Remembering the Days,* a podcast dedicated to University of South Carolina history, host Chris Horn tells the story of students from opposing universities giving chase to Spann in an effort to steal his feather duster tail. Spann recalled that most of those students were wearing loafers and tended to be quite inebriated. The undeterred Spann, meanwhile, always wore track shoes.

"Waldo," another student funded and built effort, appeared at home football games in the mid-1960s. Though little information remains, one photo survives on the Gamecock News.net site. The photo shows a helmeted Waldo standing in front of the student section along the east stands of Carolina Stadium, "hands" on hips, taking in the action. He was a barrel-chested, saucer-eyed bird, with a diagonal *USC* emblazoned across his garnet jersey. He had a

Early mascot "Waldo" during a 1961 pep rally at Davis Field. Courtesy of the *State* Newspaper Archive, Richland County Public Library.

large yellow beak and a look of perpetual surprise. In the background students can be seen in the more formal dress of the day—slacks and Arrow shirts, some wearing ties. The exact date and game are lost to history, but it appears to have been a crisp fall afternoon, perhaps mid-October, the early-season Columbia humidity blessedly passed. Perhaps it was October 16, 1965, when the Gamecocks dismantled Wake Forest 38–7. It was a good day for Waldo.

After years of nonsanctioned, student-led efforts, the university officially recognized its first costumed mascot in 1971, when undergraduate biology major John Nelson debuted as "the Rooster." Nelson's mother built the costume, which included garnet and black fabric feathers, a cardboard bill, Styrofoam spurs, and a calf-length garnet cape. The Rooster stalked the sidelines of Gamecock football and basketball games until Nelson graduated in 1973. He eventually returned to his alma mater as a professor, where he worked for three decades, ending his career as the curator of the university's A. C. Moore Herbarium. His Rooster costume can still be seen at McKissick Museum on the USC campus.

During the fall semester of 1978, Chuck Eaton, an interdisciplinary studies major from Mauldin, South Carolina, went to work on the next Gamecock mascot. He conceived the costume, which he called "Big Spur," as a way to bring more excitement to the annual Carolina versus Clemson game and undertook a fundraising campaign as a fraternity pledge project. "Everything was going great," Eaton told Becky Lafitte of the *State* in recalling the story of Big Spur in 1979. "We ordered a $400 costume and had raised over one fourth of the money when I decided to drop out of the fraternity. After that the fraternity dropped the idea," Eaton said. A local pizzeria came to the rescue, donating the remaining balance.

Eaton introduced Big Spur during a USC-Clemson basketball game on December 6, 1978, at Carolina Coliseum. Standing nine feet tall and six feet from the front of his beak to the end of his tail, Big Spur was massive and unwieldy. "The costume takes its toll on me after about eight hours, because it's so tremendous," said Eaton. "Because of the size, I'm restricted as to what I can do during games." He was an aggressive-looking bird, with, as Horn described, "spooky eyes." Even still, Big Spur was a hit with fans, despite frequent reports of his tail feathers hitting people on the sideline.

Over the course of 1979 and 1980, Big Spur was a regular at men's and women's basketball, baseball, and football games, but by the spring of 1980, the costume was showing wear. Designed by a local theater company, Big Spur was "falling apart game by game," according to Linda Singer, assistant athletics director for women's sports, who also oversaw mascots at the time. Singer knew a new mascot costume was needed and wanted to take the opportunity to do something different. She wanted a more durable yet versatile costume, one that would allow the wearer to move more freely in order to engage with fans. And so Singer commissioned a Texas manufacturer to build a shorter, chubbier, more huggable bird.

A Legend Is Hatched

Cocky debuted at the homecoming football game versus Cincinnati on October 18, 1980. "It was instant antagonism," said Singer. "A lot of people didn't like him. He was little on top and big through the middle and he looked, well,

Cocky and Big Spur perform at women's basketball game, circa 1981.
Courtesy of University Archives, South Caroliniana Library,
University of South Carolina.

pregnant." Fans commented that Cocky "just didn't look dignified enough." After the chilly fan reception, Cocky was benched for the following game, a top-fifteen contest on national television at powerhouse Georgia. Pressed back into service, Big Spur represented the Gamecocks through the Gator Bowl and into basketball season. Cocky reappeared at women's basketball contests during the 1980–81 season as "Super Chick," complete with lipstick and accessories. He caught the attention of baseball coach June Raines, who invited Cocky to attend baseball games that spring, and he soon became a fixture at Sarge Frye Field. Cocky shared the stage with Big Spur through the fall of 1981, gaining more prominence as the Big Spur costume continued its slow decline.

Fans eventually warmed to Cocky with his mischievous antics. "You can get away with anything," said John Routh, the first Cocky performer. At a

1981 football game, Cocky grabbed a highway patrolman's hat and handcuffs and ran off with them. As he patrolled the sidelines with his goofy, oversized feet, putting hexes on opposing players, presenting eye charts for baseball umpires to examine, and interacting with fans in his exuberant, wordless manner, Cocky won the hearts and minds of Carolina faithful.

By the start of the 1981–82 basketball season, Cocky was firmly entrenched, and the athletic department began advertising the mascot's availability for photographs and autographs during pregame events. He even received a shout-out from men's basketball coach Bill Foster. In a March 4, 1982, interview about the benefits of increased television exposure for college basketball, Foster noted, "You can't put a dollar figure on (that) exposure. That's why we take the cheerleaders and Cocky. You get a total upbeat image out."

Cocky gained a wider audience when he traveled with USC's baseball team to the 1981 College World Series in Omaha, Nebraska. He proved such a hit with the fans that he was invited back as the official CWS mascot when the Gamecocks returned in 1982. A June 8, 1982, article in the *State* titled "Mr. Popularity" described Cocky's crowd-pleasing antics. "He scratches around in the batter's box, falls off the mound, harasses the umpires, dances to the house organ music and generally has a good time. During rain delays, he kept the crowd relaxed and informed, marching to the pitcher's mound under a comically tiny umbrella to check for rainfall, and when it was time to play, donning gigantic sunglasses."

Following his national exposure in Omaha, Cocky won the first of his national mascot championships—this at a time when no Gamecock team had ever won a national championship. He became a point of pride for the university and Gamecock fans everywhere.[1]

Over the decades Cocky ingrained himself into the very fabric of university culture. He has held court with visiting dignitaries, including Presidents Ronald Reagan and George H. W. Bush, as well as Pope John Paul II. Perhaps his greatest work has been in the community, where he frequently visits terminally ill children and adults, among other good works. In 1987 he was named by the South Carolina legislature as a goodwill ambassador for the State of South Carolina.

Evolution of the Gamecock Logo

In the early decades of varsity athletics, South Carolina teams were represented by a variety of Gamecock logos. They were nondescript roosters crowing or strutting in some fashion. Generic barnyard portrayals, not officially
sanctioned by the university.

In the late 1950s, officials with the Gamecock Club approached Jack
Smyrl, a staff artist with the *State* newspaper from 1947 to 1986, about drawing an image they could put on napkins and other memorabilia for club
events. Smyrl obliged, creating the first official Gamecock mascot, for which
he was paid the princely sum of ten dollars, equivalent to about one hundred
dollars in 2002. He created a more aggressive bird in fighting pose, wings
spread, spurs up, and poised for combat. The logo adorned the USC Field
House court during the final decade of that building's existence and served as
the official Gamecock logo until the arrival of head football coach and athletics director Paul Dietzel in 1966.

Dietzel made it an early priority upon coming to Columbia to update the
Gamecock logo with something more defiant looking. An accomplished artist himself, he possessed a flair for creative branding. He asked talented artist
and team dentist Bill Smith to draw a new gamecock, and Smith's version was
introduced on the cover of the Carolina versus Memphis State game program
on September 24, 1966.

The updated logo faced left to right, with wings and spurs extended in
an aggressive, advancing posture while tail feathers flowed behind. The bird
clutched a streaming banner bearing the words "Scholarship-Leadership" in
its lower claw.

Legend has it that Dietzel craftily incorporated his initials among the
tail feathers. Andy Demetra, a former radio voice of Gamecock basketball
and baseball broadcasts, penned an article for his "Inside the Chart" series
in the October 2, 2013, edition of *Spurs and Feathers Magazine*. Demetra had
recently been told of the well-hidden initials and tried unsuccessfully to con-
firm the rumor with Dietzel prior to the coach's passing in September of that
year.

Had Dietzel taken Smith's design and modified the feathers to form his initials, Demetra pondered, or had Smith added them on his own as a sly tribute to his friend? Or was it all just blissful coincidence? The full answer may be obscured by time and uncertainty, but upon focus, the *PD* does come into view, and it remains a fitting tribute to the man most responsible for modernizing Gamecock athletics.[2]

When Jim Carlen replaced Dietzel as head football coach and athletics director in 1975, Smith once again assisted in updating the Gamecock logo. The revised Gamecock appeared sans banner and framed with a bold block *C*. It debuted on USC's revamped football helmets in the 1975 season and remains in use today.

In 1983 Lewis Brierly, a USC professor of graphic arts, proposed a more modern logo update. Brierly argued the current logo was too complex, and when reduced in size or viewed from a distance, it became a "glob." "It has all the personality of a Gamecock, but not the thrust," he judged. Brierly's simplified logo included a forward-leaning block *C,* with a pared-down gamecock head and what appeared to be racing stripes to emphasize "thrust." The *State's* editorial board panned the proposed logo, noting that while they made no claim to an understanding of thrust or of the finer points, or even the broad ones, of graphic art, all they saw was something resembling a demented, high-tech rooster. Fan reaction was similarly cool, and the Brierly rooster was summarily thrust into oblivion.

But Brierly was onto something with his emphasis on branding and identity. The Gamecock logo, like logos across the spectrum of collegiate and professional sports, is a dynamic marketing tool. The block *C* emblem is synonymous with the university itself and is a powerful economic driver for the university and retailers. Branding drives apparel sales, and Gamecock fans soon purchased all manner of items with the block *C* logo. Shirts and other memorabilia drove profits for booksellers on and near campus long before the rise of internet sales.

Branded apparel sales at the University of South Carolina and across the collegiate landscape of the early 1980s was on the cusp of a decades-long boom. Nike, the surging sportswear behemoth from Beaverton, Oregon, released their first television ad in 1982, and by 1985 had inked a revolutionary sponsorship deal with rising NBA star Michael Jordan. By the 1990s Nike and its competitors Adidas and Russell, among others, began signing increasingly more lucrative apparel and shoe deals with prominent athletics departments. By the 2000s Under Armour, an upstart brand founded by former University of Maryland football walk-on Kevin Plank, entered the competition, and the arms race of apparel deals truly took off.

By 2016 Nike, Under Armour, and Adidas pumped more than $300 million into athletics departments. In 2013 South Carolina signed a ten-year, $71.5 million deal with Under Armour, which was the seventh most valuable deal in college athletics at the time and second highest in the SEC. In the 2016–17 fiscal year, South Carolina earned $8.5 million from this deal, including $4.5 million in equipment and apparel and $4 million in cash. A short time later, Nike signed $252 million and $250 million extension deals with Ohio State and Texas, respectively. UCLA's Under Armour contract guarantees that school $9 million in cash payouts annually.

Indeed, apparel money has been a boon to the largest and most prestigious athletics departments across the country during a time when state funding for public universities has been in major decline, and a vast majority of departments operate in the red. Of the 1,100 schools across 102 conferences throughout the NCAA, only 25 athletics departments (.02%) made a profit in the 2018–19 fiscal year.[3]

So what's in it for the shoe companies? A lot, as it turns out. Sales of collegiate-licensed apparel generated an eye-popping $4.6 billion in annual sales in 2012 and has continued a steady climb over the decade since. Collectively collegiate-licensed apparel is second only to Major League Baseball ($5 billion) and ahead of the National Football League ($3.25 billion), the National Basketball Association ($3 billion), and the National Hockey League ($1.3 billion). Branded apparel accounts for 65 percent of the retail marketplace for collegiate licensed merchandise.

Moreover, the demographics of college sports fans include an estimated 190 million people—approximately 56 percent of the US population who have some rooting affinity for a college team. This group is diverse and largely wealthy, accounting for 80 million females, 60 million minorities, and more than 30 million earning over $100,000 annually.

So while the block *C* and gamecock is garnet and black, manufacturers of apparel and the merchants who sell them find the logo a deeply satisfying shade of green.

2001: A Space Odyssey

Tommy Suggs, longtime color analyst for the Gamecock Radio Network and a former Gamecock quarterback (1968–70), has enjoyed more than a few notable highlights throughout his decades-long association with the University of South Carolina. He captained the 1969 ACC champion Gamecocks, still the only team in program history to win an outright conference championship. He was a three-year starter who went 3–0 against Clemson and passed for 4,916 total yards, still good for tenth all-time in program history. Perhaps his greatest contribution though, was an idea inspired by none other than Elvis Presley.

In February, 1977, just six months before Pressley's death, Suggs attended Elvis' concert at Carolina Coliseum and was struck by the King's dramatic stage entrance to music from *2001: A Space Odyssey,* Stanley Kubrick's iconic 1968 sci-fi epic. Presley used the theme to open his shows from 1971 until his death a few months after the Columbia concert in 1977.

Suggs thought, "If it's good enough for the King, it's good enough for USC," and pitched the idea of using the music, the opening theme from Strauss's tone poem *Also sprach Zarathustra,* for the Gamecocks to head coach Jim Carlen. In the final two home games of 1981, Carlen's final season, the marching band played *Zarathustra,* but Suggs says nobody heard it, and he realized it needed to be played over the stadium sound system.

The university was installing an updated sound system during 1982, Richard Bell's lone season as head coach, so did not use the entrance. By 1983, Coach Joe Morrison's first season, "it all came together," says Suggs, "and the rest is history." Since the opening game of the 1983 season, Gamecock football teams have made their dramatic stadium entrance to *Zarathustra.* It is a spectacle to behold. *Sports Illustrated* and *ESPN* have listed it as one of the top five entrances in college football.

Strauss's original tone poem, composed in 1896, was inspired by Friedrich Nietzsche's philosophical novel of the same title. It was first performed in

November 1896 in Frankfurt, Germany. The version used in Kubrick's film was recorded by the Vienna Philharmonic and became a pop-culture phenomenon following the film's release. The music was often used as a portent for a significant event, as in Kubrick's film, and was an effective means to enhance the drama of Elvis's entrances. Professional wrestler Ric Flair also used the theme for his ring entrance throughout much of his career.

The theme is hypnotic, building in progression from a low-humming organ introduction to the repeating sequence of three trumpeting notes, each ending more urgently than the last, before ascending to a dramatic and triumphant fanfare. The three sequences represent the evolution of man in both Strauss's music and Kubrick's film, with the fanfare representing the final stage of evolution. And though obscure literary themes may not be top of mind on fall Saturdays at Williams-Brice Stadium, the musical effects are no less profound. A stadium full of garnet-clad Gamecock fans enters a frenzied state as Cocky, timed with the third sequence of notes, appears from his "magic box" at midfield, and as the theme crescendos, the team explodes out of the locker room, streaking through white smoke and the human tunnel formed by USC's marching band, which immediately strikes up a rousing rendition of "Step to the Rear."

The grandiosity of the entrance can seem somewhat misplaced, even awkward when times are bad, such as during the Gamecocks' 0–21 streak of 1998–99. But on those fall Saturdays when competitive Gamecock teams face a strong rival, particularly night games, when fans have enjoyed a day of tailgating, the *Zarathustra* entrance is transcendent and provides the Gamecocks a truly intimidating home-field advantage. It is a feast for the senses, and one of the truly special traditions in all of college football.

"If It Ain't Swayin', We Ain't Playin'"

Fans first noticed it on a crisp early autumn evening in 1983. South Carolina soundly defeated legendary power Southern Cal 38–14 before a rowdy sellout crowd at Williams-Brice Stadium. First-year coach Joe Morrison brought a renewed sense of enthusiasm and swagger to the USC program and to its long-suffering yet eternally optimistic fanbase.

Through four games, the Gamecocks' record stood at 2–2, after an opening loss to an eleventh-ranked UNC Tar Heel team and two wins versus Miami (Ohio) and Duke followed by a 31–13 setback at fourteenth-ranked Georgia. Next up was "the other USC," the mighty Trojans of the University of Southern California. The 7 PM kickoff allowed for day-long tailgating, and by the time *Zarathustra* blared over the stadium speakers, the Gamecock crowd was in full voice.

Following a pivotal third-down stop late in the third quarter, with the crowd jumping and boisterous, the upper-east deck began to sway noticeably. One unnamed fan described the motion as a "resonant up and down movement rippling from north to south." He elaborated, "I thought it [the upper-east deck] was going to fall. It scared me to death."

Dave Rinker, the USC vice president for facilities, downplayed the movement in an October 5, 1983, article in the *State,* saying, "it is well known and normal that a structure of this type will exhibit some deflections and vibrations." The matter died down until fans again reported swaying during a highly competitive loss versus third-ranked Nebraska in October 1986.

Following the Nebraska incident, USC hired engineers to thoroughly inspect the upper-east deck. Engineers pointed to "harmonic resonance," a phenomenon in which vibrations, in this case from thousands of excited fans, can increase drastically, sending resonant vibrations traveling through a structure in the form of torsional waves. If unchecked and severe enough, these vibrations can cause damage and even the catastrophic failure of a structure. Harmonic resonance is most often cited in bridge collapses, the most famous example being the 1940 collapse of the Tacoma Narrows Bridge in Washington, otherwise known as "Gallopin' Gertie."

Though engineers provided assurances that the deck was structurally sound, there was enough concern among fans and in local media that South Carolina governor Dick Riley weighed in, saying state officials should go the extra mile to determine that the swaying deck was safe. USC announced plans to police the upper east stands, asking the band not to play a fan-favorite party song, "Louie Louie," that led to dancing among the student section, a portion of which was then located in the suspect upper-east deck.

Told of the swaying back in 1983, head coach Joe Morrison quipped, "If it ain't swayin', we ain't playin'," and the saying caught on, predictably appearing on bumper stickers and T-shirts around Columbia.

By 1989 the USC Board of Trustees, led by Michael Mungo, cited plans to "open up" Williams-Brice Stadium to non-football activities in an attempt to lure lucrative concerts, such as the Rolling Stones. The university had previously passed on a Stones show due to concerns over structural stability of the stadium but now lobbied the State Commission of Higher Education for funding to stiffen the east upper stands with steel support struts. The commission ultimately endorsed up to $600,000 for the work, and in April 1990 a series of five-thousand-pound beams were installed along the upper-east deck, largely eliminating swaying.

But the saying stuck and became part of Williams-Brice Stadium lore, a testament to the raucous game-day atmosphere and home-field advantage created by Gamecock fans.

The Cockaboose Railroad

Talking with the *State*'s Bob Gillespie in 2006 about the idea behind the Cockaboose Railroad, which had by then become a cherished Gamecock tradition, Columbia businessman Ed Robinson said he wanted South Carolina fans to have the best parties, even if they didn't have the best teams. What started as an eccentric notion became a legendary monument to college football tailgating.

Robinson's vision began in the late 1980s when he, along with fellow businessman F. "Doc" Howard, purchased an abandoned railroad spur between the south stands of Williams-Brice Stadium and Carolina Park, the first private condo parking facility in the stadium vicinity, also owned and managed by Robinson and Howard. They purchased the spur from the CSX and Southern Railroads, which jointly owned it. It was a reminder of the industrial history of the stadium area, which is still populated to a lesser degree today by warehouses and machine shops.

Robinson and Howard spent two years purchasing twenty-two vintage caboose cars at auction from the Illinois Central Railroad to place on the spur.

The cars were painted garnet and emblazoned with "Cockaboose Railroad" signage and an outline of the state of South Carolina with the Fighting Gamecock logo. The duo began selling the cars for $45,000 (roughly $94,100 in 2021 dollars) apiece in the spring of 1990. "People would look at you and they would give you this kind of wild-eyed look, like 'you're nuts!'" Robinson told the *State's* Tom Fladung in March 1990. "Then they'd say, 'Yeah, I want one.'"

The cars were forty-five feet long and ten feet wide and could accommodate seventy people inside and on the exterior deck. They included central air, water and sewer lines, electrical wiring, telephone, and access to a satellite dish for televisions, among other amenities. Robinson and Howard sold twenty of the twenty-two cars in two days, keeping the last two cars for themselves. The university eventually purchased one of those two.

New owners set about refurbishing the unfinished caboose interiors, spending on average $75,000 apiece to upgrade and furnish the units with luxury finishes, including oak floors, mahogany paneling, granite countertops, marble fireplaces, and high-end fixtures.

The Cockaboose Railroad was an immediate hit with fans and became an integral part of USC football. Former athletics director Mike McGee told the *State* in 2006 that the Cockabooses had "become kind of an icon for Carolina football and have gained such attention around the Southeast in particular. It's become one of those things that identifies Carolina." Indeed, they have been profiled in the *New York Times* as well as *Southern Living* and *Smithsonian* magazines and are frequently featured on ESPN broadcasts.

On the rare occasions that one of the 270-square-foot cars is sold, the market is robust, commanding $200,000 or more. One reportedly sold in 2013 for around $300,000. With a value between $750 to $1,100 per square foot, these units constitute some of the most valuable property south of Manhattan.[4] Such is the premium to own an iconic symbol of Gamecock lore and college football culture.

Columbia was further solidified as the home of "railgating" in 2000, when another line of caboose cars was installed in an adjacent parking lot northeast of the stadium. The University of Louisville even copied the caboose idea with a line of their own, although as Cory Nightingale of *Saturday Down South* noted in a 2016 article about the trend, imitation is flattery, but there is nothing like the original.

The Chicken Curse

There are times in the life of a Gamecock fan when rational explanations for the sometimes bewildering and seemingly endless array of inexplicable bad luck are no longer enough. Consider the following:

- John Roche's ankle sprain late in USC's 1970 ACC tournament quarterfinal win versus Wake Forest. Roche, Carolina's all-everything guard, was hobbled in the championship game, and the Gamecocks lost by three in a slowed-down affair versus NC State. The loss was devastating for South Carolina's greatest basketball squad, a team who went 14–0 during regular-season conference play in an era when only the conference tournament champion received an NCAA tournament bid. To compound the loss, Carolina Coliseum had been named a host site for the 1970 NCAA East Regional, which would have given the Gamecocks a compelling home-court advantage in rounds one and two and an inside track to an Elite Eight berth in their first NCAA tournament.

- The 1984 Gamecock football squad, 9–0 and coming off a nationally televised thrashing of Florida State, climbed to number 2 in the national rankings with two games remaining. A trip to Annapolis to face a 3–5–1 Navy team coming off a 29–0 defeat to Syracuse the prior week and the annual rivalry game versus Clemson were all that remained of the regular season. An Orange Bowl bid and the opportunity to play for a national championship all but certainly awaited the Gamecocks should they manage to win in Annapolis. Gamecock fans had become so confident of the possibility they had taken to throwing oranges on the field during the prior week's FSU game. *Pride goeth before a fall* . . . Indeed, the fall seemed biblical in scope as Navy played their best game of the season, dominating the Gamecocks 38–21 in college football's greatest upset of 1984. The raucous crowd of Midshipmen received quite a workout that day as they rushed to the end zone to complete push-ups matching the point total every time Navy scored.

Navy became the ultimate four-letter word for any Gamecock fan old enough to remember. Adding salt to the wound, first-ranked Nebraska lost the same day to Oklahoma, which would have . . . *should have* . . . propelled South Carolina to its first-ever number 1 ranking, making the Gamecocks a lock for the Orange Bowl. Following the Navy loss, USC salvaged a 22–21 win over Clemson and accepted a bid to the Gator Bowl, where they lost in an uninspired performance to ninth-ranked Oklahoma State. BYU, meanwhile, was awarded the national championship after defeating a 6–5 Michigan squad in the Holiday Bowl to complete a 13–0 season, becoming the last non–Power Five school to win a football national championship.

- In a 1988 Metro Conference matchup versus powerhouse Louisville at Carolina Coliseum, the Gamecocks held a seemingly insurmountable fourteen-point lead, 72–58, with 1:22 remaining. After Louisville's LeBradford Smith hit a three-point bucket to cut the lead to eleven with 1:06 remaining, South Carolina's Darrell Martin and Louisville's Pervis Ellison became tangled under the basket. They were separated, but Martin punched Smith, and a wild brawl ensued, in which a South Carolina fan hit Louisville's Herbert Crook and several other players scuffled. It took ten minutes for USC security and Columbia police to restore order and officials to sort out the various transgressions. When the dust settled, officials tagged USC with three technical fouls and Louisville two. Gamecock coach George Felton was ejected, as were Martin and Terry Gould for South Carolina and Smith and Crook of Louisville. Louisville connected on six of eight free throws for the technical fouls, plus a personal foul called prior to the fight. Meanwhile South Carolina's best player, Terry Dozier, missed three of four free throws, and the Gamecock lead fell to 73–67. Eventually Louisville's Craig Hawley drilled a three-pointer as regulation expired to send the game into overtime with a 74–74 tie. Louisville ultimately left Columbia with an improbable double-overtime win.

- The 1997 SEC champion Gamecock basketball team, guided by coach Eddie Fogler and boasting college basketball's most talented backcourt trio of BJ McKie, Larry Davis, and Melvin Watson, earned a number

2 NCAA tournament seed, the program's highest ever. Many pundits predicted a Gamecock run to that season's Final Four. The Gamecocks never showed up in the opening game, however, losing by thirteen in a listless opening-round loss to a school most Gamecock fans had never heard of, Coppin State of the MEAC.

- The next season was another strong one for Fogler's Gamecocks, in which they went 23–7, placing second in the SEC East behind Kentucky and earning a number 3 seed in the NCAA tournament. The result? Another opening-round loss, this time by one point to Richmond. After that the life seemed to go out of Fogler's program. He coached three more mostly unmemorable seasons before stepping down following the 2000–2001 season.

Taken as individual occurrences, any one of these events is explainable. Upsets happen. Injuries are commonplace. Great players miss free throws. But viewing them cumulatively, over the course of years and decades, one starts to wonder if something larger, more sinister might be at play. When logical answers fail to explain accumulated emotional trauma, one begins to search the mystical, the paranormal, the preternatural. An otherwise rational being might begin to ponder hexes, sorcery, and the darker arts. One might begin to wonder, Are we cursed?

Some began to see patterns of futility in the larger sports world anytime a Gamecock letterman or South Carolina native was involved in improbable losses. In an October 1977 *Columbia Record* article, columnist Doug Nye noted that that season's Chicago Cubs, who boasted a commanding eight and a half game lead in the National League East standings halfway through the season, did not begin to falter until signing Gamecock pitcher Randy Martz. The Cubs suffered one of their greatest collapses, finishing fourth in the division with an 81–81 record.

Similarly, the 1978 Boston Red Sox took a fourteen and a half game lead over their rival New York Yankees into mid-July when the Sox called up former Gamecock Gary Hancock as a reserve outfielder. Almost from the moment Hancock was signed, the team's commanding lead began to melt away. By season's end the Yankees had tied the Red Sox, forcing a one-game playoff to determine the division title, which the Yankees won on the strength of a Bucky Dent three-run homer. The Yankees went on to win the World Series, relegating Red Sox fans to a long off-season.

Nye pointed to the 1972 US Olympic men's basketball team as further evidence. The US team had won gold every year since basketball had been introduced as an Olympic sport in 1936 and boasted a 63–0 record in Olympic competition heading into the 1972 final, in which the US team faced a powerful yet underdog Soviet Union team in Munich. In the context of the US-Soviet political rivalry, the gold medal game took on greatly enhanced significance. The US team ultimately lost by a point in the final seconds, in what remains the most controversial game in Olympic basketball history. Prominent on the roster? Former Gamecock great Kevin Joyce.

In a tongue-in-cheek explanation for these and other misfortunes, Nye proposed the existence of a "Chicken Curse," and it resonated with Gamecock faithful. In a follow-up article about the theory in 1990, he expanded, "a major weapon of the Curse is its damnable tendency to tease—to take Gamecock fans to the brink, make them think that their team is about to accomplish the ultimate, and then hit 'em with a dream-shattering slam to the gut."

The Chicken Curse entered popular culture in South Carolina, and many have speculated about its origins. One theory goes back to "Pitchfork" Ben Tillman, former US senator and South Carolina governor who was instrumental in the establishment of Clemson University. Legend holds that Tillman, indignant after the state legislature blocked his initial efforts as governor to fund a new agricultural institution, drove a pitchfork into the ground on the USC Horseshoe, which sits a stone's throw from the State House. He reportedly declared that a curse would befall the University of South Carolina henceforth.[5]

Some believe the curse goes back even further, cosmic payback visited upon the state's flagship institution for South Carolina's firing on Fort Sumter in April 1861, which sparked the American Civil War. Perhaps it is payback for the ultimate sin of slavery itself, an institution from which wealthy South Carolina planters profited mightily.

Others see impacts of the curse well beyond the sports world, pointing to the fall of the Alamo in 1836, in which the Texas garrison was led by South

Carolina native William Travis. Commander of US troops during the heaviest fighting of the ill-fated Vietnam War was South Carolina native William Westmoreland. Elvis Presley died just a few months following his concert at Carolina Coliseum in 1977, though his famously indulgent lifestyle may have been more to blame. Gary Hart, US senator from Colorado, was the front-runner for the Democratic presidential nomination in 1988 before revelations surfaced of an extramarital affair with Donna Rice. Rice was a Columbia native, USC alumna, and former Gamecock cheerleader. Speculation about the curse's origins and reach go on.

The Chicken Curse was often blamed for South Carolina's dismal 0–8 record in the school's first eight bowl appearances, as well as decades of mostly sustained mediocrity, although coaches generally took a more practical approach. When asked to comment on the curse, Lou Holtz quipped, "the Chicken Curse affects us most when we don't block or tackle."

Steve Spurrier, upon replacing Holtz in 2005, thought the real curse had more to do with the fast-food chicken restaurant across the street from Williams-Brice Stadium, which he learned players often frequented. "From what I understand, this team doesn't eat correctly, or hasn't been eating correctly," Spurrier told the *State*'s Ron Morris. "We're not going to try to load up on fried chicken or things like that."

Talk of curses is not unique to Gamecock sports, of course. Baseball in particular is synonymous with superstition and curses. Consider the "Black Sox" scandal of 1919, in which members of the Chicago White Sox conspired to fix that season's World Series. Chief among those accused was Greenville, South Carolina, native "Shoeless" Joe Jackson. Despite Jackson's outstanding performance in the 1919 series, in which he led both teams in numerous statistical categories and set a World Series record with twelve base hits, Major League Baseball's first commissioner, the splendidly named Kennesaw Mountain Landis, banned Jackson from baseball in the prime of his career after the 1920 season.

Many have protested Jackson's innocence through the years. After all, his efforts in the 1919 series seem inconsistent with a man involved in a conspiracy to throw games. Some have drawn inevitable connections to the Chicken Curse. Besides being a native South Carolinian, Jackson was a former teammate of Alfred Von Kolnitz, who played for the Cubs in 1916 and was a gifted third baseman for the 1912 and 1913 Gamecock baseball teams.

Red Sox fans frequently cite the Curse of the Bambino to explain their eighty-six-year championship drought between 1918 and 2004, pointing to Boston's trade of the legendary Babe Ruth to the New York Yankees in 1920.

The Chicago Cubs championship futility was famously blamed on the Curse of the Billy Goat. Legend holds that during game four of the 1945 World Series, William Sianis placed a curse on the Cubs after he and his pet billy goat Murphy were asked to leave Wrigley Field. Sianis, a Greek immigrant and local tavern owner, had gained local celebrity after adopting the goat when it wandered into his establishment years before. Sianis grew a goatee, renamed his bar Billy Goat Tavern, and frequently appeared at Cubs home games along with the goat. After being tossed out during game four, Sianis reportedly declared, "Them Cubs ain't gonna win no more." The Cubs lost the 1945 World Series and did not return to the October Classic until 2016, when they won the National League Championship Series on the forty-sixth anniversary of Sianis's death. The Cubs ultimately won that season's World Series in six games versus the Cleveland Indians.

As USC approached the 1992 football season, its first as a member of the mighty Southeastern Conference, fans who believed in such things were eager to vanquish the Chicken Curse once and for all. USC booster Floyd Bowie Jr. arranged for a public exorcism to be held outside the gates of Williams-Brice Stadium the day before USC's season-opening matchup with Georgia. "We are tired of the curse rearing its ugly head," Bowie told Dave Moniz of the *State*. Bowie, who was assistant general manager of marketing for the minor league Columbia Mets, was no stranger to generating publicity in his professional role.

Bowie reportedly asked a witch doctor if the curse could be "redirected." "He said yes, so we're going to redirect," Bowie said. Asked where they might redirect the Chicken Curse, Bowie simply stated, "Upstate."

On the afternoon of Friday, September 4, Bowie's hired witch doctor, Archibald Thibeaux of Blythewood, just north of Columbia, performed his black magic ceremony to rid USC from the dreaded curse. A small crowd gathered to watch the brief ritual, and when it was finished, Thibeaux declared, "The curse is gone. We will be victorious. Call me if it doesn't work, but we will win." Thibeaux cited a 98.5 percent success rate for lifting curses. It's hard to argue with a witch doctor who uses metrics to track performance.

Thibeaux likely changed his number, however, as USC began the 1992 season 0–5 and head coach Sparky Woods had to quell a growing player revolt. Curses are stubborn things.

An Eventful Era

There were other events, too, including the use of black uniforms under Coach Joe Morrison, a trend adopted by other Gamecock teams over the years. Garnet had always been the predominant color for Gamecock home uniforms (football) and away uniforms (basketball), with black and white used as trim. Morrison, known for strolling the sidelines dressed in black with his trademark aviator sunglasses, introduced all-black uniforms to much fanfare for the season-ending Clemson game in 1983. And while the game resulted in a 22–13 loss, black began to appear in uniform combos throughout the athletics department and continues today.

Black football uniforms have ebbed and flowed throughout the decades, with some coaches preferring the traditional garnet. Men's and women's basketball in particular have embraced the use of black away uniforms, first introduced by Coach Bill Foster for his men's team during the 1985–86 season.

Morrison also introduced garnet helmets, which featured a block *C* logo encircled in a field of white. USC football used garnet lids throughout the Morrison, Sparky Woods, and Brad Scott eras between 1983 and 1998.[6]

Another Morrison-era trend was the "Script Carolina" logo, which appeared on the coach's sideline cap. The logo was popular with fans but faded into disuse after the Morrison era before enjoying a resurgence three decades later during Will Muschamp's otherwise unremarkable tenure as head football coach. "Script Carolina" gained official status as an alternate logo of sorts, appearing on helmets in place of the block *C* logo a number of times during the Muschamp years.

Innovation in logos, mascots, and traditions defined the independent era. They were two decades in the long history of the University of South Carolina unsurpassed by any other era in shaping the culture and defining the brand of South Carolina athletics.

Lost in the color and pageantry of a Carolina gameday are the sepia-toned echoes of bygone people and things. A long-forgotten tone poem by an eighteenth-century composer, an abandoned railroad spur, the mothballed tatters of an old mascot costume, the initials of a former coach craftily disguised within an otherwise ubiquitous logo. They are whispers now, lost amid the more pressing sensory diversions of drum and brass, the din of the crowd, and the wafting aromas of mustard-tinged pork and concession stand fare.

But these are the things of which tradition is made.

5

A National Power Emerges

Richardson, Raines, and the
Rise of Gamecock Baseball

We have been after Bobby for a year and a half. I'll say this, we got the coach we wanted. The only one we wanted.

—Athletics director Paul Dietzel

Gamecock baseball had been a fixture in Columbia for the better part of eight decades by the time Paul Dietzel coaxed Sumter, South Carolina, native and New York Yankees legend Bobby Richardson into accepting the position of head baseball coach in 1970. Prior to Richardson, mediocrity was a consistent theme for the program, which had compiled a 646–638–14 (.503) record between the first game in 1892 through the 1969 season. Carolina had not enjoyed a winning decade on the diamond since the 1930s, a decade fueled largely by the success of coach Billy Laval, who led both the Gamecock football and baseball teams between 1928 and 1934.[1]

Gamecock baseball got its start on a Friday afternoon, April 8, 1892. The *State*'s headline proclaimed excitedly, "Ball Game Today! The Mechanics and the College Team at the Ball Park."

The "ball park" was located at the old fairgrounds, on Elmwood Avenue, future site of Logan Elementary School, which still stands today. The Mechanics, described as a "famous Columbia amateur organization," was one of several area teams comprising union or trade workers. Professional baseball would not come to Columbia for another dozen years, with the start of the South Atlantic (Sally) League in 1904,[2] but the area boasted a thriving amateur scene, including both White and Black clubs. Baseball clubs from various organizations had come and gone since the very first games were played around 1867 between loosely assembled local teams and federal troops that were encamped near USC's Davis Field, enforcing martial law following the Civil War.

Columbia was a city on the move in the 1890s, some two-plus decades removed from the disastrous fires that swept the city in February 1865 during Sherman's march through the Carolinas. Columbia boasted a population of more than twenty-six thousand residents by 1900, then the largest city in the Carolinas outside of Charleston. Commerce thrived along the main retail thoroughfare of Richardson Street, soon to be rechristened Main Street to reflect its prominence. Main would become the first paved street in Columbia in 1908, but in 1892 Richardson, like all Columbia streets, was a "miry bog," as described by the *Charleston News and Courier*. The mud was often so thick that horse-drawn streetcars frequently strayed from their tracks. The bicycle craze of the 1890s gripped Columbia, and "wheelmen," as cyclists were then called, were often pitted against walkers as they avoided muddy streets in favor of firmer, if more kinetic, sidewalks.

Electricity was slowly coming to the Capital City, thanks to hydropower from the recently expanded Columbia Canal. The world's first textile mill powered exclusively by electric power, Columbia Mills, rose on a bluff along the west bank of the Congaree River and began operations in 1893.[3] Richland Mill (later known as Whaley Mill) opened by 1895, while Granby and Olympia Mills began operations a few years later, cumulatively providing Columbia's defining industry for generations.

The cumbersomely named Columbia Electric Street and Suburban Railway Company soon replaced horse-drawn trolleys with cleaner, if not faster, electric trolleys. The stately Governor's Mansion on Arsenal Hill, then occupied by the demagogic populist "Pitchfork" Ben Tillman, had been recently electrified, enlightening for the first time the staterooms and hallways of the great house, if not the race-baiting politics of the governor himself.

A few hundred curious onlookers made their way to the old fairgrounds for that Friday afternoon contest between Mechanics and the "College Nine," as Carolina's team was called.[4] They came in their Victorian-era foppery, by trolly on the "Cemetery Line," which ran along Elmwood Avenue, by foot and by buggy, and on rudimentary mud-caked bicycles, navigating as best they could to the old wooden grandstands amid the fragrant mix of mire and manure that defined Columbia's streets.

Temperatures approached eighty degrees before first pitch, the balmy Columbia air punctuated by the earthy aromas of tobacco smoke and dung and woolen clothing damp with perspiration. Spectators paid a nickel to sit in the grandstands. A few gathered at the Sweeney house, at 901 Elmwood Avenue, to sit languidly on the home's large wraparound porch, which provided a free view of the field. Settling in for the contest, men removed their hats to pat their damp foreheads with folded handkerchiefs. Many removed jackets, rolling shirt sleeves for a bit of relief, while some took furtive glances at gold-plated pocket watches as the 1 PM start approached. The day was clear, the grandstands full, the mood festive.

Back in the business district, on the southwest corner Richardson and Taylor Streets, Al Meehan's Billiard Parlor in the Columbia Hotel arranged to post inning-by-inning telegraphic reports for patrons, some of whom enjoyed a local pilsner on tap from C. C. Habenicht's or one of the several other German breweries in town.

The *State* captured the action in Saturday morning's edition, taking note that many of the spectators were ladies, attesting to the great enthusiasm aroused by the game. "It was a beautiful battle," the article enthused, in which the "college boys" played badly early on and found themselves down by six after two innings, but a five-run third inning and a four-run fourth propelled South Carolina into the lead. Improved pitching hamstrung the Mechanics from there, giving up only two more runs the rest of the way. The College Nine won handily, 14–8 in seven innings. Highlighting the win was the pitching of James (no first name listed), who, despite yielding eight runs, pitched three scoreless late innings and recorded fifteen strikeouts. Catcher James P. Shand had three hits on the afternoon, leading all batters despite a tough day behind the plate, with four passed balls.[5]

Though the spectators had no way of knowing it that day, they had witnessed the birth of a program that would come of age more than three quarters of a century later, under the direction of a baseball legend who arrived from Sumter by way of New York City.

A Legend Comes Home

At the dawn of a new year and decade, athletics director Paul Dietzel called a secretive press conference to be held at the Market Restaurant on Assembly Street on the evening of January 16, 1970. Dietzel, who had been in Washington, DC, for the annual NCAA American Football Coaches Association meetings, gave no details, only promising "a major announcement will be made." Reporters sniffed it out soon enough, and headlines in that morning's *State* noted the Gamecocks were expected to name Bobby Richardson head baseball coach. It was well-known that Dietzel had been pursuing Richardson for some time and had offered him the head job on two previous occasions, only to be politely declined.

Dietzel was looking for yet another splashy hire for the university, which had hired national championship credentialed coaches in Frank McGuire for basketball and Dietzel himself for football in 1964 and 1966, respectively. The hire would also allow Dietzel's football assistant and coach of the freshman team, Jack Powers, to step away from his duties as head baseball coach to focus on football full time.

Dietzel did, in fact, introduce the thirty-four-year-old Richardson as his new baseball coach during the press conference, attended by university president Tom Jones, Frank McGuire, and local dignitaries. It was a major announcement indeed, providing the university with yet another prestige hire. Dietzel proclaimed it "one of the great moments in athletics at Carolina." Upon hearing the news, Clemson's Frank Howard pondered dryly whether the University of South Carolina might next hire Arnold Palmer to coach its golf team.

Richardson addressed the assembled press that evening, saying, "I'm thrilled to become associated with the University. I'm a Gamecock fan. It's a particular thrill for me to become associated with Paul Dietzel and Frank McGuire. I have so much respect and admiration for them." The ever-humble

USC athletics director Paul Dietzel (center) at press conference
welcoming new baseball coach Bobby Richardson (right) to campus in 1970.
Courtesy of the *State* Newspaper Archive, Richland County Public Library.

Richardson expanded on the thought process for entering coaching: "I had
thought about it, sure. I didn't know whether I would like it or not. But as
you grow older, you begin to wonder if maybe you wouldn't like to try your
hand at managing or coaching. But I figured I would try it at the Little League
level, or something like that. Then Coach Dietzel got after me about coming
to South Carolina."

Richardson was a certified baseball legend. The Sumter product, who grew
up a mere forty-five miles from the Carolina campus, enjoyed an illustrious
career over ten-plus seasons as the starting New York Yankees second baseman, playing alongside the likes of Mickey Mantle, Roger Maris, and Yogi
Berra. He formed a lethal double-play combo with shortstop Tony Kubek
from the mid-1950s to the mid-1960's. The hard-partying Mantle and the
clean-as-a-whistle Richardson were close friends, despite their divergent life-
styles. Legendary Yankees manager Casey Stengel once said of the clean-living

but light-hitting Richardson, "Look at him. Doesn't drink. Doesn't smoke. Nothing. But he still can't hit .220."[6]

Richardson played in 1,400 games and collected 1,432 hits prior to his retirement on "Bobby Richardson Day" at Yankee Stadium in 1966. He won five Golden Gloves, designating him the best-fielding second baseman in all of baseball in those seasons, and appeared in the All-Star classic seven times. He won nine American League pennants and four World Series championships during his time with the Yankees, and in 1960 became the only player in Major League history to win the World Series MVP from the losing team— a distinction he still holds.[7]

Of his 1960 MVP, Richardson recalls he was more surprised than anyone. "They walked into the clubhouse, and Mantle was crying—we thought we had a better team. But they told me I'd been chosen Sport Magazine's MVP, and I said, tell me that again?" he laughed. "And they said, 'yes, you get a 1960 Chevrolet Corvette. You can pick it up in New York at the dealership.' I heard from a couple of Pirates over the years, and they would call and say, 'are you still driving my Corvette?'" Richardson, ever the family man, with two young boys and a daughter on the way, ultimately traded the Corvette for a new station wagon and a Jeep. "And that fit my family perfect," he said.

Despite all the success, by 1965, though only twenty-nine years old, Richardson says he began to realize he was missing out on some important things. "Kubek and I roomed together all during our minor and major league [careers], and both of us realized that although we were playing for the Yankees and we had won (the pennant) nine out of ten years, we were missing out on a priority of our lives, and that was our families." So the legendary double-play duo went to Yankees management and simultaneously announced their retirement. Richardson ultimately ended up playing one last season, 1966, at the request of the Yankees, and signed a five-year contract through 1970 to scout talent after the 1966 season. Meanwhile Dietzel and home were calling.

James Dickey, the novelist and poet in residence at the University of South Carolina from 1969 until his death in 1997, wrote a 1981 article for *Esquire* titled "The Starry Place between the Antlers—Why I Live in South Carolina." Dickey wrote of the pull he felt to return to his native South after years of living abroad, and in California and the Pacific Northwest. "I was feeling the magnetic pull that draws from pine roots and kudzu vines for those born among them, and was being pulled south, deeper and deeper, not only by the sun-moon opposition over Lake Katherine but by a root-system, something like veins, the whole of an underground as well."

Likewise, Richardson increasingly felt the pull of home as the end of his contract with the Yankees approached. After resisting Dietzel's first two offers, he was ready to listen the third time. "I told the Yankees I wanted to go coach the Gamecocks. Lee McPhail was general manager at the time and he said 'if you want to, you can be our radio broadcaster, you can be our Triple-A manager, or you can be our Major League coach.'" But Richardson, citing the desire to be with his family and the university's proximity to Sumter, held firm. The acquiescent McPhail told Richardson to let him know once he got settled, promising to bring the Yankees down and play his ballclub. With that offer in his back pocket, Richardson concluded his duties as Yankee scout and headed south, and a new era of Gamecock baseball began.

Speaking at a Columbia Chamber of Commerce ceremony on March 17, 1970, with Richardson's first season set to begin that evening in Greenville versus Furman, South Carolina governor Robert McNair noted the impact of the university's big-name hires. "When Coach McGuire came here, he built such a basketball program that we had to build a Coliseum. Then Paul Dietzel came along with a strong football program and now they need a larger stadium." With a big grin, McNair added, "When Bobby Richardson took the job as baseball coach at Carolina, I told him, 'Bobby, for gosh sakes, don't have a good season. We can't afford it."[8]

Richardson's young 1970 team featured six seniors on the thirty-two-man roster. Two freshmen earned a starting nod: left fielder Howard Barfield, from Hartsville, and second baseman Tommy Moody of Columbia's A. C. Flora High School, who "just hustled his way right into the lineup," Richardson noted to the *Columbia Record*'s Doug Nye. Another freshman of note that joined the squad was Jackie Brown of tiny Jonesville, South Carolina, just southeast of Spartanburg. Brown made history as the first Black scholarship athlete at the University of South Carolina.[9]

Returning to the squad were juniors Buddy Caldwell at first and Butch Anderson at short, while sophomore Billy Petosky would work at third base. Senior Don Stanley and junior Ronnie Fulmer would get the start in center-field and right field, respectively, while versatile Craig Wolfrey would handle utility duties. Senior right-hander Jimbo Smith of Charleston led the pitching staff and would start the first game versus Furman. Freshman lefty Alan Hilliard would be the number two pitcher.

Assisting Richardson in 1970 was a holdover from Jackie Powers's 1969 squad, June Raines, whom Richardson noted had been a tremendous help because of his knowledge of the roster. Raines served as a student assistant in 1969 and 1970 while working toward his bachelor's degree and another two seasons as full-time assistant while pursuing his master's degree at USC. This followed a ten-year career as a catcher in the Cleveland Indians and Washington Senators minor league systems.

The opening game versus Furman, an 8–1 loss to the Paladins, provided an inauspicious opening to Richardson's tenure. The Gamecocks went on to a 14–20 overall record in 1970, with a 9–12 finish in Atlantic Coast Conference play—good for sixth place, ahead of UNC and Wake Forest. The Gamecock offense was anemic for much of the season, producing only 117 runs to opponents' 157. It was the final losing season for Gamecock baseball for the next twenty-six years.

Richardson's 1971 squad, the program's final campaign as a member of the ACC, showed marked improvement in both hitting and pitching, with the Gamecocks producing 149 runs to opponents' 111 en route to an overall 18–12 record and a 7–7 ACC tally, good for a three-way tie for fourth with UNC and Virginia and ahead of Duke and Wake Forest.

Richardson noted that the rancor of USC's conference exit generally did not spill over onto the baseball field, citing the warm friendships he enjoyed with the likes of NC State coach Sammy Esposito, among others. Of the ACC split, Richardson opined, "It was the worst thing that could have happened to us. ACC competition was what people enjoyed seeing. And as an independent, it was tougher to get a bid [to the NCAA tournament]. You had to work up an incredible record to get a bid, and you didn't have the advantage of winning a conference for the automatic bid." He further noted that he was never consulted about the conference exit and never bothered approaching Dietzel about it. "It was a done deal," he said.

The 1972 and 1973 campaigns saw continued improvement and expanded schedules, going from thirty games in 1971 to forty-one and forty-three games, respectively, the next two seasons. The Gamecocks went 25–16 in 1972 and 26–16–1 in 1973. Though neither squad received an NCAA tournament bid, big things were happening within the program. Richardson added two program-changing recruits in 1972, dominant right-handed pitcher Earl Bass, whom Richardson called "probably the best athlete I've ever coached," and power-hitting first baseman Hank Small. The duo powered Carolina's surge into the national spotlight over the following two seasons.

Following the 1972 season, assistant June Raines, having earned his MA in teaching at USC, accepted a position as catching instructor with the Philadelphia Phillies organization. Richardson hired Johnny Hunton to replace Raines. Hunton, a longtime Richardson friend, had been an infielder in the Yankees farm system in 1952–54 and coached high school baseball in Virginia for many years. Of Hunton's role in the program, Richardson reflects, "All good coaches have somebody like that, that they can depend on, that doesn't get the notoriety, but who does most of the work. Johnny would search out the players, and I would go talk to the parents. Recruiting became easy."

Beyond elevated talent, Richardson points to an event in early April 1974 as the catalyst for elevating the profile of Gamecock baseball. Feeling that he was ready to call in the promise made by Yankees general manager Lee McPhail to bring the Yankees to Columbia to play his club, Richardson contacted his old boss. The Yankees were wrapping up spring training and headed from Florida back to New York, traveling with the crosstown-rival Mets. McPhail asked Richardson if he wouldn't mind hosting both clubs, to which Richardson enthusiastically agreed.

And so on a Tuesday, April 2, Richardson shuttled the Yankees and Mets from the Columbia airport to the Enright baseball diamond for a daylong event, featuring a home run contest between Carolina's Hank Small, the Yankees' Thurman Munson, and the Mets' Duffy Dyer, followed by two six-out contests during which the Gamecocks squared off with both the Yankees and Mets. The nightcap was a Yankees-Mets exhibition game under the lights.[10]

When Richardson arrived at the airport to pick up the Mets, a confused Yogi Berra, his former Yankees teammate and then the Mets manager, asked him, "Richardson, what are you doing driving this bus?"

Richardson says everything fell into place for the event. "It looked like rain, and Sarge Frye went over to the football stadium and got their big tarp—we didn't have one—and brought it over and it covered the whole field," he laughed. "And the sun came out about five o'clock, we took the tarp off, and it was just a wonderful night for baseball. It couldn't have been any better."

An overflow crowd of sixty-nine hundred fans jammed into the Enright Athletic Complex ballpark, which had a listed capacity of only two thousand seats at the time. The *Columbia Record*'s Dick Hughley captured some of the scenes in his column the next day: "Whitey Ford was pitching to Elston Howard. Yogi Berra donned his catcher's equipment. Tom Seaver messed around with some kids. Bobby Murcer took time to speak to everybody. Superstars past and present walked around like actual human beings yesterday. Bobby Richardson succeeded in bringing Major League baseball to Columbia, and he didn't waste anyone's time by bringing in a couple of second-hand clubs."[11]

Of the overflow crowd, Hughley wrote, "Several homeowners along South Marion Street benefitted by selling parking in their yards. Fans nested on rooftops and completely surrounded the outfield, and in some cases, hung over fences. Some opened peep holes in the green canvas that draped the outfield fence."

Hank Small won the home run contest, and the Gamecocks defeated both the Yankees and Mets, thanks in no small part to some friendly pitching.[12] Yankees pitching coach Whitey Ford pitched to his son, Eddie, a senior on Richardson's Gamecock squad, who singled to right on the first pitch. The younger Ford said it was a straight fastball, "and I knew it was coming," he grinned. "As a matter of fact, we talked about it before we took the field."

Richardson commented in the 1975 baseball media guide that "a lot of people who had never seen a college baseball team in action came out to see the major league players and saw that Carolina had a great college baseball program." He later described it as a perfect day. "The fans stuck with us after that. They were there, on board, and the next year we went to the College

World Series, went 51–6, losing to Texas in the championship game. I think that was a key, to have all those fans come out and see the team, and then stick with us after that."

The Gamecocks surged to a 48–8 finish in that 1974 season and earned the program's first-ever NCAA tournament bid, coming just shy of a trip to Omaha in a 2–1 defeat in the Starkville, Mississippi, regional to rising power-house Miami. The Gamecocks had defeated the Hurricanes 3–1 earlier in the day, and the nightcap determined the regional champion.[13]

Omaha in 1975

Legendary Rosenblatt Stadium was built in 1948 as Municipal Stadium, later named in honor of longtime Omaha city commissioner Johnny Rosenblatt. In 1950 the stadium hosted the fourth-annual College World Series, which had previously been played in Wichita, Kansas (1949), and Kalamazoo, Michigan (1947 and 1948). By the mid-seventies, the college classic had become the most coveted destination for college baseball players, coaches, and fans and a firmly entrenched symbol of summertime Americana. The Gamecock baseball program had never sniffed that rarified air before June 1975, having only one NCAA tournament appearance to its credit the prior season. In-state rival Clemson had gone in consecutive seasons, 1958 and 1959, but no Palmetto State team had returned since.

The Gamecocks rode hot pitching all season long, with staff ace, right-hander Earl Bass, compiling a 17–1 record and fellow righties Greg Ward and Raymond Lavigne going 13–4 and 8–0, respectively. Lefty Tim Lewis, meanwhile, went 11–0 on the season. The squad was rich with experience and leadership from upperclassmen like seniors Bass, Small, Ward, Lavigne, catcher Donnie Branham, and relief pitcher Mike Cromer, as well as junior pitcher Lewis, outfielders Gary Hancock and Steve Cook, and shortstop Jeff Grantz. Of the 1975 Gamecocks, Richardson reflects, "They felt like they could beat anybody." And they did almost exactly that.

The fourth-ranked Gamecocks rolled into regional play sporting a pro-gram-best 49–4–1 record, good enough to earn them the program's first-ever regional host site. South Carolina played nearly perfect baseball in the Columbia regional, dominating the Citadel 11–3 and Temple 15–0 before

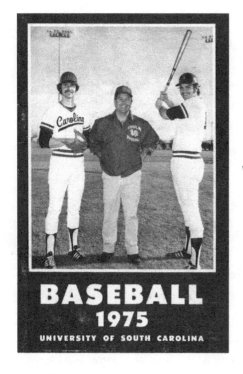

Baseball coach Bobby Richardson with Earl Bass (left) and Hank Small. Source: Cover of the 1975 USC baseball media guide.

punching their ticket to Omaha with a 4–3 win over former ACC rival NC State, winner of that season's ACC regular season and tournament championships.

Traveling with the Gamecocks to Omaha was a team mascot and a talisman of sorts, in the form of a springer spaniel named Rinky-Dink—the team's foul-ball chaser throughout the season. Owned by a friend of the team, retired army sergeant Bennie Estes, the pup made the charter flight after a sedative administered by team trainer Jim Price. When the Gamecocks held batting practice at a local Little League field, Rinky-Dink got quite a workout, as Jeff Grantz powered nine consecutive balls over the short left-field fence and into the tall weeds beyond. Power-hitting Hank Small made things even more difficult, as Herman Helms noted in the *State,* but Rinky-Dink eventually found them all. Richardson estimated the team would have lost fifty balls if not for the canine heroics, the pup more than earning his seat on the plane.

Joining the Gamecocks for the twenty-ninth College World Series was top-ranked Florida State, paired in the opening game with Eastern Michigan; traditional powers Arizona State and Texas, opening with Oklahoma and surprising Cal State Fullerton, respectively. USC, meanwhile, opened with Seton Hall, whom they had defeated earlier in the season during a Florida tournament.

Staff ace Bass got the nod against Seton Hall and turned in a very Bass-like performance, scattering six hits over seven complete innings before departing in the eighth after giving up consecutive singles. Lefty Mike Cromer cruised in relief to secure a 3–1 win, placing the Gamecocks in the winner's bracket, where they would meet Eastern Michigan, who had pulled a shocker over the top-ranked Seminoles. Arizona State and Texas, meanwhile, would meet in the other winner's bracket game. Bass picked up his sixteenth win of the season versus Seton Hall, against no losses.

Greg Ward gave up only two hits and an unearned run through six innings in game two, as the Gamecocks cruised to a 5–1 win over Eastern Michigan. The game was called in the sixth following a long rain delay. Before the delay South Carolina had the bases loaded with no outs in the bottom of the sixth.

Rain throughout the next day delayed the scheduled matchup of unde-feated USC and Arizona State until the following evening. The delay caused Richardson a dilemma—go with scheduled game three starter, the highly capable and undefeated Tim Lewis, or Bass, his ace, who was available after the extra day of rest. Not a bad dilemma. Richardson ultimately decided on Bass, with Lewis available in relief. After a shaky first inning, in which he gave up two runs on two hits and three walks, Bass settled in, giving up only one additional run in the sixth inning on a solo homer by the Sun Devils' Ken Phelps. He enjoyed ample run support on the evening, and when the Gamecocks scored four runs in an explosive fourth inning surge, a confident Bass turned to catcher Greg Keatley in the dugout and said, "My friend, it's all over now."

The Gamecocks came away with a 6–3 win over the Sun Devils squad, some members of which had spoken openly to reporters before the game of Arizona State's superiority to Bass and the Gamecocks. Bass threw 126 pitches, striking out nine, in a complete game performance that he called his "greatest win."

South Carolina found itself in the enviable position of being the only undefeated team in Omaha after three games, just one win shy of the school's first-ever national championship in any sport. The Gamecocks would face

Texas in the fourth game, which proved to be a night of horrors for the USC pitching staff. The Longhorns racked up eighteen hits, scoring seventeen runs in a 17–5 blowout. The Gamecocks went through four pitchers that evening, starter Greg Ward and relievers Ray Lavigne, Mike Cromer, and Chuck McClean. The *State*'s Hamp Rogers quipped that Richardson spent more cumulative time at the mound than any of his four pitchers on the night, given his many trips from the dugout.

USC found itself knotted with Texas and Arizona State as the only teams left standing in Omaha, all with a 3–1 record. In a strange twist due to rules in place at the time, a drawing determined which team would receive the bye to automatically advance to the national championship game, forcing the other two teams into a one-game playoff. Texas won, allowing the Longhorns a rest day, while South Carolina prepared for a rematch with Arizona State.

Starter Tim Lewis was steady in the Gamecocks' fifth game, scattering eight hits and three walks, giving up just one run in a complete game performance, and the Gamecocks sent the Sun Devils packing with a 4–1 win. The game was a thriller, scoreless through eight and a half innings before ASU scored one run in the bottom of the eighth for a slim lead. Lewis stewed in the dugout, assuming he had cost his team a trip to the championship. But the Gamecocks staged a furious rally in the top of the ninth, scoring four runs, aided by two Sun Devil errors. With that Lewis grabbed his glove and coolly took down the side to close it out, keeping his season record perfect at 11–0. The win set up a national championship finale versus the well-rested Longhorns.

Columbia was abuzz, with the action in Omaha dominating radio chatter, television sports coverage, and conversation among the regulars at Humphrey's Barber Shop in Trenholm Plaza. WIS-TV broadcast the contests, which increased in viewership game by game. Following the second win over Arizona State, placing USC in the championship, even Gov. James Edwards flew in to join other Gamecock fans already assembled. Richardson noted the number of telegrams pouring into the Omaha Hilton, where the team had taken up residence, particularly after the shelling by Texas. The messages of support "really gave our fellows a lift when they needed one," the coach added.

A total of 10,717 fans assembled in Rosenblatt Stadium under a big Nebraska sky and enjoyed weather the Omaha Chamber of Commerce might have had a hand in ordering. It was a perfect night for baseball. The Gamecocks once again ran into a hot Texas team in the Saturday evening finale, and though the score was closer, the result was the same, as Texas captured the national championship over South Carolina, 5–1. Texas starter Richard Wortham worked efficiently, giving up only four hits on the night. The solitary Gamecock run came on a Hank Small fourth inning solo blast, which cleared right center field's 390 mark. Bass, working on two days of rest, took his first loss of the season, finishing with a 17–1 record and proving even he was human. Two costly Gamecock errors assisted the Texas scoring. The final game was swift, at only two hours, twenty minutes, as the two masterful pitchers did their thing, racking up seventeen strikeouts between them.

And just like that, it was over. The Gamecocks had reached the championship game in their first-ever trip to Omaha, beating powerful Arizona State twice in the process. Though the two losses to Texas stung, there was a lot to admire about the performance of Richardson's squad. The *State's* Hamp Rogers wrote of USC's "new status" in the college baseball world, noting that Richardson's program was "one of the big boys" now. Herman Helms reminded fans in his own *State* column to take joy in remembering Bass and Small and the rest of Richardson's scrappy, overachieving crew. Speaking of the professional careers sure to follow for Bass and Small and the path forward for Richardson and Gamecock baseball, Helms wrote that fans would hear from them all in the future, adding, "In the meantime, there's joy in remembering them for what they were: the second-best college baseball team in America. That isn't as good as winning the championship, but it's better than any team from the State of South Carolina has ever done in any sport."

✗   ✗   ✗

Nineteen seventy-six was a rebuilding year by the new standards of Gamecock baseball. With the loss of Bass, Small, and Ward, Richardson had plenty of gaps to fill. The team won thirty-eight games (38–14) and qualified for its third-straight NCAA tournament appearance—still significant success by the historical standards of the program. The postseason was brief and forgettable this time around, as the Gamecocks lost two straight in the Clemson regional, 10–6 to the host Tigers and a humbling 11–1 defeat to Furman.

Following the 1976 season, Richardson surprised many when he resigned his post with USC to pursue a political career. At the urging of President Gerald Ford, he ran as a Republican in the Fifth Congressional District election—a district that included portions of Richardson's native Sumter County in the east, Spartanburg County in the west, and a wide swath of territory north of Columbia to the North Carolina border. Ford, whom Richardson had come to know through a mutual friend, hoped to unseat the Democratic incumbent, Ken Holland. A one-term congressman elected in 1974, Holland was a Gaffney native who had earned his BA and JD degrees from USC and practiced law in Camden. Democrats had held a virtual monopoly on the seat going back to the 1880s.[14]

Buoyed by Democratic presidential nominee Jimmy Carter's successful White House bid that fall, Holland won a close victory, carrying 51.5 percent of the vote to Richardson's 48.3 percent. Richardson reflects now with a grin, "I lost, but my wife said I won, because I didn't have to go to Washington."

Following the election defeat, Richardson turned his attention to his varied ministry activities and, from 1985 through 1990, returned to coaching, with a two-year stop at Coastal Carolina followed by four seasons at Liberty University in Lynchburg, Virginia. He has remained close to the South Carolina program and is viewed as the "founding father" of South Carolina's modern baseball success.

The June Raines Era Begins

Born in Greenwood, South Carolina, June Raines grew up in the small Newberry County town of Whitmire, about fifty-five miles northwest of Columbia. He grew up in a baseball family, his father a former semipro player in the 1940s and 1950s and his two brothers both scholarship baseball players, one at Newberry College, the other at Erskine College in the Abbeville County town of Due West. Likewise Raines earned a baseball scholarship at Furman University in 1957. He signed a professional contract as a catcher with the Cleveland Indians following his freshman season and went on to play eight

Head baseball coach June Raines. *Columbia Record* staff photo by Jeff Amberg, May 24, 1982. Courtesy of Richland County Public Library.

seasons with the Indians organization and another two with the Washington Senators farm system, ranging from Class D to AAA during those ten years.

In 1969 USC baseball coach Jack Powers asked Raines if he had any interest in coming back to college to finish his degree. Raines did, and Powers offered him a student assistant position while he completed his undergraduate work. Coach Richardson retained Raines as an assistant, and upon completion of his BS degree in 1971, he moved to full-time assistant while pursuing his master's degree. Upon completing his master's requirements, Raines left Carolina following the 1972 season, returning to professional baseball in the Philadelphia Phillies organization as a minor league catching instructor and, later, Rookie League manager for the Phillies' Auburn, New York, Class A team for the 1975 season.

When Bobby Richardson decided to pursue political office following the 1976 season, Raines says he was surprised when he surfaced as a candidate for the USC job. "I was in Columbia at the time, and they [USC] called me and said, 'Why don't you come in and interview for the job?' To be honest, I just thought they'd promote Coach Hunton. But they hired me, and fortunately for me, Coach Hunton decided to stay on. That helped a lot. We made a pretty good team. I was in the right place at the right time."

Indeed, when USC named Raines head coach in August 1976, his first official act was to ask Hunton to stay on.[15] Hunton served as Raines's top assistant for seventeen of his twenty seasons as Gamecock coach. "We used to travel in three vans [for road contests]. I'd drive one, Coach Hunton would drive one, and our trainer would drive one. We didn't fly back then," Raines reflects. "Times have really changed since those days."

Raines compiled a record of 763–380–2 (.667) between 1977 and 1996, taking his Gamecock program to the College World Series in 1977, 1981, 1982, and 1985 and making it to the national championship game in 1977.[16] To understand the full sweep of his USC career, consider that Raines holds the distinction of being the only Gamecock coach to have taken part in all four eras of modern athletics competition—the ACC (as an assistant in 1969–71), independent (assistant, 1972; head coach, 1977–83), Metro Conference (1984–91), and SEC (1992–96).[17] Between his time as an assistant and head coach, Raines saw six football coaches and four basketball coaches come and go and worked under seven different athletics directors.

Raines launched his two-decade run in grand fashion, his 1977 squad quickly putting to rest any fears of a backslide to mediocrity in the post-Richardson era. "Bobby had left some key players there. We had [pitcher] Randy Martz walk on from the football team, who we didn't know anything about. He said he was a pitcher," Raines recalls with a chuckle, "and he turned out to be the player of the year in the country that year, going 14–0." Raines continued, "You had Ed Lynch from the basketball team, and he pitched in the big leagues for a long time, so I was fortunate that those guys fell right into my hands, and we had several players left over from Bobby that could play. And Coach Hunton had recruited guys like Mookie Wilson to come in, and you know, Mookie turned out to be a pretty good player. And it all sort of fell together."

Raines recalls an interaction with pitcher Jim Lewis in the opening game of 1977—his first as Gamecock head coach—that set his mind at ease about the type of team he was leading. "My first game, we were playing Coastal Carolina, and Lewis was the starting pitcher. I'll never forget, he loaded the bases in the first inning with no outs. And I walked out there to him, and he said, 'Coach, I've got 'em right where I want 'em,'" Raines laughed. Lewis worked out of the inning without allowing a run, and Carolina won 11–0. Raines says with guys like Lewis on the squad, he knew the Gamecocks would compete day in and day out and had a chance to be something special.

The 1977 season started out well, as the Gamecocks rolled to a 10–1 record through the first eleven games, the lone setback coming in an unlikely 2–1 extra-inning loss to tiny Baptist College in Charleston in the season's second game.[18] Following the nine-game win streak after the Baptist loss, Carolina encountered a rough stretch, losing five of the next nine and tying another for a pedestrian 13–5–1 record coming into a rare Monday game at top-ranked Clemson. The Tigers boasted a gawdy 26–0 record going into the contest. Raines started his ace, the six-foot-four righty Martz, on an overcast day at Tiger Field.[19]

The Gamecocks scored their only two runs in the top of the first inning, beginning with a two-out triple by speedy center fielder Mookie Wilson. Fellow outfielder Don Repsher doubled next, pushing Wilson home to put Carolina up 1–0. Designated hitter Steve King then singled to score Repsher, and the Gamecocks carried a 2–0 lead into the Clemson half of the first. The two runs would be all that Martz would need, as he pitched a four-hit shutout through eight innings to preserve the 2–0 lead going into the ninth.

A light rain settled over the Tiger Stadium by the final inning, creating slippery conditions on the pitcher's mound. By the bottom of the inning, the Upstate red clay was a sticky mess. Struggling with footing, Martz ran into trouble, giving up a single, two wild pitches, and a walk and putting the potential tying and winning runners on the corners with one out. The crowd of twenty-five hundred mostly Tiger partisans came alive, sensing a comeback win over the rival Gamecocks.

While the converted quarterback took a moment to clean his cleats, Raines asked Clemson's Bill Wilhelm for some sand to stabilize footing on the mound. Wilhelm told Raines that not only did he not have sand, but further, he didn't have anyone to spread it if he did. Following the game, Wilhelm told reporters, "We went out to the road and got something as close to sand as we could find," which the coach personally applied. With better footing, Martz ended the game with a sacrifice fly, scoring Clemson's only run, and two harmless infield grounders to preserve the biggest win of Raines's young coaching career.

The newly confident Gamecocks went 30–6 the rest of the way, finishing with a 43–12–1 record, including two more wins over the high-powered Tigers in Columbia for a series sweep. South Carolina played host for the NCAA regionals but faced a tough opening round Friday game versus second-ranked South Alabama. The Gamecocks carried a lead into the late innings, but the bullpen could not hold it, and South Alabama won the opener 7–6.

The loss meant Carolina would need to win four consecutive times in the double-elimination regional round in order to get back to Omaha. It started with a 4–1 win in the loser's bracket game versus East Carolina on Saturday, powered by the complete game performance of Jim Lewis. The ECU win set up a Sunday rematch with South Alabama, who lost the winner's bracket game to Wake Forest.

Ed Lynch, the convert from McGuire's basketball squad, drew the assignment and pitched a superb game, stifling the normally hot-hitting South Alabama en route to an 11–2 win and setting up an evening matchup with Wake Forest. Righty Hal Hutchens got the start versus the Demon Deacons, and the Gamecocks beat Wake 5–2, forcing a deciding Monday rematch. Randy Martz got the nod on two day's rest and struck out twelve while scattering ten hits over a complete game effort. The Gamecocks rode home runs from Johnny Hinkel, Mark Van Bever, and Mookie Wilson and completed the loser's bracket comeback, defeating their former ACC rivals 6–2. The win sent South Carolina back to Omaha for the second time ever, and their second trip in three seasons.

South Carolina faced Baylor of the Southwest Conference in their opening College World Series matchup on June 11, and it proved to be the most dramatic game of the 1977 Omaha classic. Martz got the start opposite Baylor's Panamanian right-hander, Jaime Cocanower, and the two battled to a 1–1 deadlock through nine innings. When Baylor plated a run in the top of the tenth to go up 2–1, Raines replaced himself as third-base coach in the bottom of the tenth in favor of Hunton, "to change up the luck a little," as Raines described it. The move proved fortuitous.

After Van Bever doubled to open the inning, he advanced to third on a Wilson ground out, bringing outfielder Chuck McClean to the plate. McClean roped a first-pitch line drive over the center fielder's head, scoring Van Bever to tie the game. As the speedy McClean approached third, Hunton waved him in. McClean slid into home, just beating the relay and completing an improbable extra-inning, walk-off, inside-the-park home run on the biggest stage in college baseball.

McClean told reporters after the game he thought it was a safe triple, but when he saw Hunton waving him in, he just tried to run as fast as he could. "I've never seen him run so fast," Raines said in a postgame interview, adding, "I'm just so proud of these guys." Raines credited Hunton for the call, saying he would have held McClean at third.

In the winner's bracket game, Carolina faced upstart Cal State Los Angeles, who had defeated Big Ten champion Minnesota in their opening game. The Gamecocks enjoyed steady pitching and fourteen strikeouts from starter Lewis in a 6–2 win.[20] In round three Martz pitched on short rest, and the Gamecocks survived a challenge from Missouri Valley Conference champion Southern Illinois by a score of 5–4. They were now 3–0 and the only undefeated team for the second time in two trips to Omaha.

Carolina ran into an Arizona State buzz saw in the next two games, starting with a 6–2 loss in the semifinal matchup. The Sun Devils then avenged an earlier loss to Southern Illinois, eliminating the Salukis and setting up a championship rematch versus South Carolina.

The championship game proved a low-scoring pitcher's duel between ASU's Jerry Vasquez and USC's Jim Lewis. The Gamecocks' lone score came on a seventh-inning solo blast to right field by Steve King, which briefly knotted the game at 1–1. In the bottom of the inning, the Sun Devils' Chris Bando homered off Lewis to go ahead 2–1, and that proved to be the final margin, providing Arizona State with their fourth College World Series championship.

It was a second runner-up finish in three seasons for the Gamecocks. Randy Martz, the former third-string quarterback and tight end, earned national player of the year and first-team All-America honors for his 14–0 record. Martz, Chuck McClean, and Mookie Wilson were named to the all-tournament team, while Arizona State third baseman and future Atlanta Brave Bob Horner won tournament MVP honors.[21] The Gamecocks finished 1977 with a 43–12–1 record, and though the championship had eluded them, South Carolina had established itself as one of the elite programs in college baseball.

Of reaching the national championship game in his first season as head coach, Raines reflects, "I thought to myself when it was all over, this is a lot of fun, and it seems to be easy. I later learned, it ain't easy." The coming years for Carolina baseball, if not easy, would prove to be fun indeed.

Following Raines' successful debut season as head coach, athletics director Carlen wrote to President Patterson on June 9 recommending him for a 6.7 percent raise, from $16,000 to $17,072.

Sarge Frye Takes a Bow

One thing that did prove to be easy and predictable for Raines, and Richardson before him, was the playing conditions at USC's home field, thanks to the efforts of a retired master sergeant from Fort Jackson.

Weldon B. "Sarge" Frye's biography reads like a profile in Tom Brokaw's *The Greatest Generation*. He was born May 7, 1913, in the tiny farming community of Medon, Tennessee, a stop along the Illinois Central Railroad about ten miles south of Jackson. Frye joined the army in 1931 and spent the next twenty-three years in service, rising to the rank of master sergeant. He was wounded during the Allied invasion of Europe and received a Purple Heart and the Bronze Star for meritorious service in combat. He later received a second Bronze Star for his service in the Korean War.

His final post was Fort Jackson, where he was placed in charge of maintaining the fort's athletic facilities. Upon retirement from the army in 1953, he was hired by USC and placed in charge of maintaining the university's athletic fields. "I never had a class in it (groundskeeping), and those early years were a growing process for me," Frye recalled in a 1984 interview. "Warren Giese was the football coach then and he let me go with him to other schools to look at their facilities and learn from them."

He learned well, and in 1968 took charge of maintaining all of USC's grounds throughout a rapidly expanding campus. Upon retiring from his expanded university-wide duties in 1977, he continued in a supervisory role, overseeing USC's athletics facilities through the 1996–97 academic year. Over a half century of service to the university, Frye became a legendary figure within the athletics department and gained particular renown for the playing surfaces at Carolina's football and baseball facilities. Richardson, the man who spent over a decade plying his trade at Yankee Stadium and Major League facilities across the nation, said the field at Carolina's baseball diamond was "as good as any I'd ever played on."

In 1980 the university recognized Frye's twenty-seven years of service by renaming the baseball stadium at the Enright Athletics Complex Weldon B. "Sarge" Frye Field. In pregame ceremonies before a May 11 game with archrival Clemson, USC president James Holderman and athletics director Jim Carlen recognized Frye's many years of service, rechristening the field into which he had poured so much energy and care over the years. Attending the ceremony were members of Frye's family, including his son, Jerry, a USC football letterman from 1958–60, and his grandson, Jay, who was set to join the Gamecock football program that fall. Frye ended an emotional speech, with a nod to his old army buddy, Clemson's Coach Wilhelm. "I want to thank Bill for being here, and I hope he doesn't go away today too mad," Frye quipped with a grin, bringing laughter and a minutes-long round of applause from the overflow crowd of six thousand.

The Gamecocks scored runs in the fourth, sixth, seventh, and eighth, and Sarge Frye Field debuted with a satisfying 4–1 win, capping a two-game weekend sweep of the Tigers.

Raines, reflecting on a conversation he had with Frye several years later, remembers that "they put Astroturf in Williams-Brice Stadium [in 1971], and Sarge didn't like that. That was his baby, and he wanted to take care of the grass. Then they took the Astroturf out and put grass back in [1984], and I got worried. I said, 'Sarge, all your time's going to be over at the football stadium,'" Raines said, indicating concern that his baseball diamond might

Sarge Frye, supervisor of facilities at USC and later namesake of the Carolina baseball stadium, standing at the pre-expansion Carolina (later Williams-Brice) Stadium in 1970. Courtesy of the *State* Newspaper Archive, Richland County Public Library.

be neglected. Sarge replied, "June, look on the scoreboard out there. Whose name is on it?" Raines recalls, laughing. "He said, 'Don't worry about it,' and I never did have to worry about it."

Omaha Becomes a Regular Stop, and Metro Play Begins

Following Raines's successful debut season in 1977, Jim Carlen asked him what his program needed to sustain and enhance the recent success. "I said we needed more seats at the ballpark," recalls Raines. The stadium's official capacity was two thousand—unchanged since opening in 1969—although overflow crowds were commonplace since the successful Major League exhibition weekend of 1974 and even more frequent in the wake of the program's inaugural College World Series trip and second-place national finish in 1975. Carlen obliged, and prior to the 1978 season, an additional two thousand seats were added along the third-base line, doubling capacity.[22]

Raines's Gamecocks returned to Omaha in 1981, 1982, and 1985, and while those teams did not reach the tournament finals, finishing fourth, seventh, and eighth, respectively, South Carolina's five trips to Omaha in eleven seasons put the program in rare company.[23] Led by names like Chris Boyle, Jim Curl, Paul Hollins, Rob Lowry, Greg Morhardt, Joe Kucharski, Mark Calvert, Mike Werner, Joe Datin, Mike Cook, and Rob Rinehart, Raines's program maintained elite national status during the independent and Metro Conference years. Carolina baseball was the most consistently successful program on campus during that time, achieving twelve NCAA tournament appearances between 1974 and the final season of Metro competition in 1991.

Of the Metro Conference, which Carolina entered prior to the 1984 season, Raines remembers it as a marriage of necessity for USC, which needed the stability of a conference home during a time when the ACC or SEC were not options. "I don't think anyone was thrilled with it, but we needed it for scheduling purposes, not only for baseball, but for basketball. Being an independent, all of the conference teams had weekend series, so we had trouble scheduling weekend games."

The geography of the conference was a challenge. "It was so far-flung. We went from Florida State in Tallahassee to Memphis to Cincinnati, and it was just tough because of the way we traveled. We didn't fly back then, so it was tough on the young men." But beyond the challenges of travel, Raines says Metro baseball was good, particularly the rivalry with Florida State, which boasted a strong program and a baseball culture comparable to South Carolina's. "We loved playing Florida State."

Raines, while praising Founders Park, remembers Sarge Frye Field with great fondness. "It was a fun atmosphere. We had the third-base hecklers. And I used to get heckled all the time [by opposing fans] because of my name. People would say, 'April showers, May flowers, and June Raines,'" he says with a laugh. "I remember the train stopping out there" on the tracks beyond right field, "and between innings one of our guys from the bullpen ran down there and gave the conductor a baseball. Well, about a week or two later, the train stopped again, and the conductor wanted an autograph on that baseball!" He adds wistfully, "It was just a fun time."

Winning tends to make everything more fun, and Richardson and Raines won a lot. Combined they won 983 games versus 471 losses and four ties (.675), most of which took place during the independent and Metro years.[24] The foundation they laid set the stage for even greater success under Ray Tanner. Upon leaving NC State to take over the Gamecock program in June 1996, Tanner told the assembled media at his introductory press conference, "I had a wish-list. South Carolina was a program I hoped to be a part of one day." He was quick to credit Richardson and Raines for the foundation they had established. He continued to share credit with his predecessors throughout his sixteen seasons at the helm, including during the celebrations that followed the program's back-to-back national championships in 2010 and 2011.

Following the 2010 championship, Tanner told the *State*'s Neil White, "I was given the responsibility of carrying it forward. Without question, on a number of occasions, I've thought about Coach Richardson's seven years, and Coach Raines' 20, and being able to carry on their legacy at South Carolina." He added, "I didn't build a tradition here. They did."

Baseball is a sport steeped in tradition. Unlike football and basketball, which are nearly unrecognizable from their earliest forms, baseball is still fundamentally the same game played on that dusty, makeshift field at the old fairgrounds in 1892. The rhythm of the game, with its balls and strikes and progression of innings, the warm kiss of sunlight, the loamy aroma of grass and soil, the pop of a ball into cowhide, and the crack of a bat. (Well, that last one has changed a bit.)

But if you settle into a quiet spot along the outfield fence at Founders Park on a warm April evening, it is hard not to sense the presence of all the players who have gone before. Hard not to see Sarge Frye in the lovingly manicured turf. Hard not to detect an old Yankees legend in the crisp garnet-pinstriped home uniform, and hard not to sense the legacy of a former minor league catcher turned coach. And though the clank and horn blast of lumbering trains beyond the outfield fence is gone, you can still see the old ballpark in the carefully replicated dimensions of the new.

Like the Congaree River on whose banks its home now sits, the tradition of Carolina baseball flows deep and sure.

6

Pullets, Chicks, and Lady Gamecocks

The Evolution of Women's Sports at USC

As the Women's athletic director at Carolina, I feel extremely fortunate to have found a school with such fine interest in women's athletics, in me as a person, and all sports in general.

—Pam Parsons, women's athletics director
and head basketball coach, 1977

The evolution of women's sports at the University of South Carolina is a prism through which one can view larger trends in women's social advancement throughout the twentieth century. The advancement of intercollegiate competition in women's sports to a station on par with men's sports, though, has been a relatively recent development. Title IX of the Education Amendments of 1972, signed into law by President Richard Nixon in June of that year, was a watershed law, which fundamentally changed the face of collegiate athletics and marked the culmination of decades of struggle by women to secure an opportunity to compete in intercollegiate sports.

The first women's intercollegiate contest was a basketball game between club teams at the University of California, Berkeley, and Stanford in 1896, a mere five years after James A. Naismith invented the game. As early as 1922, female students at the University of South Carolina played basketball contests at an intramural level and against club teams from other colleges across the state. Those early teams, known as the "Pullets," played intermittently throughout the coming decades, interrupted at times by war, lack of resources, or momentary waning interest.

The women's suffrage movement of the late nineteenth and early twentieth centuries resulted in passage of the Nineteenth Amendment in 1920, which extended to women the right to vote and, in turn, renewed emphasis on women's freedoms. A rising interest in women's sports led to early efforts at organizing and governing these activities under the Women's Division of the National Amateur Athletic Federation (NAAF).

Led by Col. Henry Breckenridge, a former assistant secretary of the navy and prominent attorney, the goals of the NAAF reflected the entrenched paternalism of the time, as the group sought, among other objectives, "play for play's sake," limiting travel and awards, protecting participants from exploitation, limiting "sensational exposure," and promoting the use of "suitable costumes" for athletic activities.[1]

During the Great Depression of the 1930s, millions of American men found themselves out of work, resulting in a loose campaign to keep women in more traditional roles in the home. When the 1940s brought World War II and the deployment of millions of men to Europe and the Pacific, women filled the void in offices and factories and, in some cases, were deployed in uniform themselves. The popular image of Rosie the Riveter reflected a new sense of strength and self-reliance, and as the war ended, there was a renewed focus on intercollegiate competition for women.

Throughout the 1950s and 1960s, the social fabric of America continued to evolve, and with it attitudes concerning women in sport. In 1957 the Division for Girls and Women in Sport (DGWS), a successor of the NAAF, modified their stance on women's participation ever so slightly, stating that intercollegiate programs for women "may" exist. In 1963 DGWS liberalized their stance further to state that it was, in fact, "desirable" for women's intercollegiate programs to exist. This was followed closely by the Civil Rights Act of 1964, which served to bolster status and opportunities for minorities and women. As the feminist movement renewed focus on women's changing place in society and debate over the Equal Rights Amendment grew in volume, events again evolved to raise consciousness around opportunities for women in intercollegiate competition.

In 1967 DGWS established the Commission for Intercollegiate Athletics for Women to assist in governing intercollegiate competition—another step toward moving women's sports to an equal footing with men's. Between 1969 and 1972, the commission introduced a schedule of national championships for women's college sports, including basketball and volleyball.

In 1971 the Association for Intercollegiate Athletics for Women (AIAW) largely replaced the commission and brought governing structures more in line with the NCAA. Throughout the late 1970s, the NCAA and AIAW struggled over who would control women's athletics. With the establishment of Title IX, Congress legislated women's right to participation and funding in intercollegiate sports, mandating that it must be on equal footing with men's sports. The landmark legislation established a six-year window during which institutions would be required to develop plans for bringing their athletics departments into compliance. Thus 1978 marked a critical year in the history of women's athletics.

As Title IX enforcement became a reality, the AIAW threatened the NCAA's position as the preeminent governing body for collegiate athletics, along with the financial and political power such a governing body enjoyed. The NCAA initially attempted to limit the scope of Title IX application, arguing that because athletics departments did not receive federal funds, they should be excluded from compliance. As women's sports continued to grow in popularity, however, the NCAA shifted its focus toward increasing its financial base and political power by wresting control of women's sports from the AIAW.

The NCAA introduced its own series of women's championships in the mid-1970s and used its long-established wealth and political influence ultimately to vanquish the AIAW. The NCAA offered a series of enhancements, offering to pay all expenses for teams competing in a national championship, charging no additional membership fees for schools adding women's programs, creating financial aid packages, promoting recruitment and eligibility in alignment with men's sports, and guaranteeing enhanced television coverage for women's sports. The AIAW sued the NCAA for violation of the Sherman Antitrust Act but received unfavorable court rulings.

University of South Carolina Reflective of National Trends

By 1968 the University of South Carolina boasted women's club teams for gymnastics and tennis and provided a small budget for uniforms. The administration placed these teams in the Physical Education Department. Basketball and volleyball were added in 1970, softball in 1971, and swimming in 1972. In 1973 the women's basketball team appeared as a preliminary to several men's games at Carolina Coliseum. Frank McGuire's men's squads were still a big draw at that time, and these double-header contests raised the profile of women's sports on campus.

Noting student and fan support and the competitiveness of those early teams, the university moved the "Carolina Chicks," as they were then known, under the administration of the athletics department for the 1974–75 season, making basketball the first women's varsity sport at South Carolina.[2] The athletics department also created the position of associate athletics director for women's sports. Helen Timmermans, a professor in USC's School of Health and Physical Education, was the first to hold that role. Timmermans also served as the gymnastics coach for the first six seasons of that program's existence. Pam Backhaus, formerly the basketball club coach, was named the program's first head coach. Backhaus had played college ball at Kansas State University and was a USC faculty member. Peggy Harden, a former club player, assisted Backhaus.

The first women's varsity game provided an inauspicious beginning for the program, resulting in a 99–60 thrashing at the hands of tiny Anderson College on December 2, 1974. The first home game in program history was played against Francis Marion College at Booker T. Washington High School gymnasium in Columbia on January 14, 1975, resulting in a 62–50 win, the program's first.[3] That initial varsity squad was a winning one, compiling an overall 18–12 record and advancing to the AIAW regional playoff.

Frankie Porter took over coaching duties in 1975–76, and the first women's scholarships were awarded to Charlene DuBose, Denise Nanney, and Martha

Suber. Porter's lone season resulted in a 7–15 final record. In 1976–77 Pam Backhaus resumed head coaching responsibilities, but the team finished a disappointing 8–18. USC stood three seasons into their varsity existence with an overall 33–45 record. Change was needed, and change would come in the form of a young upstart coach from powerhouse Old Dominion University.

Pam Parsons Transforms South Carolina

The cover of the 1980–81 South Carolina women's basketball media guide boasts a photo of Pam Parsons, resplendent in a striking red dress, leaning confidently against a brick planter on the university's historic Horseshoe. Behind her bloomed the verdant flora of a lovingly manicured campus. Her short auburn hair was perfectly coifed, and her eyes reflected singular focus. Perched dramatically atop her left wrist was a live gamecock, proud and poised for battle. The two exchange a knowing gaze, an alliance of arch fighters.

Parsons, a native of Richfield, Utah, began her head coaching career during the same season (1974–75) as another young up and comer, Pat Head (Summitt) at Tennessee, and the two drew comparisons in those nascent years of the women's game. Parsons spent a successful three seasons at Old Dominion, where she quickly built that program into a powerhouse. She compiled a 23–9 record in her third and final season in Norfolk and earned a national reputation as a coach on the rise. The Monarchs went on to win two national championships in 1979 and 1980, powered largely by two of Parsons's highest-rated recruits, Nancy Leiberman and Inge Nissen.

Meanwhile South Carolina athletics director Jim Carlen set out to hire the best available coach for his women's basketball team. He thought initially of fellow Tennessee native Pat Head, but realizing she was firmly entrenched in Knoxville, he set his sights on Old Dominion's twenty-nine-year-old coach. Parsons had recently squabbled publicly with ODU athletics director Jim Jarrett, and when Carlen came calling, she listened. In May 1977 Parsons became the third women's basketball coach at the University of South Carolina in as many years, also taking on the role of associate athletics director for women's sports. She immediately went to work building her program into a winner.

Parsons quickly jettisoned the Chicks nickname and adopted the less patronizing, if slightly awkward, Lady Gamecocks.[4]

1980–81 USC women's basketball media guide, featuring head coach Pam Parsons.

Parson's first South Carolina team (1977–78) enjoyed a fourteen-game improvement over the prior season, finishing 24–10 and notching the program's first twenty-win season. The team finished strong, winning nine of their final ten games, the lone loss during that stretch a 77–52 setback versus fifth-ranked NC State in the AIAW Region II Tournament played in Chapel Hill.

The 1978–79 team went 27–10, continuing a trend of twenty-plus-win seasons and overall improvement under Parsons's tutelage. The Gamecocks turned in their best performance of that season against Parsons's old team, handing top-ranked Old Dominion a humiliating 73–49 loss in Columbia. The loss to South Carolina was the Monarchs' lone blemish during a dominant 35–1 season, which culminated in the first of two straight national championships. The Gamecocks also achieved a program-first appearance in the Associated Press Top 20 following the upset of ODU. Parsons's Gamecocks finished the season ranked fifteenth, after winning the Women's National Invitational Tournament (WNIT) with a 74–71 win over Drake University in Amarillo, Texas.

As women's athletics director, Parsons oversaw the growth and success of USC women's athletics that stretched beyond the basketball court, with four teams claiming top-twenty finishes by 1979: tennis in eighth place, swimming in tenth, and softball in thirteenth in addition to basketball's fifteenth-place finish). Indeed, Parsons had substantially elevated women's sports at South Carolina during her two years in Columbia, but bigger goals lay ahead.

A headline in the 1979–80 media guide proclaimed, "This year the Lady Gamecocks are shooting for the stars," and Coach Parsons noted that her third team at South Carolina would be "the strongest total team I've ever coached."

Her optimism was understandable, given the talent of four returning starters, highlighted by Sheila Foster, the six-foot sophomore guard/forward combo from Boiling Springs, South Carolina, who averaged fourteen points and almost nine rebounds over thirty-seven games during her freshman campaign. Foster ranked among the top ten freshmen in the nation in both scoring and rebounding. Newcomers were highlighted by Evelyn "Sweet E" Johnson, the five-ten freshman from Lansing, Michigan, and kid sister to Earvin "Magic" Johnson, the second-year phenom for the Los Angeles Lakers. Becky Parker, a five-eleven guard from Maryville, Tennessee, who averaged 34.7 points as a high school senior, and local product Sharon Rivers, an all-state selection for three straight seasons at Lexington High School, added additional excitement at the guard positions.

Parsons's third Gamecock squad compiled a sterling 30–6 record, highlighted by the program's first-ever win over Tennessee, and made it to the AIAW final four round in Mount Pleasant, Michigan. South Carolina faced its third matchup of the season with Tennessee in the semifinal, coming just short of qualifying for a national championship appearance in a 75–72 loss to the Lady Vols. Parsons's squad won their next and final game, defeating favored Louisiana Tech 77–69 for a third-place national finish. Old Dominion, meanwhile, largely powered by Parsons's recruits, capped their second straight national championship in a win over Tennessee.

After three seasons Parsons boasted an impressive 81–26 (.757) record at South Carolina, with a third-place national finish and a WNIT championship to her credit. As the team moved toward the 1980–81 season, possibilities seemed limitless, and the Gamecocks were ranked fifth in preseason polling. Parsons added highly regarded transfers in a pair of "lightning fast" five-foot-seven guards, Frani Washington from Ohio State and Pat Mason from Kansas. Washington and Mason joined a solid nucleus of returning players, including Foster, who averaged 16.4 points during her sophomore campaign, and Evelyn Johnson, who averaged 13 points as a freshman.

Warning Signs, then Stormy Weather at South Carolina

The 1980–81 Gamecocks went 21–9, Parsons's fourth-straight twenty-plus-win season. A successful campaign, if not on par with the achievements of her prior two squads. However, South Carolina ultimately forfeited eight games when the AIAW ruled transfer Frani Washington ineligible due to academic discrepancies at Ohio State, giving the Gamecocks an official 13–17 finish. The eight-game forfeiture was an early indicator that, despite unprecedented success, all was not right within Parsons's program.

During a December tournament in Los Angeles, Parsons angrily chastised Washington at courtside and in the locker room during halftime for asking assistant coach Karen Brown for advice on strategy. In early January, following a nineteen-point home win versus top-ranked NC State, Parsons did not return to the bench until two minutes into the second half. Following what should have been a celebration after a second top-ten win in as many days, Parsons reportedly fled to the Carolina Coliseum parking lot, crying and threatening to quit, only to be surrounded by players at her car for an impromptu and tearful team meeting in the chilly January night. Two days later assistant coach Brown left the team, as did administrative assistant Linda Singer, both citing irreconcilable differences with Parsons.

Parsons's stormy demeanor continued during the remainder of the 1980–81 season as friction grew with both Washington and Mason. As a transfer under AIAW rules, Mason was not eligible for university-subsidized housing, although she was eligible to play without sitting out a season. Upon receiving an $800 invoice from the university for housing, Mason told reporters Parsons had promised to cover all such expenses during her recruitment.

At a team meal prior to a January 8 game at Ohio State, Parsons reportedly asked players to bow their heads in prayer for Washington and Mason, "for they are troublemakers." Following a January 15 home win over Mercer, Mason reported to the *Daily Gamecock* that she left the team after Parsons told her she would not play the rest of the season because "you don't believe in me." Mason told the *Gamecock* that "the basketball program is a cult, and Parsons is Jim Jones."

Suspicious of Parsons even prior to resigning her position as assistant coach, Karen Brown had hired a Columbia detective to stake out Parsons's home in November 1980 in order to substantiate what she suspected to be recruiting improprieties. The detective established surveillance near Parsons's Irmo-area home at 233 Broken Hill Road at 6:50 AM on the morning of Sunday, November 2, 1980. He reported that Parsons and a visiting high school recruit from Atlanta, Tina Buck, left Parsons's home at 9:58 AM. Brown concluded from the surveillance that Parsons had hosted Buck overnight, which was a violation of AIAW rules against off-campus recruiting.

Brown shared the surveillance findings, in addition to evidence of other improprieties, with athletics director Carlen as well as NCAA delegate William F. Putnam. Additionally Brown claimed Parsons had given her $800 in cash to pay for Mason's housing. Perhaps more damning, Brown claimed that she and Parsons had collaborated to write as many as a half dozen term papers for players in cases when grades threatened eligibility. She claimed the scheme was Parsons's idea and that the coach had written the papers, after which she typed them.

In another troubling development, forward Evelyn Johnson claimed that administrative assistant Linda Singer had given her money to purchase drugs for Parsons. Though Johnson denied ever purchasing the drugs, she suspected it was a setup of sorts, an attempt to compromise the sister of Magic Johnson. The university made no obvious attempt to investigate further, although Carlen relieved Parsons of her assistant athletics director duties when he hired former Miami Dolphins cornerback Ron Dickerson to fill that role. It would be the following season before Brown's allegations became public knowledge in the form of a blockbuster *Sports Illustrated* exposé.

As Parsons approached the 1981–82 season, her fifth in Columbia, outward appearances indicated that she had achieved sustained success, and the Gamecocks were poised to mount a serious challenge for that season's national championship. She had compiled an impressive 94–43 record (.686) over her first four seasons. Washington and Mason were gone, but Parsons had secured the number-one recruiting class in the country, including two of the top five recruits.

This group included the nation's consensus number 1 prep senior, six-two Medina Dixon of Boston, and fellow top-five recruit Brantley Southers, a six-one shooting guard from Columbia. Rounding out the impressive class were Mona Nance, a power forward whom Parsons envisioned as a potential heir to Sheila Foster; Marci McAlister, a highly rated five-ten guard from Columbia; and Tina Buck, a five-seven shooting guard who averaged 29.9 points per game as a high school senior and possessed lockdown defensive skills.

This impressive group of freshmen joined a solid returning nucleus of returning players, including the senior all-American Foster, junior Johnson, point guard Rivers, and six-six center Philicia Allen. In an interview with the *Gamecock,* Parsons said of her fifth USC team, "They are as good as any other team I've had, if not the best."

The Gamecocks were ranked in the preseason top five, and excitement around the team's potential caught further national attention in the form of a three-page profile on forwards Dixon and Johnson in the November 30, 1981, issue of *Sports Illustrated.* The article contrasted the style of the two—with imagery of the powerful five-ten Johnson "bulling her way inside, leaning for position, forcing the action, working hard, while Dixon is smooth—the glider, slider, flyer." If all went well, the article posited, the two could make South Carolina a contender for the women's title, now under the purview of the NCAA. Also noted, as "slightly more notable" than Parsons's 94–43 record, was the number of players (seventeen) who had either quit or been dismissed during her tenure, a result of Parsons's "my way or Trailways" coaching philosophy. Another, less flattering *Sports Illustrated* article would appear in just over two months.

The Gamecocks opened the 1981–82 season in Manhattan, Kansas, in the Converse Little Apple Classic. They won the tournament with two double-digit wins over William Penn University (Iowa) and Kansas State to take the tournament championship. Freshman Medina Dixon was dominant, scoring forty-nine combined points in her first two collegiate games and winning tournament MVP. South Carolina jumped to number 3 in the polls on the strength of their opening performances.

The next stop was Hawaii, as the women's team joined the men's basketball team and the football team on a package trip to Oahu. The football team suffered a twenty-three-point loss to the University of Hawaii's Rainbow Warriors—a game that proved to be Jim Carlen's final outing as South Carolina's head football coach. The men's basketball team fared no better, losing to tiny Chaminade University, followed by a twenty-four-point setback to Hawaii. Parsons's Gamecocks proved South Carolina's lone bright spot, dominating the Hawaii women's team in consecutive games, 84–52 and 74–46.

The road show continued in a top-twenty matchup at archrival Clemson, where the Gamecocks took a hard-fought eight-point win in Littlejohn Coliseum. A thirteen-point win at Pittsburgh capped the six-game road stretch to start the season, followed by an 83–57 win over Tennessee Tech in the home opener and final game before a short holiday break. Now 7–0 and ranked number 2 in the country, Parsons and company were living up to preseason hype. It proved to be the high-water mark for Parsons and for the women's program for many years to come as whispers of improprieties continued to dog the coach.

On the afternoon of December 31, assistant athletics director Dickerson visited Parsons's home to confront her about rumors surrounding the program and Parsons's own conduct. He emerged a short time later with a brief handwritten note from the coach. The subject line simply noted "Resignation," followed by a two-sentence declaration: "I am formally resigning my duties as head basketball coach due to serious conditions with my health. I will not be able to continue at this time to do my duties and therefore want to have this be effective as soon as possible."

The following day, on January 1, 1982, Parsons's thirty-fourth birthday, the coach attempted to contact university officials to revoke her resignation. She also contacted reporters at the Associated Press and the *State* to dispute the resignation, claiming her health was perfect and that she intended to lead her team to South Carolina's first national championship. University president James Holderman, in response to questions from the AP, noted that Parsons's resignation had been accepted and that twenty-eight-year-old assistant coach

Terry Kelly had been promoted to acting head coach before a January 2 game at St. Joseph's in Philadelphia.

After a narrow 50–48 road victory over St. Joseph's pushed the Gamecocks' record to 8–0, the situation grew stranger still. As the team arrived back in Columbia late that night, Parsons appeared on the tarmac, greeting the team plane and holding a banner proclaiming "WELCOME HOME. I HAVE NOT RESIGNED!" The saga had taken a turn for the surreal. Later that night Parsons sent a single red rose to each of her players, which she described as a "sign of love."

On January 4, 1982, Parsons resigned a second and final time after reaching a settlement with the university that paid her $20,111.68. Parsons cited "philosophical differences" with the university. During an interview with sports anchor Craig Sager on the nascent Cable News Network in Atlanta, Parsons expanded, "I believe there should be an independent status of women's athletics and I believe women ought to run that program. Without that kind of cooperation, I felt no desire to coach at South Carolina."

Citing the terms of the agreement with Parsons and her attorney Jean Toal, the university refused public comment on the circumstances surrounding Parson's resignation.[5] However, in a February 8, 1982, *Sports Illustrated* article titled "Stormy Weather at South Carolina," reporter Jill Lieber quoted senior vice president for university relations Chris Vlahoplus, who stated the mother of one South Carolina player, Brandley Southers, had complained to the university that Parsons was engaged in a romantic relationship with a player.

The player was USC freshman guard Tina Buck, as confirmed by Southers to Lieber in the *Sports Illustrated* account. This was also confirmed to Lieber by Vlahoplus, though after learning of Vlahoplus's statement, university attorney Paul J. Ward contacted *Sports Illustrated* to say Vlahoplus subsequently denied making such a statement.

Southers, the six-two freshman forward from Columbia, alleged she witnessed Parsons and Buck behaving romantically and heard them on multiple occasions express their love for one another. The alleged incidents took place at Parsons's home when Southers was present. Parsons's attorney Toal dismissed the allegations, calling them "Karen Brown's hatchet job."

The *Greenville News,* meanwhile, reported on January 20, 1982, that Parsons had resigned after a player's mother accused Parsons of being romantically involved with one unnamed player while making sexual advances toward another, which Toal rejected as an "unsubstantiated rumor."

Parsons vehemently denied the accusations, and later sued Time, Inc., the corporation that owned *Sports Illustrated,* for libel in a $75 million civil suit. The case was tried over the course of two weeks in May 1984 at the federal courthouse in Columbia. Accounts of the trial are a reminder of how explosive accusations of homosexuality were in that era, compounded by the divergent power dynamics between a high-profile coach and a player at the state's flagship institution.

In a May 27, 1984, article in the *State* titled "Just Friends—or Lesbian Lovers?," staff writer Margaret O'Shea described the carnival-like atmosphere surrounding the trial as gawkers descended upon the courthouse. A US marshal describing the unusually large crowds noted that nothing like the Parsons trial had ever happened before in Columbia.

Federal employees from the Strom Thurmond Building next door spent coffee breaks and lunch hours in the courtroom of US District Judge Clyde H. Hamilton. Some spent entire days, burning vacation time or taking advantage of absent bosses. Jurors from other jury pools and other trials down the hall drifted in and out.

A favorite pastime of the mesmerized onlookers was pointing out Parsons and Buck, commenting on a new dress or leaning in to decipher their whispers to council. Lip-reading became a celebrated skill set. Standing in the courtroom was not allowed, and to leave a seat was to lose it. There was always a line at the courtroom door. A gaggle of would-be spectators gathered outside the courtroom waiting to get in, gathering snippets of information from those filtering out.

A late surprise defense witness provided a jolt to the courtroom on par with the most sensational television courtroom drama. The defense called as their final witness Babs DeLay, a Salt Lake City radio personality and gay rights activist whose testimony severely undermined Parsons's libel claims.

DeLay, who also worked as a Saturday night disc jockey at Puss and Boots, a Salt Lake City gay bar, testified that Parsons was a card-carrying member of the club and frequented the establishment over a period of several months in 1983. DeLay testified that she had seen Parsons and Buck dancing intimately on several occasions. Once, after approaching Buck for a dance, DeLay said she was refused, quoting Buck as saying, "My lover doesn't let me dance with anyone else."

DeLay said she was angry upon hearing reports of Parsons's libel claim and felt betrayed by Parsons's denial of the truth. She called Time, Inc., to volunteer her testimony, and defense counsel flew her overnight from Salt Lake City to Columbia for her day in court.

On cross examination things took a turn for the surreal, as Parsons's attorney J. Lewis Cromer turned street-corner preacher, deploying a ham-handed line of questioning in an attempt to score cheap points with what was almost certainly a socially conservative jury.

"Do you believe in Jesus Christ?"

"I believe that he existed," DeLay responded, clearly perplexed.

"Do you believe that Jesus Christ was the Son of God?" Cromer drawled, leaning fully into the non sequitur.

"I believe that he may have been," DeLay answered, irritation rising.

In questioning DeLay's testimony, the following day Cromer addressed the jury in a full lather. "Here's a woman who doesn't even believe in Jesus Christ," he said, turning to ask DeLay if she really expected the jury to believe her testimony. She said that she did.

Enraptured by his own performative outrage, Cromer closed in with a lupine grin. "Well then, you're pretty naïve for a lesbian and a news commentator and a public person, aren't you?" he snarked in an overly dramatized Southern accent, more oily carnival barker than urbane barrister.

"No sir, I am not, and I am offended at your accusations," a defiant DeLay retorted.

Describing the effects of DeLay's appearance on the courtroom, the *State's* O'Shea wryly observed when the witness was dismissed from the stand, "she took her duffle bag and whipped out of the courthouse, leaving some spectators convinced they had just seen an apparition."

When the trial drew to a close, Judge Hamilton observed during his charge to the jury that "quite obviously someone or *someones* have lied." Unbeknownst to the jury and courtroom onlookers, the judge had already initiated an investigation to find out who was not telling the truth, setting the stage for a perjury indictment later on.

Just after midnight on Saturday, May 26, the jury ruled that Parsons and Buck had lied when they denied under oath being involved in a romantic relationship. The libel suit against Time, Inc., was dismissed. The jury took over seven hours to reach their decision, one juror said later, because older members of the jury found it hard to believe any two women could really be romantically involved. Other jurors said they were reluctant to "brand" Parsons a lesbian, though they believed she was.

It was a stinging defeat for Parsons, and the consequences were steep. Judge Hamilton asked the FBI to investigate criminal perjury against Parsons and Buck. Charges were filed in November 1984, and both Parsons and Buck pleaded guilty after acting in their own defense, unrepresented by counsel. In February 1985 the couple were sentenced to three years in prison, ultimately serving 109 days in a Lexington, Kentucky, minimum-security facility.

In an April 1996 interview with Liz Chandler of the *Charlotte Observer,* Parsons discussed the factors that led to her downfall and efforts to put her life in order following prison.

"The rules didn't apply to me. It got so bad I couldn't even bear to stand in line. I'd sit back there thinking, 'I should be at the front of this line. I'm Pam Parsons.'"

She also felt she had no choice but to lie about her sexuality.

"I constantly wore a mask. I constantly had to lie. There wasn't anyone to talk to. When you're under that much stress, you don't think clearly. Only murder ranked worse than homosexuality in my religion," said Parsons who grew up in the Mormon faith. "I didn't know what to do. It was a terrible struggle."

"I want to apologize," Parsons tearfully told Chandler, "to all those players I hurt, and I want to apologize to their parents. They gave me their most prized possessions—their daughters. Those girls had hopes and dreams, and I let them down."

After release from prison, Parsons and Buck moved to Buck's native Atlanta, where they struggled to scratch out a living, some years living on as little as $5,000. They found work painting houses and did other labor as they could find it. They endured snide remarks and harassment, including a mocking play titled *To the Top*, about Parsons, Buck, and the drama of the 1981–82 season, which ran at a Columbia theater.

The incident rocked women's collegiate basketball to its foundation. Parsons's missteps lent credence to ugly stereotypes of the day, that lesbians pervaded women's basketball, enticing impressionable young women. Even more significantly, it revealed pervasive abuse of power within the South Carolina program. No scandal of the scale and consequence of Parsons's has taken place in the women's game in the four decades since. As *Sports Illustrated*'s Lieber testified during the libel trial in 1984, "This was not a story about two consenting adults. It was a story about a coach and a player. It was a breach of trust."

A Season on the Brink, a Season Salvaged

Meanwhile, the 1981–82 Gamecocks won their next two games, a six-point win at Mercer and a ten-point win in Columbia versus Rutgers, which ran the team's record to 10–0. But Parsons's stormy departure and the change in coaches rocked the team. Carolina would lose six of its next eight games, starting with a 71–58 loss to eventual national champion Louisiana Tech. Roster defections reduced the team to six scholarship players, as Dixon, Allen, and Buck, along with Pam Reeves and Mona Nance, left the squad.

Acting coach Kelly and his assistants were reduced to participating in team scrimmages, and in January they held a campus-wide tryout. Kelly added four players, including junior Pat Dufficy, who previously played on the team as a freshman but had switched to softball as a sophomore. Sisters Cindi and

Candi Rawl joined Liz Holland to round out the group of newcomers, who seemed to breathe new life into the struggling team.

The team began to gel when they battled valiantly with only six players during a late January home game versus Tennessee. USC risked having to finish the game with less than five players on the court, as three Gamecocks had four fouls late in the game. Though no one was ultimately disqualified, it was testament to the ravages of roster defections following the early-season drama. Following a minutes-long standing ovation by an appreciative home crowd, Tennessee coach Pat Summit visited the Carolina locker room following the game to commend the Gamecocks' courageous performance. USC's Kelly, after enduring weeks of turmoil, told reporters, "An emotional burden is lifted. This team wants to play."

A one-point win at Florida State and a hard-fought overtime loss at number 16 Georgia over the following week seemed to further galvanize the team, which had by then slipped to a 12–6 record and seventeenth in the polls. USC won ten of their next eleven games, its only loss coming at fourth-ranked Old Dominion. The regular season culminated in a rousing 71–70 upset win at tenth-ranked NC State in Raleigh. The 22–7 record was good enough for a bid to the first-ever NCAA Division I women's basketball tournament.[6] Terry Kelly's steady, improvisational leadership was rewarded when the university named him the program's fourth head coach prior to the tournament on March 8.

USC notched its first-ever NCAA tournament win in the opening round, defeating East Carolina by fifteen points at Carolina Coliseum on March 14. Four days later Kentucky avenged an earlier loss in Columbia, beating the Gamecocks 73–69 during round two of the Midwest Regional semifinals in Ruston, Louisiana. All-American forward Sheila Foster scored 23 points and pulled down nineteen rebounds in her final game, finishing a sparkling career with 2,266 points, good for first in program history.[7]

The loss ended USC's season at 23–8, in what would have to be considered one of the most drama-filled episodes in the often drama-filled history of South Carolina athletics.

The Gamecocks started the 1982–83 campaign ranked thirteenth but fell out of the rankings following a 6–4 start and a forty-point thumping at the

USC women's basketball legend Sheila Foster in game action at Carolina Coliseum, from the back cover of the 1979–80 USC women's basketball media guide. Foster's number 52 was the first to be retired for the women's program.

hands of second-ranked Louisiana Tech. South Carolina was 1–6 versus top-twenty teams, the lone bright spot a double-overtime win at home versus twelfth-ranked NC State in December. The Gamecocks finished 16–12 on the season.

The 1983–84 season, Kelly's second full season as head coach, was also South Carolina's first season of competition in the Metro Conference. The Gamecocks compiled an 18–12 overall record and were a respectable 7–3 in Metro play. But lackluster performances in big games had become a trend, as Kelly's Gamecocks compiled a 1–4 record versus top-twenty opponents, including two losses to archrival Clemson. The Gamecocks also lost by a point to an overachieving Francis Marion College team coached by Sylvia Hatchell, who soon went on to a long, successful run at the University of North Carolina.

Rumors of dissension in the locker room were rampant. Marsi McAlister, a junior on that season's team, tells of a January trip to face Metro Conference foe Cincinnati, during which a fight occurred among players at the team hotel. Following the altercation, McAlister and her sister Amy (also on the team), drove back to Columbia overnight with their father, who was there for the game. "It was a rough time," says McAlister.

Following a February loss to Tennessee, the team voted 9–2 in favor of Kelly's resignation and asked the coach to step down immediately. It was an assertion confirmed in media reports by five players but which Kelly denied publicly. Team dissension again boiled over when a fight broke out among teammates in the locker room following a loss at the Metro Conference tournament.

Kelly ultimately did resign following the final regular-season game, a ten-point win in Blacksburg versus Virginia Tech. He went on to coach during the Metro Conference Tournament in Cincinnati, Ohio, winning in the first-round matchup against Tulane before losing versus Memphis State and Virginia Tech to finish fourth in the seven-team tournament.

Citing the desire to pursue "other outside interests," Kelly told the *Columbia Record,* "I have enjoyed my association with the University of South Carolina and wish the team, the athletics department, and the University well in their endeavors." With that the embattled Kelly departed.

The Gamecock program had achieved seven straight winning seasons and established itself as a nationally prominent program under Parsons. Though the two seasons under Kelly had been winners, the program needed a new direction. Athletics director Bob Marcum noted in a March 1984 article in the *Gamecock* that he was "out to find the best man for the job."

The Nancy Wilson Era Begins

That "best man" turned out to be thirty-two-year-old Lake City, South Carolina, native and College of Charleston coach Nancy Wilson, who became the program's fifth head coach on April 1, 1984.

A graduate of Coker College in Hartsville, South Carolina, Wilson brought sterling credentials from her eight seasons in Charleston. After serving as an assistant under Joan Cronan at Charleston for three seasons, Wilson took over as head coach in 1976. She quickly built the Cougars into one of the most consistent programs in the country, ultimately compiling a record of

Press conference introducing Nancy Wilson as the new head coach for the women's basketball team at the University of South Carolina. Courtesy of the *State* Newspaper Archive, Richland County Public Library.

193–64 (.751) and leading her team to four straight AIAW Division II national runner-up finishes in 1979–82. In her final season in Charleston, Wilson was named AIAW Coach of the Year, along with Hatchell of Francis Marion.[8]

During her introductory press conference, Wilson noted that "I love the State of South Carolina and it's always been in the back of my mind that if this job opened up, I'd like to have it. I would like to be, as anyone else would, a national contender. We were at the College of Charleston and I think we can do the same thing here. I think it's very possible, and we plan to start with the Metro."

Wilson says now that her challenges off the court equaled any on-court challenges she may have inherited. "They had just experienced some very difficult times that had been publicized. Everybody had preconceived notions of the program." To compound that, Wilson points to the Parsons trial, which was unfolding in Columbia around the time she took the job, opening old wounds. Though only two players, Marsi McAlister and Brantley Southers, remained from Parsons's turbulent final season, other controversies had unfolded during Kelley's two seasons as head coach. Wilson inherited a battle-weary group.

"I was just tired," McAlister says now. "I really didn't feel like playing [by her senior season], and it took a lot to overcome." She added, "I hate drama."

Recognizing early that off-court challenges would perhaps be her biggest obstacle to success at USC, Wilson says, "we poured a lot of positivity into the girls, and asked them to be the best of themselves." She added, "We did a lot of going out into the community. I knew once people actually met them, they would see past the image." The team responded to Wilson's leadership, happy to focus on basketball in a newly stable environment. Stability led in turn to wins.

Wilson's mention of a focus on conference play during her introductory press conference was prophetic, as her teams largely dominated the Metro over the next seven seasons. The Gamecocks compiled a 70–15 (.824) record in conference games, winning five out of six regular-season Metro championships between 1986 and 1991. Wilson's program added three consecutive Metro Tournament championships between 1986 and 1989.

In the program's seven seasons of Metro play under Wilson, only two seasons, 1985 (her first) and 1987, resulted in neither a regular season nor tournament championship. In each of those seasons, the program finished second in conference standings. During these years Wilson's teams compiled an eye-popping 41–3 (.931) home record at Carolina Coliseum, enjoying undefeated Metro play in Columbia six out of seven seasons.

Two of the greatest to wear the garnet and black led Wilson's Metro-era teams, combining to lead the program to four Metro titles and three conference player of the year awards. Brantley Southers (a holdover from the Parsons/Kelly years) earned the program's first-ever conference player of the year award in 1986. She was a three-time all-American and led the program to its first Metro regular-season and tournament titles in 1985–86. Her 1,982 points is still good for fourth in program history.

Martha Parker, a five-nine guard/forward from Columbia's Hammond Academy, led the Gamecocks to three Metro titles and three NCAA tournament appearances between 1986 and 1989. She earned three all-America honors and two consecutive Metro player-of-the-year recognitions. She still ranks eighth on the all-time program scoring list, with 1,725 points, and her number 13 jersey was the second, after Foster's, to be retired by the Gamecock program.

Quite simply, South Carolina was the preeminent program in Metro Conference women's basketball during the Wilson era.

✗   ✗   ✗

As good as Wilson's teams were in conference play, the program benefited from the relative weakness of Metro teams during this era. Wilson's program compiled an 119–335 (.250) record versus ranked teams during this seven-year stretch. Of the forty-four games against ranked teams, only five contests involved Metro teams, with the Gamecocks winning two. From 1985 through 1988, the program experienced a combined 0–18 versus ranked competition, though the following three seasons were relatively more competitive.

South Carolina's lack of competitiveness versus the best teams in the women's game would be further exposed beginning with the 1991–92 season after joining the high-powered Southeastern Conference. Over the first seventeen seasons of SEC play, spanning the final six seasons of the Wilson era and the full eleven-season tenure of Susan Walvius, the Gamecocks compiled a 64–157 (.289) record in SEC play. There were two winning conference ledgers during this period, highlighted by the 2001–2 squad, which achieved a 25–7 overall record, 10–4 in SEC play, and an Elite Eight finish in the NCAA tournament.

Wilson points to her focus on in-state recruiting as a factor—a strategy that had served her well over the years but faced a reversal as the program approached SEC membership. "When we were at our best [her Sweet Sixteen club], we had ten of twelve players from South Carolina, the other two from North Carolina. Being such a small state, it tends to either be rich in talent or not. When we went into the SEC, we hit kind of a dry spell in the level of talent in the state."

More than the wins and losses and the eight Metro Conference championships during her long tenure at South Carolina, Wilson says perhaps her greatest achievement was the stability she brought to a program that had been anything but in the years prior to her arrival. "I think the stability is something we enjoyed."

What Was and What Could Have Been

Amid the phenomenal and sustained success of Dawn Staley's program over the last decade and a half, it is easy to forget that South Carolina women's basketball first tasted elite status some four decades earlier. Over the course of four seasons in the late seventies and early eighties, Pam Parsons drove her program to an NIT championship (1978–79), a third-place national finish (1979–80), a preseason number 5 ranking (1980–81), and a number 2 ranking through seven games to start her final season (1981–82).

Had her better angels prevailed, there is no reason to believe that Parsons wouldn't have enjoyed a career on par with that of Tennessee's Pat Summit. She was a brilliant tactician and one of the dominant personalities in the early era of the women's game. It is easy to imagine, had things gone differently for Parsons and South Carolina, that Parsons's Gamecock teams would have continued their run of elite play throughout the 1980s and entered SEC play as an instant conference rival to Summit's Volunteers. One could imagine, had Parsons completed a dominant run at South Carolina on par with Summit at Tennessee, that Gamecock teams might currently be playing on a court named for her, as they do for Summit in Knoxville. She possessed talent and charisma in abundance. Her track record as a winner and an innovator was firmly established.

Pam Parsons could have been a legend. Instead, she became a cautionary tale.

On December 1, 1998, Parsons gave testimony before the House Judiciary Committee on the consequences of perjury during the impeachment trial of President Bill Clinton. Though she bore little resemblance to the resplendent thirty-three-year-old firebrand on the cover of South Carolina's media guide those many seasons ago, a fifty-year-old Parsons could still command a room. She spoke forcefully, her eyes full of conviction and regret.

"Anything I ever denied about myself was what created a spiraling journey through hell. I enjoyed creating the opportunity to say that I was good at some things in my life. I loved trophies and medals and winning. But to turn around and look at the other side of me took more guts than it ever took to win a ballgame," she said, choking back tears. "Now I truly know what it's like to be part of a team. But when that team can't trust you, you've lost it all. And I would rather be who I am today than to have continued coaching with a lie."

Saying of her reduced prison sentence, "I picked up cigarette butts for four months in Lexington, Kentucky. But I did it with a smile on my face to pay back humanity for my ignorance. I finally found what I was looking for . . . peace. I'm not afraid of being found out. I don't have to lie or concoct an image." She concluded, "It's an amazing space to be in. It's something I've wanted more than a national championship."

As for Tina Buck (who has long since gone by Kristina), she says of her brief time at South Carolina, "I just want to say how deeply sorry I am for all of it. I walked into a storm and had no concept of what it meant. I had no idea to be afraid of it, because I was too young. As an eighteen-year-old"—she was seventeen when the relationship with Parsons began—"given my circumstances, trying to navigate and be a part of that team in that situation, it was very, very difficult, and really, impossible." She adds, "I was witnessing the slow implosion of the program from behind the scenes and also, being a part of the team, kind of witnessing it from both sides."

Buck says of the abuse of power element that defined her relationship with Parsons, "I tried to justify it, to deny it, for many, many years, because I didn't want to think of it that way, but a part of it was that," adding that the recent Me Too movement has had particular resonance with her. "There has been a reckoning," she says.

She has not seen Parsons for many years but tells the story of a trip to the coach's south central Utah hometown soon after the explosive *Sports Illustrated* exposé. Parson's parents wanted her to come home, and Buck says Parsons thought it would be a good idea, "to figure out what to do, to be around family." Parsons's parents were devout Mormons, deeply religious people, and Buck recalls Parsons's father saying he would drive all over, buying up all the *Sports Illustrated* magazines he could find, so nobody would see it. "The level of shame [among Parsons's family] was crushing. There was no support. It was 'let's move on and pretend it didn't happen.'"

"Certainly," she says, "If I would have had a crystal ball when I was seventeen, it would have told me, 'Don't go anywhere near this. This is not a healthy scenario.'" She says of the experience, "it's been the biggest teacher of my life."

"I've worked hard and shed a lot of tears," she says, adding that she has used her experience to help others who have found themselves in similar relationships involving toxic power imbalances. She hopes to be able to help on a broader scale at some point. "I try to put as much good into the world as I can, and when I make a big, giant mistake, I do my best to take responsibility and make amends."

Of her former Gamecock teammates, she says, "I think it affected everybody differently," before adding through tears, "I just hope that people have found their own healing."

Staley Takes Program to Unprecedented Heights

Following the 2007–8 season, South Carolina athletics director Eric Hyman achieved a monumental hire in luring Dawn Staley from Temple to lead the Gamecock program. A native of Philadelphia, Staley was already a luminary of the game, having starred at point guard for the University of Virginia, where she led the Cavaliers to three Final Four appearances and one national championship game.

From there she led the US National team to three gold medals in the 1996, 2000, and 2004 Olympic Games, while also forging an all-star career in the nascent women's professional leagues, first with the American Basketball League (ABL), then with the WNBA. She returned to her native Philadelphia to coach Temple in her first head coaching role, leading the Owls to a 172–80 record, including six NCAA tournament appearances and four Atlantic 10 titles over eight seasons. All that while still competing as a player in the WNBA until her retirement in 2006.

What she inherited at USC was a program far removed from Parsons's high-octane teams, or Wilson's dominant Metro squads, or even Wavius's excellent Elite Eight team. She often tells the story of being able to hear— word for word—the cellphone conversations of fans in the largely empty Colonial Life Arena during her first season.

She built her program methodically, elevating recruiting and weathering a few storms along the way, including losing records in her first two seasons and the transfer of her highest-profile recruit in those early years, Kelsey Bone, to Texas A&M in 2010.

By the 2011–12 season, Staley's fourth at South Carolina, the Gamecocks went 25–10 (10–6) and surged to a Sweet Sixteen appearance in the program's first NCAA tournament appearance in a decade. It was just the start. Staley's program compiled seven SEC regular-season titles and seven tournament titles between 2014 and 2023. Starting with the 2011–12 team, the Gamecocks have finished no worse than the Sweet Sixteen in NCAA tournament play, with one Elite Eight and five Final Four appearances during that span.

In 2016–17 the Gamecocks broke through with the program's first national championship, led by all-America junior forward and Columbia native A'ja Wilson. South Carolina went 32–1 during the 2019–20 season, including a perfect 16–0 in SEC play, capturing the regular-season and tournament championships. They were the number 1 overall seed and odds-on favorites to capture the program's second national championship before the tournament was canceled amid concerns over the rising COVID-19 pandemic.

The Gamecocks captured their elusive second national championship to cap the 2021–22 season. Led by the consensus national player of the year, six-five junior forward Aliyah Boston, USC defeated old nemesis Connecticut 64–49 in the championship game. It was a contest that may well have marked a passing of the torch from UConn's Geno Auriemma, the undisputed greatest women's coach of the post–Pat Summit era, if not all time, to Staley.[9]

The Gamecocks continued their dominance in 2022–23, completing an undefeated regular season for the first time in program history and capturing the SEC regular season and tournament titles. The team made it to its fifth Final Four, finishing 36–1. The dominant senior class of 2023, including Aliyah Boston, Zia Cooke, Brea Beal, Laeticia Amihere, and Olivia Thompson—affectionately known as "The Freshies"—enjoyed an astounding four-year record of 129–9 (.934).

"I couldn't be a bigger admirer of what she's done," former USC coach Wilson says of Staley. "I just think it's phenomenal." Wilson points to the increase in spending on women's sports during her three decades as a head coach. "People started putting money into the programs and being more intentional about who they were hiring." As some programs led the way, others fought to catch up. Facilities and resources improved, and momentum around women's sports continued to build.

Wilson says she happened to be at the Colonial Life Arena along with two of her former assistants when Staley's 2014 team captured its first SEC regular-season championship. During the trophy presentation she told her former assistants, "Don't feel bad, girls, that trophy wouldn't have fit in our locker room, anyway," she recalls with a laugh. "Things have just changed a whole lot, and it really came down to the money that was put into it."

✗   ✗   ✗

A few days after Staley's Gamecocks brought home the 2021–22 national championship, thousands of fans, or "Fams," as Staley proclaims them, lined both sides of Columbia's Main Street for a victory parade to honor the team's historic achievement. Among the VIP cars and parade floats, an assemblage of former players, mostly from the Staley era, joined in to celebrate what they had helped build.

Among them was a Gamecock legend from the Parsons years, Sheila Foster. From its lofty perch among the rafters of Colonial Life Arena, her long-retired 53 jersey has borne witness to the highs and the lows, the challenges and the triumphs of the Gamecock program over the course of four decades since Foster herself roamed the old tartan floor of Frank McGuire Arena, generally having her way with opponents while collecting 2,266 points and 1,427 rebounds.

Her scoring record stood until 2016, finally broken by A'ja Wilson, who now has a statue at the entrance to Colonial Life Arena. Though her double-double record was broken by Aliyah Boston in 2023, Foster still holds the program record for rebounds. Staley's players refer to her simply as "the Legend."

Foster has been in remission since a scare with breast cancer in 2014 and has battled back from two knee replacements. She was hospitalized briefly in 2020 with double pneumonia and retired after fifteen seasons coaching the Boiling Springs (in her native Spartanburg County) Middle School girls' basketball team to focus on her health.

Like the South Carolina women's basketball program of which she remains such an integral part, Foster has seen the greatest highs and the darkest lows.

But on that warm April Wednesday in Columbia as the championship parade made its way south along Main, Foster smiled her thousand-watt smile, absorbing the love of thousands of well-wishers, many of whom had never seen her ply her trade under the Coliseum lights those many years ago.

In that moment, a radiant spring sun reflecting on her face, the universe came full circle in a beautiful and healing way. Foster says of the experience, "It was the greatest feeling in the world."

7

Any Port in a Storm

USC Joins the Metro Conference

The Metro is not merely the best option for the moment, it is
the only one.

—Herman Helms, sports editor,
Columbia State

In fits and starts throughout the 1970s and early 1980s, the University of South Carolina looked toward a return to conference affiliation, preferably a return to the ACC or, perhaps less likely, an opening in the SEC. Given its history as a founding member of the ACC and the geographical proximity to member institutions in both conferences, those two options made sense on paper, and certainly from an aspirational standpoint. But when Georgia Tech accepted an invitation to membership in the ACC in 1978, the door effectively closed on South Carolina's chances of a return to the conference it helped found. The SEC, meanwhile, was content and stable with ten members. A withdrawal of any team from either conference seemed highly unlikely.

Yet the University of South Carolina increasingly found its major independent status a hindrance in all sports other than football. Men's basketball particularly suffered from decreased fan interest and attendance. Dwindling prospects for NCAA tournament invitations in the wake of a 1974 decision to begin inviting two teams per conference rather than just conference winners beginning with the 1974–75 tournament reduced the at-large bid possibilities for independent teams. This led in turn to the hasty formation of several new makeshift conferences that cobbled together independent programs with an eye toward achieving automatic bids and possibly a second-place at-large bid for members.

In the early 1970s, St. Louis University athletics director Larry Albus envisioned the formation of a new basketball-focused athletic conference, whose membership would comprise schools from large metropolitan cities across the upper South. By June 1975 Albus's vision had become a reality with the formation of the Metropolitan Athletic Conference. Founding members included Cincinnati, Georgia Tech, Louisville, Memphis State (now Memphis), St. Louis, and Tulane. The fledgling conference was known less formally as the "Metro Six."

Florida State University joined the Metro in 1976, becoming the seventh member institution. When Georgia Tech left to join the ACC two years later, the Metro promptly returned to seven members with the addition of Virginia Tech. Founding member St. Louis withdrew its membership in 1982, but the league grew to seven members once again with the addition of Southern Mississippi later that year. The geographical footprint of the conference was expanding, and the movement of member institutions foreshadowed a more widespread fluctuation in NCAA conference affiliation in the decades to come.

When Albus was named the Metro's first commissioner in 1975, he immediately targeted the University of South Carolina as a desirable expansion target. Just four years removed from ACC membership, South Carolina still enjoyed a nationally ranked basketball program, and Columbia fit the profile of other Metro Conference cities.

Albus pursued USC through informal conversations and at least one letter to USC assistant coach Donnie Walsh, dated February 6, 1976, wherein Albus extolled the virtues of the nascent conference and in closing wrote: "Since expansion will be discussed in the near future, I would like to determine if there would be any interest on the part of South Carolina in this conference."

Walsh, in turn, notified President Patterson of Albus's inquiry in a February 20 letter, writing on behalf of McGuire, "At this point Coach McGuire has no definite feelings one way or the other about the Metro Six, but feels that it should be brought to your attention."

Though nothing came from those initial conversations, McGuire's interest in the Metro grew in the coming years, as it became evident that a return to the ACC was unlikely. The Metro officially invited USC in 1979, which generated extensive debate among fans, local media, and university officials.

There was vocal interest from some segments of Gamecock boosters. The Columbia Tipoff Club, a USC basketball booster organization unaffiliated with the university but closely associated with Coach Frank McGuire, was the most vocal. On Sunday, August 5, 1979, the Tipoff Club placed a full-page ad in the *State* with the all-caps headline "ATTENTION: GAMECOCK SUPPORTERS." The ad went on to state the club's endorsement of USC's affiliation with the "Metro 7 Conference" and urged fans to contact the USC Board of Trustees to "let their feelings be known" before the board's scheduled meeting later that week.

What followed in fine print was an elaborate series of questions and answers designed to inform the public and place pressure on the board to consider the Metro Conference invitation. It included quotes supporting conference affiliation from USC head coaches, including women's basketball coach Pam Parsons and baseball coach June Raines. Also included were quotes from various Metro coaches extolling the virtues of the conference and expressing heartfelt wishes for the addition of South Carolina.

The ad ended with a final plea: "The Time Is Urgent—If we cannot get the Board of Trustees to look into the Metro 7 on Thursday, the opportunity may be gone for this year and for many years to come." At the bottom of the ad was a cutout petition titled "Our plea to the Board," which could be signed and mailed into the Tipoff Club for collection and presentation to the university.

McGuire's desire for Metro membership was pragmatic. With more attractive options momentarily out of reach, the Metro provided the opportunity to shore up a basketball program that by then was eight years removed from the ACC and struggling with fewer wins, reduced fan interest, and lower attendance. McGuire reasoned the establishment of new conference rivalries would interject renewed enthusiasm into his program. "I don't say that games with Metro teams will be as exciting to our fans in the beginning as games with North Carolina, Duke or N.C. State," McGuire told reporters. "But I believe we could cultivate good rivalries with some of the outstanding Metro teams over a period of years."

Indeed, the fledgling conference boasted two elite basketball programs in Louisville and Memphis State. A McGuire-led South Carolina, even somewhat diminished from its prime, would only add excitement and prestige to the Metro.

McGuire was not alone in his advocacy for Metro affiliation. Baseball coach June Raines said he liked "the idea of being able to play for a conference championship" and "especially like[d] the advantage which conference affiliation gives a school for the playoffs." The NCAA tournament selection process in recent years had shifted toward awarding bids to conference-affiliated teams rather than independents with better records.

USC swimming coach Scott Woodburn added, "Conference membership would give more incentive to our athletes. It would add some identification to the program. I'm in favor of conference affiliation." Woodburn went on to say, with a hint of resignation, "The Metro 7 would be fine, but only because there is no alternative. By that, I mean I would prefer the ACC or the Southeastern Conference."

During the summer of 1979, some speculation swirled that Vanderbilt was considering a withdrawal from the SEC, given its difficulty competing in football. This gave some Gamecock fans a glimmer of hope for membership there and created a short-lived buzz on local sports talk shows. During an interview with a Columbia radio station in August 1979, SEC commissioner Hootie Ingram put those rumors to rest, citing Vanderbilt's competitiveness in basketball and its ability to consistently sell out its fifteen-thousand-seat arena despite an enrollment of just seven thousand. "I can't imagine the Commodores wanting to end relations with the SEC rivals who help them fill all those seats," Ingram said. The Commodore withdrawal chatter soon faded.

The talk of conference affiliation served to exacerbate a growing rift between athletics director and head football coach Jim Carlen and McGuire. Despite statements supporting conference affiliation early in his tenure at USC, Carlen had become entrenched in his support for retaining independent status. While head coach at West Virginia in 1968, Carlen had been instrumental in leading WVU out of the Southern Conference into major independent status. Soon after leading that move, Carlen bolted Morgantown for his next stop at Texas Tech following the 1969 season.[1]

Since Metro affiliation did not include competition in football, proponents argued, membership would be a win-win for the entire athletics department. Football could retain independent status, keeping 100 percent of revenue from home games, while the other programs, most notably basketball, would benefit from ease of scheduling, budding rivalries, and the potential for an automatic bid to NCAA tournaments.

Metro supporters highlighted other benefits as well. Given the energy crisis of the late 1970s, travel costs were a major source of concern for athletics departments across the country. Conference play in the Metro, proponents argued, would serve to reduce the scope and cost of travel for athletic teams. The trouble with the Metro 7, according to the *State*'s sports editor Herman Helms, was "a move into the conference seems so logical that the wishy-washy Board of Trustees may not make it."

University president James Holderman commented in an August 22, 1979, interview with the *State* that the USC Board of Trustees desired to see the Gamecocks in a conference that has both athletic and academic quality. Further, Holderman expressed the belief that the board wanted Carolina to be in a "full and comprehensive conference," meaning an "all-sports" conference. Holderman elaborated that the Metro Conference "does not enjoy that status at this time" and predicted that it would be some time before it did.

Angling to control the narrative, Metro commissioner Albus released comments a few days later, stating that while "the door is still open for expansion," it was too late for USC to join the conference for the 1979–80 school year due to scheduling difficulties. Thus ended the initial rounds of talks between the Metro Conference and South Carolina. It would not be the last.

Efforts to Rejoin ACC Stumble Out of the Gate

Talk of a South Carolina/ACC détente sputtered along in fits and starts between 1971 and 1978, when the ACC invited Georgia Tech rather than USC to restore its membership to eight schools. In May 1975 the USC Board of Trustees authorized James Patterson to engage in negotiations with ACC commissioner Bob James. Talk picked up momentum in January 1976, and the topic of reunification appeared to be on the verge of serious consideration by the ACC.

Patterson noted in the *Daily Gamecock,* USC's student newspaper, that Carolina would apply for readmission prior to the ACC's winter meeting February 10–12 in Greensboro. However, in a follow-up article, Patterson reversed field, noting that "enthusiasm had begun to wane for us getting back into the ACC." He went on to state that although the matter would not be taken up during the ACC's February meetings, the possibility remained that it would be addressed during meetings in May, by which time the ACC's expansion committee would have made a determination on their intent to expand. "We are not going to submit a formal application until we can see what definite plans the ACC has," Patterson stated.

By April it had become painfully obvious that ACC reentry for South Carolina would be a long shot. In an April 8, 1976, Associated Press article, a number of conference athletics directors gave tepid commentary on the topic of expansion in general and South Carolina in particular. USC, or any school, would need affirmative votes from an in-state sponsor as well as two additional members. By this time both South Carolina and Virginia Tech had expressed strong interest in joining the league. East Carolina University, too, had announced plans to leave the Southern Conference and apply for admission in the ACC.

While South Carolina received support from Clemson and NC State and Virginia Tech received support from Virginia, athletics directors from the other schools demurred. Wake Forest's Gene Hooks said, "We have no burning desire for expansion"; UNC's Bill Cobey noted, "I believe the membership is satisfied right now with seven." Maryland's Jim Kehoe expressed a desire for better "geographic balance" within the league, which would make entry from any North or South Carolina school a nonstarter from his perspective. Duke's Carl James (no relation to ACC commissioner Robert James) noted concerns with further diluting distribution of coveted ACC basketball tournament tickets by the addition of an eighth member. Notably James mentioned that Georgia Tech would be "a better addition than any other school."

On May 19, 1976, during their meeting in Myrtle Beach, ACC athletics directors established criteria for any school seeking entry into the ACC. While specifics were not released immediately, ACC officials were clear that entry into the league would require an "equity payment" in addition to meeting other criteria both academic and athletic. Said Commissioner James, "Quite frankly, the terms we set for admission might not be acceptable to certain schools seeking admission."[2]

Indeed, South Carolina did find those terms a nonstarter. University officials viewed the substantial equity payment, estimated to be as much as $400,000, a particularly ungracious approach. Other perceived slights included a questionnaire sent to USC president Patterson, which included generic questions about USC's student enrollment, sports programs, and the city of Columbia. Five years removed from their school's status as a founding member of the ACC, many at South Carolina found this galling.

Despite this, conversations between USC and the ACC lingered throughout the summer. When the Metro's Albus wrote directly to Patterson on July 7, 1976, providing additional information about his conference and again attempting to gauge USC's interest in affiliation, Patterson replied in a July 14 letter, stating, "It is our conclusion at this time, in part because of our recent action concerning the Atlantic Coast Conference, that we will remain independent of all conference affiliations."

In a June 2 letter from board of trustees chair T. Eston Marchant to Patterson, Marchant detailed recent conversations with James. Specifically with regard to the controversial "contribution" required of USC for reentry, James explained the thinking of ACC members. USC had received an $88,704 equity distribution in 1971, "notwithstanding the fact that South Carolina had already left the conference." Marchant went on, "He [James] explains it was the feeling of the [ACC] membership that if we received a distribution payment upon withdrawal, we should make a contribution payment upon re-entry—to equalize matters." James further detailed that the "monetary" item could be handled by withholding of future equity distributions "until such time as the amount was fully credited."

Marchant ended the letter by expressing his own position on the reentry matter. "My personal feelings about this matter are that it would be in our best interest to formally process the application, do all that we can to secure its approval, and to reaffiliate as soon as possible."

Media and fan speculation continued to swirl around the potential of ACC membership throughout the remainder of 1976 and into 1977, leading President Patterson to seek some resolution on the matter. In an April 25, 1977, letter from Patterson to board of trustees members, the president asked for clarification from the board regarding their interest in pursuing ACC membership, in light of "continued public speculation," prior to Patterson's communicating further with ACC commissioner James.

A May 4 letter to Patterson from Peter Becker, chairman of the faculty Athletic Advisory Committee, noted that consensus could not be reached among the university community with regard to desires for ACC membership due to insufficient knowledge of the terms for reaffiliation. The committee offered three recommendations (underline in the original):

- A detailed study of all pertinent information relevant to conference membership should be undertaken with full participation of the Athletic Advisory Committee.
- All public statements by university officials should be withheld until the issue is resolved.
- As a long-range goal, a single athletics director, in charge of all intercollegiate sports, and responsible to the president of the university.

In short order Patterson arranged a meeting between an unnamed university liaison and Commissioner James on Wednesday, May 18, at the Myrtle Beach Sheraton Hotel. The unnamed liaison documented the meeting in a May 19 memorandum to Patterson, noting that the commissioner was asked if the "mechanics" for admission had changed since James's communication in May 1976—namely, that USC would need an in-state sponsor (Clemson) and two additional conference sponsors. Commissioner Edwards replied, "No," conditions had not changed, and that the entire process would hinge on USC submitting an application for admission. James noted that there were several schools from whom an application would not be welcome, and that was the reason for the ACC's relative secrecy about the entry process.

Of the money question—the equity payment that had been so unsavory to USC officials—James confirmed that was still a requirement as well, also noting that the ACC was doing so well that he "feared the sum might well be greater," but it could not be set exactly, as the fiscal year had not ended. James confirmed that the equity payment would secure "full membership," meaning the incoming institution would be guaranteed a full member distribution during the fiscal year after admission. He estimated that future distribution to be anywhere between $275,000 and $700,000, "depending on details of participation in various activities by individual schools."

About the ACC's recent rejection of applicant Virginia Tech, James said that should not be taken as an indication of conference members' intent to hold at seven schools. "We're not wedded to a certain number," James noted. As the meeting ended, James said he did not feel the matter demanded immediate action on the part of USC, stating as he walked away, "The lines [of communication] are open."

By 1978, Carlen and anti-ACC factions among USC's power structure had gained advantage, bolstered by what they perceived as the ACC's ungracious approach. The ACC, meanwhile, moved on. On April 3, ACC officials announced that Georgia Tech would become their eighth member, effectively closing the door on a South Carolina return.

Board chair Marchant lamented that his "greatest mistake" was allowing Paul Dietzel to lead the university out of the ACC. He believed the split had hurt USC's reputation, and the chaotic environment within the athletics department made that point inarguable.

With Georgia Tech and the Atlanta television market secured, the ACC soon signed a lucrative media contract that guaranteed each conference school $1.5 million annually. USC, meanwhile, found itself tossed about in a sea of institutional and administrative upheaval, a once-proud basketball program on the decline, with no safe (or acceptable) port in sight.

A Three-Headed Monster

This period also marked a low point of political and institutional stability within the athletics department. Following Paul Dietzel's resignation as head football coach and athletics director in 1974, the board of trustees expressed their intention to separate those two posts, going so far as to pass a resolution prohibiting one individual from holding both head coach and athletics director positions.[3] At the same time, supporters of Frank McGuire lobbied the board to hire him as athletics director.[4] In an effort to maneuver around delicate egos within the athletics department, the board created a tangled web of administration, in which President Patterson essentially functioned as athletics director.

Marchant met with the media on December 13, 1974, to announce that Jim Carlen had accepted the dual role of head football coach and associate director of athletics. Meanwhile Marchant announced that McGuire would be granted additional responsibilities and the expanded title of associate director of athletics for basketball, in addition to his continuing role of head basketball coach. Both men, Marchant noted, would report only to university president Patterson and would enjoy full control over their programs.

Marchant went on to announce that Harold "Bo" Hagan, formerly a department administrator and Gamecock football letterman, would be the director of athletics, overseeing all other athletic affairs. It was a nominal title, as he had no authority over Carlen or McGuire or their programs. Hagan too would report to Patterson. South Carolina had created a three-headed administrative monster.

It was this unorthodox arrangement, with no strong athletics director to unify the department, that sowed unprecedented dysfunction and created a chasm between the university's highest-profile coaches. Rather than enjoying a collegial and mutually beneficial relationship, Carlen and McGuire's relationship eventually deteriorated to the point where the two men did not speak.

Adding to the general dysfunction was a board of trustees with members sharply divided along McGuire-supporting pro-ACC and Carlen-supporting anti-ACC sentiments. Students and fans became divided as well, with Carlen backers and McGuire backers firmly entrenched respectively in for or against camps. Despite early public statements in support of rejoining the ACC, Carlen soon reversed field, citing concerns over sharing the wealth from his lucrative football program with conference schools who did not generate revenue at the same level.[5]

✗   ✗   ✗

Despite the board of trustees' stated intentions to separate the positions of head football coach and athletics director, politics still held sway. By

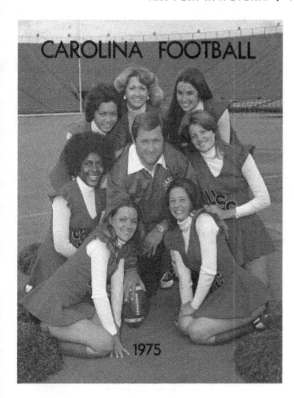

CAROLINA FOOTBALL

1975

1975 USC football media
guide, featuring new head
coach Jim Carlen with
cheerleaders.

September 1976, in an effort to streamline the bewildering web of athletic administration, the board rescinded their 1974 prohibition against one individual holding both head coach and athletics director positions and named Carlen athletics director, granting him control over all sports except the basketball program. Carlen's stock was on the rise after a successful seven-win season in 1975, his first in Columbia. His inaugural team also managed a 56–20 thrashing of archrival Clemson and the program's third-ever appearance in a bowl game.[6]

Another driving factor in the board's attempts to streamline athletics administration was a requirement for membership the ACC presented to Patterson during readmission talks in May 1976. The ACC commissioner outlined a requirement that only "one voice" speak for a prospective university regarding athletic affairs. USC had three. Though the board found the ACC's requirements galling and ultimately did not pursue readmission, it had become clear that change was needed.

With Carlen's ascension to the director of athletics post, McGuire kept his associate director of athletics title and control over his basketball program. Bo Hagan's responsibilities shifted from the athletics department to the newly formed alumni association. Streamlined, yes. Simplified, no. The new arrangement still left the university president essentially in charge of overseeing the athletics department and managing the egos of both Carlen and McGuire.

By this time McGuire's relations with one-time allies Sol Blatt Sr. and Jr. had soured. Though the Blatts were no longer Speaker of the House or on the board of trustees, respectively, they still maintained an outsized influence over university affairs generally and Gamecock athletics specifically.[7] The Blatts had aligned themselves with Carlen, compounding the deleterious effects of a declining basketball program and waning attendance. Though still wildly popular and influential with fans and students, McGuire's stock had declined significantly with the power brokers at USC, and it seemed his days as basketball headman were numbered. Dislodging McGuire, however, would fall to a new president.

Soon after James B. Holderman was appointed to replace James Patterson as university president on June 30, 1977, Holderman publicly proposed that McGuire's duties as basketball coach would cease following the 1977–78 season. In an effort to remove McGuire from Columbia, Holderman further proposed the coach would assume the position of athletics director for the university's branch campuses, with headquarters on the campus of USC-Coastal in Conway. McGuire roundly rejected the proposal, stating that he only wanted to coach basketball, and demanded the opportunity to complete his contract, which expired following the 1979–80 season. Media and the student body ardently supported McGuire, and the optics were not good for the new president. Amid rising pressure, Holderman retracted his proposal.

In short order Holderman and the board of trustees again tried to oust McGuire by enforcing a newly changed retirement age, which the board had recently lowered from seventy to sixty-five, effectively forcing McGuire out after the 1977–78 campaign. Once again fans and the media rallied with highly vocal support for McGuire and condemnation for Holderman and the board. Several faculty members challenged the legality of the new retirement rule in court. Stinging from criticism and still working to establish credibility as president, Holderman discovered truth in the old adage that there is rarely an education in the second kick of a mule. He would not risk a third. McGuire would be allowed to coach the final two seasons of his contract.

Controversy continued to trouble the athletics department and Holderman's fledgling presidency over the next year. When Holderman appointed James A. Morris, a former dean of the College of Business Administration at USC and one-time vice president of the ACC, to the newly created position of vice president of athletic affairs, the move initially seemed a stroke of genius. Morris could take the burden of athletics department oversight off of Holderman's full plate and bring some stability to the scene. Morris was also a McGuire ally who would bring balance to Carlen's growing power and influence in athletic affairs.

The move backfired when Carlen hired an attorney and threatened legal action over a breach of his contract, as he felt his powers of administration were being usurped. The Gamecock Club, led by USC football letterman Ed Pitts, sided with Carlen and publicly disputed Morris's authority over its considerable funds, even threatening to sue the university. Morris eventually resigned, and the position of vice president for athletic affairs was allowed to lapse, handing Carlen a significant victory. In the midst of this, the university suffered yet another embarrassment when the State Law Enforcement Division began an investigation into alleged misappropriation of $95,000 in concession funds by the athletics department.

Holderman found his presidency increasingly threatened by the chaos and even corruption within the athletics department. In a few months on the job, he had alienated both Carlen and McGuire, as well as Gamecock Club leaders, fans, and the student body.

Carlen and McGuire continued their entrenchment, each working to solidify their power and influence within the university and among fans.

In 1977 Carlen donated $200,000 of athletics department profits to the university's academic fund. Later, wealthy supporters threw a lavish roast for Carlen, attended by notable political dignitaries. McGuire, meanwhile, held a VIP cocktail party for influential boosters, and well-heeled Tipoff Club and Gamecock Club members following the final Carolina Classic basketball tournament in 1978. Before one home game, fans were asked to wear green if they supported McGuire, and the Coliseum was awash in verdant hues. USC athletics had become a garish, partisan spectacle.

The board of trustees determined that if South Carolina ever had a chance of joining an all-sports conference, they would have to set the university's athletic house in order. They developed a two-pronged approach, which included permanently separating the positions of head football coach and athletics director and convincing Frank McGuire to step down. Setting the plan in motion, the board informed Carlen two days before the beginning of the 1979 football season that his contract as USC athletics director would not be renewed at expiration in 1982. McGuire, meanwhile, eventually agreed to step down following the 1979–80 season and received a settlement of $400,000.

These moves resulted in predictable backlash from Carlen, who gave a blistering interview in the September 17, 1979, issue of *Sports Illustrated,* in which he criticized the board as "foolish" and portrayed Holderman as "this little ole president we have," who, rather than expressing gratitude for the athletics department donation, asked if he could expect that every year. Likewise McGuire backers protested loudly at his planned ouster. Players threatened to quit. Nearly five hundred students gathered on the Horseshoe in front of the President's House to protest the decision. But McGuire had agreed to the deal, and the board had reached an important, if clumsily executed, goal of bringing stability to the athletics department.

With McGuire's exit determined and Carlen's athletics directorship due to expire at the end of his contract in 1982, it appeared that Carolina had finally charted a path toward a unified athletics department. Though the board succumbed to political pressure from Carlen backers and extended his athletics director and head football coach contracts to 1986 following consecutive eight-win seasons in 1979 and 1980, they ultimately returned to their stated intention of separating those two posts.

Following a disappointing 6–6 campaign in 1981, which ended with three straight losses, including a 23–21 defeat at home to lowly Pacific, the board found the impetus they needed to oust Carlen. After a dismal 33–10 defeat in the season's final game at Aloha Stadium against Hawaii, rumors swirled about Carlen's future. On Friday, December 11, the board of trustees met in a contentious, hours-long meeting, during which they voted "overwhelmingly" to fire Carlen. Holderman communicated the decision to Carlen by telephone that evening. The board declined comment on the reasons for the decision, but few were surprised given Carlen's combative relationship with the president, the board, some prominent Gamecock boosters, and local media.

On January 2, 1982, Carolina introduced its new athletics director, Bob Marcum, who formerly held the same position at the University of Kansas. Marcum's arrival at USC marked the first time in twenty years in which the director of athletics was someone other than the head football coach.[8] As college athletics became big business over that twenty-year period, nearly all Division I universities had long since moved to a strong athletics director format. USC's athletics department had suffered for its failure to evolve, and progress had been stymied by a lack of accountability and a toxic cult of personality.

That failure was most glaring when Dietzel led the charge to pull USC out of the Atlantic Coast Conference over football-related concerns. But the instability and dysfunction had only deepened in the intervening years. Marcum's hiring marked a positive change of direction. The *State's* Herman Helms opined that Marcum's hiring would mark an end to a system that had "caused so much divisiveness. Coaches will no longer wage a contest for the AD post and control over other coaches. Coaches will coach and administrators will administrate. USC will be one school again, a whole institution, and that's worth cheering about." Indeed, Marcum's first order of business would be to hire new head football coach not named Bob Marcum. A new day had dawned at Carolina.

Aside from the search for a head football coach, the new AD soon turned his attention to the matter of conference affiliation. He noted in an early press conference the obvious benefits of affiliation with a strong conference, and his experience with the Big Eight as Kansas AD certainly would have guided his thinking. After appointing former Carlen defensive coordinator Richard Bell as head football coach, Marcum turned his attention to exploring conference possibilities.

New Leadership, NCAA Snub Propel Carolina toward Metro

Almost as soon as McGuire announced his retirement at USC, rumors connected Duke's Bill Foster to the South Carolina job. Foster, a Pennsylvania native, had established a name for himself as a builder of programs during stints at Bloomsburg State, Rutgers, Utah, and then Duke. South Carolina's program needed rebuilding, and Foster soon became their number one target.

Foster's credentials were sparkling. One of college basketball's most respected coaches, he had served as president of the National Association of Basketball Coaches in 1975–76 and in 1978 guided his Blue Devils team all the way to the national final before losing in the championship game to Kentucky. Foster masterfully rebuilt a proud Duke program that had suffered a dramatic reversal of fortunes in the post–Vic Bubas era, compiling a pedestrian 73–61 record under Bucky Waters and Neill McGeachy, including a 10–16 record in McGeachy's lone season.

Foster came to Duke in 1974, following a successful three-year stint at Utah, including a 22–9 record in 1973–74 and a runner-up finish in that season's National Invitational Tournament. He quickly set about rebuilding Duke's fortunes. Following three rebuilding seasons that hovered around the .500 mark, Foster's Blue Devils broke out in 1977–78 with a 27–7 record, including a second-place regular-season finish in the ACC, an ACC tournament championship, and a surprising run to the NCAA tournament final, finishing as that season's national runner-up.[9] Foster saw continued success over the next two seasons, his Duke teams hovering at or near number 1 in the NCAA rankings for portions of both seasons. Foster's Blue Devils won a share of the regular-season ACC championship in 1978–79 and made it to the second round of that season's NCAA tournament, finishing with a 28–8 overall record. His 1979–80 team finished a disappointing 7–7 in ACC play but went 24–9 overall, won the ACC tournament, and made it to the Elite Eight in NCAA tournament play.

Despite Foster's success at Duke, he felt increasingly frustrated and out of his element in Durham. There were perceived slights by Duke AD Tom Butters, which included failure to pave the coaches' parking lot behind Cameron Indoor Stadium and the frustration of being overshadowed by UNC's Dean

Smith, who had become something of a deity in North Carolina since replacing Frank McGuire in 1961. Foster also felt a general unease—a sense that he did not fit in culturally at the school and was not appreciated by the Duke people—that perhaps they thought he was lucky to be at such a prestigious institution, given his Elizabethtown College pedigree.

By his sixth and final season in Durham, with South Carolina rumors swirling and criticism mounting as ACC losses accumulated, Foster had become reclusive, speaking infrequently to reporters and refusing to address the South Carolina rumors, which only added to the speculation. By the end of the regular season, Foster had reached a verbal agreement with South Carolina, becoming Carlen's final hire as USC athletics director. The deal done, Foster's Duke team played angry during the ACC tournament and went on an improbable tear, beating NC State, UNC, and Maryland to win the tournament, securing an automatic bid to the NCAA tournament in the process.

Twenty-four hours after beating Maryland for the ACC championship, Foster found himself at the Roost athletic dorm in Columbia, standing alongside AD Carlen and university president Holderman at a press conference, where he was introduced as the new head basketball coach at the University of South Carolina. He had tendered his resignation to Duke AD Butters, to be effective at the end of NCAA tournament play. Following an emotional third-round loss to Purdue, Foster's Duke tenure ended, and his South Carolina tenure began.[10]

Foster called rebuilding the USC program "maybe my biggest challenge" during his introductory press conference on November 3, 1980. It proved to be challenging indeed, though there were early signs Foster would work his rebuilding magic at South Carolina just as he had in his previous stops. He inherited four returning players from McGuire's final squad, three of whom figured prominently in Foster's first Gamecock team: rising seniors Zam Fredrick and Kevin Dunleavy and rising sophomore Kevin Darmody. A fourth returnee was an academic casualty. Foster quipped upon seeing the numbers, "it takes at least five to play."

The new head coach and his assistants, Bob Wenzel, Ray Jones, and Steve Steinwedel, all of whom had followed Foster from Duke, hit the recruiting trail quickly. Foster and staff signed six freshmen and one junior college transfer and added three "run-ons," Foster's spin on the traditional walk-on. The incoming freshmen included Jimmy Foster (no relation)—a scrappy six-eight power forward from Greenville, South Carolina; six-eight forward Brad Jergenson from Manitowoc, Wisconsin; six-five shooting forward Kenny Holmes from Savannah, Georgia; and six-three guard Scott Sanderson of Tuscaloosa, Alabama (son of University of Alabama coach Wimp Sanderson). Joining this talented group of freshmen was six-foot point guard Gerald Peacock, a junior transfer from Brevard Junior College in Florida. These five newcomers plus the returning nucleus of Fredrick, Dunleavy, and Darmody played the lion's share of minutes in 1980–81.

Foster's first USC team far exceeded expectations, winning seventeen of twenty-four games after a 0–3 start to finish a respectable 17–10. The season was highlighted by wins over Texas, Florida State, and Penn State and a thrilling two-point win in Milwaukee versus high-powered Marquette in a nationally televised game.

Throughout the season, and particularly over the final thirteen-game stretch, senior Zam Fredrick distinguished himself as a prolific scorer. He finished the season with a 28.9 points per game average to take the national scoring championship. He secured that title with a forty-three-point performance in a season-ending home win versus Georgia Southern. Fredrick had been mostly a role player under McGuire but flourished in Foster's system.

Another pleasant surprise was hard-nosed rebound machine Jimmy Foster, who was a promising prospect but had been out of organized basketball for two years prior to signing with the Gamecocks. The rationale given for Foster's missing senior season at Wade Hampton High School was "personal reasons." It would not be the last basketball he would miss or the end of his personal struggles. Foster was a blue-collar scrapper who quickly became a fan favorite for his all-out, Tasmanian Devil style of play. He started twenty-six of twenty-seven games, led USC in rebounding, and was second on the squad in scoring behind Fredrick.

Disappointingly, the 1980–81 Gamecocks did not receive an NIT bid, but the new coach and his young squad brought a new energy back to the Gamecock program and notched the program's fifteenth consecutive winning season.

The 1981–82 Gamecocks would be a disappointment. Foster's second team was still one of the younger squads in the country, with five incoming freshmen, five sophomores, and only two juniors who would log significant minutes. There were no seniors. The Gamecocks missed the firepower of Fredrick, who by then was playing professionally in Europe. Top returning scorer and rebounder Foster was also missing during the season's first eight games, a period that saw the Gamecocks go 3–5, including ugly losses to Chaminade and Hawaii during a week-long junket in which the men's and women's basketball teams and the football team all traveled to Honolulu for sightseeing and competition.[11]

USC finished 14–15, the program's first losing season since 1966. Despite that outcome, the Gamecocks finished on a strong note, winning their final three contests, versus Florida State in Tallahassee, the Citadel, and a talented UNLV team in Columbia. The encouraging finish plus the return of Foster's entire roster bode well for the 1982–83 season.

Foster's third season in Columbia marked the seventy-fifth season of varsity competition for USC basketball. It would be a season of milestones, dramatic wins, and a serious health scare for Foster, which sidelined him for seventeen games. Following a dramatic six-point win versus fifteenth-ranked Purdue in early December, Foster was taken to the hospital after collapsing in the locker room. He was diagnosed with a moderate heart attack and underwent quadruple coronary bypass surgery four days later. Assistant coach Steinwedel took charge of the team in Foster's absence and coached USC to twelve wins and five losses. The Gamecocks notched a win over a strong Vanderbilt team and a split in two games with Clemson during this stretch, as well as an eight-point win against Georgia Tech, spoiling Coach Bobby Cremins's highly emotional homecoming.

Foster returned to the bench for a game versus Holy Cross on February 19 and led the inspired Gamecocks to a lopsided win, as well as four wins in their last five regular-season games, including thrilling final-second wins versus power programs Marquette and DePaul. The Gamecocks finished with twenty wins for the first time in nine seasons, and optimism abounded for an NCAA tournament bid.

Photo media guide of 1982–83 USC basketball team. Bill Foster left Duke to replace legendary coach Frank McGuire for the 1980–81 season. Foster's best season in Columbia was his third, 1982–83, when the Gamecocks finished 22–9. Foster was integral in leading USC into Metro Conference membership.

Despite a solid résumé, the Gamecocks were on the outside looking in when NCAA bids were awarded and settled for an NIT bid. It was a bitter pill to swallow for Foster and Marcum and highlighted the need for conference affiliation. USC's twelve seasons of major independent status had produced a frustrating array of troubles for both McGuire and Foster. As conference-affiliated programs focused their efforts primarily on conference play, USC faced increasing difficulty in scheduling quality opponents. Subpar schedules with little to no regional interest led in turn to a steady attrition in fan interest and low ticket sales.

To complicate matters, the NCAA had also begun shifting away from awarding postseason bids to independent programs in favor of conference-affiliated teams with comparable records. In 1974 the NCAA opened invitations to second-place conference teams, further reducing the possibility of an at-large bid for independent programs. There remained as well the promise of an automatic bid with a conference tournament championship, a goal to which independent teams could not aspire. North Carolina State, the eventual winner of that season's national championship, had ended their regular season a pedestrian 17–10 but achieved an automatic bid after an improbable run and championship in the ACC tournament. The Wolfpack entered NCAA play with an identical win total to South Carolina's regular-season twenty wins.

Another factor had entered the equation by the early 1980s—television contracts. The ACC had just inked a lucrative new contract for its television games with Raycom Sports, guaranteeing each of its members $1.6 million in television revenue from basketball during the 1982–83 season. Other conferences were negotiating similar deals. There was no such financial opportunity for major independent schools.

The Gamecocks achieved two wins in that season's NIT, versus Old Dominion and Virginia Tech, both played before home crowds in Columbia. The third-round game was a disappointing, lopsided loss on the road to former ACC foe Wake Forest, which left the Gamecocks one win shy of a semifinal trip to Madison Square Garden. It would prove to be the final contest for USC as a major independent.

Athletics director Marcum moved decisively to guide Carolina toward the Metro in the days following the basketball team's failure to secure an NCAA tournament bid. Just two weeks later the USC Board of Trustees accepted an invitation from the Metro Conference, becoming the eighth conference member. It had become increasingly clear that major independent status was an unsustainable model in the modern world of collegiate athletics. With more appealing "all-sports" options in the ACC and SEC out of reach for the time being, the Metro proved the best, and for all practical purposes the only, option for South Carolina in 1983. The timing allowed Gamecock men's and women's basketball teams and baseball team, among others, to begin conference competition with the 1983–84 academic year. The football team, meanwhile, would retain its independent status (and more importantly, 100 percent of that program's revenue) as the Metro did not offer a football championship.

South Carolina had now taken major steps toward putting its athletic affairs in order, in hiring a strong athletics director to unify the department and securing conference membership within the Metro. Moreover, coaches Frank McGuire and Jim Carlen had departed, taking with them the acrimony that had so destabilized the university's athletic affairs and kept USC from returning to the ACC in 1976. These events, while producing mixed results in the win-loss column, cumulatively provided the cohesion the athletic department and university sorely needed. Moreover, they set USC along the path toward bigger and better things to come.

8

Good Times, Bad Times

Heisman Highs and Losing Lows

George has all the moves. He twists and turns and changes
direction so fast, he's being drafted by three NFL teams and
two political parties.

–Bob Hope

I n a deep baritone that sounds like the voice of God, John Facenda of NFL
Films fame narrated the 1983 documentary short *George Rogers—South
Carolina Legend*. In his iconic style, Facenda described Rogers's "sprinter
speed and lumberjack power . . . like a loaded .38, exploding toward the end
zone." The faded Kodachrome images are a time capsule of the university as
it was, set to the tune of "Step to the Rear" and pulse-quickening trumpet.
Faded glimpses of a flowering campus, an asymmetrical Williams-Brice Stadium in the years before the upper-east deck, the rough-as-a-cob early Astroturf field. "The University of South Carolina," Facenda intones. "Excitement.
Challenge. A daring new world for George Rogers."

Rogers gallops, sprints, and bulldozes his way through and around defenders, his garnet number 38 swaying like a matador's cape. His trademark smile
and "aw shucks" persona belied an elite athlete in his prime, raw muscle and
speed and 220 pounds of battering ram menace. As Facenda described it,
"Many defenders chased his lightning, and shrunk beneath his thunder."

Duluth, Georgia, today is a bustling Atlanta suburb, but in the 1970s a more pastoral setting welcomed a young Rogers and his four siblings, when his mother moved them there from inner-city Atlanta to be closer to family. The town became a haven for Rogers, and he thrived in the supportive environment. He soon found football and eventually fell under the tutelage of Duluth High School coach Cecil Morris. Rogers says Morris was "like a dad to me," and the coach filled a void left by the absence of Rogers's father.

Morris arranged tutors for his young charge, and Rogers put in the work, positioning himself to graduate. Meanwhile his talent on the football field attracted suitors from across college football. Rogers won all-state honors following his junior and senior seasons and, by the spring of his senior year, had his pick of college destinations. In the 1983 documentary, Morris notes in a stately drawl that Rogers wanted to stay in the South, and by the end he had narrowed his choices down to Georgia Tech, Tennessee, and South Carolina.

The Gamecocks' Jim Carlen was the only coach, Rogers says, who promised him the opportunity to play as a true freshman. That was enough for Rogers, and he chose South Carolina to the surprise of many. In the 1977 football media guide, Carlen noted of his incoming freshman class, "We feel like we had a relatively good recruiting year." It was his staff's third recruiting season, and things were getting easier now that his program was established. "Relatively good" would prove in time to be a monumental understatement.

Carlen made good on his promise, and Rogers earned the starting fullback spot his freshman season, with fellow freshman Johnnie Wright at starting tailback. Rogers impressed early, gaining 623 yards on 143 carries during the 1977 campaign, a freshman record for the program. Carlen commented on his young fullback's modesty, noting that Rogers was reluctant to start over upper-class teammates. That modesty would become a defining trait over the coming years, as Rogers consistently shrugged off his own accomplishments, crediting his offensive linemen for any individual success.

Still at fullback in 1978, Rogers gained another 1,006 yards in just over eight games as a sophomore. He suffered a shoulder injury during a homecoming win over Ohio University and missed most of the next two games versus Mississippi and UNC. By late season he was again at full speed and gained

237 yards on 27 carries, scoring two touchdowns in a dazzling performance versus Wake Forest.

A knee injury to Wright prior to the opening game of the 1979 campaign thrust Rogers into the starting tailback spot—a defining moment. In the opener versus UNC, he gained 98 yards in an otherwise forgettable 28–0 drubbing at the hands of the Tar Heels. It would prove to be Rogers's final game below the 100-yard mark, and the start of a historic two-season run to greatness. Rogers gained 1,681 yards on 311 carries as a junior, for an impressive 5.4 yards per carry. He earned first-team all-America honors from the AP and the Newspaper Enterprise Association, while earning second-team recognition from United Press International and *Football News*.

Rogers finished 1979 second in rushing behind Heisman winner Charles White of Southern Cal and boasted a string of ten straight 100-yard games to finish the season, including a career-best 237 versus NC State. He ended his junior season as the program's single-season and career leader in rushing. His 3,310 career yards through three seasons surpassed the nearly three-decade-old record of 2,878 set by the legendary Steve Wadiak between 1948 and 1951. In a preview of the hype that would come in his senior season, Rogers finished seventh in Heisman voting, the first South Carolina player in program history to earn consideration for the prestigious award.

Moreover, Carlen's program was thriving. The 1979 squad completed an 8–3 regular season, tying a school record for wins.[1] The Gamecocks earned an invitation to the Hall of Fame Bowl in Birmingham, Alabama (which later moved to Tampa and became the Outback Bowl). It was just the fourth bowl game in program history, but the second since Carlen's arrival in 1975. The bowl resulted in a 24–13 defeat to future SEC rival Missouri, then of the Big Eight, which dropped Carolina's season record to 8–4. Despite that disappointment, optimism abounded within the program.

Big George Runs to the Heisman

The cover of USC's 1980 football media guide features a smiling George Rogers, clad in his familiar number 38 jersey, sitting atop a footlocker in the Gamecock dressing room. Jim Carlen is attired in garnet polyester pants, the kind universally beloved by coaches of the era, with a double-snapped waistband capable of weathering barbeque buffet indulgences. He leans confidently against Rogers's locker with a flinty stare and a Mona Lisa smile, exuding confidence as only a coach with a Heisman Trophy candidate can.

Rogers spent a good portion of the off-season making the rounds with other high-profile college players at promotional events across the country, including the Kodak All-America television show, an NCAA-sponsored tour for ABC-TV to promote college football, and even a trip to Chicago to be photographed for the *Playboy* All-America team. Of meeting Hugh Heffner at the Playboy Mansion, Rogers commented to the *Columbia Record*, "He's a real nice guy. The funniest thing was how he dressed—he's got a beard and wears boots and fishing clothes all the time, and smokes that pipe."

The media exposure seemed to bring out a side of Rogers's personality few had seen since his arrival in Columbia. The quiet, humble kid from Duluth was becoming more comfortable in the public eye. His thousand-watt smile and good-natured persona made him approachable and familiar. It was easy to like George Rogers, and an entire state looked at once to a new football season and the start of a new decade through the lens of a single, tantalizing word: *possibility.*

The Gamecocks opened the season on a two-game home stretch versus outmanned Pacific and Wichita State squads. Through two games South Carolina outscored its beleaguered opponents by a combined score of 110–0. Rogers, playing only in the first half of both games, rushed for 153 and 108 yards, respectively, to push his consecutive streak of 100-yard performances to twelve. The Gamecocks debuted at number 20 in the following week's AP poll, setting the stage for a top-twenty matchup against powerful number 4 Southern Cal at the Los Angeles Coliseum during week three.

The USC West versus USC East matchup was a rare opportunity for South Carolina to showcase its program and Heisman candidate running back to a West Coast audience in a time when most games were broadcast only regionally if at all. Two thousand Gamecock fans journeyed west to the legendary LA Coliseum and witnessed a spirited defensive struggle in which the Trojans came out on top, 23–13. The Gamecock defense played with their backs against the wall most of the night, as three South Carolina turnovers kept Southern Cal in favorable field position. A stirring fourth-quarter goal-line stand by the Gamecocks kept the score from getting out of hand, stopping future Heisman Trophy winner Marcus Allen on four straight attempts from inside the five yard line.

Rogers pushed his consecutive 100-yard streak to thirteen with 141 hard-fought yards on twenty-six carries. "It's no use to care about the yards," he told reporters, after managing to bolster his Heisman credentials despite the loss. "We came to win, not just gain yards."

The 2–1 Gamecocks wouldn't have to wait long for a crack at another legendary opponent, as they traveled to face number 17 Michigan in Ann Arbor the following week. More than 104,000 spectators, mostly clad in Michigan maize and blue, with a smattering of garnet-hued visitors, gathered at the "Big House" on a crisp early fall afternoon to witness what would be a landmark game in the history of South Carolina football.

From the start the Gamecocks held their own in a hostile Michigan Stadium, taking a fleeting 3–0 lead early in the second quarter on a twenty-six-yard Eddie Leopard field goal. The Wolverines' offense picked up steam, though, as two drives resulted in end zone connections from quarterback John Wangler to receiver Anthony Carter, to take a 14–3 lead at the half.

An air of confidence pervaded the partisan crowd during halftime as fans milled about for concessions and the Michigan band performed their kaleidoscope maneuvers set to Tchaikovsky's Fourth Symphony. When the Wolverines took the second-half kickoff and embarked on an efficient seventy-two-yard drive to first and goal at the USC eight yard line, Carolina was on the ropes, as a 21–3 deficit would almost certainly have put it out of reach. But Michigan fullback Jerald Ingram fumbled into the end zone, recovered by USC linebacker Walt Kater for the harmless touchback, and the Gamecocks had new life. A two-yard Rogers touchdown capped an eighty-yard Carolina drive following the touchback, tightening the score to 14–10 with 1:21 remaining in the third.

The Carolina defense held Michigan to third and inches at the Wolverine thirty yard line on their ensuing possession, and coach Bo Schembechler—normally as conservative as a Baptist preacher—turned riverboat gambler with "tragic results," as the State's Herman Helms described it. The Wolverines attempted a fake punt, sending "heavy footed" fullback Stan Edwards on an attempted sweep around the right end. Carolina's sophomore defensive back Chuck Finney sniffed it out and crushed Edwards for a one-yard loss at the twenty-nine, where the jubilant Gamecocks took possession. Six plays later, fullback Johnnie Wright barreled in for a one-yard touchdown, and the Leopard point after put Carolina on top 17–14 with 4:49 remaining. But there was plenty of drama left in store.

With efficient passing from Wangler, Michigan stormed down the field, reaching the Gamecock three yard line with eighteen seconds remaining. On third and goal, junior defensive end Hal Henderson sacked Wangler for a seven-yard loss, setting up a fourth-down play in the final seconds. Wangler attempted an end zone pass under heavy pressure to his prize target Carter, but Carolina's Finney batted it down as time expired, sending dismayed Wolverine partisans to the exits and the small assembly of Gamecock fans into hysterics.

Rogers was impressive once again on a big stage, racking up 142 yards against the vaunted Wolverine defense and further burnishing his Heisman credentials. Carolina moved to 3–1 on the season, and Carlen now had a program-defining win in addition to his individual highlight machine Rogers.

The Gamecocks reappeared in the AP poll at number 18 and rolled through the next three weeks with convincing wins over NC State (30–10), Duke (20–7), and Cincinnati (49–7). Rogers continued his impressive run, tallying 193, 224, and 128 yards, respectively, the latter in first-half action alone. An open date followed the Cincinnati game, as the Gamecocks, by then ranked fourteenth, prepped for yet another challenging road contest with national implications on November 1 versus that old nemesis and border rival, the fourth-ranked Georgia Bulldogs.

The battle between the 6–1 Gamecocks and 7–0 Bulldogs garnered the attention of ABC-TV, which made the matchup its national game of the week, marking the first regular season appearance by a South Carolina team on national television. The nation tuned in to watch a duel between two of the nation's leading running backs, Rogers and Bulldog freshman phenom Hershel Walker. Both runners featured a physical, attacking style and open-field speed. The six-two, 223-pound Rogers averaged 156 yards per game, while Walker, at six-two and 215 pounds, averaged 153. Legendary announcer Keith

Jackson, the very voice of college football, described the action for viewers in his iconic style.

Under a clear, autumn sky between the fabled Sanford Stadium hedges, a capacity crowd of 62,200 and millions tuning in across the country witnessed what the *State*'s Herman Helms called "a grim, hard-hitting battle between Southern football powers." Style points were few that afternoon in a low-scoring, defensive slugfest. It was a battle that would have been more recognizable, perhaps, to the mud-caked Scots and English at Bannockburn and Falkirk than to anyone more accustomed to high-scoring passing affairs tuning in from the West Coast. This was a different brand of football altogether. Three yards and a cloud of bruises.

At halftime, the score stood 3–0 Georgia.

In the third stanza, Walker broke open for a seventy-six-yard touchdown run and the Bulldogs added a field goal to take a commanding 13–0 lead. Carolina finally found some momentum with a forty-five-yard Eddie Leopard field goal, and on their next possession, fullback Carl West rambled for a forty-five-yard touchdown to make it 13–10 after the Leopard extra point.

The Bulldogs and Gamecocks traded punts through the early minutes of the fourth quarter, before Carolina took over at the Georgia forty-seven with 7:20 remaining. Rogers took the first-down handoff and rumbled left for what looked like a fifteen-yard gain but was called out of bounds just shy of the first-down marker. On second and a half yard, Big George crashed off the right tackle for the first down.

Rogers again took the first-down carry, slashing and spinning for eight yards, down to the Georgia twenty-seven. On second down he carried again, picking up seven to the Bulldog twenty for another first down. But he was slow to get up.

Officials called an injury time-out as trainers rushed to check on the big back. Rogers, doubled over with fatigue, eventually staggered to the Carolina sideline, clearly favoring his battered left hand, which had absorbed blow after blow while cradling the football.

Fullback West took the first-down carry, bulling for three down to the Georgia seventeen and setting up second and seven for perhaps the most consequential play in the history of Carolina (and Georgia) football.

An audible cheer from the Carolina faithful greeted Rogers as he checked back in for the second-down play. The 62,200 fans and all eleven Georgia defenders knew who would carry the ball next. Rogers, with good blocking, ran off the right end, avoided a would-be tackler, and shifted his carry from left to right when the ball popped out, landing on the turf behind him.

Rogers, on his knees in disbelief, could only watch as Georgia lineman Tim Parks recovered among a Bulldog celebration. Dazed and battered, the big back struggled to the sideline amid the consolation of teammates and coaches, his hands visibly bloodied.

The defiant Carolina defense rose up, forcing a three-and-out punt. A roughing the kicker penalty gave Georgia a fresh set of downs, however. From there the Bulldogs milked the clock on a drive down to the Gamecock one. Carolina's defense held again, their third goal-line stand of the afternoon, and the Gamecocks took over with forty-five seconds remaining inside their own one. Quarterback Harper hit senior flanker Tim Gillespie for a seventeen-yard gain, but a miracle finish was not in the cards, as a Georgia interception two plays later ended the game. Georgia had survived, 13–10.

In announcing the players of the game, Keith Jackson waxed poetic: "It was expected to be, it was advertised, it was billed, it was dramatized as a battle between these two young men." He went on, "It has been that way, they have been the prime players in the drama. They have performed nobly."

Carlen accepted responsibility for Rogers's fumble, for sending his star back into the game, for calling on number 38 once too often. Georgia's Walker told reporters after the game, "I'd vote for him if I could. I don't think I'm as good as George right now. I hope he wins the Heisman." Walker praised the Carolina defense, calling it "the hardest-hitting team we've faced."

As with the loss to Southern Cal, the Gamecocks and Rogers were valiant in defeat, on the road against a traditional football power. Although they could take a healthy measure of pride in that, thoughts of what could have been hung over the season like funeral crepe. Georgia, meanwhile, went undefeated, winning their first-ever recognized national championship and illustrating that the fortunes of a season can turn on the vagaries of a single play.[2]

The Gamecocks rebounded with consecutive wins over the Citadel and Wake Forest, the first of which included another matchup between two of the nation's premier running backs in Rogers and the Citadel's Stump Mitchell— then the NCAA's leading rusher. Rogers racked up 179 and 266 yards in those two games, respectively, giving him twenty consecutive games over the 100-yard mark ahead of the Gamecocks' annual matchup with Clemson. During halftime ceremonies of Rogers's final home game versus the Demon Deacons, his number 38 was retired—the third retired number in program history and the first to have his jersey retired while still an active player.

The 8–2 Gamecocks entered the regular-season finale ranked fourteenth and slim three-point favorites against the 5–5 Tigers. Both teams had plenty to play for. South Carolina was looking for the first nine-win season in program history and hoped to burnish its credentials ahead of the recently announced Gator Bowl matchup with top-five Pittsburgh. Clemson, meanwhile, hoped to avoid its first losing season since 1976.

Looking for a way to spark his team after a demoralizing 34–7 loss at Maryland the week before, Clemson's Danny Ford allowed them to wear orange "britches" for the first time. Of the all-orange combo, Ford said, "Maryland whupped us pretty good. We had to do something."

The uniform tweak worked as intended. Carolina took at 6–3 lead into halftime at Death Valley, but Clemson turned two second-half interceptions into touchdowns—one of them a pick-six—and played shutout defense on the way to a 27–6 upset. Rogers gained 149 yards, but the Clemson defense kept him out of the end zone, denying the soon-to-be Heisman winner a rushing touchdown in all four career meetings versus the Tigers.

Disappointment over the Clemson loss lingered through the long Thanksgiving weekend, but a new month brought renewed excitement, as Rogers, along with fellow Heisman candidates defensive stalwart Hugh Green of Pittsburgh and Georgia's fabulous freshman Walker, traveled to New York City's Downtown Athletic Club for the Heisman Trophy presentation on Monday, December 1. When the voting was tabulated, Rogers was the winner, with 1,128 total votes to Green's second-place 861 and Walker's 683.

Rogers's teammates and an estimated ten thousand fans greeted the conquering hero when he returned to Columbia Metropolitan Airport that evening. The love for Rogers was infectious and palpable, evident in the smiles, the handmade signs, and the size of the crowd itself. After deplaning to a minutes-long round of cheers and applause, the humble Rogers made a brief speech. "I wanted to come back to Columbia tonight, y'all. I wanted to be with the guys, and I have to go to school. This is the biggest moment of my life, and I want to thank my teammates and the offensive line for doing this." He paused before adding, "I've never been so happy."

And with that two highway patrolmen whisked Rogers through the cheering crowd to a team bus, waiting to carry the newly minted Heisman Trophy winner back to campus. The marching band played the Carolina fight song as the bus lumbered forward. The jubilant crowd lingered in the cool evening air. No one seemed ready to let the moment go. Loman Green, a twenty-seven-year airport employee, looked on through tear-filled eyes, telling a reporter, "This is the proudest I've been in quite some time."

✗   ✗   ✗

The Gamecocks, who fell to number 18 in the AP poll following their loss to Clemson, were overmatched in their Gator Bowl matchup with third-ranked Pitt, coached by Bear Bryant protégé Jackie Sherrill. The matchup was a compelling one, featuring the top two Heisman finishers, made even more interesting in that the two—one a tailback and one a defensive end—would be on the field at the same time.

Pitt took a 17–3 lead into the half and used a 17–0 third quarter to build an insurmountable 34–3 lead by the fourth stanza. Carolina finally crossed the end zone late in the game on a Harper connection to flanker Tim Gillespie. A miss on the extra point provided the final score, Pittsburgh 37, Carolina 9. Rogers extended his streak of 100-plus-yard performance to twenty-two, with 113 yards on twenty-seven carries, but it was a disappointing ending to a brilliant career.

All four of Carolina's losses came away from home in 1980, with three of the four coming against top-eleven teams in the final AP poll: number 1 Georgia, number 2 Pitt, and number 11 Southern Cal. After another eight-win season—a comparatively excellent result set against the history of the program—Carlen's squad was achingly close to so much more.

Rogers's Legacy

George Rogers finished his career with an astounding 5,204 rushing yards. To put that into perspective, the second-place rusher in program history, Brandon Bennet (1991–94), rushed for 3,055. Rogers still owns the program standard in numerous other statistical categories some four-plus decades after his final game. To name a few:

- Rushing (season): 1,894 in 1980 (he also owns second place with 1,681 in 1979);
- Rushing attempts (career): 954;
- Rushing attempts (season): 324 in 1980 (his 311 attempts in 1979 is second);
- 100-yard rushing games: 27 (second place is a four-way tie with Brandon Bennett, Mike Davis, Harold Green, and Marcus Lattimore, each of whom had 11);
- All-purpose yards (career): 5,932;
- All-purpose yards (season): 1,917 in 1980.

His thirty-one rushing touchdowns are still good for second in program history, tied by Harold Green (1986–89) and surpassed only by Marcus Lattimore's thirty-eight (2010–12).

But more than the records, the awards, the accolades, what Rogers meant to the University of South Carolina and its fans was a matter of pride and legitimacy. He represented a program mired in mediocrity throughout its football history and showed that the University of South Carolina could compete on par with the blue bloods of college football. He was the lovingly adopted son of a small, poor state with a lurid history of racial strife and discrimination, demonstrating the power of sport to transcend even the most deeply rooted social ills. He was the first Black player from the Deep South to win the Heisman, soon to be followed by Georgia's Walker and Auburn's Bo Jackson, among others.

Rogers was selected by the New Orleans Saints as the first overall pick in the 1981 NFL draft and went on to lead the league in rushing with 1,674 yards during his rookie season—an NFL rookie record and still the single-season

George Rogers watches his teammates from the sidelines during a game in his Heisman Trophy–winning season of 1980. This photo was the inspiration for Rogers's statue, unveiled at Springs Brooks Plaza outside Williams-Brice Stadium in 2017. Rather than a photo reflecting his individual achievements, Rogers liked this one, because it showed him as part of a team. He insisted that the names of the entire 1980 USC squad be inscribed at the base of the statue.

record for the Saints. After four seasons in New Orleans, Rogers was traded to Washington, where he played the final three seasons of his career and contributed to the club's 1987 Super Bowl victory in his final professional game. Rogers rushed for 7,176 yards and fifty-four touchdowns during his seven seasons in the NFL.

Shortly after Rogers's Heisman campaign, Stadium Road, which runs between Shop and Bluff Roads just outside the north gates of Williams-Brice Stadium, was renamed George Rogers Boulevard. In May 1981 Columbia-area artist Ralph Waldrop completed a larger-than-life, thirty-by-fifty-foot mural of Rogers on the east facade of USC's Booker T. Washington Center on Blossom Street—formerly the site of Booker T. Washington High School. In 1987 Rogers was selected for the University of South Carolina Athletics Hall of Fame, and in 2015 a bronze statue of Rogers was erected outside the northwest gates of Williams-Brice Stadium, a part of the newly completed Springs Brooks Plaza.

For four decades Rogers has run the George Rogers Foundation, with a mission to provide financial assistance to first-generation college students. He can be found around Williams-Brice before most home games, signing auto-graphs and posing with his Heisman Trophy for photos as he raises donations for his foundation.

George Washington Rogers no longer boasts "sprinter speed and lumber jack power," as John Facenda intoned in that long-ago documentary, but he is arguably the most beloved of all Gamecock lettermen from the independent era or any other.

The Foster Era Begins, and a Scoring Champion Emerges

Bill Foster's first South Carolina squad, by some estimates the youngest in NCAA Division I basketball, stumbled out of the gates to a 0–3 to start the 1980–81 campaign. But the young Gamecock squad gelled and won seventeen of the following twenty-four contests. Paced by Zam Fredrick's sensational 28.9 points per game average, the Gamecocks far exceeded expectations and achieved the program's fifteenth consecutive winning season, highlighted by a win over Texas, two wins over Florida State, a road upset over traditional power Marquette on national television, and a triple-overtime win versus the Citadel in the longest contest in program history.

During a six-game stretch in late January, Fredrick was a man possessed, his dunks and jumpers filling the air of arenas with the sound of scorched cotton. His scoring average jumped 5.2 points per game. He averaged 35.2 points per game on 56.7 percent shooting, including highs of 41 versus Davidson and Furman. His scoring average surged from twentieth in the country to second by the first week of February 1981.

Foster said of Fredrick's emergence, "We figured we had a fine athlete who we could work with," adding, "we didn't plan to accentuate him like we have." Indeed, Fredrick blossomed during his senior campaign under the new coach. He had languished during his first three seasons under the legendary McGuire, whose game was based on patterns, passing, and patience, as the *State*'s Bill Gillespie noted in a February 3 article. Foster's system, by contrast, was based on the fast break and running—a system tailor-made for Fredrick's run-and-gun style. "Basketball is fun again," Fredrick told Gillespie.

And fun it was. Following Fredrick's many electrifying dunks, Coliseum public address announcer Gene McKay would shout, "Shaaa-zaaam!" to the

Zam Fredrick dunking the ball during a game between USC and Temple at the Carolina Coliseum in 1981. Courtesy of the *State* Newspaper Archive, Richland County Public Library.

delight of fans. And the fans were coming back, curious to see this over-achieving young team of upstarts and their phenom senior captain. Average attendance jumped by 850 per home contest from the prior season to 6,787. Still modest numbers in the 12,401-seat arena, but it reversed a trend of nine consecutive seasons of decreased attendance. Several games drew crowds of over 10,000, which had become a rarity in the latter McGuire years.

In the next to last game, a 93–86 road contest at Boston University, Fredrick poured in 39 points, bumping his average to 28.4 and overtaking Cal Irvine's Kevin Magee for first place nationally in scoring. After twenty-six games, the Gamecocks owned a surprising 16–10 record. Most pundits thought a seventeen-win season would result in postseason play, with the NIT the most likely destination. It would be a heady achievement for the young squad and their first-year coach. Optimism reigned within the team, among fans, and in local media coverage.

The season ended on February 23 with a dominant 106–69 victory over outmatched Georgia Southern in front of 10,477 fans at Frank McGuire

Arena. Fredrick scored a season- and career-high forty-three points on senior night to secure the national scoring championship, while freshman Jimmy Foster pulled down a season-high twenty rebounds. Coach Foster speculated about his team's tournament chances during his postgame comments. "I think we have to be someplace," he said, before adding, "if we don't get a bid somewhere, I'll start my own tournament." The *State*'s Bob Cole noted that Foster was only joking about starting his own tournament, since his team's 17–10 record and the attraction of the nation's number one scorer would virtually guarantee that the Gamecocks a slot in postseason play.

Carolina could only wait to learn their fate, as teams in the ACC and SEC, among others, competed in conference tournaments to determine automatic bids for the NCAA tournament. As the team waited, year-end accolades rolled in for Fredrick, who was named to the National Association of Basketball Coaches District Five all-star team, the only non-ACC player to be so recognized, joining the likes of Virginia's Ralph Sampson, Duke's Gene Banks, Clemson's Larry Nance, and North Carolina's James Worthy. Adding to his list of achievements, Fredrick earned honorable mention all-America honors from the Associated Press.

Meanwhile several upsets in conference tournaments caused unexpected jostling among the projected NCAA and NIT tournament fields. Ole Miss, a 13–13 club, got hot at the right time, winning the SEC tournament and securing an automatic bid. Mercer, a 17–12 team, won the Trans-America tournament, likewise securing an unexpected automatic bid.[3] A twenty-win Clemson team was bounced from the ACC tournament after a one-and-done showing and was passed over by the NCAA tournament, landing instead in the NIT, leaving one less spot available for the hopeful Gamecocks. The long-standing preference for conference teams among the NCAA and NIT selection committees was as pronounced as ever, as only five independent programs received bids among the eighty available slots in the NCAA (forty-eight) and NIT (thirty-two) tournaments. Unfortunately for Foster and his young squad, South Carolina was not among them.

The 17–10 Gamecocks were passed over for the NIT in favor of numerous conference-affiliated teams with the same or worse records. The SEC's Alabama had an identical 17–10 record, as did the Big Ten's Minnesota,

Michigan, and Purdue and St. John's of the Big East. More galling for the Gamecocks, Foster's former Duke team received an NIT bid with a 15–12 record in Mike Krzyzewski's first season. Even Frank McGuire, who by then had taken on the role of director of intercollegiate athletics at Madison Square Garden, the home of the NIT's semifinal and final games, was unable to leverage what influence he may have had on the selection committee in favor of his former team.

Reaction to the snub in Columbia was profound disappointment. Coach Foster told Bill Gillespie of the *State*, "The staff is down, the players are down. I'm still down." Fredrick, realizing his college career had come to a close, described his reaction as "shock," while fellow senior Kevin Dunleavy said he was "stunned." Jimmy Foster, the fan-favorite freshman, sat outside his coach's office looking lost. "Every season ought to have an ending," he said. "Georgia Southern wasn't one. We thought it was preparation for more seasons. And then one day the phone rings and you find out your season is over." He added, shaking his head, "That's an ending?"

It was an ending, but also a beginning, and in March 1981, despite the sting of no postseason play, the future looked bright for Gamecock basketball. Foster's first team had exceeded expectations, infused enthusiasm back into the program, and brought fans back to the Coliseum. Fredrick, along with his 28.9 scoring average, was lost to graduation in 1981–82, as was legacy guard Kevin Dunleavy, but a solid nucleus of players would return, including rebound machine Jimmy Foster and his fellow rising sophomores Jergenson, Sanderson, and clutch-shooting Holmes. Rising junior Peacock would be a steady hand at point guard for two more seasons, and forward Kevin Darmody, the final holdover from the McGuire era, would likewise be a steadying mainstay. To this mix Foster added an exciting freshman class, including vaunted Columbia product Harold Martin of Lower Richland High School and the program's first seven-footer since Danny Traylor, Mike Brittain from Clearwater, Florida.

The University of South Carolina achieved a distinction not matched by any other institution before or since in claiming both the Heisman Trophy winner and basketball's national scoring champion in the same academic year.[4] Adding to the fun, June Raines's baseball squad reached the College

World Series that spring (equivalent to the NCAA basketball tournament's Elite Eight), making the 1980–81 academic year one of the best ever for Gamecock sports.

Three Coaches in Three Years

The eighties were a turbulent period within the USC athletics department and the university itself. Marked by unprecedented successes and an elevated national profile, the decade also brought a steady stream of controversies and uncomfortable media exposure. Perhaps no time demonstrates that pattern better than the years between 1981 and 1983, when three different head football coaches roamed the Gamecock sidelines.

Jim Carlen's seventh season at South Carolina started promisingly enough. Coming off George Rogers's Heisman season of 1980, which included a second straight eight-win season and bowl appearance, all indications were that Carlen's program was on the rise. The incoming freshman class for 1981 was arguably his deepest and most talented ever, including the likes of Ira Hillary, Quinton Lewis, James Seawright, James Sumpter, Kent Hagood, Chris Wade, Frank Wright, Bill Barnhill, Tom Garner, Hinton Tayloe, and Emory Bacon—all names that figured prominently in the success of future seasons, and some of whom contributed immediately in the 1981 campaign.

Five games into the season, their record stood at a disappointing 2–3, with wins over Wake Forest and Duke and losses to Ole Miss, number 14 Georgia, and number 4 Pitt. The Gamecocks rebounded from there, with a road win at Kentucky and a home win versus Virginia ahead of a tilt with third-ranked UNC in Chapel Hill. The Tar Heels, at 6–0 and atop the ACC, were favored by two touchdowns over the visitors from Columbia.

Behind the stellar, sixteen-for-seventeen passing of junior Gordon Beckham, which included a dazzling eleven-for-eleven performance in the first half, the Gamecocks turned in perhaps the most impressive performance of the Carlen era with a shockingly easy 31–13 win. The South Carolina defense dominated the shellshocked Tar Heels, collecting three sacks and forcing five turnovers while limiting North Carolina's outstanding running back Tyrone Allen to just 52 yards, well below his season average. Beckham threw for 195 yards, including a touchdown pass to tight end DeWayne Chivers, in what was his greatest performance in a Gamecock uniform. Some five hundred fans braved a cold rain to great the Gamecocks at the Columbia airport that evening.

Carlen was named coach of the week by UPI for leading his team in the upset. Now 5–3, with the program's first-ever win over a top-five opponent and a three-game winning streak, the Gamecocks enjoyed a wave of momentum. A first-ever nine-win season was not out of reach. But distractions abounded.[5]

As with many instances during the era, personal grievances, perceived slights, and ugly diatribes stole the spotlight from the deserving young men and women who wore the garnet and black. Since arriving in Columbia seven years prior, Carlen had styled himself as a straight shooter who did not play "the political game," as he called it. He was notoriously caustic with some fans and media members and publicly clashed with the university president in a national media publication.

Carlen's infamous disputes with Frank McGuire over power within the athletics department and conference affiliation created toxic chasms within the university board and among the fanbase. And while Carlen had a healthy share of vocal supporters who saw his candor as refreshing and delighted in his willingness to poke the university's entrenched power structure, others notably took exception.

In an October 27, 1981, *State* op-ed titled "Carlen's Words Differ with His Actions," sports editor Herman Helms, a frequent Carlen critic, publicly rebuked the coach in the most direct and strident language yet employed. Helms fired the first of what would be a litany of shots across Carlen's bow in opining, "He urges a positive attitude, but no one is more negative about people or life." Helms recounted an incident immediately following South Carolina's thrilling win in Chapel Hill, in which an enthusiastic fan rushed to embrace Carlen. "The Gamecock coach, his face flushed with rage, shoved the startled fan aside and said angrily, 'keep your hands off me.'" (A photo capturing the incident ran in the *State* three days later.)

Helms pointed to a bizarre Carlen rant during his coach's show, which aired Sunday following the win over UNC. "Good Carolina people," Carlen began, "honorable people are running their mouths and letting the rumors flow. And that's not fair. If you don't like me, that's your privilege. But if you want to know the truth, you call me." One can imagine the rising discomfort of genteel show host Bob Fulton at this point, as Carlen continued, "You help our football team if you're a Carolina fan. If you're not, that's your problem."

Helms called out what he described as Carlen's lack of respect for both fans and the university itself, noting the egregious incident from two years earlier when Carlen was quoted in the September 17, 1979, issue of *Sports Illustrated,* ranting about Holderman's reaction to a $200,000 gift from the athletics department to the university's general fund, "This little ole president we have didn't even say thank you. Know what he said? 'Can I count on this every year?'" However graceless Holderman's reaction to the gift might have been, Carlen's exposure of internal university squabbles in a national publication was indefensible.

The op-ed continued, with Helms describing Carlen as "a troubled man," who had attempted to blame his problems on a myriad of perceived enemies, including fans, the media, the university administration, and a basketball coach (McGuire). Helms alluded to Carlen's "personal problems"—a veiled reference to his recent marital separation and rumors that he had been seen about town in the company of other women. Helms complained that the media had remained silent on that issue but had received the brunt of Carlen's derisiveness nonetheless.

Concluding, Helms wrote, "In truth, his own worst enemy is the person he sees in the mirror each morning. The damage he is doing to his own reputation and the University of South Carolina is considerable."

The Helms op-ed prompted a flood of letters to the editor, a majority of which took exception to Helms's frequent criticisms of Gamecock coaches through the years and Carlen in particular. Some pointed out Helms's hypocrisy in decrying Carlen's negativity, given the negative slant of his own op-ed. Pinkey Dukes of Winnsboro wrote to say that Helms should be made "executive gossip editor" if not fired outright. A smattering of letters agreed with Helms, including Columbia attorney Leigh Leventis, who turned Carlen's own trademark words around, noting, "Mr. Carlen, don't take this negatively. I'm just being 'straight-up.' You may not like what is being printed, but 'I'm just telling it like it is.'"

Don T. Simmons of Columbia pointed to the relative absurdity the incident had caused in light of larger social ills, among them drugs and violence and . . . R-rated movies. "It amazes me that two men who mutually dislike each other so much can, with their venomous verbiage and backbiting, throw so many thousands of people into a state of frenzy, while more important things go unnoticed."

By November 4 the *State*'s editorial board published a plea to readers to move on from the Helms article, noting the topic had been adequately covered and the continuous flow of letters was now largely repetitive of opinions already expressed. "After today, we are discontinuing letters on that subject to devote the limited space available to other contributors who have important matters to discuss."

Amid the Helms/Carlen ruckus, Monte Kiffen brought his 4–3 NC State team to Columbia for a Halloween Day matchup. The Wolfpack, who started the season 4–1, were coming off two consecutive top-five losses, to archrival UNC and to Clemson in a spirited 17–7 contest. Carlen's squad managed to overcome a ghastly offensive performance, in which it gained only 124 total yards while tossing four interceptions, and held on to win a "weird, unbelievable" game, as Kiffen described it, 20–12.

The Gamecocks, now 6–3, looked to finish strong with a home matchup versus lightly regarded University of the Pacific, followed by an opportunity to play spoiler at home versus undefeated Clemson and a then-rare twelfth regular-season game versus Hawaii in Honolulu. Unbeknownst to Carlen and crew, the Halloween win versus the Wolfpack would prove to be the final treat of 1981, followed by a veritable bag of late-season tricks.

The Tigers of the University of the Pacific, hailing from Stockton, California, made the cross-country trip to Columbia as a presumptive late-season patsy for the Gamecocks ahead of a much-needed open date. Pacific, a middle-of-the-pack member of the Pacific Coast Athletic Association, entered the game a pedestrian 3–5. Most Gamecock fans had never heard of them and rightly expected an enjoyable afternoon of pre- and postgame tailgating, interspersed by a fifth straight Gamecock win. Representatives from the Hall of Fame, Peach, and Tangerine Bowls were in attendance to scout the Gamecocks.

By the time the final whistle blew, fans must have wondered if those orange-helmeted Tigers might have been Clemson in disguise. Pacific blitzed an injury-riddled and hapless Carolina defense, completing thirty-one of fifty-eight passing attempts for 335 yards. Their defense and special teams were even more impressive, as the Tigers held Gamecock rushers to twelve total yards on thirty-seven attempts and controlled the ball for more than thirty-four minutes. Adding to that, the Tigers blocked two Gamecock punts, one resulting in a safety. Entering the final minutes, the slim 23–21 Pacific lead belied just how dominant the Tigers had been in every facet of the game. Seventeen Pacific miscues resulting in 163 penalty yards kept it close.

It was one of those penalties that gave the Gamecocks a final chance at victory. Carolina took over on their own thirty-six yard line with 2:32 remaining. A thirty-two-yard Gordon Beckham strike to Ira Hillary set the Gamecocks up with a first-and-ten at the Pacific twenty-two, breathing new life into what had largely been a funereal Williams-Brice crowd. On the next play, Beckham connected with fullback Dominique Blasingame on a short screen pass, but Blasingame was stripped of the ball by defenders and Pacific recovered, halting the Gamecock drive.

Pacific picked up a game-clenching first down, rushing six yards on third and five, enabling the Tigers to run out the clock and preserve a shocking 23–21 win. The first-down run was one of only two rushing plays on the afternoon for the pass-happy Tigers.

Following the game, Carlen pointed to injuries as a factor in the loss. "In defense of our football team, and I've never made excuses since I've been here, we've had the most unusual group of injuries I've ever had." Indeed, the shorthanded Gamecocks were without key players tight end DeWayne Chivers, offensive guard Cas Danielowski, linebacker James Seawright, and defensive end Phill Ellis. They suffered another major blow eight plays into the game when defensive line stalwart senior Emanuel Weaver, whom Carlen described as "a great player and an emotional leader," went down with a season-ending knee injury.

Now 6–4, with bowl hopes dimmed, Carolina looked to an open date to recover and prepare for another set of Tigers, undefeated and second-ranked Clemson, which had built a compelling national championship résumé.

An ailing South Carolina squad limped into the final home game looking to play spoiler versus their vaunted archrival and, early on, set the tone to do just that. In front of a boisterous, sell-out Williams-Brice Stadium crowd on a brilliant late November Saturday, Carolina held Clemson to a three-and-out on the game's first series. Starting with excellent field position near the fifty yard line, quarterback Gordon Beckham engineered an impressive drive down to the one, setting up Johnnie Wright's leaping touchdown for the early 7–0 lead.

Momentum swung to the Tigers later in the first, however, when Clemson's Rod McSwain came untouched around the left end to block a Chris Norman punt. Clemson recovered in the end zone for a touchdown, and though Carolina maintained the lead after a missed extra point, Clemson never looked back, outscoring the Gamecocks 29–6 from that point en route to the 29–13 final score.

By late game a weakening late November sun cast chilly shadows of the stadium's distinctive west-deck light stanchions beyond the Gamecock bench headlong to midfield, like massive, grasping fingers. Meanwhile a celebratory Clemson squad basked in still-warm sunlight along the east sideline, the shadow and light dichotomy emblematic of two programs headed in divergent directions.

Following the game, Carlen again pointed, almost uncomprehendingly, to the plague of injuries, noting that at one point reserve Paul Martin was forced into the game to temporarily relieve a shaken-up Andrew Provence at defensive tackle. "Two weeks ago, Martin was an offensive guard on the jayvee team," Carlen moaned. He also noted as a pivotal factor a controversial third-period defensive interference call against the Gamecocks while the game was still close. Rather than facing fourth down, the call gave Clemson a first-and-ten at the Gamecock fourteen yard line, leading in short order to a touchdown that transformed the Tiger lead from tenuous to comfortable. "But I don't want to take anything away from Clemson," a weary Carlen added. "I want to congratulate them. They're an excellent team, and well-coached."

At 6–5, South Carolina headed into its matchup at Hawaii needing a win to salvage the program's first streak of three winning seasons since the 1950s. The rare December contest and tropical locale combined to give the game a bowl-like feel, which would have to suffice for the Gamecocks, as postseason suitors had shied away following the loss to Pacific. Hawaii, coached by Dick Tomey, entered the game 8–2 and stood second in the Western Athletic Conference standings behind thirteenth-ranked BYU. In a strange twist, one of their two losses had also come at the hands of the Pacific squad, who finished 5–6 on the season.

A practice injury to starting quarterback Beckham pressed two freshmen, Bill Bradshaw and Rich Ingold, into the lineup, with Bradshaw receiving the starting nod. The young signal caller ran the offense with some effectiveness during the first half, and the Gamecocks remained within striking distance, 17–10, at the half. However, Hawaii scored on a touchdown and field goal within a seventeen-second span during the third period to go up 26–10 after a failed extra point attempt. The "generous Gamecocks," as the *State*'s Bob Spear aptly described them, gave away six turnovers to Hawaii's zero during the game, which negated any chance of a comeback. Hawaii added a fourth-quarter touchdown to win going away, 33–10.

"I felt if we didn't beat ourselves, we'd have a chance of winning," Carlen told reporters after the game, "but we did beat ourselves." The coach struck a more optimistic tone in discussing the role of injuries during the 1981 season. "The good thing is, we've played a lot of young football players, and they'll go into next year with experience."

The three-game losing streak to end 1981 continued a longstanding pattern under Carlen of late-season collapses and provided President Holderman and the board of trustees the impetus they needed to remove the combative coach. In a contentious December 12 executive session, the board voted to fire Carlen, citing the 6–6 season and a 2–5 overall record versus archrival Clemson. The move surprised many, including Carlen, coming as it did a year removed from consecutive eight-win seasons and a Heisman Trophy winner. But astute observers noted Carlen's abrasive personality, which had alienated many and spoiled whatever goodwill he might have otherwise built.

Indeed, Doug Nye of the *Columbia Record* wrote of Carlen that the one thing the coach could never conquer was himself. The late-season struggles year in and year out, the 0–3 bowl record, the public squabbles with McGuire and Holderman, the combative comments during speaking engagements, postgame press conferences, and even his weekly television show all combined to derail what was at times a highly promising seven-year stretch. The win over number 3 UNC, followed by the devastating loss to Pacific during a stormy fifteen-day period that included open feuding with fans and the media, seemed a perfect illustration of the thrilling highs and toxic lows during Carlen's regime. "Some don't like me because I don't play the game," Carlen was fond of saying. "That's their problem." It turned out to be Carlen's problem too.

Moving forward, the board looked to separate once and for all the positions of head football coach and athletics director, another factor that may have contributed to the timing of Carlen's dismissal. Assistant athletics director and business manager John T. Moore was named interim AD. The board next turned its attention to hiring a permanent athletics director, who would, in turn, hire a head football coach.

The era of football coaches doubling as athletics directors at the University of South Carolina, a once-common arrangement in collegiate athletics but long since abandoned by most schools, was mercifully over. It was an administrative structure that had caused untold harm to the university, including the self-defeating ACC exit and decades of wildly destabilizing power struggles.

✗   ✗   ✗

USC hired Bob Marcum as athletics director on January 2, 1982. Marcum, bespectacled and cerebral, had held the same position at the University of Kansas and brought with him an appreciation for conference affiliation that dovetailed with Holderman's ambitions for USC. He inherited two high-profile openings in the vacant football post and the women's basketball coach position, as Pam Parsons had resigned in a swirl of controversy a day before Marcum's introduction.

With Marcum in place, rumors of candidates for the football opening ebbed and flowed as they tend to do. Arkansas coach Lou Holtz's name was prominently bandied about in media reports as it had been in 1974 following Dietzel's resignation. By this time the former South Carolina assistant under Marvin Bass had taken his Razorback program to five consecutive bowls for the first time in program history. When Holtz quickly put the South Carolina rumors to rest, talk turned to USC graduate Dick Sheridan of Furman and West Virginia coach Don Nehlen.

Meanwhile, Carlen's former defensive coordinator, Richard Bell, who was still on staff and actively recruiting, approached Holderman to express interest in the head job. A nineteen-year coaching veteran and Carlen's top assistant at West Virginia, Texas Tech, and USC, the affable Bell was immensely popular with players and fans. Several rising seniors, led by defensive tackle Andrew Provence, drafted a letter to Holderman backing Bell.

When Nehlen opted to stay at West Virginia and with Holtz off the table, any hopes Marcum may have entertained of a splashy hire evaporated. With recruiting season ramping up, USC needed a head coach, and Marcum yielded to popular support for Bell, naming him USC's new head football coach on January 9, 1982.

The "Bell System"

In 1982, before cellular technology became widely available and affordable, Ma Bell still ruled the telecommunications industry just as it had for the better part of a century. Named for the inventor of the telephone, Alexander Graham Bell, the Bell Telephone Company, which later became American Telegraph and Telephone (AT&T), was a mammoth enterprise, with more than a million employees and a net worth roughly equivalent to today's Walmart. And though it faced headwinds by the early 1980s from the US Justice Department, which accused the company of violations of the Sherman Antitrust Act, it is hard to overstate the power and reach of the telecom behemoth.

When USC's new head coach moved away from Carlen's grind-it-out rushing attack in favor of a wide-open, pass-first system under new offensive coordinator Dave Fagg, newspapermen didn't have to look far to find a catchy nickname for the new-look scheme—the Bell System.

The USC job was a homecoming of sorts for Fagg, a native of High Point, North Carolina, who had spent time as an assistant at the Citadel and Davidson before leading the Davidson program from 1970 to 1973. In 1974 Fagg moved to Georgia Tech, where he served as an assistant for five seasons under Pepper Rogers prior to joining Dick Tomey's staff at Hawaii. At Hawaii, Fagg served as offensive coordinator and top assistant, engineering the record-breaking Rainbow Warrior offense that had dominated Bell's defense in Jim Carlen's swan song a few months earlier.

Bell called the USC job "a dream" and "an opportunity, a chance I've always wanted," before adding, "the name of the game is to win, and I do not expect any grace period." Indeed, Carolina returned the bulk of its starting lineup from Carlen's final team, including eight starters on both sides of the ball, starting quarterback Gordon Beckham, and an all-America candidate, defensive tackle Andrew Provence.

It started promisingly, with a cathartic 41–6 rout of the prior campaign's spoiler Pacific to open the season in a newly expanded Williams-Brice Stadium. The gleaming, new, mirror-image upper-east deck boosted capacity to 72,400, and a record crowd of 61,524 witnessed the win. Senior cornerback Harry Skipper electrified the big crowd when he snatched a Pacific fumble out of midair one-yard deep in the Gamecock end zone and returned it the length of the field for a school-record one-hundred-yard interception return for a touchdown in the second quarter.

Bell's Gamecocks advanced to 2–0 after drilling Richmond 30–10 but dropped their first game of the young season when they could find no answer for Duke offensive coordinator Steve Spurrier's dynamic play-calling in a 30–17 loss in Columbia. A 34–18 loss to number 7 Georgia followed before the Gamecocks bounced back to defeat Cincinnati 34–10, moving to 3–2 on the season.

With in-state rival Furman coming to town to cap a season-opening six-game home stand, Carolina looked for an opportunity to build momentum before a brutal back half of the schedule. It was not to be, as the Dick Sheridan–led Paladins built a surprising 21–3 lead and held on for a shocking upset, 28–23.[6]

Now 3–3 and facing the toughest portion of their schedule, Bell found his debut season on the brink of disaster. Carolina would salvage one win over the final five contests, a narrow 17–14 win versus Navy. Perhaps their best performance of the year came in a losing effort on the road versus number 14 LSU, in which the Gamecocks played valiantly and kept it close, 14–6. That was followed by lopsided losses to NC State and FSU, before the win over Navy and a season-ending 24–6 loss to defending national champion Clemson. The Gamecocks finished a disappointing 4–7 on the season, and questions abounded about Bell's future with the Gamecocks.

"We're just going to have to re-establish a winning tradition at South Carolina," Bell told reporters after the Clemson loss. "Winning is not easy. We're just going to have to figure it out."

But just as antitrust litigation would spell the demise of the Bell System telecommunications monopoly at the dawn of 1983, a similar fate befell its namesake in Columbia.

Days later, Marcum and Bell met for a season-ending review. They discussed where the season had gone wrong and, specifically, which assistant coaches did not perform to expectation. Marcum asked Bell to replace four assistants, all of whom had previously been part of Carlen's staff: defensive coordinator Larry New, defensive end coach Bob Roe, secondary coach Keith Colson, and receivers coach Jerry Sullivan. When Bell refused, Marcum said he was left with no choice but to dismiss his head coach. He told reporters, "Richard Bell is a fine person, a man of integrity." But he was no longer the head football coach at the University of South Carolina.

Reflecting on the 1982 season in a 2020 interview with the *State*'s Bob Gillespie, Sullivan pointed to offensive coordinator Dave Fagg's pass-heavy offense as a major factor in the season's troubles. "Beckham was highly-recruited, great kid, but marginal passing skills. Bradshaw was a running quarterback, very limited. We were trying to put a square peg in a round hole." Perhaps, given time and the right personnel, Fagg's system would have worked, and Bell would have gone on to much success at South Carolina. As it was, Bell's lone season represents a brief interlude between the seven seasons of Carlen, with his three bowls and Heisman Trophy–winning tailback, and the swaggering "Black Magic" era that followed.

Former defensive end John Dantonio, who played under Bell when Bell had served as defensive coordinator between 1975 and 1978, submitted a letter to the *State*'s editor in December 1982, writing of his former coach, "I still do not believe I have uncovered all of the facets about life which he instilled in me. He is a man who has always stood by his convictions and principles, and who taught people the facts about life, not just football." Speculating that

Bell would soon find success as a head coach, Dantonio continued, "Then we will have our answer to the question of what it takes to develop a winning program at South Carolina: faith, dedication and a little patience in a sincere, loyal man."[7]

Of Bell's firing, Marcum told reporters at the time, "I have no intention of paying off Bell's contract," pointing to the coach's refusal to fire the four assistants in question. "I gave him a directive involving his staff, and he didn't follow through. I asked him to make certain changes, and he did not make those changes."

Marcum's refusal to honor Bell's contract and public comments suggesting insubordination led Bell in turn to sue the university and Marcum himself for slander and libel. He joined Carlen in the ranks of former coaches with active lawsuits against USC. An additional two former coaches were still on the payroll, with Frank McGuire receiving $150,000 per year through July 1, 1983, and Pam Parsons receiving pay through the end of her contract, which expired in June 1982.

By July 1984 Bell's lawsuit resulted in a $171,000 settlement. A short time later, Carlen collected $557,000 from USC resulting from his own lawsuit. Bell went on to serve as defensive coordinator under Steve Sloan at Duke from 1983 until 1987, among other stops in a career that spanned nearly six decades before his retirement in 2017.

As for USC, Marcum installed his new coach in short order. Joe Morrison, formerly of New Mexico, was announced as the new head coach at South Carolina on December 5, 1982. Morrison, a fourteen-year NFL veteran, whose number 40 had been retired by the New York Giants, earned the nickname "Old Dependable" during his long playing career. He would bring a new swagger, toughness, and style to South Carolina football and in two short seasons would have the Gamecocks positioned to compete for a national championship.

Things were about to get interesting in Columbia, as the cowboy-boot-wearing, Marlboro-smoking "man in black" brought unparalleled excitement (and controversy) to USC football.

9

The Man in Black

Joe Morrison Brings
Unprecedented Excitement,
Notoriety to South Carolina Program

He had hands that looked like a blacksmith's. He was grizzled.
Tough. Everything he did, it looked like a man who played in
the NFL for more than a decade. We just all felt like he was
invincible in a lot of ways.

—Todd Ellis

USC athletics department historian Tom Price recalled in his book *The '84*
Gamecocks that upon Joe Morrison's arrival in Columbia, the coach was
asked if he felt intimidated by a schedule that included the likes of Georgia, Southern Cal, Notre Dame, LSU, Florida State, and Clemson. "Heck
no," Morrison replied, in his refreshingly aw-shucks manner. "I've never seen
Southern Cal and Notre Dame play in person. I'm looking forward to seeing
them."

Indeed, the Gamecocks and their third head coach in as many seasons
would face a powerful North Carolina team ranked just outside the top ten
as the Morrison era kicked officially kicked off at Williams-Brice Stadium on
September 3, 1983. The Gamecocks took the field to the theme from *2001: A*
Space Odyssey for the first time ever, electrifying the near-capacity crowd.

Morrison had abandoned the Gamecocks' traditional white helmets for garnet, with black face masks and a smaller block *C* and gamecock emblem against a circular white field. *Gamecocks* replaced the *Carolina* emblazoned across the jersey chest during the Carlen/Bell era. Morrison had commissioned team dentist Bill Smith, a talented graphic artist, to design the new uniforms, a snazzy sartorial upgrade. A professional look. Morrison was putting his stamp on the program early. Despite a 24–8 loss to the Tar Heels, the modern era of Gamecock football had begun.

Morrison collected his first win as Gamecock skipper the following week, in a 24–3 win versus Miami (Ohio). Asked during his postgame press conference if there was any special reason for his all-black sideline attire, Morrison quipped, "Yes, there were two. It fit and it was clean." Fans liked it, and in the grand tradition of retail capitalism, merchants began carrying all manner of Gamecock apparel in black. They would soon have trouble keeping it in stock.

A 31–24 win at Duke was followed by a hard-fought setback at number 14 Georgia, in which the Gamecocks entered the fourth quarter down by just a field goal before costly turnovers led to a rapid succession of fourth-quarter Bulldog scores and a 31–13 final. Still, Morrison had the 2–2 Gamecocks playing with great effort and enthusiasm. The team seemed to be having fun, and fans were buying into Morrison's style.

A date with Southern Cal awaited back in Columbia.

It was the long-awaited home contest versus the "other USC" in a home-and-home series, the first game of which resulted in a 23–13 Trojan win during George Rogers's Heisman campaign of 1980. The 7 PM kickoff and sellout crowd promised a rowdy atmosphere. Fans who had spent the day tailgating in the dusty State Fairgrounds parking lot or the old farmer's market across Bluff Road descended on the stadium well-oiled and sensing possibility.

The game was tied 14–14 late in the third period when the Gamecocks exploded for twenty-four points in a span of 7:41. Sophomore running back Thomas Dendy broke loose for a fourteen-yard touchdown to start the deluge. A few plays later, Gamecock defensive end Tony Guyton hit Trojan quarterback Sean Salisbury just as he released a long pass. Free safety Bryant Gilliard intercepted and returned the ball thirty-eight yards to the Sothern

Gamecock football players Roy Hart and James Sumpter carry
coach Joe Morrison off the field after the University of South Carolina
defeated the University of Southern California in 1983. Courtesy of
the *State* Newspaper Archive, Richland County Public Library.

Cal one. Kent Hagood bulled into the end zone for the easy score, and Mark
Fleetwood's extra point pushed the Gamecock lead to 28–14.

The Gamecock defense held on Southern Cal's next possession, and a
bad snap on a fourth-down punt resulted in excellent field position and an
eventual Fleetwood field goal to make it 31–14 Gamecocks. A few plays later,
junior linebacker James Sumpter recovered a Trojan fumble at their seventeen,
setting up a Quinton Lewis touchdown for the final 38–14 margin.

On a pivotal third-down defensive stand, fans were so exuberant that the
upper-east deck began to sway visibly, as engineers had intended. Still the
movement startled those who saw it. When told of the swaying upper deck
following the game, Morrison quipped, "If it ain't swayin', we ain't playin'."
It was a Morrison classic, setting loose once again the machinations of retail
opportunists, as bumper stickers with the quote began to appear around
Columbia.

Southern Cal quarterback Salisbury pointed to the crowd as a factor in the game. "They had that good ol' twelfth man working for them out there. I don't think the crowd rattled us, but our guys were having trouble hearing the signals, and it took away our audibles." Trojan linebacker Jack Del Rio told reporters, "They were all fired up, and the crowd sparked their enthusiasm. It's a great crowd."

The 3–2 Gamecocks would lose the next game to another traditional power, Notre Dame, 30–6 on a rainy night in Columbia, dampening any thoughts of a second-consecutive big-name upset. Still, at 3–3—the same record after six games as the prior season—things felt different within the program. Players had bought into Morrison's system. The energy and optimism among fans were palpable.

A 20–6 loss at LSU dropped the Gamecocks to 3–4, but it hardly seemed to matter. Another rowdy home crowd greeted the third former ACC rival of the season, NC State, for a homecoming matchup on the final Saturday in October. The Gamecocks, clad in all garnet for the first time, largely dominated the Wolfpack, sparked by Todd Berry's touchdown return of the opening kickoff. Of the all-garnet uniforms, Morrison commented in his low-key way, "I thought with homecoming and all that, it was something to do. Our young men enjoyed it. They came out with fire and enthusiasm."

The Gamecocks entered November at 4–4, having already exceeded the expectations of most pundits, who predicted two to three wins at best in Morrison's first season. They traveled next to Tallahassee for a matchup with fellow independent Florida State. Carolina played well in a tough environment and were tied at 24 midway through the third quarter with an opportunity to move ahead, driving to the Seminole six yard line before stalling. FSU blocked a Mark Fleetwood field-goal attempt from twenty-three yards out, which sparked a ten-play touchdown drive to go up 31–24. A few moments later the FSU defense intercepted a Bill Bradshaw pass attempt, setting up the final Seminole score, and 38–24 proved the final margin.

Following a 31–7 win over Navy the next week, one of the more notable Morrison-era traditions debuted. During intrasquad scrimmages, Morrison and defensive coordinator Tom Gadd required their defensive players to either be in on a tackle or running full speed toward the play by the time the practice camera clicked off. Gadd, having watched film of the all-garnet-clad Gamecocks from the NC State game a few weeks before, commented that his defense "looked like a bunch of fire ants" swarming around the ball carrier. Reporters picked up on the phrase following the Navy game, during which the Gamecocks again wore all garnet, and the "fire ant" defense was born.

With USC sitting at 5–5 and the season-ending game versus Clemson coming up, speculation on radio talk shows and in Columbia media turned, as it often does, to uniforms. Specifically rumors circulated that the Gamecocks would take the field versus Clemson in all black—a tip of the cap to their charismatic coach. Indeed, Morrison encouraged fans to wear black to the game, a boon to retailers. "There's nothing on the racks in black," D. H. Jeffcoat, the manager of a Columbia Sears, told a reporter. "Black shirts, black caps, black pants. They're all gone."

To the delight of fans, Carolina did, in fact, take the field to the strains of *Also sprach Zarathurstra* wearing all black for the first time that Saturday afternoon. The game itself was less than delightful, as the charitable Gamecocks gave up two interceptions, two fumbles, and a blocked field goal to the thirteenth-ranked Tigers. It was a sloppy game all around, as Clemson gave up three turnovers of its own, though they were not as costly. Statistically, the Gamecocks held tough, outgaining the Tigers 317 to 304 and nineteen first downs to Clemson's eighteen. Time of possession was nearly equal, with Clemson holding the slight 30:01 to 29:59 advantage. The Tigers, though, came out on top in the only statistical category that counts, winning a hard-fought game 22–13.

Clemson finished the season 9–1–1 and 7–0 in ACC play, winning the ACC championship. However, they missed out on postseason play, serving the second of a three-season suspension following recruiting improprieties uncovered after their 1981 national championship run. Clemson's bowl misfortune was cold comfort to the Gamecocks, though, as Carolina's seniors were the first class in forty-four years not to experience a win over their archrivals.

Morrison told reporters after the game, "We'd heard so much about the Carolina-Clemson rivalry, it's been a great experience to go through this week, to see the great enthusiasm, the great interest the people of South Carolina have towards their two major football programs." He added, "It's great to be a part of it." In observing his team and hopes for continued progress, Morrison noted, "I believe this football team will mature a little bit and somewhere on down the line will be able to turn some of these things the other way."

"On down the line" came sooner than anyone could have expected.

"Next Year" Finally Arrives: 1984 Brings Big Success, Lofty Rankings

Just days after the 1983 season ended, workers, backhoes, and dump trucks descended on Williams-Brice Stadium to remove the old, threadbare Astroturf playing surface. The Astroturf, originally installed following Paul Dietzel's "Carpet the Cockpit" campaign, arrived in conjunction with the new upperwest deck, which debuted in 1971.[1] Thirteen seasons later, new athletics director Marcum made the calculation that natural grass was more economical than installing a new artificial field, safer for players, and more aesthetically pleasing.

Crews faced quite a job. Under the watchful eye of groundskeeper Sarge Frye, the old carpet had to be cut up and rolled away, along with the half-inch sponge directly underneath. Next, nearly thirty-two thousand tons of asphalt and twenty-nine thousand tons of gravel a foot deep had to be broken up and hauled away. It was essentially 120 yards of roadbed within the stadium. It was replaced with a foot of sand and clay topped by the new Bermuda turf. The crown of the new field was about half that of the fifteen-inch rise between midfield and sidelines built into the old Astroturf field. "It will be a surface where your athletes are not running uphill, sidehill or downhill." Marcum told reporters. Beyond the return to a natural grass playing surface, new hedges were planted along the back of both end zones. They were scrawny in that first season but soon filled in, softening the spartan, industrial look of stadium.[2]

Entering fall practice, the Gamecocks boasted four potential starting quarterbacks, including junior Allen Mitchell from nearby Batesburg-Leesville, the presumptive favorite who took over starting duties from Bill Bradshaw in 1983. Mitchell was impressive at times as a sophomore, producing 1,324 combined passing and running yards but also tying a school record with eighteen interceptions. Junior Mike Hold, an intriguing transfer from Mesa (Arizona)

Community College, junior Jim Desmond of Miami, and redshirt freshman Kevin White of Charlotte rounded out the quartet. The Gamecocks featured the veer offense, a triple-option-style attack engineered by coordinator Frank Sadler once again, and all four quarterbacks showed proficiency during the spring.

Beyond quarterback, the Gamecocks featured perhaps the nation's best and most experienced offensive line, a quintet of seniors who had been at Carolina since the Carlen era: center Tom Garner, guards Jim Walsh and Del Wilkes, and tackles Carl Womble and Bill Barnhill. Wilkes in particular would enjoy a stellar season, becoming only the second consensus all-American in program history.[3]

The Gamecocks were similarly stacked at the running back position, led by junior Thomas Dendy, whose 1,573 career yards put him close to Gamecock legend George Rogers's pace after two seasons (1,629). Fellow junior Kent Hagood, recruited by Carlen, had left school shortly after Carlen's firing and sat out the 1982 season, working as a press operator at J. P. Stevens mill in Greenville, near his native Upstate hometown of Easley. Hagood told *Sports Illustrated*'s Jack McCallum, "I was sitting around watching television with my little nephew one day when I heard a car door slam and saw this big, tough-looking guy get out all dressed in black," adding, "I said to my nephew, 'Yeah, that must be the man.' He asked me to come back and I'm glad I came." Dependable senior Quinton Lewis and sophomore speedster Raynard Brown rounded out a deep and talented running back corps.

Senior Ira Hillary led the receivers, joined by fellow seniors Chris Wade and Emory Bacon, junior Eric Poole, as well as tight ends Chris Corley and Danny Smith. Another promising receiver who had played sparingly as a freshman in 1983 watched the 1984 season from the sidelines as a redshirt—future all-American Sterling Sharpe.

The unquestioned leader of the fire ant defense was senior linebacker James Seawright, who enjoyed an all-American season in 1984. Joining him at linebacker were headhunter Paul Vogel from Greenville and Carl Hill, a sophomore from Memphis. Willie McIntee, James Sumpter, Glenn Woodley, and James Wright anchored a stout defensive front, while free safety Bryant

Gilliard headlined a stingy defensive backfield, joined by Chris Major, Otis Morris, and Joe Brooks.

The Gamecocks hardly missed a beat at placekicker following the loss of Mark Fleetwood to graduation, as dependable Scott Hagler took over extra point and field goal duties, while Tom O'Connor handled punts.

Beyond all-Americans Wilkes and Seawright, the 1984 Gamecock roster comprised what *SI's* McCallum called "a bunch of Joe Morrisons—players who are tough and consistent." This scrappy, resilient group took Gamecock fans on a thrilling ride in the fall of 1984. But nobody was predicting that early on.

The general feeling among fans and pundits alike was that South Carolina should be somewhat improved in 1984; however the Gamecocks again faced a murderer's row of opponents, including Pittsburgh, Clemson, and Notre Dame, who ranked third, fourth, and eighth in preseason polls, respectively. Florida State ranked number 20 preseason, while always tough Georgia, who owned a commanding 30–6–2 series record versus the Gamecocks, hovered just outside the top twenty. Most journalists who covered the program predicted six, maybe seven wins if things went well.

At press day transfer quarterback Mike Hold, who had yet to play a down for the Gamecocks, boldly predicted, "This year we're going to a bowl game," and added, "There's no doubt. The attitude of this team is great and that's our main goal."

The Gamecocks entered the 1984 season with precisely a .500 record over ninety years—386 wins, 386 losses, and 38 ties. Looking to tip the scales ever so slightly toward the win column, South Carolina welcomed in-state rival the Citadel to Columbia for the season opener before a near-capacity crowd of 71,200 at Williams-Brice Stadium. The Gamecocks owned a 37–6–3 record versus the Bulldogs in forty-six previous meetings and had not lost in the series since 1950. During the 1950 game at the Citadel's Johnson Hagood Stadium in Charleston, USC coach Rex Enright debuted black jerseys for the first time in program history. The Citadel pulled a 19–7 upset, and Enright promptly deep-sixed the jerseys, not to be seen again until Morrison famously introduced the all-black combo versus Clemson in the 1983 season ender. Most considered that a one-and-done novelty, much like Enright's failed experiment.

To the surprise of many, the Gamecocks took the field in black jerseys and white britches that night, which became a frequent alternating home uniform during the Morrison years and beyond.

The scrappy Bulldogs gave Carolina all it could handle on a steamy night in Columbia. With the game knotted at 26 deep into the fourth quarter, South Carolina's Mitchell engineered a late-game eighty-three-yard drive, completing passes of six and twenty yards to Hillary and Corley, respectively. Raynard Brown provided balance to the attack with four carries to push the ball to the Bulldog forty-five with under 1:30 remaining in regulation. On second and two, Mitchell pitched to tailback Quinton Lewis, a former high school quarterback in his native Midway, Georgia. Lewis swept left and tossed a forty-yard strike to wideout Chris Wade for the deciding touchdown with a minute showing on the clock. A Hagler extra point put the Gamecocks up 31–24, allowing the USC faithful to exhale, but only briefly.

The Citadel's Mike Lewis returned the Carolina kickoff seventy-seven yards up the Gamecock sideline before being brought down at the USC eighteen yard line. The Citadel offense took over, eighteen yards away from a tie or perhaps the opportunity to win with a two-point conversion.[4] The Gamecock defense rose up, forcing two incompletions and an interception to end the game. Carolina escaped with what fans considered a "closer than it should have been" victory at home over a lightly regarded Citadel team, forcing many to reevaluate expectations for the season.

After an early open date, the Gamecocks next hosted old ACC nemesis Duke. Though the Gamecocks had beaten the Blue Devils more often than not in the post-ACC era, Duke still enjoyed a comfortable 24–13–2 margin in the series, which dated to 1930. South Carolina won only five of seventeen games versus Duke as a member of the ACC.

The Gamecocks returned to an all-garnet uniform combo for the Duke game and maintained that look for the remainder of their home games in 1984. The fire ant defense turned in a gem, shutting out an overmatched

Blue Devil team and holding them to fifty net rushing yards on thirty-seven attempts and less than three hundred total yards. The Gamecock defensive performance allowed Mitchell and his offense to overcome a sputtering early game. Carolina won 21–0 in workmanlike fashion.

The Gamecocks moved to 2–0 with an opportunity to go to 3–0 for the first time since 1977 in their next game versus Georgia. The twelfth-ranked Bulldogs, meanwhile, had notched a stirring 26–23 win over number 2 Clemson the week before, on the strength of a sixty-yard Kevin Butler field goal with eleven seconds remaining.

Before a crowd of 74,325, the third largest ever at Williams-Brice Stadium, the Gamecocks staged a stunning 17–10 upset, spurred by Mike Hold's fourth-quarter sixty-two-yard strike to Ira Hillary to the Bulldog six yard line. The long pass set up a Hold keeper off the right side to give the Gamecocks the final margin with 8:04 remaining.

Hold had entered the game to spot Mitchell, who experienced numbness in his throwing arm after a hit to his funny bone. In only his second varsity appearance, Hold forever endeared himself to Gamecock faithful, not only with the sixty-two-yard strike to Hillary but also with his scrappy style of play, which seemed to encapsulate the Gamecock brand. Sports editor James Beck of the *Charleston Post and Courier* wrote that Hold's long bomb "must have been the prettiest pass ever thrown in Williams-Brice Stadium." Hold was quick to put down any rumors of a quarterback controversy, telling reporters after the game, "Next week we'll get back to practice and Allen will be No. 1. I'm ready to back him up one hundred percent. Allen played a great game and we're a team."

Morrison called the win bigger than Southern Cal in 1983. "I've never been prouder of a group of young men," he said. "You could see it in practice and the first of the week. There was just a different feeling. More intensity, I guess is the best way to describe it. We didn't have to tell those guys anything extra. They knew we were playing Georgia."

The fire ant defense held Georgia to 272 yards and four first downs on sixteen attempts. "I guess they thought they'd intimidate us," linebacker Paul Vogel said; "they ran right at us all night. But we just lined up and played defense."

For the first time since 1980, the Gamecocks appeared in a top-twenty poll, coming in at twentieth in the UPI poll while remaining unranked by the AP.

A week later, the Gamecocks continued their season-opening homestand versus Kansas State of the Big Eight. The two schools had met only twice, a two-game series in 1940 and 1941, with each team winning once. The Gamecocks and Wildcats played the second of those games on November 8, 1941, in Manhattan, Kansas, a mere twenty-nine days before the attack on Pearl Harbor that ushered the United States into World War II.

Carolina overpowered the visiting Wildcats on the first Saturday of October, and the first daytime contest of the season, winning 49–17 to go to 4–0 for the first time since 1928. Carolina set the early tone with 61 rushing yards in four plays on their first possession, en route to 350 rushing yards for the day, as the Gamecocks controlled the game from opening kickoff of final whistle.

Up next was Pittsburgh, which had embarrassed the Carolina program twice in recent years. The Panthers won in a lopsided affair over an eight-win Jim Carlen team, led by freshly minted Heisman Trophy winner George Rogers in the 1980 Gator Bowl. The Dan Marino–led Panthers came to Columbia the following season and rolled to a 28–0 halftime lead, prompting ABC-TV to switch to another regional broadcast. It was an embarrassment for Carlen's program during his final season in Columbia and a headache for ABC Sports executives, who endured days of invective from fans across South Carolina and Pennsylvania. Carolina scored a couple of late touchdowns in that contest to make the final score (48–24) look closer than it actually was. Marino threw for six touchdowns, four in the first half alone, on the way to all-America honors and ultimately a hall of fame professional career with the NFL's Miami Dolphins.

The seventeenth-ranked Gamecocks redeemed themselves this time, rolling to a convincing 45–21 win, including a 24–7 advantage in the second half. Carolina surged to 5–0, matching the 1928 season for the best start in program history. National media began to take notice of the undefeated Gamecocks, who found themselves ranked eleventh in the AP poll the following week, tying the loftiest perch ever for the program.[5]

After a thrilling five-game homestand, the surging Gamecocks took their fire ants and black magic show on the road to the holiest of holies in college football, the University of Notre Dame in South Bend, Indiana. It was the home of bronze-cast, sepia-toned legends Knute Rockne, the Four Horsemen, George Gipp, Johnny Lujack, Paul Hornung and more recent legends like Joe Theismann and Joe Montana.

South Carolina had visited Notre Dame once before, on October 27, 1979, and as Gamecock historian Tom Price wrote, "found out what it was like to be stabbed in the heart by a leprechaun." The Gamecocks held a 17–3 fourth-quarter lead in that contest, only to see Notre Dame score two late touchdowns and a two-point conversion to win 18–17. South Carolina had hosted Notre Dame in 1976, a 13–6 loss, and in 1983, a 30–6 Irish rout.

Notre Dame had started 1984 ranked in the top ten, as they almost always did, despite a pedestrian 7–5 record the previous year. Gerry Faust's squad entered the South Carolina game unranked, at 3–3, and looking for some momentum after consecutive losses to Miami and Air Force. The Gamecocks, meanwhile, hoped to continue their good vibes and undefeated start, while also removing that pesky leprechaun from the backs of a program that had yet to taste success versus the legendary Irish.

Tom Price relays the story of a conversation between team dentist Bill Smith and Gamecock linebacker James Seawright, demonstrating that the history and tradition that is so often the focus of fans and sportswriters doesn't always resonate with nineteen- and twenty-year-old players. During warm-ups Smith asked Seawright if he knew that he was walking on hallowed ground.

"What does that mean?" Seawright asked, according to Smith's telling afterward.

"This is where the Four Horsemen rode," Smith replied. "This is where the Gipper played. This is where Knute Rockne coached."

"Means nothing to me, 'cause they're all dead," Seawright retorted.

In a post-game interview, Seawright expanded. "That tradition stuff doesn't bother me. This felt the same as any other game."

The Gamecocks and Irish met in a cold drizzle, under steel-gray South Bend skies. Despite the rain, 59,075 fans filed in before kickoff, the 105th sell-out in 106 games at Notre Dame Stadium, dating to 1964. An estimated 5,000 Gamecock fans made the trip from South Carolina, their garnet and black ponchos in a distinct block, surrounded by Irish blue and gold.

Carolina took an early 7–0 lead on an Allen Mitchell sneak from the one, capping a thirty-one-yard drive after recovering an Irish fumbled punt a few plays earlier. The score was tied at 14 late in the second corner before a long Notre Dame field goal pushed their lead to 17–14 as the halftime whistle blew.

The third quarter started in disastrous fashion, as the Gamecocks turned the ball over on their first three possessions, two fumbles and an interception, leading to an Irish field goal and touchdown. When Notre Dame decided to go for a two-point conversion after the touchdown, Carolina's Bryant Gilliard sacked Irish quarterback Steve Beuerlein on a safety blitz, leaving the score 26–14 late in the third period.

A one-yard Mike Hold sneak capped a sixteen-yard drive by the Game-cocks, and Hagood barreled in for the two-point conversion just a minute into the final period, pulling the Gamecocks within four, 26–22. The teams next traded turnovers before South Carolina regained possession at their own twenty-five after a Notre Dame punt with twelve minutes remaining. The Gamecocks moved the ball to the Irish thirty-three, helped by a face-mask violation against the Irish. From there Hold narrowly avoided a sack before setting off on a mad scramble to the end zone, pushing the Gamecocks in front 29–26 after the Hagler extra point.

Gamecock safety Rick Rabune recovered a Notre Dame fumble at their own seventeen, and three plays later Quinton Lewis took it in for a seem-ingly comfortable 36–26 lead with seven minutes remaining. Though Notre Dame did not go away quietly and pulled to within 36–32 after another failed two-point conversion, time ran out on the Irish, and South Carolina held on for a historic win. *Sports Illustrated*'s Jack McCallum, who had spent the prior week in Columbia covering the team and traveled to South Bend for the game, wrote of the feeling that settled over the stadium after Carolina's final score: "In the next moments, the sense of one school on the rise, the other in decline, was inescapable."

The Gamecocks, now a sparkling 6–0, had won six straight during the same season for the first time in program history. And in doing so, they had finally vanquished that leprechaun. As Tom Price put it, "The Gamecocks had slogged through the rain, in the shadows of the Golden Dome and 'Touchdown Jesus,' and had conquered a legend." Even the stoic Morrison couldn't contain his enthusiasm during a postgame press conference, telling reporters with a wide grin, "Damn, it's exciting when you take Georgia, Pittsburgh and Notre Dame in the same year."

Proving that the significance of the Gamecocks' win was more than just symbolic, the following week the Irish went on to upset number 7 LSU in Baton Rouge, one of the most hostile environments in all of college football. They won four straight to end the regular season, including a 19–7 win versus cross-sectional rival number 14 Southern Cal, before an Aloha Bowl loss to number 10 SMU.

South Carolina, meanwhile, was greeted by an estimated twelve thousand fans at Columbia Metropolitan Airport. Seventy-two-year-old Victor Floyd summed up the feelings of many in attendance, noting that he had been following the Gamecocks for fifty-two years, since 1932. "I wouldn't miss this. I love them."

South Carolina cracked the top ten for the first time in program history, climbing to number 9 in the AP and eighth in the UPI.

Back in Columbia for week seven, the Gamecocks kept it rolling, with a 42–20 trouncing of East Carolina. Each time the Gamecocks scored a touchdown that afternoon, which was often, fans showered Sarge Frye's new grass field with oranges, signifying their hopes for an Orange Bowl bid and a shot at the national title.

In an odd scheduling twist, it was the first Saturday in November before the Gamecocks faced their second road contest, and this one was a familiar foe, old ACC rival the NC State Wolfpack. The Gamecocks had defeated State in the first game ever played at Carter-Finley Stadium (then known as Carter Stadium) when it opened on October 8, 1966. It also happened to be Paul Dietzel's first (and only) win during his inaugural season at South Carolina, an otherwise miserable 1–9 campaign.[6] The Gamecocks had not won in Raleigh since, losing seven of eight contests and battling to a 7–7 tie in 1970.

The Wolfpack looked to play spoiler to the undefeated Gamecocks, who had by then risen to number 5 in the polls. An estimated eight thousand South Carolina fans snapped up every ticket available, some traveling ticketless to Raleigh in hopes of finding scalpers before the kickoff on a cold, raw afternoon in early November.

The Gamecocks were sluggish in the first half, as if laboring under the burdensome and unfamiliar load of high ranking and national attention, and the Wolfpack built a 15–3 halftime lead. Carolina scored quickly to open the second half on an eleven-play, eighty-six-yard drive, capped by a twelve-yard Raynard Brown touchdown scamper. Hagler's point after cut the lead to 15–10 and, more important, put some wind in the Gamecocks' sails. The teams traded scores on a wild, seesaw afternoon, in which USC lost tailback Kent Hagood to a season-ending broken leg before clawing out a 35–28 win. Carolina had captured its eighth consecutive win, defended their top-five national ranking, and won consecutive road games for the first time since 1981.

There was a growing mystique around this Gamecock team. Some spoke of "black magic," a nod to Morrison and the intangible elements of confidence and faith the coach had infused into players and long-suffering fans as much as to his sideline garb. Prior to the NC State contest, Hagood spoke with the *State's* Teddy Heffner about the Gamecocks' magic sauce in 1984, citing team chemistry. "My freshman year (1981), I'd go to the dining hall and nobody would be talking. The black athletes would be sitting at one table, and the white athletes at another," Hagood recalled. "Now everybody is mixing. The blacks with the whites, the offense with the defense. Everybody is together and trying to bring about one goal. There are no conflicts."

The Gamecocks, who remained at number 5 in the polls, now turned their eyes toward a top-ten matchup with Bobby Bowden's Florida State Seminoles in Columbia. ABC-TV had announced that the matchup would be their national game of the week. It marked only the third nationally televised appearance in USC program history and the first such broadcast from Williams-Brice Stadium.[7] In the days before ESPN's *College GameDay,* ABC's game of the week with legendary play-by-play man Keith Jackson was the pinnacle of college football broadcasting. Carolina had officially reached the big time.

The game set up like a college football fan's dream. FSU boasted the nation's highest scoring offense at 38.6 points per game, while South Carolina was seventh, at 34.5. The 8–0 Gamecocks were ranked fifth, while the 6–1–1 Seminoles were ranked tenth and eleventh by the UPI and AP polls, respectively. Florida State had dismantled in-state rival and defending national champion Miami 38–3, their only loss coming in a 42–41 shootout versus number 16 Auburn. South Carolina, meanwhile, had spent the season turning in Houdini-like escapes with four thrilling come-from-behind victories. It was the Cinderella Gamecocks versus the perennial national power Seminoles on ABC's prime weekly broadcast before an overflow Williams-Brice crowd. Morrison noted in his understated way, "Yeah, it might turn out to be a pretty good offensive game."

Morrison was prophetic, as the Gamecocks and Seminoles combined for sixty-four points and almost a thousand yards in a wild game, which saw the Gamecocks build a 17–7 halftime advantage and 38–7 third-quarter lead before a furious Seminole fourth-quarter comeback. It was the fire ant defense, though, that carried the day, collecting seven pass interceptions and recovering two fumbles—all in the second half—to snuff out nine Seminole possessions, preserving a 38–26 Gamecock win. Safety Bryant Gilliard accounted for five of the seven takeaways—four interceptions (tying a program record) and a fumble recovery. For his efforts Bryant was named defensive player of the week by *Sports Illustrated*.

Raynard Brown, famously, opened the second half with a dazzling ninety-nine-yard kickoff return for a touchdown, though ABC-TV replays appeared to show that his right knee touched down at the Gamecock one-yard-line. Brown was adamant in talking with reporters after the game that his knee didn't touch, though by that point it was all academic, as the whistle never blew and Brown raced down the east sideline for a school-record kickoff return, setting off pandemonium among the Williams-Brice crowd.[8]

The Gamecocks, now 9–0, surged to number 2 in the AP and UPI polls on the strength of their top-ten win, aided by losses higher up by Texas and Washington. Meanwhile Nebraska rose to number 1.

Nick Moschella of the *Fort Myers News Press*, one of twenty-nine writers representing nineteen Florida newspapers in Columbia to cover the game, noted, "On this afternoon, it would have been more appropriate if Florida State Seminole fans had worn black, for they were the ones who left Williams-Brice Stadium in mourning." Of Columbia, Moschella wrote that it was "a town consumed by its team." FSU's Bowden said, in a backhanded compliment of sorts, "I thought we were lousy. But, I don't want to take anything away from South Carolina. They are a good team, better than I thought they would be."

The win placed Carolina squarely in contention for a shot at the national championship. Fans knew it and again threw oranges on the field after touchdowns throughout the game. They reveled in the heady reverie unknown to a century of Gamecock football fans before 1984 unfolded as the often promised but never realized "next year." The stars were aligning for Gamecock Nation. A win against Navy the following week would all but assure an Orange Bowl berth, no matter what happened at Clemson in the regular-season finale.

A 3–5–1 Navy squad was all that lay between South Carolina and the promised land.

The Midshipmen had been riddled by injuries in 1984, most notably losing their all-America tailback Napoleon McCallum to a broken leg earlier in the season. The week before South Carolina's visit, their starting quarterback, Bill Byrne, went down with a broken leg of his own. Morrison warned, though, that the Navy squad would be "ready emotionally and mentally" for the Gamecocks and maintained that Carolina would need to play perhaps a better game than they had against FSU. Few took him seriously. And who could blame players and fans for looking beyond? Talk of a Nebraska versus South Carolina national championship matchup dominated college football media. Moreover, not a single player on the South Carolina roster had tasted victory over archrival Clemson, the Gamecocks' last win in the series coming in 1979. With the Tigers waiting in the wings a week later, thoughts turned naturally to bigger stages and brighter lights beyond Annapolis.

Sunk

There are certain maritime disasters that naturally come to mind when pondering the 1984 USC-Navy game. A sinking of the "unsinkable" in the cold, unforgiving waters of the North Atlantic, perhaps, or in this case the

Chesapeake Bay. It remains the single most haunting loss in the long, often fraught history of Gamecock football. Nearly forty years later, the "what-if" conversations ebb and flow like Lowcountry tides, filling the pluff mud channels and fecund estuaries of fan message boards with revisionist histories, written on the fly but pondered over decades. A single word, coldly sinister in the context of South Carolina athletics, has come to embody the myriad cruel plot twists that have bedeviled Gamecock fans through the years. For them it is the ultimate four-letter word . . . *NAVY.*

It was sunny and cold, with highs in the mid-forties and gusty winds out of the north when the number 2 Gamecocks and Midshipmen took the field at thirty-four-thousand-seat Navy-Marine Corps Stadium. A smattering of garnet-clad South Carolina fans made the trip and sat among a sea of Navy blue and gold, both local fans and the brigade of midshipmen in their wool peacoats and crisp Academy uniforms. It was a near perfect day for football.

After a first quarter in which the Gamecocks forced two Navy turnovers but came no closer to scoring than a blocked Hagler field goal attempt, the Midshipmen led 7–0. Navy maintained a touchdown advantage, leading 14–7 at the half. A disastrous third quarter followed, in which it was Navy who looked like the top-five team. They had built a 31–7 lead by the start of the fourth quarter and scored again two plays into the final period, capping a seventy-eight-yard, seven-play drive to make it 38–7. The game, and Carolina's dreams of a national championship, were all but over. Each time Navy scored, members of the brigade of midshipmen poured out of the stands behind the north end zone to do pushups corresponding to their point total. They got quite a workout that afternoon.

The Gamecocks scored two touchdowns in the fourth quarter to pull to 38–21, but that was as close as it got, with turnovers and a ticking clock killing any hopes of another miracle comeback. The fourteen-point underdog Midshipmen had beaten the country's second-ranked team by seventeen points.

To compound the Gamecocks' disappointment, news came while boarding the flight home that Oklahoma had upset top-ranked Nebraska 17–7 that afternoon. Had Carolina taken care of business in Annapolis, they would have taken over the number 1 ranking. It was a gut punch, a twist of the knife, salt in the wound. Pick your cliché—it hurt.

Awaiting the team when they arrived at the Columbia airport were an estimated five thousand fans, gathered to commiserate and cheer their Game-cocks, even in defeat. Local celebrity Joe Pinner, the longtime weatherman and host of the *Mr. Knozit* children's show on WIS-TV, led cheers from a flat-bed truck. "We did beat Pitt. We did beat Notre Dame. We did beat Florida State. We paid a lot of people back," Pinner shouted to a cheering crowd. "I think we needed this defeat so we could trample Clemson!"

Coach Morrison told the gathered faithful, "Coming home after the Notre Dame game, it was good to see the fans here. This means a lot more."

The next day Morrison gathered the team for a Sunday meeting. Colum-nist Andrew Miller of the *Charleston Post and Courier* relayed a story of the meeting in a 2011 column about the aftermath of the Navy loss:

He [Morrison] entered the meeting room a few minutes late, which was unusual for the coach, and with no preamble, went to the blackboard and wrote down five items.

1. National championship
2. No. 1 ranking
3. Orange Bowl bid
4. $2 million
5. Toilet

Morrison turned to face his team.

"Guys, you just blew the chance at a national championship, you're not going to be Number 1, we're not going to the Orange Bowl, and you just lost your university two million dollars," Mor-rison said, pointing to each of the first four items on the list.

Then he put the chalk on number five and said with empha-sis, "That's where you are right now."

Morrison paused, making eye contact with each player in the room, which was silent as a crypt. "Ok, let's go beat Clemson."

Without another word, Morrison dropped the chalk and walked out of the room.

Indeed the Gamecocks did drop seven spots in the AP poll, down to number 9. Undefeated Brigham Young University, which had been behind Carolina at number 3 the prior week, surged to the top spot. Oklahoma moved from number 6 to 2 on the strength of their upset of previous number 1 Nebraska, while Oklahoma State and Florida each moved up one spot to third and fourth, respectively. Washington, who had been number 1 two weeks earlier, rounded out the new top five.

Despite the good feelings at the Columbia airport after the Navy game, a pall hung over the Capital City during the week leading up to Carolina's regular-season finale. Already talk about what could have been dominated conversations as businesspeople, politicians, students, and fans met to commiserate over coffee, eggs, and grits at the Capitol Restaurant and the Elite Epicurean downtown, or the Lizard's Thicket on Beltline Boulevard. All over Columbia, the stages of grief found people in various states of denial, bargaining, anger, depression, and acceptance. Monday was dark and funereal. By Thanksgiving Thursday, as families gathered for the annual feast, thoughts turned ever so slightly away from the disappointment of Navy and to the many milestones the Gamecocks team had accomplished.

By Friday thoughts turned to Clemson, as students and fans gathered on campus for the annual Tiger burn. The ritual burning of a giant papier-mâché tiger that year doubled as a funeral pyre of sorts, an opportunity to collectively grieve and release whatever national championship hopes they may have harbored just a few short days before. As the glowing embers floated skyward on that chilly November evening, dancing among autumn leaves and the brass notes of the pep band, healing and perspective took hold. There was still much to play for: a state championship, a tenth (and perhaps eleventh) win in reach, the first win over Clemson since 1979, the first win at Clemson since 1970, and a yet-to-be-named bowl destination. Not the Orange Bowl, perhaps, but a good one nonetheless, and only the sixth bowl berth in program history.

There was wide speculation and media reports pointing to a Gator Bowl invitation, but that would not be official until after the Clemson game.

Hold That Tiger

South Carolina wasn't the only team coming off a humiliating defeat in the state of Maryland. Thirty miles north of Annapolis, the Tigers took a thumping from the Maryland Terrapins to the tune of 41–23 at Memorial Stadium in Baltimore. Clemson was 7–3 entering the season finale and serving the last of their three-season probationary period. Even with Carolina's 9–1 record and a top-ten ranking, oddsmakers set Clemson as a two-point favorite, owing largely to their historical dominance in the rivalry and home-field advantage.

The Tigers carried a twenty-five-game home winning streak into the contest, and its seniors had never tasted defeat at home or to their archrivals from Columbia. Moreover, Clemson was 10–0 in orange britches, which they reserved for big games and had debuted against the Gamecocks in 1980. The Tigers ran down the hill that day in all orange after clandestine pregame warmups in nearby Littlejohn Coliseum, which Tom Price called a "psychological ploy" on the part of Clemson coach Danny Ford.

Another psychological ploy, according to Price in *The '84 Gamecocks,* was the Clemson band's playing of "Anchors Aweigh," the Navy fight song, to needle Gamecock players and fans about the prior week's loss. Clemson fans threw oranges on the field, mocking Gamecock fans who had done the same during Carolina's win over FSU. Mixed with the oranges were several lemons. Several fans carried signs taunting, "Welcome to your Orange Bowl, South Carolina."

The Gamecocks took the field in visiting white jerseys and (a surprise to many) black britches. They had lost versus Clemson in all black the prior year and struggled versus the Citadel in black jerseys during the season opener. Most assumed black had been shelved for good. If it was an unsettling omen to the 12,000 Gamecock fans scattered around 80,500-seat Memorial Stadium, Carolina's first-half performance did little to comfort them.

The Gamecocks trailed 21–3 in the second quarter and 21–10 at the half. In the third quarter, Tony Guyton caught Clemson quarterback Mike Eppley in the end zone for a safety, closing the score to 21–12. Hagler missed a forty-yard field goal attempt on Carolina's ensuing possession, and the score remained at 21–12 entering the final period of play.

Hagler connected on a forty-one-yard field goal early in the fourth, bringing the Gamecocks to within six points, 21–15. Building on the momentum generated by Carolina's late-second-quarter touchdown, the fire ant defense held Clemson to just one first -down in the third period, sacking Eppley for the safety and securing a Bryant Gilliard interception. Though still trailing, the Gamecocks were surging, and Clemson fans could only watch the clock in its agonizingly slow countdown.

When the Gamecock defense forced a Clemson punt with just over three minutes left, Carolina took possession at their fourteen yard line, eighty-six yards from paydirt. On third and six, quarterback Hold, who had started for the first time all season, hit receiver Chris Wade, who weaved his way along the right sideline for a thirty-six-yard gain, keeping the drive alive just inside Clemson territory. Lewis and Dendy carried for sixteen yards and eighteen yards, respectively, and the Gamecocks were in business, first and ten at the Clemson eleven yard line.

Two Hold keepers picked up nine additional yards, and a Clemson face-mask penalty gave Carolina a first and goal at the Tiger one. Hold kept once again off right tackle, breaking the plane of the goal line for a Gamecock score, 21–21.

Fifty-four seconds remaining.

Scott Hagler trotted onto the field, having connected on forty-two consecutive point after conversions, one shy of the school record. Just as the ball was snapped, yellow flags flew, and Hagler, following through with the kick, missed left. The Clemson crowd roared, but the penalty soon became obvious. Twelve men on the field for the Tigers.

Do-over.

Hagler lined up to kick it again, and this time he was true, giving Carolina a 22–21 lead, its first of the day. Gamecock special teams executed the kickoff brilliantly, as Jay Frye, the grandson of USC's legendary groundskeeper Sarge Frye, tackled Clemson's Ray Williams at the eight yard line, putting the Tigers sixty yards away from realistic field goal range.

Clemson's Eppley completed one of six passes for twenty-two yards to the Clemson thirty, but a fourth-down pass dropped harmlessly beyond its intended target, and Carolina took possession, needing only to take a knee as the clock expired. The Memorial Stadium scoreboard went dark within seconds of time elapsing, but the impotent gesture meant little to jubilant Gamecock players and fans who lingered to celebrate in Death Valley long after the stadium emptied of orange-clad partisans.

Sweet redemption.

The Gamecocks, now 10–1, officially received their Gator Bowl invitation in the visitor's locker room and were greeted as conquering heroes by more than six thousand fans as the team buses arrived at the Roost that evening.

USC's Gator Bowl opponent was the 9–2 Oklahoma State Cowboys of the Big Eight, who had lost their in-state rivalry game to number 2 Oklahoma earlier that day. The Cowboys entered their regular-season finale at 9–1 and ranked third in the country, their only previous loss to powerful Nebraska. The Cowboys were a highly talented team, led by future NFL players quarterback Rusty Hilger and running back Thurman Thomas.

Though Jacksonville was well north of the Florida destination the Gamecocks had hoped for, players and fans looked eagerly to the December 28 matchup and the opportunity for postseason play.

Outgunned at the Gator:
Carolina's Bowl Futility Continues

Seventh-ranked South Carolina and number 9 Oklahoma State had met just once before, a 23–16 Gamecock win in Columbia during the 1979 season. It was the Gamecocks' third visit to the Gator Bowl, having appeared in the inaugural contest in 1946, a 26–14 loss to fellow Southern Conference member Wake Forest, then coached by the exquisitely named Peahead Walker. Carolina returned to Jacksonville for the 1980 contest, a 37–9 dismantling at the hands of Pittsburgh in Heisman Trophy winner George Rogers's final college game.[9]

Following the script of so many games in 1984, the Gamecocks found themselves in a hole and needing a comeback, down 13–0 at the half this time around.

The Cowboys received to start the second half, but a promising drive stalled at the Gamecock twenty-nine when the fire ant defense held on fourth down. The defensive stand shifted momentum Carolina's way, as Hold connected with Eric Poole for a forty-five-yard gain on first down, putting the Gamecocks at the OSU twenty-six. A few plays later, Quinton Lewis threw a perfect halfback pass to Chris Wade for a twenty-four-yard touchdown strike to pull within 13–7 after the Hagler extra point.

The Gamecocks forced a punt on the Cowboy's ensuing possession, but Carolina promptly handed it back on a Lewis fumble. The Gamecock defense held again, and Oklahoma State missed on a forty-yard field goal attempt.

Carolina took just forty seconds and two plays to surge ahead on a fifty-seven-yard touchdown strike by Hold to Ira Hillary. Hagler's point after put the Gamecocks up 14–13 heading into the final period. In a statistical anomaly, Carolina had outscored Oklahoma State 14–0 in the third quarter despite a 13:18 to 1:42 time-of-possession advantage for the Cowboys.

The score remained 14–13 until 1:04 remaining in regulation, when the Cowboys' Hilger found receiver Jamie Harris open in the end zone to cap an efficient eighty-eight-yard drive. OSU went for the two-point conversion and made it, pushing their lead to 21–14.

On the Gamecocks' next and final possession, Hold hit Dendy for a fourteen-yard pickup, then threw a long bomb in to Poole, which appeared to be on target before OSU defensive back Demise Williams stepped in front at the last second for the interception and thirty-four-yard return, ending Carolina's chances of yet another comeback.

It was a disappointing end to a magnificent season. Morrison said following the game from the USC locker room, "Both teams can be proud of this one. And there are some things learned from tonight's game that will go with these young men later in life. I'm still proud of our players' accomplishments."

All-American linebacker senior James Seawright said, "This is not the way we [the seniors] wanted to go out, but I think we accomplished something. We came here to start a tradition, and we did. We can say that we are the best Carolina team ever." He added, "Now, when people ask me where I went to school, I can say, 'South Carolina' and be proud."

South Carolina finished just outside the top ten, at number 11 in the final AP poll, the highest finish in program history. The Gamecocks made a lot of history in that year of fire ants and black magic. Fans spent the off-season reflecting on the thrilling and unexpected ride of 1984—the exploits, the upsets, the personalities, and the unbridled joy shared by so many.

The future seemed bright. Anything seemed possible.

10

The Backside of the Storm

Football Scandal and Basketball Probation Mar Late '80s Success

Certain wind, moisture, and heat conditions were coming together and staying together long enough to form something called Tropical Depression Number Eleven. A day later, Tropical Depression Number Eleven strengthened into a Tropical Storm and was given a name. It was called Hugo, which means heart and mind; a strange name with an Edgar Allan Poe sound about it; it was ominous. It would get stronger and more ominous as the next seven days went by.

—William Price Fox, *Lunatic Wind*

After twelve seasons without a conference home, South Carolina began Metro Conference competition during the 1983–84 basketball season. The new conference home seemed a move in the right direction for a program that had suffered a long decline in results and prominence since departing the ACC. Conference membership would also give the Gamecocks an opportunity for an automatic bid to the NCAA tournament, which had been unavailable since 1971. With a talented and experienced team returning from 1983's twenty-three-win NIT squad, all signs pointed to a bright future for South Carolina basketball under fourth-year head coach Bill Foster.

Despite the loss of team captain Gerald Peacock and forward Kevin Darmody to graduation, most of the Gamecocks' production would return.[1] Most prominent among them was senior forward Jimmy Foster, who once again led in scoring (17.3) and rebounding (8.9) as a junior. Foster also established a new school record for single-season field goal percentage (.611), which still ranks first in program history.

Foster earned honorable mention all-America as a junior and traveled to Australia over the summer with an NIT all-star team. Despite a minor knee injury suffered during the tour that necessitated arthroscopic surgery, he returned at full health for his senior season.

The trip to Australia would not be his last.

While Foster's senior season provided continued highlights to round out a superb career, team successes were rare. A preseason academic casualty to key sixth man and rising senior Kenny Holmes, and an unexpected medical redshirt for six-foot-ten junior Duane Kendall foretold of struggles to come. Foster says of his senior season, "Expectations were big because of the success of the prior season, and then all of a sudden Kenny wasn't there, and it all started to unravel. [Coach] Foster was not as involved after his heart attack. [Assistant coach] Ray Jones was a recruiter, not much of a floor coach. There was Steinwedel, but that season everybody was going in different directions. We had no common purpose, and that was reflected in the way we played."

Indeed, the loss of Holmes haunted the team. The forward from Savannah possessed a deadly baseline jumper and had been responsible for many of the last-second winning baskets in 1982–83. Further, the loss of point guard Peacock's steady leadership and school record 182 assists was sorely missed, as the Gamecocks turned to freshman Michael Foster (no relation to Jimmy or Bill) to run the point. The six-two Foster was a highly regarded recruit from Greensboro and would prove a steady performer for the Gamecocks throughout his career, but he was still a freshman cast into a difficult situation.

Jimmy Foster at USC basketball photo shoot. Of the photo Foster quipped, "That picture captured the only time I ever passed the ball."

South Carolina struggled to a 12–16 record on the season, going 5–9 in Metro Conference play. After fifteen consecutive winning seasons, the program had now suffered its second losing campaign in three years.

As the long season drew to a close on senior night, Jimmy Foster's last home game provided a fitting finale for the blue-collar scrapper in the form of a 70–62 win over Metro foe Southern Mississippi. With five seconds remaining in regulation and the Gamecocks comfortably ahead, Foster took a half-court pass from fellow senior Scott Sanderson and went for a dunk attempt before the Golden Eagles' Kenny Siler fouled him hard at the basket. A melee ensued between Foster and Southern Mississippi's James Williams, which spilled over into press row. Both benches cleared before coaches and Coliseum security eventually managed to separate the combatants.

As officials did their best to restore order, the pep band broke into a raucous war chant, shouting rhythmically, "Don't mess with Jimmy, don't mess with Jimmy!" Paramedics took one spectator away after she was pressed against her seat by fans leaning forward to see the fight. Security ushered Siler to the visiting locker room as boos rained down, after which Foster exited to a rafter-rattling, minutes-long standing ovation. He finished with nineteen points and eight rebounds in a classic lunch-pail performance.

The Gamecocks and Foster lost their final two games, a nine-point loss at DePaul and a seven-point defeat to Florida State in the Metro Conference tournament, the program's first conference tournament game since winning the ACC in 1971.

Foster finished his career with 1,745 points, good for third in program history. The final of his 10 rebounds in the Metro tournament game gave him an even 1,000 for his career, one of only five Gamecocks (named in the Introduction) to achieve that milestone. He remains one of only three players in program history to reach both the 1,000 point and 1,000 rebound thresholds. His .596 career field goal percentage still stands as a program standard.

The "Dick Dyer Incident" Leads to Startling Revelations

Foster's celebrity in the Columbia area was a key that opened many doors. He was handsome, with an easy smile. Most who knew him described him as affable and popular. People wanted to be around him and to do things for him, favors he was happy to accept. These favors were not unique to Foster, nor were they unique to student-athletes at USC. In many ways the atmosphere surrounding major college athletics in the 1980s reflected the excesses of broader society. For the best athletes, and those open to such things, the world was their oyster. As long as discretion ruled, the good times rolled.

In the summer of 1986, some of those chickens—or gamecocks, as it were—came home to roost.

Columbia-area Mercedes-Benz dealership Dick Dyer and Associates filed a complaint against Foster in August 1985, alleging the South Carolina player had borrowed a 1984 Mercedes 380 SL from them, promising to return it in three days. Foster failed to return the car as agreed, and the vehicle was repossessed in Foster's hometown of Greenville several months later. Charges were also filed against Foster by the Fifth Circuit solicitor's office in Columbia, and a trial was set for June 1986.

By the time of the trial, Foster was playing professional basketball in Australia. His attorney, Rus Templeton, said he had not been in contact with Foster about the trial, and his client would be unlikely to return for the hearing. Foster was tried in absentia and convicted by a Richland County jury of breach of trust with fraudulent intent, a felony, which carried a maximum penalty of ten years in prison.

The only witness to appear during the trial was David Thornton, a Dick Dyer sales associate. Thornton testified that Foster had completed the paperwork to purchase, not borrow, the car on June 26, 1985. According to Thornton, Foster claimed his mother controlled his money, so he would need to take the car, valued at $36,000 (approximately $87,500 in 2022 dollars), to Greensboro to show her to secure the funds for purchase. Foster, according to testimony, agreed to return to Columbia with the funds in three days. Thornton said he agreed to release the car because of Foster's relationship with the dealership. Foster had borrowed cars on two previous occasions and in both instances brought them back in time. Despite Thornton's testimony about completed sales paperwork, no such documentation was entered into evidence.

Judge John Hamilton Smith issued a sealed sentence, which was to be opened when Foster returned to the United States, at which point he would be arrested and the sentence revealed.

Reached for comment by Dan Foster (no relation) of the *Greenville News,* Foster confirmed the loans and said he had also been loaned cars by a Greenville dealership while playing at South Carolina. Foster the player said Coach Bill Foster had been unaware of the loans, and he had no intention of harming the Gamecock basketball program. He stated further that he did "not want to be the one to open the doors, but if I go down for this thing, I'm going to take a lot of people with me."

A media frenzy ensued over the coming weeks, leading to further revelations from Foster about alleged improprieties, both within the basketball program and by prominent boosters. In a *Columbia Record* article, Foster alleged he received gifts of cash, deals on loans, cars to drive, free meals at restaurants, and weekend trips to Myrtle Beach courtesy of boosters while a student-athlete at South Carolina. USC boosters "answered all of my wishes," Foster said.

He pointed as an example to the DePaul game in early March 1983, a Gamecock win, saying an unknown booster shook his hand and handed him an envelope with ten one hundred dollar bills in it. A former girlfriend of Foster's, Susan Kensey, confirmed his story in an interview with the *Hilton Head Island Packet.*

A few days later, yet another Foster allegation leaked out, this time concerning an operation overseen by a former Gamecock assistant basketball coach in which players were able to sell their ticket allotments to boosters for cash. Players were issued four books of complimentary tickets for home games in those days, which they could distribute to friends and family. Players who participated in the scheme were alleged to receive as much as a 100 percent markup over face value. There was no direct interaction between players and boosters—all money went through the assistant coach.

Bill Foster had resigned as USC head coach following the 1985–86 season and by this time had taken the same position at Northwestern University of the Big Ten. Reached for comment in Chicago at the time, the former Gamecock coach denied knowledge of any of the allegations. Four other former Gamecock players confirmed the setup: Duane Kendall and three other players who spoke with media outlets on the condition of anonymity.

Over a period of three weeks, Foster's allegations unleashed three separate and distinct scandals on the University of South Carolina and its men's basketball program: the allegations of car loans; the separate implications of illicit money, meals, and favors from boosters; and a third allegation of the prohibited sale of student-athlete-allotted tickets for profit, managed by an assistant coach. It was the last allegation that attracted the attention of NCAA investigators. The University of South Carolina, led by athletics director Bob Marcum, launched its own investigation and cooperated fully with the NCAA.

On March 3, 1987, the NCAA's Committee on Infractions announced the results of its investigation and the associated penalties for the Gamecock program. The violations revealed six findings, including:

- the loan/lease of cars to a prospective athlete and enrolled student-athletes;
- provision of transportation to or from Columbia at no cost for a prospect and several enrolled athletes;
- short-term lodging at no cost for several perspective athletes;
- provision of meals at no cost at several restaurants in Columbia;
- out-of-season practices in the summer and fall of 1984, involving prospective athletes and enrolled student-athletes and men's basketball coaching staff; and
- sale of student-athletes' complimentary tickets by members of the men's basketball coaching staff

The report found that following Coach Bill Foster's health issues in the wake of his heart attack in December 1982, he delegated much of the day-to-day operation and supervision of the Gamecock men's basketball program to members of his staff. During the 1984 recruiting season and 1984–85 academic year, the absence of institutional constraints permitted members of the basketball staff to engage in most of the violations reported to the committee. Although Foster's accusations of improprieties had prompted the investigation, most, if not all, of the violations described in the NCAA findings occurred after he had departed campus.

The NCAA imposed sanctions on the South Carolina basketball program, including public reprimand and censure, a two-year period of probation, and a postseason ban for the 1987–88 season. With Bill Foster moved on to Northwestern, new head coach George Felton, a Gamecock letterman from the McGuire era and former top assistant under Bobby Cremins at Georgia Tech, was left to deal with the aftermath of a mess he had no hand in creating.

Of the Dick Dyer incident, Foster now says, "I drove their loaner cars for two of the four years I was at Carolina. I absolutely didn't bring it back [the Mercedes in 1985]. I didn't think it was a big deal at the time," he said. "So I'll plead guilty to stupidity or whatever. I don't know how it got to that point. I wasn't there at the time [of the trial]. Maybe it was somebody seeing me drive a Mercedes around Greenville, and of course, it wasn't like I didn't want everybody to see me driving it around. I wasn't the smartest, you know. I take all the responsibility."

Foster continues, "They probably intended to sell me the car, and they figured they could get me financed. They probably figured 'Hey, he's going to play [professional] basketball somewhere.' But I kept it to the point where I think they realized they weren't going to be able to get it financed, and that's when they came and got it."

Of the conviction and sealed sentence, Foster says, "I'm not sure if it's settled or not. I'm pretty sure I'm not on the FBI's most-wanted list. I don't think anybody wanted to put Jimmy Foster in jail," he says, referring to himself in third person, as he does frequently when talking of his days at USC. "I don't think that was the point. I just think . . . I blew it. That's what it came down to. I think it got to the point where they [Dick Dyer and law enforcement] didn't have any other place to go. I think if cooler heads had prevailed, mine especially, it wouldn't have ended up like that. I have no idea what it [the sealed sentence] said. I would be curious to know. It may not even exist anymore if you tried to find it. I don't think there's anybody left alive that knows what it said."

Fifth Circuit solicitor Jim Anders, now deceased, said in 1986 that he had placed the notice of Foster's legal status in the database of the National Crime Information Center, which would alert passport authorities to his fugitive status if he tried to reenter the US. However, according to a Richland County Sheriff's Department spokesperson in 1987, the warrant was deleted from the database on December 24, 1986. "No one in this office deleted the warrant, and I don't know who did," the spokesperson said.

The sealed sentence is another mystery. The *State*'s Bob Gillespie interviewed Richland County clerk of court Barbara Scott for a June 1997 article inquiring into the sentence. When Scott retrieved the document from court archives, the envelope was open. "The sentence is in there, but it's no longer sealed," Scott said. "There should be a record of why it was opened, but there's no record. If it was never opened and published, it should still be sealed." Scott speculated the envelope could have been opened by mistake. But as with many things in Foster's story, time and uncertainty have obscured the details.

Years of Regret and Rambling

In 1997, at the age of thirty-five, Jimmy Foster contacted the *State*'s Gillespie to say his life had changed. He claimed to have a wife and ten-month-old son in another state. Yet he said his fondest memories were of his four years at USC. He expressed regret for the lying and cheating and the hurt he had caused family and friends. "I've got a lot of fences to mend," he told Gillespie.

Of the bridges he burned in South Carolina by way of his allegations, Foster said in 1986 that it didn't matter to him. Because of the warrant awaiting him, he said then he was planning to marry an Australian woman and become a citizen there. But he told Gillespie in 1997 that he never forgot South Carolina and expressed a desire to mend fences in Columbia. "I'm not the same person I was then. I think I've matured. I do realize I made a mistake. It was my fault. I implicated people. I didn't make any friends. But I was cocky. I was in Australia, and didn't think I wanted to come back," Foster explained to Gillespie.

He lived a vagabond life for years, spending time in Southern California, Missouri, Montana, and the Wilmington, North Carolina, area.

He tells a story of living for a time in Malibu, where, he says, "I was the only one living there that didn't have any money." In a bar one night, he struck up a conversation with a local surfer. Foster had learned to surf but said with a laugh, "tall people are not conducive to surfing." After numerous drinks, the surfer offered Foster a place to stay for the night so he wouldn't have to drive. Walking out of the bar a limousine waited for them, which Foster says "impressed nobody, because everybody has a limo in Malibu."

He continued, "The limo took us into the hills and to the gates of this mansion." After drinking late into the night, he settled into one of the "million guest rooms." He says, "The next morning I was in the kitchen and started looking at all these gold albums on the wall, and about that time, Olivia Newton-John comes around the corner." The surfer, as it turned out, was Matt Lattanzi, Newton-John's first husband. Foster says of Newton-John that "she was polite, nice. She cooked us breakfast."

He tells another story of befriending Martin and Charlie Sheen, both noted basketball fans. "They did their research. They knew I was who I said

I was. And I treated them just like regular people, and they wanted to spend time with me as much as I wanted to spend time with them."

Foster describes these stories as "nonreality moments for a country boy like me." One could be forgiven for doubting the validity of these tales. He has been known to spin a yarn. But he tells them convincingly, off the cuff, with just enough obscurity in the details to ring true.

Peace in Northern California and Dreams of South Carolina

Foster now lives in Northern California. He drives an eighteen-wheeler and says he finds satisfaction in the job. "It gives me a lot of time to be by myself and think." He says the materialistic tendencies of his youth, the desire to drive fancy cars, to see and be seen, are long gone. He owns a simple cabin and drives an old pickup—an existence fitting for a guy nicknamed "Truck" back in his playing days. The pace of Northern California suits him much better than the hustle and glitter of Southern California. There is a verdant natural beauty there that reminds him of his native environs in the Carolina foothills.

He says now that he has never married and has no children. He has a girlfriend who keeps him on his toes and encouraged him to engage in the interviews for this book. He says he is at peace, and although he can't do everything he used to do on the basketball court, he is in the best shape of his life. He plays the occasional pickup game. He still likes the feel of a basketball in his hands, still harbors that competitive fire.

He says from time to time over the years, he has driven through Columbia on the way to or from visiting his parents. He has on occasion stopped his car behind the Carolina Coliseum along Park Street where he used to enter the arena as a player.

"When I sit there and close my eyes, all the good memories come back." He remembers the games, which he describes as "heaven," the camaraderie with teammates, the feeling of being young and talented, with limitless possibilities.

When asked what he would say to former teammates and coaches, to fans, and to the university community if given the opportunity, he says, "Thanks for the best four years of my life. I'm sorry for the way it ended. I just want to be remembered for what I did on the court. I loved to entertain the crowd, and the fans drove me. I lived my life like I played, my emotions on my sleeve. That had to be harnessed, and that took some time."

After a pause, he added, "I love the University of South Carolina."

Like all of us, Jimmy Foster has made mistakes. Compared to most of us, his stage was a little bigger, the lights a little hotter, and the repercussions more severe. Foster has paid a steep price for the mistakes he made as a young man. He spent the bulk of the last four decades effectively disowned by his university and by a program to which he gave so much. He says the most disappointing part was when he did not receive an invitation to attend a commemoration of the program's one hundredth anniversary in 2008. He calls that "the most hurtful thing."

Even so, he dreams of returning to Columbia and of a return to the program in some fashion. He says he has no great desire to visit the "new place," twenty-year-old Colonial Life Arena but would love nothing more than to walk through the old Coliseum, which he calls "Frank's House," where he spent so many of his younger days and nights.

Thirty-five years of Congaree River water has flowed under the Blossom Street Bridge since the debacle of 1986. Foster readily acknowledges his mistakes. And to be certain, the program for which he played was not blameless in his saga.

One could argue it is time to leave those things in the past, that youthful indiscretions nearly four decades old could and should be set aside in the name of embracing one of the program's very best.

Foster turned sixty in January 2021. For a long time, he told those closest to him that he would never again discuss his days at the University of South Carolina. That changed.

Time has a way of accomplishing things like that.

Successful 1987, 1988 Seasons Belie Trouble Ahead for Morrison's Program

Despite great expectations heading into the 1985 season after a ten-win result in 1984, the Gamecocks faced a rebuilding year after heavy losses to graduation. The season began promisingly enough, in a 56–17 rout of the Citadel, but the Gamecocks struggled to put away a scrappy Appalachian State team in week two, winning a close one 20–13.[2] Losses to number 19 Michigan, Georgia, and Pitt followed, the last of those an ugly 42–7 pasting at the hands of the Panthers in Pittsburgh. If style points and memorable plays count for anything, though, the Gamecocks' lone touchdown against Pitt was one for the ages.

On the first play of the second quarter, facing a long third down from their own twenty yard line, the Gamecocks lined up for what would be the most memorable play of a mostly forgettable season. Under heavy pressure from Pitt defenders, USC quarterback Mike Hold, as the *Columbia Record*'s Doug Nye described it, "squirmed and slithered" away from would-be tacklers, scrambling backward all the way to the Gamecocks' own end zone before finding space to unleash a 60-yard bomb toward intended receiver Anthony Smith. The ball bounced off Smith's shoulder pads and into the waiting arms of Raynard Brown, who dashed 40 yards for the score. The play was recorded as an 80-yard passing touchdown but covered closer to 125 yards in total.

Carolina next picked up a homecoming win over Duke, in which sophomore wide receiver Sterling Sharpe took the second-half kickoff 102 yards for a score, tying an NCAA record and revealing to Gamecock fans a glimpse his brilliant career to come. Carolina next traveled to Greenville, North Carolina, for the first time ever and enjoyed a dominant afternoon versus the outmatched East Carolina University Pirates. A close home loss to NC State and a blowout loss in Tallahassee to FSU preceded a narrow 34–31 win over Navy in what was a revenge game of sorts but felt more frustrating than satisfying for players, coaches, and fans.

South Carolina and Clemson, both 5–5, squared off before a record crowd of 74,025 at Williams-Brice Stadium for the annual season-ending rivalry game on a sunny and cool afternoon. A bid to the Independence Bowl in Shreveport hung in the balance as an additional incentive for the winner. It looked promising early for the Gamecocks, who held a 14–3 lead five minutes into the second quarter. But Clemson tied the score at 14–14 before intermission, and second-half turnovers doomed a hard-fought Gamecock effort. Clemson, having concluded their three-year NCAA probation, collected a

24–17 win and punched their ticket to Shreveport, while Morrison's club remained at home with a disappointing 5–6 record.

It was later revealed that representatives from the Peach Bowl were on hand for the game and were prepared to offer a bid to the losing team if Northwestern upset 5–5–1 Illinois in their season finale. Illinois prevailed, however, earning the bid and preventing an awkward scenario in which the Gamecocks would have been presented a bowl bid despite a losing record, which the *State*'s Herman Helms rightly called a "ridiculous situation."

If it could ever be said that a 3–6–2 season was fun and entertaining, 1986 was that season. Offensive coordinator Frank Sadler switched the Gamecocks from the run-oriented offense that had been in place since Morrison's arrival in 1983 to the pass-oriented "run and shoot" offensive scheme. Despite a losing record, the Gamecock offense ranked third in the nation in passing and sixteenth in total offense.

Running Sadler's new offense was a highly acclaimed redshirt freshman quarterback out of Page High School in Greensboro, Todd Ellis. The freshman thrived in the new offensive scheme, piling up an incredible 3,020 passing yards on the season, still a South Carolina record and an NCAA freshman record at the time. Ellis ranked third place on the program's career passing list behind Tommy Suggs (4,916) and Jeff Grantz (3,440) after just one season. His twenty touchdown passes on the season was second nationally, only surpassed by Heisman Trophy winner Vinny Testaverde's twenty-six. Working through a complex new offensive system as a freshman quarterback, Ellis had difficulties as well, throwing twenty-two interceptions on the season. However, his performance was roundly praised, earning first-team freshman all-America honors from the *Football News* and second-team all-America honors from the AP.

Ellis enjoyed a bevy of highly talented targets, including deep ball threat Ryan Bethea and emerging star Sterling Sharpe, as well as returning starter Danny Smith. Sophomore tailback Harold Green balanced the pass-forward attack.

Defensive coordinator Tom Gadd's unit had talent, including noseguard Roy Hart, linebacker Derrick Little, and defensive stalwart Brad Edwards, but struggled to contain opponents all season. Morrison made a change in coordinators following 1986, tapping Joe Lee Dunn, who had previously coached under him at Chattanooga and New Mexico.

Ellis and the run-and-shoot offense debuted in a 34–14 loss at home against number 3 Miami on national television. The Hurricanes would go undefeated during the regular season before losing 14–10 in the national championship game to Penn State. A win versus Western Carolina was bookended by losses at Virginia and to Georgia in Columbia, giving the Gamecocks a 1–3 start on the season.

Third-ranked Nebraska rolled into Columbia on an unseasonably hot first Saturday in October, and the grain-fed Cornhuskers expected an easy win. Before a near-capacity crowd, the Gamecocks were valiant throughout, holding a 24–20 lead and the football with 3:09 remaining. But a Raynard Brown fumble set up a Nebraska score to go ahead 27–24 with 1:26. Brown redeemed himself with a forty-one-yard return on the ensuing kickoff. A face-mask penalty and two Ellis passes later, USC was threatening at the Cornhusker nineteen, before an Ellis interception ended any hopes of what would have been a massive upset. Despite the loss, which dropped Carolina's record to 1–4 on the season, coaches and fans were encouraged with the team's fight and tenacity throughout.

South Carolina next tied Virginia Tech on the road, 27–27, and picked up win number two versus East Carolina, 38–3, preceding the annual matchup with sixteenth-ranked NC State in Raleigh. The Gamecocks, up 22–17, stopped the Wolfpack on the last play of regulation, but as Carolina players and fans began to run onto Carter-Finley Field in celebration, a defensive offside penalty was called. Since the game cannot end on a defensive penalty, NC State had one last play with no time on the play clock. State quarterback Erik Kramer threw a desperation thirty-three-yard pass into the Gamecock end zone, where Wolfpack split end Danny Peebles, covered by several USC defenders, somehow came down with the ball, handing State a miracle finish and South Carolina a devastating gut punch.

Carolina led FSU at halftime of the following game, but the Seminoles went on a 32–7 second-half romp to win going away, 45–28. A win over Wake Forest followed to improve Carolina's overall record to 3–6–1 on the strange season, ahead of the annual tilt with number 19 Clemson at Death Valley.

Gamecock football players Sterling Sharpe (2), Todd Ellis (9), and
Ryan Bethea during press day at Williams-Brice Stadium in 1987.
Courtesy of the *State* Newspaper Archive, Richland County Public Library.

Carolina surged to a 21–18 lead at the half, and the game looked to be a high-scoring affair before both defenses battened down in the second half. The only second-half score was a David Treadwell 31-yard field goal with 2:51 remaining to knot the score at 21. The game ended in Carolina's second tie of the season, after the Gamecocks could not score on their final possession. Carolina's efforts were highlighted by a Brad Edwards 61-yard interception return for a touchdown in the second quarter, a feat he would repeat against the Tigers a year later, and by Sterling Sharpe's 167 receiving yards and touchdown.

The Gamecocks had to settle for mostly moral victories in 1986, but the pieces were in place for better things in 1987 and beyond.

✗   ✗   ✗

After two frustrating seasons, South Carolina tasted success again in 1987. Morrison fielded arguably an even more talent-rich team in that season than the ten-win squad in 1984. With a seasoned Ellis back at quarterback and an offensive unit now well accustomed to the high-octane run-and-shoot scheme, USC was explosive throughout. The pass-happy Gamecocks averaged nearly thirty points per contest through the first nine games of the season before faltering in the final two.

After opening wins versus Appalachian State and Western Carolina, the Gamecocks dropped two difficult road contests, 13–6 versus number 20 Georgia and 30–21 in another scrappy performance versus the number 2 Cornhuskers in Lincoln.

From there the Gamecocks went on a tear, averaging thirty-eight points per game over the next six contests while holding opponents to under ten points per game on average. Carolina went 4–0 versus ACC teams, 5–0 versus teams from the state of North Carolina, defeated Virginia and Virginia Tech by a combined score of 98–20, and enjoyed a particularly pleasing 48–0 shutout of NC State before a rowdy, vengeful Williams-Brice Stadium crowd.

The highlight of the season, though, came the Saturday before Thanksgiving, when the number 12 Gamecocks hosted their old rivals the eighth-ranked Clemson Tigers on a cold and raucous night in Columbia. Gamecock fans were in full voice for the contest, which was televised nationally on ESPN. Clemson struck first on a long touchdown drive in the first quarter. Two Collin Mackie field goals from USC made the score 7–6 Clemson at the half.[3]

From there the Gamecock defense took control of the game, shutting out the high-powered Clemson offense through the final two periods. South Carolina surged ahead on a Harold Green rushing touchdown to make it 13–7 with 3:58 to go in the third quarter. The scoring play was set up by a seventy-seven-yard strike from Ellis to Ryan Bethea, which electrified the already rowdy crowd.

A series of punts followed until Carolina's next score, which came on a Brad Edwards interception of a Rodney Williams pass, returned forty yards for a touchdown. The Williams-Brice crowd went into delirium as Edwards sprinted to the Tiger end zone, putting the Gamecocks up by the final margin, 20–7, after a Mackie extra point. Feeling confident and enjoying the moment, Carolina fans taunted Williams during the next possession, chanting "Rod-ney" repeatedly, seeming to rattle the accomplished Tiger quarterback into tossing another interception, also to Edwards, which sealed

Safety Brad Edwards (27) in 1987. Courtesy of the *State*
Newspaper Archive, Richland County Public Library.

the game. Edwards's performance of two interceptions and one touchdown equaled his efforts against the Tigers in the 21–21 tie of 1986.

A blurb in the *State* noted the absence of USC defensive lineman Tommy Chaiken for the game, citing the explanation of coaches that Chaiken had returned to his Bethesda, Maryland, home due to "personal reasons." The true reason behind Chaiken's absence would gain further clarity in the form of a damning *Sports Illustrated* exposé the following season.

In a scheduling oddity, the Gamecocks had one more regular-season game left after Clemson, another top-ten matchup, this time on the road against number 2 Miami on December 5. The Hurricanes prevailed 20–16 in a wild, fight-marred game. Officials did little to control the jawing by the Hurricanes, who were infamous for their "bad-boys" persona and intimidation tactics during the era. The number 8 Gamecocks, not a group to back down, returned in kind, until talking turned to brawling with 9:18 left in the final period, after Miami defensive end Dan Stubbs slung Ellis to the ground well after whistles

Head football coach Joe Morrison exits the field following USC victory
over Clemson in 1987. Courtesy of the *State* Newspaper Archive,
Richland County Public Library.

sounded on a dead-ball penalty. A melee ensued, which took officials several minutes to sort out. The Gamecocks were never able to get anything going from there, and the Hurricanes escaped with their undefeated season intact.

South Carolina, meanwhile, dropped to 8–3, with all three of their losses coming on the road, to Nebraska and Miami, both ranked number 2 at the time, and to number 20 Georgia. The Gamecocks went bowling in Jacksonville for yet another Gator Bowl matchup, this time with ninth-ranked LSU of the Southeastern Conference. The Tigers dominated Carolina, winning 30–13 in a game that was not as close as the score indicated.

It was a bitter ending to one of the greatest seasons in program history.

✗ ✗ ✗

The 1988 Gamecock team, Morrison's sixth in Columbia, steamrolled through the first six games of the season, outscoring opponents by a combined 170–43. The stretch was highlighted by a 23–10 dismantling of sixth-ranked Georgia on a scalding hot day in Columbia. South Carolina's signal caller and Heisman Trophy hopeful, junior Todd Ellis, connected on twenty-eight of forty-three attempts for 321 yards and a touchdown, marking nine games with 300 or more passing yards in twenty-seven outings. The touchdown connection was a 36-yard strike to sensational freshman receiver Robert Brooks, who made a spectacular one-handed grab in the corner of the south end zone.

Carolina's defense played dominant football, holding the vaunted Bulldog rushing game, which averaged a national-best 355 yards per game, to a paltry 102 yards. The Gamecocks jumped from number 14 to eighth on the strength of their Georgia upset and remained at that position after wins over Appalachian State and Virginia Tech.

The 6–0 Gamecocks rolled into week seven at 1–4 Georgia Tech. The Yellow Jackets' only win was a 24–10 decision over Morrison's former school, Division I-AA Tennessee-Chattanooga, in the season opener. The Gamecocks were fifteen-point favorites. The Yellow Jackets, who had not beaten a Division I team in fifteen tries, were, as Herman Helms described then, a "struggling, frustrated, basket case of athletes."

A total of 45,105 spectators at Atlanta's Grant Field looked on in bewildered awe as a formerly hapless Tech squad embarrassed the number 8 Gamecocks 34–0. It was the first shutout loss for the Carolina program since 1981. The *State*'s Teddy Heffner called it "the worst 30 minutes in the history of Gamecock football," adding, "and the second half wasn't much better." Helms agreed, calling the performance "shameful." Tech, who had averaged thirteen points through five games, could not be stopped, pushing the proud Gamecock defense around seemingly at will. Morrison said of Tech after the game, "Like [Georgia's] Vince Dooley said a few weeks ago at our place, Georgia Tech took us to the woodshed."

How to explain such an unlikely reversal? In retrospect the Gamecocks had narrowly escaped Virginia Tech with a 26–24 victory a week before, and they had not been sharp against Appalachian State. The excitement over the Gamecocks' season-opening win against North Carolina had been tempered as well by the Tar Heels' winless record through six games. USC was clearly not the eighth-best team in the country but just as clearly was not as bad as they looked against the Yellow Jackets. There was suddenly a cloud over the

Carolina program that only grew darker and more ominous as the team navigated an open date and two-week break before another road trip to NC State.

Steroid Abuse Allegations Rock the Gamecock Program

It was Tuesday, October 18, when press members received an advance copy of the story that revealed allegations of a seedy underworld of steroid abuse within the Gamecock football program. Former South Carolina defensive lineman Tommy Chaikin worked with *Sports Illustrated* senior writer Rick Telander to produce an explosive fifteen-page piece titled "The Nightmare of Steroids" for the magazine's October 24 issue. The article painted a lurid picture of an anything-goes culture within Morrison's program, wherein coaches ignored and in some cases even encouraged the use of banned performance-enhancing drugs.

Chaikin alleged that he took steroids for three years while at Carolina and that fellow players, team doctors, and coaches knew about it. A tacit permissiveness pervaded the program. Of his position coach, Jim Washburn, Chaikin wrote, "He told me to 'do what you have to do, take what you have to take.'" He further alleged that as many as half the team were taking steroids during the 1986 season and as many as a third were taking cocaine and other drugs.

Chaikin wrote that by the fall of 1987, he suffered from destabilizing depression and suicidal thoughts. The article opened with him sitting in his room at USC's Roost dormitory the morning before the 1987 Carolina-Clemson game. He had a loaded .357 Magnum revolver and was ready to end it all. His father and brother had flown in from their hometown of Bethesda earlier than usual for the game after Chaikin had spoken with his sister a few days earlier, asking for help. Upon seeing the condition his son was in, Chaikin's father promptly put him on a plane back to Bethesda. Chaikin wrote in the piece, "I can't blame others for my mistakes, certainly not for making me take dangerous drugs. But I still think of myself as someone who started out as just a normal guy, a hard worker, a studier, a kid who loved sports. And I feel part of the trouble comes from things outside of me—the pressures of college football, the attitudes of over-zealous coaches and our just-take-a-pill-to-cure-anything society."

Reached for comment on the piece by Gillespie and Heffner, several players acknowledged Chaikin's steroid use but denied the involvement of coaches. Morrison and Washburn declined comment. USC president Holderman released a statement saying, "The University of South Carolina deeply regrets the personal tragedy of Tommy Chaikin. Since earlier this year, the university has taken a variety of positive steps to strengthen our drug-testing and wellness program and assure that as far as possible, such a tragedy should never reoccur here."

Indeed, in the spring of 1988, former USC athletics director Bob Marcum had been dismissed when an internal report indicated that the drug testing program he oversaw was a "sham." King Dixon had been brought in as interim AD after the brief tenure of Dick Bestwick. Dixon's primary charge was to implement a more rigorous drug testing program. He was promoted to full-time athletics director in the days following the *Sports Illustrated* article, and his leadership of USC's efforts to cooperate with NCAA investigators paid dividends in USC's search for a conference home a few years later. For now, though, the Gamecocks faced a football season on the brink.

Besieged during a wild ten days of reporting and distraction over the steroids scandal, including comments from Fifth Circuit solicitor Jim Anders, who said a grand jury would be convened to examine Chaikin's allegations, Gamecock players and coaches did their best to shut out the noise and circle the wagons. South Carolina was in freefall in the AP poll since the Georgia Tech loss, dropping from eighth to seventeenth ahead of their October 29 game against NC State in Raleigh. What had started so promisingly seemed to be on the verge of collapse. For one week, at least, the Gamecocks came together for one of their best performances of the year.

Before a wildly hostile Carter-Finley Stadium crowd of 54,800, the Gamecocks rallied to stifle a strong NC State team in a nationally televised evening contest. The Wolfpack entered the game with a sizable chip on their shoulders after their 48–0 loss in Columbia the prior season. Unranked despite a 6–1 record and a win versus number 9 Clemson the week before, Dick Sheridan's Wolfpack team was eager to prove themselves on a national stage. The South Carolina–NC State rivalry had grown heated since State's controversial 27–21 win in Raleigh two years earlier, and the Wolfpack partisans were in full voice for the prime-time contest.

State boasted the nation's second-rated defense coming into the game, but it was the Gamecock defenders who rose up and redeemed themselves after their anemic display against Georgia Tech. Carolina sophomore linebacker Patrick Hinton sparked the Gamecocks' stingy performance with a fumble recovery and three interceptions, the first of which resulted in an eighty-three-yard return for a touchdown. The Gamecock offense dominated time of possession, 40:26 to 19:24, keeping the Wolfpack offense off the field for most of the evening and subduing the rowdy Carter-Finley crowd.

The Gamecocks carried a slim 13–7 lead until a twenty-yard touchdown strike from Ellis to speedy receiver Eddie Miller at the 8:54 mark of the fourth quarter. A Collin Mackie field goal with 1:15 left pushed the final margin to 23–7 USC. Gamecock players standing along sideline kept their helmets on late in the game, as frustrated Wolfpack fans threw cups, ice, and other detritus in their general direction. The Carolina band played "Na Na Hey Hey, Goodbye" to the delight of celebrating Gamecock fans clustered in the north end zone stands. It was that kind of night in Raleigh.

The win provided much-needed relief for the embattled Gamecocks, pushing their record to 7–1 and delivering to Morrison his one hundredth career victory. The relief, though, was fleeting.

South Carolina improved two spots to number 15 in the AP rankings ahead of another nationally televised contest, this time at home versus number 5 FSU. The Gamecocks carried a thirteen-game home winning streak into the contest, and a vocal capacity crowd looked to cheer the Gamecocks to win number eight. Kickoff proved to be the high-water mark for the Gamecocks on this evening, as the Seminoles dominated every facet of the game, winning 59–0 and handing Carolina its worst home loss in program history. The dispiriting defeat dropped the Gamecocks out of the polls for the first time all season.

Carolina overpowered a 3–6 Navy team the following week, but the Gamecock offense couldn't find the end zone for the third time in four contests. The Gamecocks scored on an Antonio Walker blocked punt returned for a touchdown and on four Mackie field goals to make the final 19–6. Despite the eighth win of the season, which equaled the second-best total in program history, optimism was hard to come by as the Gamecocks traveled to Clemson for their annual season-ending grudge match.

Clemson controlled the game throughout with strong defense and steady play from quarterback Rodney Williams. The Clemson effort received ample help in the form of three first-half fumbles and a second-half interception from a charitable Gamecock offense. Robert Brooks scored Carolina's first touchdown in ten quarters with a twenty-yard reception just before the half, but a late Mackie field goal was the only other scoring USC could muster in the 29–10 Clemson win.

In the throes of a late-season slide, the 8–3 Gamecocks received a bid to the Liberty Bowl in frigid Memphis, where they faced Indiana of the Big Ten. Carolina lost its eighth bowl appearance in as many tries, as the Hoosiers controlled the game throughout, steamrolling for 575 yards, while holding the Gamecocks to 153. For the fourth time in five contests, the Gamecock offense failed to cross the end zone. Carolina's only scores came on another Antonio Walker blocked punt, which Mike Tolbert scooped up for a thirty-four-yard third-quarter touchdown, and a forty-three-yard Mackie field goal later in the same period.

With a still-simmering steroids scandal and late-season collapse, Carolina's eight wins belied one of the uglier seasons in the history of Gamecock athletics.

Moreover, new athletics director King Dixon faced a galling dilemma in what to do with his head football coach, who remained popular despite recent setbacks. It was a dilemma that would be resolved in a most unexpected and unfortunate way.

Fade to Black

It was the first Sunday night in February 1989. Gamecock head football coach Joe Morrison gathered with his close friend and defensive coordinator Joe Lee Dunn, attorney Ed "Punky" Holler, and businessman Ken Wheat for their twice-weekly racquetball game on a court beneath the west stands of Williams-Brice Stadium. The games typically pitted the coaches, Morrison and Dunn, versus Holler and Wheat, both of whom were Gamecock letter-men from the Bass and Dietzel years, respectively.

In the days following the 1988 season, media and fan speculation swirled over Morrison's future with the program. Former athletics director Bob Marcum, the man who hired Morrison, had been dismissed in March of that year after a two-week internal investigation determined that the drug testing program under his direction had been a sham. Since that time, Dick Bestwick, a former assistant athletics director at the University of Georgia, had been hired as Gamecock AD, only to take a medical leave of absence six months later because of overwork and job-related stress. Upon Bestwick's departure, President Holderman appointed Gamecock letterman King Dixon as interim athletics director. Three days after the Chaikin article, Dixon's interim title was removed, and he officially took the helm of USC athletics.

Holderman and the board of trustees gave Dixon a mandate to clean up the program and guide the university toward membership in an all-sports conference. Dixon, a retired Marine Corps lieutenant colonel, called the appointment "probably one of the greatest challenges I've ever had, except leading young Marines into combat." During his interim role, Dixon had been openly critical of what he characterized as a lack of discipline within the USC athletics department. "If we need to take some action, we're going to do it," he said. "It would appear we need to do something."

With the scrutiny of a new boss and the weight of an ongoing steroids scandal, which included an inquiry into possible criminal activity within the USC program by the Fifth Circuit solicitor's office and State Law Enforcement Division, Morrison's future at South Carolina was in doubt. A lifelong smoker who had undergone balloon angioplasty to relieve a heart valve blockage several years prior, the fifty-one-year-old Morrison's health was in question as well. Compounding matters, he had suffered from flu symptoms in the days leading up to his standing Sunday evening racquetball matchup.

The match went on as scheduled, after which Morrison had trouble breathing and struggled to cool down, though initially he was still alert and talking with Holler, Dunn, and Wheat. Dunn summoned team trainer Terry Lewis and Dr. Robert Peele to the stadium to examine Morrison, and the coach agreed to go to the hospital for further observation. Before leaving,

Morriosn insisted on taking a shower, where he collapsed. "He looked bad," Dunn told the *State*'s Bob Gillespie in a 2009 article marking the twentieth anniversary of Morrison's passing. "I went to call an ambulance. Then Joe started making all kinds of sounds. When I pulled the curtain back, he was stiff as a board, blue from waist to head."

Peele and Lewis immediately started performing CPR, which paramedics continued upon their arrival at the stadium. Morrison was transported to nearby Providence Hospital, arriving still unconscious at 8:44 PM. By 9:03 PM, doctors pronounced him dead. Peele told reporters in the coming days, "I came over and looked at his heart and checked his blood pressure, and he didn't have any complaints of chest pains. I went out to a phone to check in with his cardiologist, but before I got back, he collapsed." Peele added, "Whatever hit him, hit him massively and irrevocably. I don't think he ever knew what hit him."

"He knew he was going to die early," Dunn told Gillespie. "His dad died when he was about 48; it was in the family. Joe never did try to quit [smoking]. [His attitude was], 'Enjoy it while I'm here.'" Former quarterback Todd Ellis added, "He wasn't going to show vulnerabilities. He was the John Wayne of football coaches."

Morrison's death left his program, the USC community, and the state of South Carolina in shock as news broke overnight and into Monday morning. Fans gathering for the USC men's basketball game versus Metro Conference foe Southern Mississippi that Monday evening found solace and an opportunity to grieve as a community. George Felton's team wore black patches on their jerseys in silent tribute and played like a team on a mission, dominating the Golden Eagles 105–63. "There was a lot of emotion about Coach Morrison," USC point guard Brent Price told reporters after the game. "Before the game, Coach Felton told us about Coach Morrison, about what a competitor he was. He told us to go out there and play like a bunch of Joe Morrisons."

"This game is dedicated to Coach Joe Morrison," an emotional Felton said in his postgame comments, a black ribbon attached to his jacket's lapel. "Athletics is a family, and one of our members is not here. But I know one thing, he's here in spirit."

Morrison remained tremendously popular with fans through several challenges, including consecutive losing campaigns in 1985 and 1986, before turning things around in 1987. Even a paternity suit by Barbara Button, the mother of Morrison's out-of-wedlock daughter, did little to hinder the coach's popularity. Morrison and Button had begun an affair during his time coaching in New Mexico, and she followed him to South Carolina prior to filing the suit. In the staunchly conservative, Southern Baptist–dominated culture of South Carolina, such a thing would have ended many public careers. Not so for Joe Morrison. "He was that popular," Holler told Gillespie.

A *State* editorial noted that Morrison endeared himself to many with his laid-back, low-key style, a stark contrast to the sometimes flamboyant and evangelistic approach of his predecessors. Indeed Morrison seemed a balm for fans after sixteen years of the loquacious salesman Dietzel and the territorial pugilist Carlen, whose hegemonic ambitions and clashes with trustees, administrators, fellow coaches, and even fans (particularly in the case of Carlen), outnumbered wins.

Morrison just wanted to coach football. He charmed fans with his direct style and subtle, often self-deprecating sense of humor. Of his coaching stops before USC, he once said, "It took me five years to spell 'Chattanooga,' and then we moved to Albuquerque." He talked little, won much, and made South Carolina football cool for perhaps the first time in its history.

Morrison's star quality was vaguely reminiscent of Johnny Cash, with his cowboy boots and man-in-black persona. His expressionless gaze behind an ever-present "script Carolina" hat and aviator sunglasses obscured any joy or disappointment he might have felt on the sidelines. He sought to project a cool calm to his assistant coaches and players and commented that his fourteen years in the NFL had prepared him for the role of head coach, having seen just about everything one could possibly see in football during that time. He embodied a quiet plainspokenness, exuding confidence that seemed to embolden players and fans alike. His foibles, the smoking, and even the out-of-wedlock child seemed to endear him to fans. They made him human, relatable. Mostly, though, it was the winning fans cared about, and Morrison presided over three of the winningest seasons in program history.

The Friday following his death, the university held a 3 PM memorial service at Williams-Brice Stadium. An estimated crowd of seven thousand braved blustery winds and temperatures in the mid-forties to pay tribute to the fallen coach. The late afternoon sun cast a cold shadow across the crowd gathered along the west-lower stands, exacerbating the cold. The painted block C and gamecock at midfield, untouched since the final home game, looked as faded and forlorn as the spirits of those in attendance.

Former Giants teammate Sam Huff and Gamecock defensive coordinator Dunn eulogized Morrison. "He fell in love with the University of South Carolina, the fans here, and '2001,'" Dunn said. "We were apart for four years when he came here and I stayed at New Mexico, and every time we'd talk, he'd talk about the tremendous fans here, and the way they love football." He added, "This place was his pride and joy."

Clemson coach Danny Ford and a contingent of Tigers personnel attended the service. Ford told reporters, "I don't know how close you can be to somebody you work against every day, but he's been very nice to us, a fair person to us. Every time you played him you knew his people were prepared. They played hard and were very competitive. He was just a good fellow to know."

Senior free safety Ron Rabune, sitting among his teammates in Morrison-inspired black jerseys, told reporters, "It was really hard for the guys who have been around here for a while to go out there today," adding, "I could see him across the field, pacing back and forth, encouraging the players the way he always did."

✗   ✗   ✗

In the days after Morrison's death, the focus of USC's unexpectedly sudden coaching search turned to Dick Sheridan of NC State. Sheridan, a North Augusta native, USC graduate, and former Furman coach, was USC's top choice almost from the moment of Morrison's passing. Media reports were that Sheridan had been offered the job in a meeting with Dixon on Monday, February 13. Just two months earlier, Sheridan had turned down the opportunity to succeed retiring Vince Dooley at Georgia, and it was widely reported that he harbored a desire to coach at his alma mater.

By Thursday of that week, Sheridan officially pulled his name out of consideration, stating he was "compelled" to turn down the USC offer because of unfulfilled commitments at NC State. With Sheridan out of the picture, Furman's Jimmy Satterfield and Air Force's Fisher DeBerry were the most likely candidates. Satterfield, a USC graduate who replaced Sheridan at Furman, had just wrapped up a Division I-AA national championship season with the Paladins. DeBerry, a Cheraw native and former coach of Wofford, had compiled a 40–21 record in five seasons at the Air Force Academy, including a 12–1 finish in 1985. Another name receiving consideration was Sparky Woods, who had compiled a 38–19–2 record over five seasons at Appalachian State.

It was Woods who ultimately received the nod, becoming the twenty-eighth head football coach at the University of South Carolina on February 21, 1989. Woods, a thirty-five-year-old native of Oneida, Tennessee, fit the profile Dixon had in mind. He was young and successful, with a squeaky-clean image and an engaging, affable presence with fans and media. A graduate and four-year football letterman at Carson-Newman College in Jefferson City, Tennessee, Woods guided his Mountaineer program to two Southern Conference championships. His youth was also a major selling point. He was fourteen years younger than Furman's Satterfield, and USC wanted a coach who could serve for an extended time and bring much-needed stability to the program.

Woods's 1989 team brought back much of the talent from Morrison's final squad, including Ellis, Brooks, and Green on the offensive side of the ball, along with defensive stalwarts Patrick Hinton, Corey Miller, and Scott Windsor and dependable junior placekicker Collin Mackie. The Gamecocks jumped out to a 5–1–1 record, including a 21–10 defeat of Georgia Tech just two days after Hurricane Hugo ravaged the Palmetto State. A 24–20 upset of number 23 Georgia in Athens followed a week later. The win over the Bulldogs propelled Woods's program into its first top-25 appearance at number 24 and also marked the final meeting between the Gamecock and Bulldog programs until they met again as conference foes three years later.

October 28, 1989, marked the untimely end of one of the most brilliant careers in the history of South Carolina football. The number 24 Gamecocks took on old rival, number 20 NC State, in Columbia before a season-best home crowd of 74,248. On the third play from scrimmage, Gamecock quarterback Todd Ellis was hit by Wolfpack linebacker Mark Thomas on third and seven from the NC State thirty yard line. Ellis, slumped on the ground and clearly in pain, tried to get up before falling backward, grasping his left knee. Reports from the locker room confirmed the worst—he was lost for the season with a torn medial collateral ligament. The Gamecocks' senior leader, all-time-winningest quarterback and holder of nearly every passing record in program history, had played his final down in garnet and black.

Dickie DeMasi, a seldom-used junior from Irmo, finished out the game and the season behind center for the Gamecocks. Despite earning second-string status coming into the season, coaches had planned to redshirt DeMasi, with durable veteran Ellis at the helm. It all changed in one play, and DeMasi was pressed into action. He connected on four of twelve passing attempts, taking five sacks, tossing an interception, and losing a fumble late in the game, which allowed the Wolfpack to salt the game away with a late field goal for the 20–10 finish.

The Gamecocks next lost to FSU, then won on the road versus a hapless North Carolina team before losing in humiliating fashion at home to fifteenth-ranked Clemson (45–0) to end the regular season. After the promising start, Carolina stumbled to a disappointing 6–4–1 finish. The six wins were good enough for a bowl bid, though the university declined the opportunity, wanting to stress academics over postseason play in an effort to clean up the program's outlaw image.

Behind transfer quarterback Bobby Fuller, who followed Woods from Appalachian State, the Gamecocks managed six wins again in 1990 but once more forwent participation in a bowl game, a decision Woods has said he regrets.

The Gamecocks fell to 3–6–2 in 1991, their final season as a major independent program. Fallout from the steroids scandal, Morrison's untimely death, Ellis's 1989 injury, and the decision to pass up the additional practice time and national exposure that comes with participation in bowl games had all conspired to severely hamper recruiting.

Though better times lay ahead, the 1990s proved to be a period of growing pains for the Gamecock program, which struggled to find its footing in the rugged Southeastern Conference starting in 1992. Woods deserves tremendous credit for accepting the challenge of stabilizing the USC program in the wake of a national scandal. And his tenure was not without exciting times, including a miraculous streak of five wins in six games after an 0–5 start in 1992 and a thrilling upset of number 14 Georgia in Athens to begin the 1993 season.

Ultimately Woods was fired by new athletics director Mike McGee at the end of a 4–7 campaign in 1993. He compiled a 24–28–3 record in Columbia over five seasons and guided the Gamecock program through its first two seasons of SEC play. Look no further for evidence of progress under Woods's leadership than the first season of his replacement, Brad Scott, in 1994. The Gamecocks went 7–5, highlighted by a dominant 33–7 win at archrival Clemson and the program's first-ever bowl win, a 24–21 defeat of West Virginia in the Car Quest Bowl. It was Scott's finest season in Columbia with a roster full of Woods's recruits, including the flamboyant fan-favorite quarterback from Altoona, Pennsylvania, Steve Taneyhill.

In 2019 Woods spoke with David Cloninger of the *Charleston Post and Courier* prior to South Carolina's matchup with North Carolina, where he had taken an advisory role to Tar Heel head coach Mack Brown. Reflecting on his time in Columbia, Woods recounted the challenges of recruiting in the wake of the steroids scandal and of guiding the program into the murderer's row of SEC competition. He said that despite the way it ended, there were no hard feelings.

"I'm not sure it was the best time to take that job," Woods said, adding, "but it was certainly the best opportunity for me."

George Felton Revives Gamecock Basketball before Unexplained Dismissal

When thirty-two-year-old George Felton was introduced as the twenty-sixth head coach of USC basketball in March 1986, the *State*'s Bob Gillespie wrote that the hire was more than a new head coach replacing Bill Foster, who had resigned under fire two weeks before. "This," Gillespie wrote, "was USC welcoming home one of its own." And the feeling was shared by Felton, who told gathered reporters at his introductory press conference, "This is a dream come true."

New USC basketball coach George Felton leads the Gamecock's
first day of practice in 1986. Courtesy of the *State* Newspaper Archive,
Richland County Public Library.

Felton, formerly the top assistant on Bobby Cremins's Georgia Tech staff, was a USC graduate and a two-year letterman in the mid-1970s under USC legend Frank McGuire. "I love South Carolina," Felton said. "It's my home. And I guarantee I'll work hard to bring USC back to national prominence."

A few days later, Felton recalled with a chuckle the surreal experience of occupying the office of his former coach. Felton told reporters he "finally went in there" a couple of days after accepting the USC job, "and I had hardly sat down when the phone rang, and Bobby Cremins asked, 'Are you sitting in Frank J. McGuire's chair?'"

A renowned recruiter, Felton was credited with landing four consecutive ACC rookie of the year award winners at Georgia Tech: Mark Price, Bruce Dalrymple, Duane Ferrell, and Tom Hammonds. He quickly built an impressive staff at South Carolina, including former Belmont Abbey coach and athletics director Eddie Payne and Virginia Commonwealth University assistant Tubby Smith.[4]

Felton's first squad surprised many pundits by achieving a winning season (15–14) in 1986–87 with mostly holdovers from the Foster era, including Terry and Perry Dozier, Michael Foster, Darryl Martin, Tony Shaw, and Bill Vernau. By year two Felton's focus on keeping Columbia's best high school talent at home began to pay off, in the form of newcomers six-five forward Michael Glover and six-four guard Barry Manning, from Keenan and Eau Claire High Schools, respectively. Felton also added six-eleven Jeff Roulston of Summerville to the mix, along with six-one sharp-shooting guard Brent Price of Enid, Oklahoma (brother of Mark Price), and athletic six-eight forward transfer John Hudson of Anderson, by way of San Jacinto Junior College. The 1987–88 squad, Felton's second, achieved nineteen wins, the most since Bill Foster's twenty-three wins in 1982–83.

Felton added more local talent for 1988–89 in the form of high-flying six-four guard Jo Jo English of Lower Richland High School and six-eight forward Joe Rhett of Eau Claire. The Gamecocks again won nineteen games and earned the program's first NCAA tournament invitation since 1973–74. Though Carolina bowed out in a first-round loss to NC State, the tournament bid was an important milestone, signifying admirable progress for the Gamecock program.

A disappointing 14–14 season followed in 1989–90 before the Gamecocks appeared to regain momentum in 1990–91, Felton's fifth season at the helm. South Carolina jumped out to an 18–5 record through twenty-three games, highlighted by a thrilling two-point victory over number 4 North Carolina in the Diet Pepsi Tournament of Champions in Charlotte on November 30. A late-season skid followed the impressive start, however, and the Gamecocks lost eight of their final ten games. Though USC finished with its first twenty-win season in eight years (20–13, 5–9 Metro) and a first-round win in the NIT before bowing out in round two, rumors swirled in local media regarding Felton's job security.

The passage of time quieted rumors considerably by the first week of May, a full seven weeks after the end of the season. Felton's top assistant, Eddie Payne, had accepted the head job at East Carolina, and Felton looked to interview a replacement on the afternoon of Tuesday, May 14, after a previously planned meeting with athletics director Dixon. Beyond that he had arranged to attend a Gamecock Club function in Raleigh the following day.

Unbeknownst to Felton, ten days earlier Dixon had gone to new USC president John Palms to recommend his termination. By the time Felton met with Dixon on the May 14, rumors of Dixon's decision had leaked, including to Felton's team. Felton himself was notified he would be fired by a member of the media the night before the meeting with Dixon. The firing "shocked those close to the program," wrote David Newton of the *State*, "none more so than Felton."

Meeting with members of the media later that afternoon, Dixon was vague when asked repeatedly about the reasons behind his decision. After all, the coach had completed the most successful first five years of any coach in program history with eighty-seven wins. He had taken the Gamecocks to their first NCAA tournament in fifteen years and had just completed the first twenty-win season in eight years.[5] Moreover, how Felton was notified, through a media outlet because of a leak, seemed particularly galling, especially given his status as a USC letterman and legacy coach from the McGuire and Cremins coaching trees.

Dixon said the decision came after "an extensive and consuming" review of the basketball program but provided no further detail on the cause of the firing, only adding that it was "in the best interest of the university." When asked directly whether reasons for Felton's firing included rumors of a drinking problem and Felton's relationship with players and the media, Dixon replied that he had looked into "any rumors concerning Coach Felton" and added, "I can tell you right now, there was not one rumor I've heard of that I could substantiate."

Point guard Barry Manning called it "pretty much a bad decision on the school's part," adding, "they should have let him finish what he started." Center Jeff Roulston took it further, calling USC fans who had expressed dissatisfaction with Felton "some of the most hypocritical in the country" and stating that the school had "no basis to fire him." Roulston pointed to the fact that Felton had never suffered a losing season at USC, also noting the coach's success in graduating players.

USC athletics director King Dixon in 1988. Courtesy of the *State* Newspaper Archive, Richland County Public Library.

Coach Perry Clark of Metro rival Tulane expressed surprise as well, noting Felton's expressed desire to keep Columbia kids at home. "He's done that. The hardest thing to do is to keep kids at home. He brought in great kids who are good representatives of the institution."[6]

In discussing the I PM meeting in which he informed Felton of the firing, Dixon became emotional. "As it ended, I was moved and so was he," he said, stopping to gather himself. "I was greatly disturbed that our relationship had to end in this manner. But I wished him luck and we shook hands."

With that handshake, Dixon set in motion a cringeworthy fifty-seven-day coaching search, in which the Gamecock opening was declined by a collection of the school's top-choice candidates, including Vanderbilt's Eddie Fogler, San Antonio Spurs coach Larry Brown, and Rutgers coach Bob Wenzel, a former Bill Foster assistant at USC. In between those rejections, other notable and noted candidates publicly pulled their names from consideration, including

Rick Barnes of Providence, John Kresse of the College of Charleston, Wake Forest's Dave Odom, former Virginia coach and Davidson athletics director Terry Holland, and Furman's Butch Estes, among others. Another candidate, highly respected Eau Claire High School coach George Glymph, never really gained the attention or traction his candidacy deserved, creating hard feelings between local high school coaches and the USC program.

By mid-June the search had taken on the acrid stench of desperation, as media scrutiny mounted over missteps, ham-handed communications with candidates, and a general lack of professionalism. Critics pointed out that Dixon seemed in over his head. By late June, Rutgers's Wenzel became the third candidate to publicly decline the job.

It was the second week of July before USC turned its attention to Steve Newton of Murray State University in Kentucky. Newton, fifty, had compiled a 116–64 record in six seasons with the Racers, winning four consecutive Ohio Valley Conference titles and two conference coach of the year awards. On July 10, after fifty-seven days of a coaching search that had been sharply, and justifiably, criticized in Columbia and beyond, the University of South Carolina hired Newton as its twenty-seventh head basketball coach.

✗   ✗   ✗

The 1991–92 Gamecocks bolted to an 8–1 start, their only loss a one-point setback to number 19 Oklahoma, led by former Gamecock guard Brent Price, who had transferred to the Sooners' program after reportedly growing homesick during his two years in Columbia.

On the first Saturday of the new year, South Carolina hosted Kentucky in the school's first-ever SEC conference matchup in any sport.[7] An overflow crowd of 12,754 fans, including a healthy showing dressed in Kentucky blue, jammed into the Carolina Coliseum. The atmosphere was charged with emotion, as legendary USC coach Frank McGuire was honored during pregame ceremonies and officials from USC and Kentucky exchanged gifts.

The raucous Carolina crowd went into hysterics after the Gamecocks jumped out to an early twelve-point lead before Kentucky hit their stride, going on a 35–10 run for a 48–35 halftime lead. Carolina started hot again in the second stanza, pulling to within five on consecutive Barry Manning

THE BACKSIDE OF THE STORM | 261

three-point plays. Kentucky forward Jamal Mashburn was too much down the stretch, though, scoring nineteen second-half points to defeat USC handily, 80–63.

Better days lay ahead for the Gamecock program, though not under Newton, who was dismissed by athletics director Mike McGee following the 1992–93 season, capping a two-year run during which he compiled a 20–35 (8–24 SEC) record.

For a few fleeting days in March 1993, it appeared that prodigal son Bobby Cremins would return to his college roots to take over the struggling Gamecock program, setting off a wave of euphoria in Columbia not seen in ages. The good feelings were short-lived, however, as Cremins had a change of heart, returning to Georgia Tech seventy-two hours after his triumphant introductory press conference in Columbia. While Gamecock fans whipsawed into the depths of despair, McGee never broke stride, hiring the reigning SEC coach of the year, Vanderbilt's Eddie Fogler, just days later. Within four seasons Fogler and his roster of mostly native South Carolina players brought home the school's first-ever SEC championship.

But the story of how South Carolina came to join the SEC is a drama unto itself.

11

A New World Order

South Carolina and the
Southeastern Conference

Out of these troubled times . . . a new world order can emerge.

—President George H. W. Bush, September 11, 1990

President George H. W. Bush famously made his "New World Order" speech before a joint session of Congress just over a month after Iraq's invasion of tiny, oil-rich Kuwait in August 1990. The phrase was a reference to the broad coalition of nations the US was building to turn back Iraqi dictator Saddam Hussein's oil grab. At that very moment, the Soviet Union, America's great rival of the post–World War II era, was slowly disintegrating as Moscow's satellite republics defected one by one amid a great democratic wave. The world was turning on its axis and realigning in new and uncertain ways.

Bush referred to a new cooperative of nations, working together to ensure peace through economic and military might. But his sentiments set the perfect tone for an event ten days later that marked the beginning of the end of South Carolina's long wilderness path through major independent status.

Indeed, the shifting world of college athletics reflected geopolitics of the time, as converging factors drove major independent institutions to seek the relative stability of conference alignment and those already in conferences sought firmer ground in other conference arrangements. Lucrative television deals for conferences highlighted a growing financial discrepancy, as television rights became a cash cow for the ACC and the SEC, among others, while major independents were cut off from this rising revenue source, with the notable exception of Notre Dame, which had entered a blockbuster broadcasting rights deal with NBC.

Further complicating matters, the NCAA basketball tournament had long trended toward awarding at-large bids to schools with conference affiliation over major independents, even those with better win-loss records. Even generally positive developments, such as the addition of more nonrevenue sports following implementation of Title IX, drove increased costs for cash-strapped athletic departments. Amid these convergent factors, athletic departments increasingly looked to television money and conference revenue-sharing arrangements to relieve budgetary concerns.

Just as major independents sought the stability of conference affiliation, conferences hoping to maximize positioning for television rights deals looked to expand into pivotal markets. As economic pressures built throughout 1980s, the tectonic plates of conference alignment were poised for a great shift at the dawn of a new decade.

"A Swollen Behemoth"

Though conference alignment had been relatively stable for decades, realignment had occurred on a grand scale before. In the late 1920s and early 1930s, the Southern Conference included an unwieldy twenty-three schools at its peak. It was a "swollen behemoth," according to Brett Weisband of the website Saturday Down South. Founded in 1921, the conference boasted schools from across the South and mid-Atlantic regions, including most of the schools that would eventually form the SEC and the ACC.

Indeed, at the 1932 annual conference meeting in Atlanta, Dr. S. V. Sanford, president of the University of Georgia, announced that thirteen schools west and south of the Appalachians would depart the Southern to form a new league which they called the Southeastern Conference. Departing members included Alabama, Georgia, Ole Miss, Mississippi State, LSU, Vanderbilt, Auburn, Sewanee, Georgia Tech, Tulane, Florida, and Kentucky.

The move left VMI, Virginia, Virginia Tech, Washington and Lee, South Carolina, Clemson, UNC, Duke, NC State, and Maryland to carry on in a diminished Southern Conference.[1]

In the spring of 1953, seven additional Southern Conference schools departed to form the Atlantic Coast Conference, including South Carolina, Clemson, North Carolina, Duke, North Carolina State, Wake Forest, and Maryland. The departure was prompted in part by the Southern Conference's ban on postseason play, which was implemented in 1951. The new conference sought an eighth member to balance out scheduling, and Virginia, Virginia Tech, and West Virginia emerged as the most likely candidates. Virginia, which became an independent since departing the Southern Conference in 1937, was ultimately invited and joined the ACC in December 1953.[2]

"There's a Lot of Interesting Things Going On"

By 1989, after USC had spent the better part of two decades as a major independent, the university's athletics department faced unprecedented financial headwinds. After years of operating in the black, USC reported a $600,000 deficit for fiscal year 1988–89. The deficit was fueled by numerous unanticipated expenses, including $300,000 to add structural supports to the upper-east deck of Williams-Brice Stadium, the cost of replacing the "Bubble" indoor practice facility after it was destroyed by Hurricane Hugo in September 1989, and a $232,000 settlement for former athletics director Bob Marcum and associated legal fees, plus expenditures from the internal investigation into the steroids scandal, totaling over $300,000. To compound matters, USC had only one televised football game during the 1989 season, with Clemson, as conferences increasingly tied up television outlets.

In fits and starts, South Carolina had sought a return to an all-sports conference home almost from the time it left the ACC in 1971. On-again, off-again back-channel talks with the ACC had narrated those efforts during most of the 1970's. South Carolina was, after all, a founding member of that conference, and many within the university community still believed it was the natural fit for USC.

The path toward reunification with the ACC seemed all but permanently blocked after Georgia Tech replaced USC as the eighth conference member in 1978, but with expansion rumors heating up in the late 1980s, the door seemed to crack open once again. By the spring of 1990, other options entered the discussion as well.

Writing for the *State* on May 20, 1990, Bob Gillespie explored the possibility of the Metro Conference adding football, among other options for USC. Since 1983 the Metro had been a viable if not entirely satisfactory conference home for South Carolina. In some ways the Metro offered the best of both worlds, with South Carolina keeping 100 percent of the revenue from seven home football games while Metro affiliation provided a vehicle for earning NCAA basketball bids and a home for nonrevenue team sports. But with the rising costs of athletics and the need to generate income, maintaining an independent status in football was increasingly unsustainable.

Gillespie suggested five paths forward for USC:

- the ACC, USC's former conference home (many still thought this the most natural fit);
- the SEC, the option preferred by some who believed it a better cultural fit for football-first South Carolina;
- the Eastern Seaboard Conference, a new conference model first proposed by Penn State's Joe Paterno—a confederation of major independent schools, including Penn State, West Virginia, Virginia Tech, Florida State, Miami, and South Carolina;
- an expansion of the Metro Conference from ten to sixteen teams, which would include football;
- maintaining independent status in football, with Metro affiliation in all other sports.

A *State* reader poll published two days later revealed a strong fan preference for the ACC, which garnered 62.2 percent of votes. The SEC was a distant second at 24.6 percent. Fans largely dismissed the Eastern Seaboard proposal, which accounted for only 4.3 percent of votes. The Metro options barely registered.

The Metro Conference had recently commissioned Raycom Sports to conduct a study into the viability of football scenarios for the conference. The study recommended conference expansion by at least two schools in order to make football an economically viable option for all members, with the preferred options being West Virginia and Miami. At their spring 1990 meeting, representatives from the Metro took the concept further, proposing a "Super 16" expanded Metro. Schools targeted for membership included Miami, Syracuse, Pittsburgh, Boston College, East Carolina, Rutgers, West Virginia, and Temple.

With the proposed expansion, twelve schools would play all sports, while three (Syracuse, Pitt, and Boston College) would play football only, remaining in the lucrative Big East for basketball and other sports. East Carolina would also play football only and remain in the Colonial Athletic Association for all other sports.

Conference officials boasted that the expanded Metro would capture more than a third of American television markets, though critics called that overly optimistic. Boston College and Syracuse, for example, would not deliver a sizable portion of the Boston and New York markets given those city's many sports options, including more than a dozen professional teams in the four major sports.

Still, Metro officials were eager to make bold moves in the hopes of retaining member institutions ripe for the picking by expanding all-sports conferences, primarily South Carolina and Florida State. The Metro also faced possible defection from Cincinnati, Louisville, and Memphis State, which were in talks to join DePaul and Marquette to form a Midwest-based basketball conference if the Metro did not expand to include football and deliver them much-needed revenue sharing.

For USC athletics director Dixon, Metro Conference football was a nonstarter. "I'm not comfortable with the eight [schools] we have going to football," Dixon told the *State*'s Gillespie. "We need at least two to five more, and I'm not sure the schools we'd want would come in with the current alignment. Frankly, a lot of our fans aren't going to be intrigued with a home-and-home series with some of these schools. There's nothing wrong with them, but there's no rivalry or relationship."

Beyond the minimal appeal of Metro football for fans, the financials were tenuous at best for South Carolina and Florida State and especially unattractive for prospective member Miami, who was the linchpin for Metro Conference football viability.

In a May 21, 1990, article in the *State,* columnist Doug Nye broke down the numbers in a sobering look at the viability of an expanded Metro arrangement. According to projections, a Metro television package was projected to yield around $1.25 million per conference team. Using real data from the 1989 season, Miami and FSU earned more than $3 million each from television appearances, all theirs to keep. Another prospective member, West Virginia, earned $1.5 million, while South Carolina and Southern Miss earned around $250,000 each. All told, these five schools earned around $9 million from football television appearances in 1989. Divided by ten teams (the current Metro, plus Miami and West Virginia), each would have received about $900,000 in 1989. Great for Louisville, Cincinnati, and Memphis State but a losing proposition for Miami and FSU.

For USC the option of maintaining status quo was dead on arrival, and Metro Conference football was on life support. Meanwhile Penn State accepted an invitation to join the Big Ten in the spring of 1990, effectively eliminating the Eastern Seaboard Conference option. With three of the five options all but gone, South Carolina looked with renewed focus to the ACC and the SEC.

ACC officials were initially coy amid rising media speculation of expansion. Commissioner Gene Corrigan told the *State*'s Bob Cole in May 1990 that the door was closed, "not just where South Carolina is concerned, but expansion in any form." Corrigan cited high demand for ACC basketball tournament tickets and the unwillingness of some within the conference to split that pie into more pieces. Some members, he said, had a "big problem" when the ACC expanded to eight teams with the addition of Georgia Tech in 1978.

Corrigan was effectively buying time with media dismissals of expansion talk while he worked to align unanimous support within the conference before moving forward. Some media outlets noted that Duke and Wake Forest were against expansion, and though it would have taken three member schools to block, Corrigan strove for a united front.

Meanwhile, on May 29, 1990, SEC member presidents gave unanimous approval to expansion at the league's spring meetings in Destin, Florida. Four teams, FSU, Miami, Arkansas, and USC, were reported to be the top candidates.

Adding to the immediacy for expansion, Notre Dame's unilateral deal with NBC to broadcast home games beginning with the 1991 season and Penn State's pending move to the Big Ten removed those two schools from the College Football Association (CFA), a loose conglomeration of the country's major conference member schools and major independents, with the exception of Big Ten and Pac-Ten members. Beginning in the late 1970s, CFA member schools wrested control of lucrative football broadcasts away from the NCAA, which since the 1950s had exercised complete control of college football television rights. The NCAA wanted to limit broadcasts out of a concern that television would suppress game attendance, while CFA sought the freedom to negotiate and expand television rights.

With Notre Dame and Penn State gone, the CFA's bargaining power declined, and conferences looked to strengthen their own credentials for negotiating broadcast deals independent of the CFA. Soon the SEC forged its own broadcast deal with CBS. Other conferences looked to follow, ensuring the irrelevancy of the CFA.

NCAA Drama Complicates Path Forward

South Carolina's hopes for landing an all-sports conference home also faced headwinds from the ongoing NCAA investigation into the Joe Morrison era steroids scandal. The investigation cast a pall over the athletic department and prompted a cautious approach to expansion talks by both SEC and USC officials, so much so that USC was not among the schools initially approached by the SEC after the conference approved expansion plans in May 1990.[3] South Carolina officials looked anxiously toward a resolution, which they anticipated sometime during the summer.

Of major concern for USC was a prior NCAA investigation into former basketball coach Bill Foster's program in 1986, which resulted in a two-year probation and one-year postseason ban. Because the steroid allegations occurred during that first probationary period, USC risked the ugly specter of

repeat offender status and resultant harsher penalties. This included the possibility of the "death penalty," which the NCAA had recently administered to
the Southern Methodist University football program.[4]

Also of concern was the fact that the NCAA had never investigated violations over steroid or drug use, which made USC's a test case. University
attorney Joe McCullough told the *State*'s Gillespie that "the committee's
never heard a case where a drug program got off track. It's a novel issue"—
McCullough paused—"and novelty causes terror."

On June 22 a delegation from USC, including outgoing president James
Holderman, interim president Alfred K. Smith, athletics director King Dixon,
USC faculty representative William Putnam, football coach Sparky Woods,
and men's basketball coach George Felton, traveled to NCAA headquarters,
then located in Kansas City, Missouri. The delegation appeared before the
NCAA's Committee on Infractions to review USC's four-hundred-page internal report into potential steroid-related violations.

Adding to the drama, former athletics director Bob Marcum attended
to provide his own testimony to the infractions committee. Under NCAA
rules, interested parties were allowed to participate in such hearings. Holderman had fired Marcum on March 1, 1988, following a presidential task force
investigation that concluded Marcum failed in his responsibility to oversee
appropriate drug testing for Gamecock athletes. Marcum subsequently sued
USC for the remainder of his contract and was awarded half, $234,425. Mar-
cum sought to rebuild his image with the appearance, as he had been unable
to obtain another athletics directorship. He had recently been passed over for
the open Oklahoma State AD job.

Gillespie's June 22 article in the *State* noted that USC profiled three cases
of football coaches providing money for steroids in their report. The report
also noted that Marcum and Coach Joe Morrison were aware of steroid use
and the involvement of assistant coaches as early as 1985 but took no action.
This raised the uncomfortable issue of institutional control, or lack therof,
which could make or break USC's case.

Former defensive lineman Tommy Chaikin's devastating October 1988
Sports Illustrated exposé led to a federal grand jury investigation following the
death of Morrison in February 1989. Four assistant coaches were indicted,

and three ultimately pled guilty to illegally purchasing and providing steroids to players. Former tight-end coach Tom Kurucz, defensive line coach Jim Washburn, and strength coach Keith Kephart were convicted, while former defensive coordinator Tom Gadd was acquitted.[5]

Following the Kansas City hearing, the normally stoic Dixon confided to the *State* that "ever since I walked into the athletics department in October [1988], this has been hanging over my head. It's probably the heaviest burden I've ever felt."

After a tense and speculative month, USC learned its fate when the NCAA handed down its decision on July 25, 1990. A collective sigh of relief emanated from the Roundhouse, USC's athletic administration building, as the association found South Carolina guilty of only three secondary violations, none involving steroids. The *State*'s Gillespie noted in a July 26 article titled "NCAA Rewards USC for Efforts" that steroids were mentioned only in passing in the NCAA's report. The penalty, a six-month extension of the existing probation, amounted to a slap on the wrist.[6]

The NCAA concluded that turnover among the athletics director, football coach, and staff positions "frustrated the university's good intentions." The NCAA did not pursue cases of coaches providing steroids to players because they did not detect that those cases were part of a pattern. "They weren't looking at particular coaches or athletes," interim president Smith noted, "but how did the institution deal with these incidents." He expanded, "We've been working for two years-plus, presenting facts and attitudes to persuade the committee that this school does have integrity and intends to operate an exemplary program. There's no perfect answer as to why they treated us lightly, but I think ultimately we convinced them this school is on track."

With the NCAA investigation favorably concluded, USC could once again focus on the future of its athletic fortunes. Indeed, two weeks prior to the NCAA's announcement of findings, the university had received a questionnaire from the SEC seeking information about its athletic budget, enrollment, NCAA compliance rules, and facilities. It was a preliminary expression of interest from the league, which buoyed the spirits of the administration in the tense days before their NCAA fate was entirely clear.

Interim president Smith told the *State*'s David Newton, "What we're doing right now is maximizing our opportunities. We're very interested in everything—proposals from the SEC, the Metro and the ACC." Smith noted USC would not commit to the Metro until they heard what the SEC and ACC had to say. With respect to the ACC, Smith sounded a rare conciliatory tone, telling Newton, "Everybody knows that removing ourselves from the league two decades ago was a mistake."

USC Plays a High-Stakes Game of Musical Chairs

Over the coming weeks, South Carolina faced another tense waiting game as the ACC and SEC expansion drama unfolded. Three schools, South Carolina, Florida State, and Miami, vied for two open conference slots, one in the ACC and one in the SEC. In the case of the ACC, Florida State was their expressed sole target, while the SEC openly considered all three schools. Media coverage was unanimous in speculating that the SEC's preferred choice was also FSU.

The SEC had, by this time, settled on limiting expansion to twelve members, after the Texas legislature pressured the University of Texas and Texas A&M to remain in the Southwest Conference. With Arkansas already on board as the eleventh member and the high-priority Texas schools then out of reach, the SEC sought to finalize its twelfth and, for the time being, final addition.

USC's Smith told the *State*'s Newton he had been working with SEC commissioner Roy Kramer on the basis of South Carolina's merit. "I really don't have a sense we're waiting in line for anybody. I'm very optimistic," Smith said, adding cautiously, "but at the same time, not supremely optimistic." Despite his guarded optimism, USC was clearly waiting in line as the Florida State decision unfolded. Further muddying the waters was the potential that the SEC might extend an invitation to rival Florida football powerhouse Miami if spurned by FSU.

On September 14, 1990, the ACC voted unanimously to invite Florida State. Before FSU could formally accept, SEC presidents voted by teleconference not to invite the Seminoles. SEC officials denied the face-saving element of the odd, hastily cast vote, but the intent was entirely transparent. Florida

State accepted the ACC's invitation in short order, becoming the ninth member of that conference.[7]

Speculation shifted to whether the Gamecocks or Hurricanes would receive the coveted final SEC invitation. Miami's powerhouse football program was in its heyday, having won two of the last three national championships (1987 and 1989). It would win another in 1991. The school had also won national championships in baseball in 1982 and 1985 and continued to play at an elite level in that sport. The Hurricanes were one of the more recognizable brands of the day, and their football prominence, in particular, would add to the SEC's prestige.

South Carolina could not compete with the national brand and championship résumé Miami brought to the table; however other factors played in USC's favor. The day after ACC expansion was settled, an anonymous SEC official told the *State*'s Newton that the SEC was interested in expanding into the ACC's television market, namely the burgeoning Charlotte metro area. The ACC had gained a foothold in SEC territory with Georgia Tech and now Florida State, and the SEC looked to respond in kind. Given Columbia's close proximity to Charlotte, a ninety-minute drive up I-77, and the large number of USC graduates and fans in the Charlotte area, this bode well for the Gamecocks. As another significant factor in USC's favor, Georgia's athletics director and legendary former head football coach Vince Dooley lobbied behind the scenes for South Carolina. The Bulldogs and Gamecocks had a long-standing home-and-home series, providing Dooley familiarity and a level of comfort with the USC program and the city of Columbia. Dooley's advocacy and considerable influence within the SEC's power structure was a major positive for the Gamecocks.

Beyond that, South Carolina's overall sports program was broadly competitive, with a highly regarded women's basketball program and a men's program back on its feet after a few years of rebuilding under McGuire-era letterman and Bobby Cremins protégé George Felton. Baseball was strong at South Carolina, with three College World Series appearances in the prior decade. USC boasted highly competitive softball, tennis, golf, and track and field programs as well. Meanwhile, beyond their elite football and baseball programs, Miami's competitiveness dropped off steeply.

Perhaps the most favorable factor for the Gamecocks was culture. The University of Miami was a small, private university in a relatively large city. The University of South Carolina, meanwhile, was a large public university, the flagship institution of South Carolina, located in a midsize southern city and more closely aligned with other SEC schools.

On Thursday, September 20, 1990, SEC commissioner Kramer traveled to Columbia, where he met with interim president Smith and other USC officials for four hours at the president's residence on the historic USC Horseshoe.[8] Afterward Smith described the meeting as "warm, very pleasant, cordial. Friendly." He elaborated, "I certainly wouldn't characterize him [Kramer] as being in a gruff mood when he left here." It was a reference to Kramer's earlier meeting with University of Miami officials, which was comparatively brief, at ninety minutes, and reportedly not as cordial. Smith told reporters he felt, "if anything, more encouraged, more optimistic than I have been."

Beyond the good feelings in Columbia, reports out of Coral Gables pointed to a Miami move to the expanding Big East Conference. Miami university officials met with Big East representatives on Tuesday, September 18, and all indications were that the Big East was their preferred landing spot.

As excitement and anticipation built at USC, Coach Sparky Woods's Gamecock football team traveled to Blacksburg in a road contest versus Frank Beamer's Virginia Tech Hokies. The Gamecocks and Hokies had played yearly beginning in 1986, with South Carolina getting the better of things, compiling two wins and two ties in the previous four contests.[9] But momentum was building around fourth-year coach Beamer's program, and though no one in Lane Stadium could have predicted it that day, he would go on to enjoy a legendary career spanning twenty-nine seasons in Blacksburg, including three Big East and four ACC championships.

It was a noon kickoff in bucolic Blacksburg. Temperatures were a balmy sixty-nine degrees with clearing skies after an overnight rain. The Gamecocks struggled throughout the first half, which ended with a 14–7 Hokie lead. Tech scored ten more in the third period, while the Gamecocks scored on a one-yard Mike Dingle touchdown run. Collin Mackie's extra point was blocked, and Tech took a 24–13 lead into the fourth quarter.

The Gamecocks came alive in the final period, scoring three touchdowns in five minutes on two Dingle rushing scores and a Bobby Fuller end zone connection with receiver Eddie Miller. Dingle finished with four rushing touchdowns and 131 yards, while Fuller threw for 251 yards and junior Robert Brooks, a future Green Bay Packer, hauled in 118 receiving yards.[10] The Gamecocks pulled off a gritty, come-from-behind road win, and the 35–24 final kept the Gamecocks perfect at 3–0 after earlier victories over former ACC rivals UNC and Duke.

That Saturday, September 22, marked the one-year anniversary of Hurricane Hugo's devastating landfall along the South Carolina coast in 1989. The win was a harbinger of better days and served to heighten the good vibes in Columbia as the SEC's decision loomed.

Deliverance, What Might Have Been, and What It All Means

The highly anticipated news came three days later. After a 10–0 favorable decision by the SEC's presidents (Arkansas did not yet have a vote), SEC commissioner Kramer telephoned USC interim president Smith to extend the coveted membership invitation. The USC Board of Trustees voted unanimously to accept, and by midday of Tuesday, September 25, media outlets were notified. After a winding, sometimes uncomfortable, and often uncertain courtship, South Carolina had officially become the twelfth member of the Southeastern Conference.

USC officials, including Smith, Dixon, and Sparky Woods, conducted a hastily convened late-afternoon press conference on the southwest ramp of Williams-Brice Stadium to officially announce USC's entrance into the SEC. The contingent, along with board of trustees chair Michael Mungo, took the podium to the strains of *Also sprach Zarathustra*. Some in the crowd sported stickers boasting "Proud to be in the SEC." Smiles were infectious. A mix of enthusiasm and profound relief permeated the air.

An emotional Dixon told the assembled reporters and smattering of fans, "I am absolutely ecstatic. This is a giant step. A new era." Then, pumping a fist, he shouted, "Let's go, Cocks!" Smith described the process of securing conference membership as a "long one," adding it had not been unpleasant

products Xavier McDaniel and Tyrone Corbin might have stayed in Columbia to play for the hometown Gamecocks rather than bolting to Wichita State and DePaul, respectively. One can imagine the Michael Jordan versus McDaniel matchups that could have taken place in Columbia and Chapel Hill.

Impacts on the football program are easier to imagine, because unlike basketball, where ACC schools refused to play the Gamecocks after 1971, the football program continued a steady diet of ACC competition throughout the 1970s and 1980s. From 1971 until 1991, South Carolina played ninety-three games versus ACC competition, compiling a 49–41–3 record (.526). The Gamecocks played Clemson yearly, of course, but UNC, Duke, Wake Forest, and NC State were also scheduled regularly. South Carolina went 4–1 versus ACC competition in 1975, 5–1 in 1981, 3–0 in 1984, and 4–0 in 1987. Might those teams have won ACC championships for the Gamecocks?

Of course, it is impossible to know exactly how events might have unfolded. Would Jim Carlen have come to South Carolina to replace Dietzel in 1975, or would Dietzel have coached longer? Had Carlen not come to South Carolina, would George Rogers have signed with the Gamecocks in 1977 and gone on to provide USC with its lone Heisman Trophy winner? Likely not, given Rogers's unique relationship with Carlen.

What we do know is that leaving the ACC caused the gradual, yet inevitable, decline of McGuire's powerful basketball program. Moreover, the power struggles within the USC athletics department caused by the lack of a strong, independent director of athletics created decades of instability. It was part and parcel of why South Carolina left the ACC to begin with, and that instability nearly cost the Gamecocks the opportunity to join the SEC when the time came.

South Carolina's eventual move to SEC membership was unquestionably a positive one for Gamecock athletics and for the university as a whole. Membership has led to financial stability beyond even the most optimistic hopes of USC administrators in 1990. But was that stability worth two decades spent traversing the wilderness of independent status? Is South Carolina better off now than it would be had it remained in the ACC?

Moreover, would conference realignments have played out the way that they did had USC not forfeited its ACC membership? Would the ACC have offered Georgia Tech membership in 1978, for example? Would the SEC and ACC have expanded the way they did in 1990? What would the ACC, the SEC, and other conferences look like now without the ripple effect created by USC's conference departure more than fifty years ago?

Through conjecture, speculation, and a little imagination, one can envision an endless variety of choose-your-own-adventure narratives to answer these questions. An alternate history of USC athletics—one with a stable administration and trophy cases sagging under the weight of conference championship hardware—would make for fun writing and interesting reading.

Bookended by seventeen years of ACC membership and thirty-plus years in the SEC, the independent era is one of the more complex periods in the history of USC and, more broadly, American society. It began on the heels of the civil rights movement, with Black athletes having only recently gained scholarship status at USC and other schools across the South. The passage of Title IX and the rise of women's sports helped define the era. College athletics evolved into big business during these years, as television rights and athletic apparel deals reshaped athletic department budgets. The arms race of athletics facilities and coaches' salaries exploded and continues unabated today. It was an era of steroids, illicit incentives, and resultant NCAA-imposed reforms. It was a time of conference realignment, when the financial viability of independent status ended for South Carolina, Florida State, West Virginia, and even Notre Dame, among others.

It was two decades of societal change and evolution as experienced through the prism of Gamecock athletics. To those athletes who wore the garnet and black during this time, to the coaches who led them, and to the fans who cheered them on, *Here's a health, Carolina; Forever to thee.*

Epilogue

Why not us? Why not the University of South Carolina
Gamecocks?

—Steve Spurrier

What a ride it's been. As this book goes to publication, the University
of South Carolina has enjoyed membership in the Southeastern Conference for thirty-two years. It is a span approaching twice as long as
their seventeen years in the Atlantic Coast Conference and longer than their
time in the ACC and Metro combined. There are fans well into adulthood
who never knew anything different, who take for granted the Gamecocks'
membership and status within the greatest conference in all of college sports.
That both astounds and delights me.

It has been a successful three-plus-decade run. At the dawn of South Carolina's entry into the SEC, Gamecock athletics could boast not a single NCAA
team national championship. Zero. The Gamecock track and field program
owned one individual championship, a four-hundred-meter outdoor title
won by Norman "Scooter" Rucks in 1948. And there was one indoor relay
championship from 1974, won by Don Brown, Mike Sheley, John Brown, and
Jim Schaper in the four-by-eight-hundred-meter event.[1] That's it; that's all.

Since joining the SEC, Gamecock programs have collected five NCAA
team national championships. The first came in 2002, with the women's
outdoor track and field title. Two in baseball followed in 2010 and 2011 and,
most recently, two in women's basketball in 2017 and 2022. Additionally, three
overall national titles (in 2005, 2007, and 2015) and two hunt-seat national

titles (in 2005 and 2006) have been collected by the equestrian program.[2] Curtis Frye's track and field program has secured twenty-two individual national titles, led by greats like Dawn Ellerbe, Lisa Misipeka, Terrence Trammell, Miki and Lisa Barber, Demetria Washington, Tiffany Ross-Williams, Jeannelle Scheper, and Rachel Glenn.

As Gamecock football entered SEC competition in 1992, the program could boast of not a single bowl victory in eight tries. Since that time, USC has won ten bowls in seventeen trips. Coaching luminaries Lou Holtz (1999–2004) and Steve Spurrier (2005–14) elevated the success and stature of the program, bringing unprecedented national attention to Gamecock football and the university community.

The famously witty Holtz, when asked upon taking the South Carolina job how he felt about playing the likes of Georgia, Alabama, LSU, and Florida every year, quipped, "I sleep like a baby," continuing with a grin, "I wake up every two hours crying." But the legendary former Notre Dame coach, famous for performing magic tricks during late-night talk show appearances, brought real magic to Columbia in turning around a program that had lost twenty-one straight games, spanning Brad Scott's final season and Holtz's first (1998 and 1999). Holtz led the 2000 team to an 8–4 record, their eight-game turnaround still tied for second best in NCAA history. The magic was highlighted by a season-opening 31–0 win over New Mexico State, snapping the nation's longest losing streak, followed by a dominant win over number 9 Georgia in week two, as goalposts became an endangered species in Williams-Brice Stadium. The Gamecocks capped their eight-game turnaround with a 24–7 whipping of number 19 Ohio State in the Outback Bowl on New Year's Day 2001. Holtz's 2001 Gamecocks improved to a program second-best nine wins and defeated Ohio State once more in an Outback Bowl rematch.

Former Florida Gator head coach Steve Spurrier took the USC program even greater heights, matching a school-record ten wins and capturing the SEC East Championship in 2010 before three consecutive eleven-win seasons between 2011 and 2013. Spurrier's most successful teams were led by South Carolina natives, including Stephon Gilmore, Marcus Lattimore, Alshon Jeffery, Jadeveon Clowney, and D. J. Swearinger. The winningest quarterback in program history, Connor Shaw, never lost a home game as a starter between

2011 and 2013. Perhaps most important to Gamecock fans, South Carolina won an unprecedented five straight versus Clemson between 2009 and 2013.

Since Eddie Fogler's thrilling 1996–97 men's basketball team went 15–1 in conference play, bringing home Carolina's first SEC championship, Game-cock programs have won more than thirty SEC regular-season and tournament titles. Carolina has added numerous SEC East division championships, including football in 2010 and men's basketball in 2009.[3]

Men's basketball broke an incomprehensible drought of forty-four years without an NCAA tournament win with their electrifying 2017 run to the Final Four, collecting the program's first-ever NCAA tournament regional championship along the way under former coach Frank Martin. Dave Odom's 2004–5 and 2005–6 teams brought home consecutive NIT championships, the first program to do so since St. John's in 1943 and 1944.

Ray Tanner's baseball program won the final College World Series championship played at Omaha's classic Rosenblatt Stadium in 2010 before becoming the first to win it all at the new TD Ameritrade Park in 2011.[4] Those back-to-back championships were bookended by runner-up finishes in 2002 and 2012. Tanner's teams won regular-season SEC championships in 2000, 2002, and 2011 and a conference tournament title in 2004. From 2000 through Tanner's final season as head coach in 2012, Carolina boasted the win-ningest program in all of Division I college baseball.

Women's sports, in particular, have enjoyed great success, led by the incomparable Dawn Staley and her women's basketball program. Staley's program has collected two national titles (in 2017 and 2022), seven SEC regular-season championships, and seven tournament titles all since 2014. The 2019–20 team compiled a 32–1 overall record, went undefeated in SEC play, and was the number-one overall seed in the NCAA tournament before concerns over COVID-19 forced cancellations of all NCAA postseason play. The 2023 team completed an undefeated regular season, a first in program history, and made it to the program's fourth Final Four appearance, finishing 36-1.

Program stalwarts A'ja Wilson and Aliyah Boston earned national player of the year honors in 2018 and 2022, respectively, and SEC female athlete of the year in those same two seasons, along with Ty Harris in 2020. A bronze statue of Wilson now graces the entrance of South Carolina's basketball home, Colonial Life Arena.

Staley replaced Connecticut's Geno Auriemma as head coach of the USA National Team in 2017 and led that elite squad to a Gold Medal in the 2020 Olympic Games in Tokyo as well as championships in the 2018 World Cup and 2019 and 2021 FIBA AmeriCup championships.[5] Her prominence on the national stage and tireless work in the community have elevated the stature not just of her Gamecock program but also of the university, the city of Columbia, and the state of South Carolina.

USC added women's soccer in 1995, and since 2001 Coach Shelley Smith has led that program. Carolina has won three regular-season SEC titles (in 2011, 2016, and 2017) and three tournament titles (in 2009, 2019 and 2022). In 2017 Smith's team achieved the program's first appearance in the College Cup (soccer's equivalent of basketball's Final Four).

USC women's golf has enjoyed success in NCAA tournament play, capturing regional championships in 2010, 2012, 2015, 2016, and 2017. The women's tennis, outdoor track and field, equestrian, and softball programs have all captured SEC titles and enjoyed successful runs.

New, Upgraded Facilities Transform Campus and Beyond

On September 25, 1990, after receiving their official invitation to join the Southeastern Conference, USC officials hosted a 7 PM press conference at Williams-Brice Stadium to announce what was, by then, perhaps the worst-kept secret in school history. Attending the press conference was SEC commissioner Roy Kramer, who told USC athletics director Dixon his biggest challenge would be upgrading facilities to a level on par with other conference members.

Indeed, the University of South Carolina had entered the most highly competitive conference in the country, and the challenge of upgrading the brick and mortar of facilities rivaled that of elevating talent on the courts and fields across campus.

Buoyed by annually distributed SEC revenue-sharing funds, USC began a dizzying array of upgrades and new construction across all sports.[6] The building craze kicked off in earnest in 1995 with a basketball practice and volleyball competition facility adjacent to the Carolina Coliseum, along with a new football press box and luxury suites atop the upper-west stands. An upper-south end zone deck came the same year, bringing the seating capacity in Williams-Brice from 72,400 to 80,000.

In 1996 the university constructed a five-thousand-seat concrete grand-stand for the men's and women's soccer programs at the same site the men's program had used since its founding in 1978, nicknamed the "Grave-yard" because of its proximity to the adjacent House of Peace Cemetery. Funding for the project came from a $1 million donation from USC graduate Eugene E. Stone, for whom the new facility was named.

In 2002, after thirty-four seasons at the Carolina Coliseum, the men's and women's basketball teams moved into the eighteen-thousand-seat Caro-lina Center, later rechristened Colonial Life Arena for its corporate naming partner. After years of uncertainty about what to do with the Coliseum, the university converted the playing arena into a permanent practice facility, accommodating both the men's and women's programs.

The baseball program moved into 8,242-seat Carolina Stadium (now Founders Park) in 2009 after four decades at Sarge Frye Field. The stadium, built off-campus along Lincoln Street, on the western edge of Columbia's Congaree Vista District, was widely acclaimed as the greatest facility in college baseball at the time and prompted many SEC rivals to upgrade investments in their own baseball facilities. Carolina's move to the new stadium heralded the golden age of Gamecock baseball, with back-to-back College World Series championships in 2010 and 2011 and another championship series appearance in 2012.

Another key 2009 addition was the Dodie Anderson Academic Enrichment Center, named for a longtime USC supporter and philanthropist. Located on Heyward Street, across from Stone Stadium, the 40,500 square-foot facility, lovingly referred to as the "Dodie" provides academic assistance resources for student-athletes and a dining hall. Upon its opening the facility was described as a "game-changer" by Steve Spurrier and other Gamecock coaches.

Adjacent to the Dodie, at the corner of Heyward and Marion Streets, Rice Athletics Center opened in 2012, housing offices for coaches and athletics administration. The Rice Center replaced the aging, mid-century vintage Rex

Enright Athletic Center, also known as "the Roundhouse" for its distinctive circular design.

Additional upgrades to Williams-Brice Stadium and surrounding areas came in several stages, including the installation of a state-of-the-art video and scoreboard atop the north stands in 2012. The "greening" and beautification of the former asphalt apron circling the stadium's exterior was completed in 2015, and the Springs Brooks Plaza debuted with its brick and iron ornamental fencing along with 340 trees planted around the promenade. A bronze statue of George Rogers was added to the northwest corner of the plaza as part of the upgrades, and a few years later, a giant bronze Gamecock statue was installed in the same area. Renovations in 2020 added luxury seating to various areas of the stadium, reducing capacity to 77,559 but offering high-end amenities and an enhanced game-day experience.

The university purchased the former State Farmer's Market site across Bluff Road in 2012, creating the fifty-acre Gamecock Park, a parking and tail-gating space for boosters and fans, which the USC athletics website describes as a "central open space, called the Garnet Way, a grassy promenade lined with scarlet oaks and providing a route for the marching band, cheerleaders, and football team to parade through the venue on the way to the stadium."

Behind Gamecock Park sit the Jerri and Steve Spurrier Indoor Practice Facility (opened in 2015) and the Cyndi and Kenneth Long Family Football Operations Center (opened in 2019), enabling a one-stop shop for football student-athletes, complete with weight room and training facilities, indoor and outdoor practice fields, coaches' offices and player locker room, lounges, and dining facilities.

Other new and upgraded facilities include the Carolina Tennis Center in 2012, Carolina Softball Stadium at Beckham Field in 2013, the Wheeler Beach volleyball facility in 2014, the Sheila and Morris Cregger Track in 2019, and the Carolina Indoor Track and Field Complex in 2019, among other projects at an ever-evolving campus.

A Final Verdict—Was Leaving the ACC Worth It?

With the hindsight of over fifty years, and three decades securely rooted in the rich, stable soil of Southeastern Conference membership, the question persists among fans old enough to remember: Should South Carolina have left the Atlantic Coast Conference? It is a topic still hotly debated on fan message boards, one likely never to be definitively answered to the satisfaction of all.

For this writer, two seemingly conflicting things are true at once. From the standpoint of stability and prestige throughout the 1970s and 1980s, it seems self-evident that the university made a mistake in leaving the ACC. The Gamecocks left behind a conference it helped found in 1953, filled with natural rivalries among institutions with deep geographical and historical ties. The stated reason for Carolina's departure, primarily their resistance to the ACC's entrance requirements, was already on course for favorable resolution in the courts and was in fact resolved just over a year after USC formally relinquished its conference membership.

In the aftermath of their tempestuous decision to bolt, the university willingly relinquished the stability of conference membership for an uncertain, often rocky path. There was seemingly no consideration beyond the immediate impediment to recruiting or a path back to conference affiliation, in the ACC or otherwise. As the 1970s progressed, South Carolina could only watch as its former ACC brethren embarked on a golden age of basketball dominance and lucrative television broadcasting agreements. It was a golden age in which Frank McGuire's basketball program would have been poised to thrive. Instead USC's most successful program entered a decades-long decline from which it still has not fully recovered.

On the contrary, South Carolina is enjoying unprecedented success, fiscal stability, and brand strength as a member of the SEC, even as additional rounds of conference realignments threaten to destabilize the ACC and its member institutions. From the standpoint of financial strength, the ACC lags far behind the SEC, distributing $36.1 million per conference member in 2022, compared to $55.6 million per member distributed by the SEC. That gap is projected to continue widening as the SEC's revenue distributions are expected to exceed $117 million per school by 2029, nearly doubling that of the ACC.[7]

As of this writing, there is rampant speculation that the ACC will be subject to the raiding or defection of its members by or to the Big Ten or the SEC, which are positioning themselves to expand into "super conference" status.[8] There is some speculation that Clemson and perhaps Florida State may at some point bolt to the SEC if invitations were to materialize. Perhaps the University of North Carolina or NC State, maybe Virginia or Virginia Tech will leave the ACC for more a more lucrative and stable future as well. It is possible that in the not-too-distant future the SEC could loosely resemble the old Southern Conference prior to the formation of the SEC in 1932 and the ACC in 1953, when most of the universities from both conferences were joined under one banner. Only time will tell.

Also of note is the new era in college athletics that began when student-athletes gained the right to earn compensation from their name, image, and likeness (NIL) in the 2021 US Supreme Court case *Alston vs. NCCA* Like the coming conference realignment drama, NIL will transform collegiate athletics in novel and unforeseeable ways.

Whatever the outcomes of these tectonic shifts, the University of South Carolina is well positioned for continued financial stability and competitive success, the likes of which fans in the independent era could have only dreamed. As that era grows more distant with the quicksilver passage of time, it is worth reflecting back and paying tribute to the players and coaches who roamed USC's fields and courts those many years ago.

ACKNOWLEDGMENTS

It has been written many times that a project like this is never the product of one person's efforts. "It takes a village," as the old saying goes, and that certainly bears repeating in the case of the book you now hold in your hands.

One of the great pleasures of seeing this effort to fruition has been reflecting on the people who helped me along the way and have provided inspiration, wisdom, guidance, and encouragement at each step, often and uncannily, just at the moment I needed it most. I am deeply grateful to each of them. While any mistakes or oversights contained within this volume are entirely my own, I am most thankful for the following:

To my wife, Melissa, without whose steadfast encouragement, infectious enthusiasm, and gentle cajoling, the idea of this book would have died on the vine years ago. Your willingness to listen patiently while I read aloud a morning's work or relayed a newly uncovered nugget of trivia; your tolerance for a dining room table littered by yellow legal pads, decades-old media guides, and dog-eared books; your embrace of all things Gamecock, and your endless positivity are amazing to me. You were an invaluable partner from the outset in this endeavor. There is no one with whom I would rather be in the trenches.

To Dad—there was nothing more special to me as a young boy than sitting with you those many winter nights in the cozy confines of Frank McGuire Arena. The games we attended were the seeds of inspiration for this book. And to Joan, for gamely encouraging those too-rare opportunities when Dad and I are still able to connect for a game.

To Mom, who passed to me your great love of reading; for taking Celeste and me to Richland County Library on those long-ago summer days, where I discovered joy in the aroma of old books and the stories waiting to be discovered inside. For the abiding encouragement of my work on this project both you and Howard have shown throughout; and for the trips to Edisto, where the tide-haunted Lowcountry marsh never fails to inspire.

To Patrick Morgan and Lyn Herr, for their consistent interest in, and encouragement of this project.

To my Columbia nephews, Chase and Evan, whose first memories of Gamecock fandom are of confident belonging in the Southeastern Conference, multisport national championships, and eleven-win football seasons. It wasn't always that way!

To Andy Shlon, beloved family member and Columbia icon. You are missed by all, my friend.

To Lee Pitts, who was like a second dad to me growing up and whose humor made every game a joy in Section 305 of Williams-Brice, even when the football wasn't so joyful. Thank you for your kind encouragement of this project, and for making a key introduction along the way.

To Norwood Smith, a fellow Gamecock expat in Tar Heel, Blue Devil, and Wolfpack country, who read an early version of chapter 1 and provided much needed encouragement during the nascent, uncertain days of this project.

To the memories of Howard Weeks and John Campbell—friends, mentors, and great Gamecocks. I miss you both.

To Lori Cove, the greatest of Clemson Tigers, whose friendship transcends rivalries and whose perseverance through unfathomable challenges provides inspiration daily.

To Mike Chibbaro, whose early guidance and advice was indispensable, and whose excellent books, *The Cadillac* and *The Mighty Generals,* provided me with vision and inspiration for what I hoped to accomplish through my own work.

To Bob Gillespie, who lived these stories as he covered the Gamecock teams of this era, took the time to speak with me early on, and introduced me to others who would also be helpful.

To Ron Morris, who patiently gave of his time, expertly editing early chapters of this book long before there was any reason to believe it would one day be published.

To Brian Shoemaker and Collyn Taylor of Gamecock Central, who, in 2021, published a series of articles from my interviews with Jimmy Foster and, later, excerpts from what became chapter 1 of this book, I owe you a tremendous debt of gratitude.

To Elizabeth West and her talented staff at the University of South Carolina's Caroliniana Library for pointing me toward the vast array of resources available through USC Libraries' Digital Collections. I am envious beyond measure for the opportunity you have to work each day in that magnificent building in the verdant heart of our university.

To Margaret Dunlap at Richland County Library, who was tremendously helpful throughout, introducing me to the Newsbank database of digitized newspapers, and going beyond the call of duty to secure many of the photos included in this book from the photographic archives of the *State* and *Columbia Record*. The Newsbank database was key to accomplishing the research for this project and saved me from the dizzying, laborious task of reviewing two decades of microfiche reels. To historians of the pre-digital age, you have my undying respect and admiration.

To my editor, Ehren Foley, who has been an advocate and partner from day one, and who knows a thing or two about great barbeque; to USC Press, for taking a chance on this project; to marketer extraordinaire, Cathy Esposito, and the entire team at the press, whose diligent and often unsung work made it all possible.

To the former Gamecock athletes and coaches who took the time to speak with me. I thank, in particular, Jimmy Foster and Kristina Buck, who took a leap of faith in sharing their stories openly, honestly, and unsparingly. Jimmy, my sincere hope is that you one day receive the recognition from our university you so richly earned on the court those many years ago. And to Kristina, your spirit, bravery, and grace have been an inspiration to me.

And to all who wore Garnet and Black during the years covered in this book, you provided inspiration throughout. Your grit, hustle, and passion planted the seeds of this book in a nine-year-old boy during his early visits to Williams-Brice Stadium, Frank McGuire Arena, and Sarge Frye Field.

Here's a health, Carolina, and to all of you.

NOTES

1: Storms in the Southland

1. The loss to Fordham was South Carolina's final basketball game as a member of the ACC. Though the Gamecocks competed in ACC baseball that spring, South Carolina left the ACC officially on June 30, 1977, three months after their greatest triumph in Greensboro.

2. Chamberlain came in fourth for the national scoring title during the 1957 season, edged by Joe Gibbon of Mississippi, Elgin Baylor of Seattle, and South Carolina senior forward Grady Wallace, who averaged an NCAA-leading 31.3 points per game. Wallace's number, 42, was the first number retired by the USC athletics department in any sport. He remains one of only two national scoring champions from the ACC, along with Erick Green of Virginia Tech, who averaged 25 points per game in 2012–13. USC's Wallace is the only national scoring champion from the original ACC schools.

3. At St. John's, McGuire also coached baseball, taking the Redmen to the 1949 College World Series, as well as his basketball team to the '52 finals, the only coach in NCAA history to accomplish both.

4. In the early days of professional basketball, wire cages were often assembled over the playing floor to keep balls inbounds and to separate players and fans. The term *cage coach* stuck around long after the actual cages disappeared.

5. McGuire nearly backed out of the South Carolina job when Dwane Morrison, upon learning that he would not continue as head coach, lobbied USC president Jones to stay on as an assistant to McGuire. Jones supported Morrison's bid and advised McGuire accordingly. McGuire advised Jones in return that he would not be forced into hiring staff not of his choosing and returned to New York. Upon learning of the situation, Sol Blatt Sr. demanded Jones travel to New York to smooth things over, telling Jones he could "get a new president easier than he could get another Frank McGuire." Jones made the drive to New York, met with McGuire, and assured him his staffing choices would be his own. McGuire promptly returned to Columbia to continue his rebuilding project. Barton and Fulton, *Frank McGuire*, 81–82.

6. LSU defeated Clemson 7–0 in the Sugar Bowl on New Year's Day, 1959, to secure its first national championship. Clemson's only other losses that season were a 13–0 shutout by Georgia Tech in Atlanta and a 26–6 setback to the Gamecocks on

Big Thursday in Columbia. The loss to Carolina was the Tigers' only ACC loss that season, and they went on to win the ACC championship. The following season, 1959, marked the final Big Thursday contest, which was played annually between Carolina and Clemson in Columbia during State Fair week. Beginning in 1960, the rivalry moved to a format where each school would host alternating years; since 1962 it has been the final regular-season game for both teams.

7. In hindsight Bass's comments about Dietzel's motivations may not have been totally without merit. In his 2008 memoir, *Call Me a Coach*, Dietzel notes the football program at USC had become "an embarrassment": "It had to be rebuilt from scratch. The season prior to my arrival, the Gamecocks' record was no wins and ten losses. The team had never won a conference championship and had not received a bowl invitation in twenty-five years." While the program was certainly in need of upgrading upon Dietzel's arrival, the picture he paints is not completely accurate. His reference to the 0–10 season in 1965 is misleading, as Bass's final team compiled a 5–5 record (4–2 ACC) and won a share of the ACC title. With the four forfeited ACC games, Carolina's record became 1–9 in the eyes of the ACC. Though the university does not recognize the '65 ACC championship, the USC football media guide still reflects a 5–5 record for the 1965 season.

8. Bill Cates of the *Roanoke Times* wrote of the ACC's dismal football performance versus other conferences that "ACC football is one of the worst frauds ever perpetrated on the southern sporting public." Quoted in J. Samuel Walker, *ACC Basketball*, 312.

9. Howard and Dietzel were not close, and their styles contrasted dramatically. Howard often referred to Dietzel as "Pepsodent Paul," a derisive reference to his toothy grin.

10. South Carolina governor Strom Thurmond famously led the Dixiecrat ticket during the 1948 US presidential election. The States' Rights Democratic Party, as it was also known, was a short-lived segregationist party formed in protest of the moderate civil rights advances under President Harry Truman, such as integration of the US military. The Dixiecrat ticket of Thurmond and Mississippi governor Fielding L. Wright carried South Carolina, Alabama, Mississippi, and Louisiana.

In the 1964 presidential election, South Carolina again joined Alabama, Mississippi, and Louisiana, plus Georgia and Arizona, in voting for Republican presidential candidate Barry Goldwater of Arizona. Goldwater ran in part to protest passage of the 1964 Civil Rights Act championed by incumbent president Lyndon B. Johnson. The Civil Rights Act was broadly popular across the United States, and Johnson won handily, with 486 electoral votes to Goldwater's 52.

11. Hayward played on the freshman team in 1969 and redshirted in 1970, finally earning his letter in 1971. Brown, who came to Carolina on a baseball scholarship in 1969, switched to football and lettered in 1970. Manning played on three NCAA tournament teams under McGuire and later became a circuit court judge and a member of the Gamecock Radio Network for basketball broadcasts. White became a longtime

fixture within the athletics department as a full-time academic counselor, serving the university for nearly forty years.

12. Solomon did not score the requisite 800 on his SAT and went on to star at the University of Tampa, from there playing eleven years for the Dolphins and 49ers of the NFL. In the 1982 NFC championship game, made famous by "the Catch," Dwight Clark's iconic leaping touchdown grab, Solomon was the primary target on the play. Quarterback Joe Montana checked off to Clark when Solomon slipped on his route. Solomon figured prominently for the 49ers on the final and deciding drive of that game.

13. South Carolina later accelerated its departure date to June 30.

14. South Carolina's 1971 season marked only the second time a squad not from the Big Four won the ACC basketball championship—the first was Maryland in 1958. In the nearly seventy-year history of the conference, there have been only fourteen non–Big Four tournament champions (20 percent), with four of those coming in an unprecedented straight stretch between 2012 and 2015. The only other consecutive non–Big Four champions were Maryland and Georgia Tech in 1984 and 1985. The original non–Big Four members of the ACC have won a combined six champion-ships: Maryland three, Virginia two, and South Carolina one. Clemson has never won an ACC basketball title. Maryland left the ACC for the Big Ten Conference in July 2014.

2: Build It, and They Will Come

1. USC experienced exponential growth as the "Baby Boom" generation came of age. The Columbia campus grew from 5,660 in 1960 to 26,000 by 1979.

2. South Carolina's and Clemson's venues were frequently cited by opposing coaches and players as the most inhospitable in the ACC, though they had competi-tion. When the ACC Sportswriters Association planned to award a sportsmanship trophy for the school that showed the "best sportsmanship" during the 1957 season, Smith Barrier of the *Greensboro News* suggested the award would end in "an eight-way tie for last place." Walker, *ACC Basketball*, 217.

3. Freeman had been McGuire's coach and mentor at St. John's, where he com-piled an impressive 179–32 (.850) record as head coach, an average of twenty-six wins over eight seasons between 1927 and 1936. Freeman also served as athletics director at St. John's. He later joined McGuire's staff at the University of North Carolina and then at the University of South Carolina, where he retired following the 1972–73 sea-son. New York Times, February 16, 1974.

4. The Omni Coliseum in Atlanta surpassed Carolina's new arena by several thou-sand seats when it opened four years later. Meanwhile, as USC opened the Carolina Coliseum, Clemson debuted its own sparkling new arena on the same night, with a 76–72 victory over Georgia Tech in the eleven-thousand-seat Littlejohn Coliseum. A few days later, Clemson recorded its first sellout crowd, which witnessed a heartbreak-ing 86–85 loss for the Tigers against Louisiana State. LSU's "Pistol" Pete Maravich led

all scorers with thirty-six points in a homecoming of sorts. Maravich's father, Press, had coached Clemson for six seasons during Pete's youth before moving on to North Carolina State and ultimately to LSU.

5. Spartanburg Junior College is now Spartanburg Methodist College.

6. The Carolina Coliseum served as the Gamecocks' home venue for thirty-four seasons, between 1968 and 2002, during which time USC compiled a 372–125 (.748) record. The playing area was named "Frank McGuire Arena" in honor of the longtime coach in 1977. The final men's game played in the Coliseum occurred on March 21, 2002, in a third-round NIT contest, an 82–47 win over Ball State. USC opened the eighteen-thousand-seat Carolina Center (later renamed Colonial Life Arena) for the 2002–3 season.

7. In the early 1950s, construction of the Russell House student union commenced in the area of Melton Field, creating the need for new athletic fields. The university purchased twenty-one acres bounded by Rosewood Drive and South Marion Street. By 1956 USC had constructed athletic offices, which became known as the "Roundhouse," and athletic facilities, including a baseball diamond, a track, and three football practice fields. Lesesne, *History of the University of South Carolina*, 94–95.

8. The one tie was 4–4 against ACC-leading Clemson on April 16. The game was played a day later than originally scheduled because of rain and was called after thirteen innings because of darkness. The teams met on the campus of the Veterans Hospital in Columbia because of soggy conditions at their new home field. USC played many of its home games at the Veterans Hospital field prior to the opening of their new spring sports complex.

9. Melton Field sat roughly at the site of today's Russell House Student Union building. The field was a former parade ground for General William Sherman's troops during the Union occupation of Columbia in 1865. Davis Field, the former baseball diamond, lay immediately to the west along Greene Street, between Melton Field and Longstreet Theater, roughly at the site of the Thomas Cooper Library's reflecting pool. The first recorded baseball games in Columbia took place on Davis Field between Union soldiers and local teams.

10. Brice was the daughter of Sumter furniture magnate O. L. Williams and the widow of Thomas H. Brice, president of Southern Coatings and Chemical Company and Williams-Georgia Pacific Furniture Company. Her interest in Carolina athletics went back decades, and her husband had been a football letterman at USC. The will further directed $250,000 gifts each to Trinity United Methodist Church of Sumter and Epworth Children's Home in Columbia.

11. Carolina's first bowl game, in 1946, was the inaugural Gator Bowl contest in Jacksonville, Florida. That game resulted in a 26–14 Wake Forest win, though the Gamecocks made a splash in their first bowl appearance. Coach Johnnie McMillan led the 1946 squad, filling in for Rex Enright while Enright fulfilled his military obligation. Enright, who was stationed in Jacksonville, had lobbied Jacksonville bowl officials on behalf of the Gamecocks and was largely responsible for USC's bid. The most notable

play in a losing effort was a ninety-yard interception return for a touchdown by USC's Dutch Brembs—a Gator Bowl record until Gamecock safety O'Donnell Fortune returned an interception 100 yards versus Notre Dame in the 2022 Gator Bowl.

3: Into the Wilderness

1. USC's baseball diamond at the Enright Athletic Complex was renamed "Sarge Frye Field" in honor of the longtime groundskeeper on May 11, 1980, in ceremonies preceding a 4–1 win over archrival Clemson.

2. Richardson played twelve seasons for the Yankees, from 1955 to 1966. A contemporary of Mickey Mantle, he became a regular starter at second base by the 1957 season and earned all-star recognition following that season. He went on to an illustrious career, which included five straight Gold Glove awards between 1961 and 1965, and was named an all-star seven times. He was a starter on the Yankees World Series championship teams of 1958, 1961, and 1962, and in 1960 he became the only player from a losing team in MLB history to garner World Series MVP honors.

3. The upgrades brought capacity from 42, 238 to 56,140 and also included a new press box, broadcast booths, and camera deck. Immediately following the 1971 season, work began to replace the lower west stands with a concrete deck and the wooden benches in the east, north and south stands with aluminum ones. Those upgrades included wider seating, which reduced capacity to 53,685. USC officially christened the venue Williams-Brice Stadium in honor of benefactor Martha Williams Brice during ceremonies preceding the home opener versus Virginia on September 9, 1972.

4. Wallace Wade Stadium, previously Duke Stadium, served as the host of the 1942 Rose Bowl between the Blue Devils and Oregon State. Following the bombing of Pearl Harbor on December 7, 1941, large gatherings were discouraged, and in many cases banned, along the West Coast. The Beavers won that contest 20–16 in front of fifty-five thousand spectators, over twenty thousand of whom sat on temporary bleachers borrowed from nearby UNC and NC State.

5. FSU had begun its rise to national prominence under Coach Bill Peterson, who built the program essentially from scratch. After fielding early football teams in the 1890s, FSU was designated a women-only college in 1902 by the Florida legislature and remained so until 1947, following World War II. The program struggled under various coaches until Peterson arrived in 1960. By 1964 Peterson's Seminoles beat Florida for the first time and earned the school its first major bowl bid. South Carolina and FSU met for the first time in 1966, Dietzel's first season at USC, when the teams began a home-and-home series. The Seminoles won that first game in Columbia, 32–10, and carried a 5–0 series record into the 1971 matchup. The two schools played frequently as independents until each joined their respective conferences in 1992. Since 1991 the teams have only met once, a 2010 matchup in the Peach Bowl, which resulted in a 26–17 FSU win. Florida State holds a 16–3 series advantage.

6. Between 1896 and 1959, the Gamecocks and Tigers met annually on Thursday of State Fair week in Columbia, which became known as "Big Thursday." The rivalry

was interrupted for six years following a 12–6 Gamecock win in 1902, after which armed conflict between the student bodies was narrowly averted. Following that season's surprise win over John Heisman's powerful Clemson squad, jubilant South Carolina students famously "borrowed" a transparency of a Gamecock crowing over a sad-looking tiger from a Main Street store. When the students displayed the transparency during Friday's annual Elk's parade, Clemson cadets (it was then a military school) took strident exception and, following the parade, marched with bayonets drawn from the State House a block south along Sumter Street to the campus gates. There a ragtag assemblage of Carolina students had armed themselves with "a few pistols and clubs and anything that would be useful in self-defense" and crouched behind the old Horseshoe wall in a hasty defense of the campus. Among those students was future USC president and namesake of the University's McKissick Museum, Rion J. McKissick. One student among the badly outnumbered Carolina defenders was reported to have exclaimed, "McKissick, make every shot count!"

Faculty members and Columbia police were able to gain control of the situation before things turned truly ugly. A joint committee of students agreed to burn the transparency between the two groups, as they took turns cheering one another. A crisis was averted, but in the days that followed accusations flew, and reports of the facts varied wildly between the two schools. Carolina's athletics committee decided to discontinue the rivalry, which eventually resumed in 1909. Barton, *Carolina-Clemson Game.*

7. South Carolina played forty-three games in front of crowds at or above capacity (12,401) at Carolina Coliseum during its thirty-four seasons as the home of Gamecock basketball, compiling a record of 32–11 in those contests. The bulk of those games were during the program's early 1970s heyday, when sellouts were commonplace. Perhaps the most notable of those games occurred December 16, 1970, a wild night when 12,686 boisterous partisans witnessed a dominant 96–70 Gamecock win over Lefty Driesell's young Maryland Terrapin squad. The contest was stopped with 4:52 on the clock after an extended brawl, in which John Ribock famously belted Driesell after the coach waded into the melee. The highest attendance in Coliseum history occurred February 2, 1991, when 12,783 fans passed through the turnstiles to witness George Felton's 16–5 Gamecocks defeat Cliff Ellis's Clemson Tigers 59–53.

As testament to the basketball hysteria that once gripped the state of South Carolina, one beyond-capacity event that did not make the record books was a crowd of 12,456 that gathered to witness the annual preseason intrasquad scrimmage in November 1970. Klores, *Roundball Culture,* 201.

8. The South Carolina–Marquette series was a fixture during Frank McGuire's remaining seasons as Gamecock coach. The two schools first met during the 1966–67 season, a 63–61 Gamecock win in Milwaukee, but did not meet again until 1970–71. Marquette largely got the better of South Carolina in this series, in which McGuire's Gamecocks went 2–11 from '66 through '80. Al McGuire took his Warriors to two national championship appearances during this time, losing to NC State in 1974 and

winning Marquette's only championship in 1977 versus another Frank McGuire protégé, Dean Smith, and his UNC Tar Heels. Following his championship, Al retired from coaching in favor of the broadcaster's booth. The South Carolina–Marquette series continued into the early 1980s, providing Bill Foster with his first signature win in 1980–81, a 91–89 upset in Milwaukee. The Gamecocks took a 66–64 thriller in Columbia during the 1982–83 season before the series was interrupted. Since then the teams have met twice, a 2005 Marquette overtime win in the Great Alaska Shootout tournament and an opening round win in the 2017 NCAA tournament for Frank Martin's Gamecocks—the program's first NCAA tournament win in forty-three seasons.

9. The consolation game win versus Southwestern Louisiana proved, incredibly, to be the program's final NCAA tournament win for forty-three years.

10. Morrison, who was a Gamecock letterman and top scorer for Frank Johnson's 1951–52 USC squad, later returned to South Carolina as freshman squad coach and assistant under head coach Doug Noe. When Noe resigned, citing "nervous exhaustion" during the 1963–64 season, Morrison took over coaching duties for the varsity, coaching the final twelve games to a 4–8 finish. When McGuire was hired in the spring of 1964, Morrison spent several years coaching high school ball before landing another college assistant gig at Georgia Tech, where he spent six seasons under coach John Hyder. After a brief head coaching job at Mercer (1970–73), where he compiled a 48–22 record, Morrison was hired to replace Hyder at Georgia Tech in 1973. He spent the next eight seasons at Tech in an eventful period that saw the Yellow Jackets go from independent status to the fledgling Metro Conference, then back to independent for the 1978–79 season, before beginning ACC play in 1979–80. He was ultimately fired at Tech after going 1–27 in ACC contests during his final two seasons.

Morrison's replacement for the 1980–81 season was fellow Gamecock letterman Bobby Cremins, previously head coach of Appalachian State. Cremins famously spent nineteen seasons leading the Tech program until stepping away in 2000. Thus two Gamecock lettermen led Georgia Tech basketball over a period of twenty-seven years.

11. The 1975 Tangerine Bowl was the Gamecock program's third bowl appearance, and the first since the 1969 Peach Bowl. Carolina lost 20–7 to a powerful Miami (Ohio) team, which had compiled a 30–1–1 record over three seasons and defeated Georgia and Florida in the previous two Tangerine Bowl matchups.

12. Walsh went on to a highly successful career in the NBA, assuming the position of head coach of the Nuggets in 1979–80, with later stints as assistant coach and then general manager for both the Indiana Pacers and the New York Knicks. He later returned to the Pacers as president of basketball operations, where he finished his career in 2013.

13. The crowds never really came back in a sustained way. During Bill Foster's best season, 1982–83, the Gamecocks drew an average of 8,793 fans. George Felton's best team, the 1990–91 squad, drew 9,964 on average. Even Eddie Fogler's SEC regular-season champion 1997–98 squad drew only 9,227 on average.

14. B. J. McKie passed English into the top all-time scoring position during his senior season of 1996–97. McKie scored 2,119 points in an illustrious career, highlighted by the 1997–98 SEC regular-season championship. His number, 3, was the fifth to be retired in program history, following Grady Wallace's 42, John Roche's 11, Kevin Joyce's 43, and Alex English's 22.

4: Legends, Logos, Mascots, and Traditions

1. It was another sixteen years before the Gamecock track and field program, under the direction of Curtis Frye, won the 2002 NCAA women's outdoor track and field championship. Since that time the University of South Carolina has accumulated an additional nine national championships, most notably women's basketball in 2017 and the back-to-back championships for baseball in 2010–11. USC's highly regarded equestrian program won six titles between 2005 and 2017.

2. Dietzel also worked with USC band director James Pritchett to update the USC fight song. After Pritchett secured an arrangement of the Elmer Bernstein song "Step to the Rear" from the Broadway musical *How Now, Dow Jones,* the band played the song during the first game of the 1968 season. The tune caught Dietzel's ear, and he approached Pritchett about replacing the current fight song with "Step to the Rear." Dietzel wrote updated lyrics, though he insisted that he not be identified as the author, fearing the basketball program might not accept the song if it was known that the lyrics were written by the football coach. The Carolina band introduced "The Fighting Gamecocks Lead the Way" during halftime ceremonies of South Carolina's home matchup with Virginia Tech on November 16, 1968, with Dietzel's lyrics printed in the game program.

According to USC Libraries, the old fight song, "Carolina Let Your Voices Ring," now simply known as "Old Fight Song," was the result of a 1933 fraternity contest to create a fight song for athletic contests. The fraternity promised five hundred dollars for the winning submission. USC student M. Carerre Salley gamely composed the winning lyrics, after which the prize was reduced to three hundred dollars. He eventually managed to collect fifty dollars and settled for that, noting that he would have entered even if there had been no prize. In a 1968 letter to Dietzel, Salley noted the song was lightly used until band director James Pritchett revived it and used it as the primary fight song from 1959 until the introduction of the new song in 1968. Salley's "Old Fight Song" lives on today as part of pregame ceremonies at home football contests.

3. In 2018–19 USC earned $140.7 million, landing at seventeenth among highest-earning athletics departments. Ten of the twenty highest-earning departments were from the SEC. The conference boasted eleven of the top twenty athletics departments in terms of royalties from merchandise sales in 2012–13, with South Carolina landing at number sixteen.

4. The median square-foot price for a home in Columbia was around $105 in 2021.

5. Tillman was an unabashed White supremacist, whose part in the persecution and murder of Black citizens in his native Edgefield County was remarkable even in post-Reconstruction South Carolina. He harbored a seething resentment toward the "Bourbon aristocracy" of the ruling class and a strident antipathy toward USC for its meager agricultural offerings, calling for a separate institution dedicated to the agricultural and mechanical arts. His spirited deprecation of Lowcountry aristocrats and Columbia pols earned him the adoration of Upstate farmers, enabling him to capture the governorship in 1890.

6. Prior to the Morrison era, white helmets of varying designs had been the modern-era standard. The only other time garnet helmets had been used was in 1964–65, over the course of two seasons under coach Marvin Bass. The helmets sported an offset *SC,* and the Gamecocks alternated between white and garnet helmets during those two seasons. A digital collection of USC Libraries hosts footage of the 1965 USC versus NC State game in Columbia, during which the Gamecocks wore those garnet helmets. During the latter portion of the Dietzel era (1970–74), seniors wore black helmets for the season-ending Clemson game, while the rest of the team wore traditional white helmets. See the USC page at the website Helmet History, helmethistory .com/south-carolina.html (accessed March 13, 2023).

5: A National Power Emerges

1. Laval compiled an 89–33–1 (.728) record as USC baseball coach, still the top winning percentage of any coach in program history. He also became the only football coach in program history to achieve seven straight winning seasons, compiling a 39–26–7 record in the process. Steve Spurrier later tied that record with seven straight winning seasons between 2008 and 2014.

2. Columbia's first Sally League team in 1904 was known as the Skyscrapers, a nod to the rapidly developing downtown business district. The twelve-story Barringer Building, Columbia's first skyscraper, had opened the prior year at 1338 Main Street. The team's name changed frequently in those early years, going by Gamecocks for a time and then Commissioners, named for the form of city government then employed. That name was shortened to the more familiar Comers or Commies, long before anticommunist hysteria gripped mid-century America.

3. The old Columbia Mills location has been the site of the South Carolina State Museum since 1988.

4. USC's early football and baseball teams played under various names, including the Jaguars. Gamecocks found permanent favor shortly after the turn of the twentieth century.

5. There was no evident relation between James P. Shand and prominent Columbia attorney and developer Robert W. Shand, president of the Columbia Land and Investment Company, who gave his name to Shandon, Columbia's first planned suburban community. Robert Shand's youngest son, Monroe, did play both baseball (1900) and football (1899) at South Carolina.

6. Richardson's career batting average was actually .266. See https://www.baseball
-reference.com/players/r/richabo01.shtml.

7. Game 7 of the 1960 World Series, which took place at Forbes Field in Pittsburgh, has been called the greatest game in MLB history. The Pittsburgh Pirates beat
the Yankees 10–9 to secure an improbable championship in a series where the Yankees
scored twice as many runs (55 to 27) and dominated practically every statistical category. Richardson hit a grand slam during a 16–4 game 3 rout, only his second home
run of the season and first since that April. At the time MVP votes had to be submitted by the start of the eighth inning, at which point the Yankees held a 5–4 lead.

8. Herman Helms, *Columbia State*, March 19, 1970.

9. Brown's athleticism caught the attention of Dietzel, who invited him to football tryouts. Brown earned a football scholarship and a starting spot in Dietzel's backfield for the 1970 season.

10. When Richardson arrived at South Carolina, there were no lights at the ballpark, which had just been completed in 1969. Richardson lobbied his contacts in the
South Carolina legislature for funding to install outfield light towers. The legislature
approved the funding for both USC and Clemson. "That worked out well for both of
us," Richardson noted.

11. The Yankees were front-runners in the American League East for most of that
season, while the Mets had gone seven games in the 1973 World Series, ultimately losing to Reggie Jackson's Oakland As.

12. Just six days later, a different Hank won yet another home run contest, as the
Braves' "Hammerin' Hank" Aaron launched his iconic 715th home run off the Dodg-
ers' Al Downing on April 8, 1974, in Atlanta's Fulton County Stadium, breaking Babe
Ruth's fifty-nine-year-old home run record.

13. Nineteen seventy-four also marked the switch from wood to aluminum bats
for college baseball in a cost-saving effort, since aluminum bats were cheaper and
more durable than wood. Besides replacing the traditional crack of the bat with a
new-age ping, aluminum bats also resulted in a power surge. Carolina scored a school-
record 336 runs in 1974, compared to 200 the season before, which had also been a
program record. The jump marked a 68 percent increase in run production, with
similar jumps in offensive output evident across college baseball.

14. Long-serving congressman John Spratt succeeded Holland in the Fifth Congressional District in 1983. He served in that seat until 2011, when he was succeeded by
Republican candidate Mick Mulvaney, a darling of the Tea Party movement and the
first Republican to carry that district since the Reconstruction era.

15. Raines was the sole major hire of athletics director Bo Hagan, who served in
that role in 1975–76 following the resignation of Paul Dietzel. Hagan's authority was
limited, as associate athletic director Jim Carlen held full sway over football operations
and associate athletic director Frank McGuire had full control of basketball operations
during Carolina's ponderous, multipronged approach to athletics administration. All

three men reported directly to university president James Patterson. The university reassigned Hagan in 1976, and Carlen was named athletics director over the full department, with the exception of McGuire's basketball program.

16. The only other Gamecock coach of a major men's sport with a comparable tenure was McGuire, who compiled a 283–142 (.665) record over sixteen seasons. Dawn Staley has completed fifteen seasons as women's basketball coach, compiling a 402–106 (.791) record

17. Harold White, who Paul Dietzel hired as the university's first Black assistant coach in August 1971, began his career shortly after Carolina's ACC exit. White served in numerous coaching and academic support roles throughout his career, eventually gaining the title of associate athletics director of academic support and student services. He retired in 2017.

18. In 1990 Baptist College achieved university status, and the South Carolina legislature approved a name change to Charleston Southern University.

19. Tiger Field was renamed Doug Kingsmore Stadium in 2003, after a generous gift by the former Clemson board of trustees member, earmarked for renovation of the stadium.

20. Cal State Los Angeles eliminated Clemson in the following round. Clemson made its second consecutive trip to the College World Series in 1977, the first of three times the Gamecocks and Tigers would make the trip to Omaha in the same season. Though the Palmetto State rivals did not meet in the CWS that year, they played twice in both the 2002 and 2010 tournaments, resulting in four Gamecock wins. The Clemson program experienced a resurgence in the mid-to-late seventies under long-time coach Bill Wilhelm, who had previously taken his first two Clemson teams to the College World Series in 1958 and 1959.

21. Horner would win the inaugural Golden Spikes Award in 1978, presented annually to the best amateur baseball player in the United States. South Carolina pitcher Kip Bouknight won the award in 2000, following a season in which he compiled a nation-leading seventeen wins and one loss.

22. A two-tier press box was added behind home plate in 1987, and additional upgrades followed in the Ray Tanner years, including chairback seats, dugout enlargements, and extensive renovations to the locker room and training facility. Restroom facilities were added to the visitor's dugout, a welcome accommodation for opposing teams. Potential for additional expansions at Sarge Frye Field was limited, shoehorned as it was between the Roost athletic dorms, the softball stadium, and the CSX railroad tracks. Following Tanner's successful teams of the early 2000s, including a runner-up finish in the 2002 College World Series, plans began to take shape for the next home of Gamecock baseball. In 2009 South Carolina opened the $35 million Carolina Stadium, situated on the banks of the Congaree River, featuring stunning views of the Columbia skyline beyond center field. With capacity of 8,242, the stadium was the premier venue in all of college baseball, leading other institutions in the SEC and

beyond to upgrade their facilities. In 2016 the stadium was renamed Founders Park for its sponsoring partner.

23. Reaching the College World Series is the equivalent of reaching the Elite Eight in the NCAA basketball tournament. South Carolina's eleven College World Series appearances rank thirteenth nationally.

24. Raines coached five seasons in the SEC, from 1992 until 1996.

6: Pullets, Chicks, and Lady Gamecocks

1. Breckinridge represented Charles Lindbergh during the Lindbergh kidnapping trial of 1935, dubbed at the time the "trial of the century," and also opposed President Franklin Roosevelt in the 1936 Democratic presidential primaries as an anti–New Deal candidate. Roosevelt won the primaries convincingly with 93.19 percent of the cumulative vote.

2. The "Chicks" moniker, like "Pullets," was a not-so-subtle reflection of the paternalism of the day, bringing to mind as it does something diminutive, weak, even cute, but not to be taken seriously—very much unlike imagery conjured by the "Fighting Gamecock" of men's teams.

3. The university acquired the campus of Booker T. Washington High after it closed in 1974. The women's team used the gymnasium at the high school as a home court when access to the Carolina Coliseum was not available because of scheduling conflicts during the first few years of the program.

4. Women's teams at USC have long since gone simply by "Gamecocks." They will be referenced in that fashion during the remainder of the chapter, unless directly quoting primary sources from the period.

5. In 2000 Toal became the first female chief justice of the South Carolina Supreme Court, serving in that role until her retirement in 2015.

6. Basketball was one of twelve women's sports added to the NCAA championship program for the 1981–82 academic year. "NCAA Division I Women's Basketball Tournament," Wikipedia, https://en.wikipedia.org/wiki/ (accessed March 8, 2023).

7. Foster remained atop USC's career scoring list until 2018, when she was passed by A'ja Wilson. Aliyah Boston surpassed Foster's double-double record in 2023. Foster remains the program leader in rebounds. Foster remains the program leader in rebounds and double-doubles. USC women's basketball media guide.

8. Cronan went on to serve as the women's athletic director at the University of Tennessee from 1983 to 2012, where she oversaw the nation's most successful program under Coach Pat Summit. Hatchell enjoyed a highly successful thirty-three-season stint as head coach at the University of North Carolina, highlighted by a national championship in 1994.

9. After serving as an assistant to Auriemma on the 2016 gold-medal-winning US Olympic team, Staley assumed the head coaching role, leading Team USA to another gold medal during the 2020 Olympic Games in Tokyo.

7: Any Port in a Storm

1. Carlen's 1969 WVU Mountaineer squad defeated Paul Dietzel's ACC-champion Gamecocks 14–3 in a rain-soaked Peach Bowl at Atlanta's Grant Field. The game was South Carolina's first bowl appearance since 1946 and only the second bowl game in program history.

2. Board of trustees secretary George Curry acted as an intermediary between the ACC and South Carolina. Curry managed to secure a confidential offer for USC's readmission, but the board refused to accept the ACC's terms and, in a sharply divided 5–3 vote, rescinded their application to the ACC. This was the high-water mark of South Carolina's efforts toward readmission to the Atlantic Coast Conference. Lesesne, *History of the University of South Carolina*, 252.

3. The USC board appointed Dietzel vice president of university relations in December 1974, which Chairman Marchant described as a "newly-created position" with vague responsibilities for overseeing "alumni activities and development." Dietzel had hoped to retain the athletics director position, but the board was ready to move on. Dietzel ultimately decided he was too and resigned the VP position a month later.

4. McGuire actively lobbied for the athletics director job, telling a *Daily Gamecock* reporter in early December 1974 that the AD job would be "not a big undertaking" and suggesting he could easily balance coaching and AD responsibilities.

5. Carlen commented to the *State* in August 1975, just prior to his first season in Columbia, that USC had made a mistake in leaving the ACC. "We'll play five ACC teams this fall. We're playing in the ACC, but we're not part of it. That's not a good situation." He soon changed his stance on the ACC.

6. USC lost 20–7 to Miami (Ohio) in the 1975 Tangerine Bowl in Orlando, Florida. The "Redskins" (now Red Hawks), a Mid-America Conference power, had accumulated a 31–1–1 record over the three seasons, going 10–1 in 1975 and finishing sixteenth in the AP poll. The loss pushed South Carolina's still fledgling bowl record to 0–3.

7. Blatt Sr. served as Speaker of the South Carolina House until 1974, and in 1973 he was named Speaker Emeritus in 1973. USC's Blatt Physical Education Center is named for him. In July 2021 the university's Presidential Commission on University History recommended removing his name from the building due to his staunch segregationist views. Blatt Jr. served as a federal district court judge for the South Carolina District from 1971 until 1990.

8. Rex Enright had served as athletics director after turning over football duties to Warren Giese in the 1950s. When Enright died, Giese took on both positions. He continued to serve as director of athletics for one year after the arrival of new football coach Marvin Bass, but in 1962 the two positions were combined again under Bass, and the jobs had remained combined over the next two decades under Bass, then Dietzel, and finally Carlen.

9. Kentucky defeated Foster's Blue Devils in the 1978 NCAA final, 94–88, largely thanks to Wildcat forward Jack Givens's forty-one-point performance. John Feinstein's 1989 book, *Forever's Team*, delves into the 1977–78 Duke basketball team.

10. Ten days later Duke hired a thirty-three-year-old Bobby Knight protégé named Mike Krzyzewski.

11. The football game versus Hawaii proved to be Carlen's final game as head football coach at South Carolina.

8: Good Times, Bad Times

1. South Carolina had previously reached the eight-win mark once, in 1903, however that schedule included two games versus noncollegiate teams. Under coach C. R. Williams, the newly christened Gamecocks, who officially adopted the mascot following the previous season's upset of Clemson and subsequent near riot, went 8–2 on the season, highlighted by shutout wins over Georgia, Tennessee, and Georgia Tech. The Gamecocks defeated Welsh Neck (later Coker College), 89–0, still a program record for points in a game. Perhaps less impressively, USC claimed shutout victories over YMCA teams from Columbia and Charleston. The two losses were to UNC and NC State, then known as North Carolina A&M. That same year also marked the beginning of a six-year stretch when South Carolina and Clemson did not meet on the gridiron, a result of the 1902 conflict. The teams met again in 1909 and enjoyed the longest-running continuous rivalry series in the South prior to an interruption due to COVID-19 in 2020, when the SEC ruled against holding nonconference games.

2. Georgia defeated UCLA in the Rose Bowl on January 1, 1943, capping a 10–1 season. The Associated Press had voted Ohio State number 1 at the end of the regular season (the 9–1 Buckeyes did not participate in a bowl) and did not conduct post-bowl polling at that time. Long before the College Football Playoffs and Bowl Championship Series did much to clarify claims to national championships, many organizations conducted polls that were used to designate a national champion, with the AP the most prominent among them. In 1942 six polls listed Ohio State as number 1, while six other polls listed Georgia. Ohio State claimed the championship because of their listing by the AP. Upon discovering this fact during a visit to the College Football Hall of Fame in the late 1980s, Vince Dooley brought the information to Georgia officials. After some research Georgia retroactively claimed a share of the 1942 title. As of 2020 there were 257 claimed national titles across 147 seasons of college football. The further back those claims go, the more murky and sometimes dubious they become. Seth Emerson, "Why Does Georgia Claim Only 2 National Titles When It Could Have More?" The Athletic, March 30, 2020, https://theathletic.com/1704920/2020/03/30/.

3. The Trans-America Conference, along with the Metro, Big East, and others, was among the numerous basketball-focused conferences that sprung up in the mid to late 1970s, as schools moved away from independent status in favor of the opportunity to compete in conference tournaments, resulting in automatic bids to the NCAA Tournament.

4. The Heisman Trophy, awarded to college football's best player each season, was first presented in 1935. The NCAA began recognizing an individual national scoring champion during the 1947–48 season, though unofficial records go back to 1935–36. The state of South Carolina dominated the national scoring champion award in 1952–57, when three players from the Palmetto State won the award over five successive seasons: Frank Selvy of Furman (1952–53 and 1953–54), Darrell Floyd of Furman (1954–55 and 1955–56), and Grady Wallace of USC (1957). Fredrick's 1980–81 title gave the state of South Carolina six national scoring champions, tied with Louisiana, and more than any other state except New York and Texas, which claim seven titles apiece. Additionally, Columbia native Xavier McDaniel took the title with Wichita State in 1984–85.

5. The 31–13 win at third-ranked UNC was the program's only win versus a top-five opponent prior to the Spurrier era and is one of only six such wins all-time. South Carolina owns the following other top-five wins: against number 1 Alabama, 35–21 (2010); number 3 Georgia, 20–17 (away, 2019); number 4 Ole Miss, 16–10 (2009); number 5 Georgia, 35–7 (2012); and number 5 Missouri, 27–24 (away, 2013).

6. Furman was in the midst of its football heyday, which included nine Southern Conference championships in twelve years between 1978 and 1990 under Sheridan and Jimmy Satterfield. The run was highlighted by the 1988 Division I-AA national championship under Satterfield.

7. Dantonio played at USC alongside his brother, Mark Dantonio, who would go on to great success as a head coach in the college ranks, including thirteen seasons at Michigan State between 2007–19, during which time he became the winningest coach in the history of the Spartan program with a record of 114–57 (.667).

9: The Man in Black

1. Dietzel's "Carpet the Cockpit" campaign provided fans with an opportunity to purchase squares of Astroturf along with certificates commemorating the donation. The program sold out in short order, largely funding the project. Dietzel admitted to the State's Bob Gillespie in a 2015 interview the decision to install Astroturf had been "a tremendous mistake," elaborating, "The traction was so good, it was easy for players to twist knees." Moreover early-season day games became untenable due to the tremendous heat absorbed and released by the asphalt base under the turf. "The only thing that saved us was playing at night," Dietzel said. Bob Gillespie, "History Runs Deep at Williams-Brice Stadium," Columbia State, April 15, 2015.

2. With fieldwork occupying Williams-Brice Stadium throughout the spring of 1984, Morrison's Gamecocks held a spring scrimmage at Spring Valley High School's Harry Parone Stadium, and the annual Garnet and Black spring game was played at Florence Memorial Stadium.

3. After failing to make NFL rosters in 1985 and 1986, Wilkes turned his considerable talents to professional wrestling, where he spent a decade performing at various times as the Trooper and the Patriot.

4. College football did not adopt overtime rules until 1996, amid rising discontent from coaches and fans over tied ballgames.

5. Gamecock football had previously reached eleventh in the AP poll under Coach Warren Giese in 1959, following a 3–0 start and week-three upset over a Fran Tarkington–led thirteenth-ranked Georgia Bulldog club, 24–14. Giese's Gamecocks had finished the 1958 season 7–3, after defeating powerful Duke, Georgia, and a tenth-ranked Clemson. Alex Hawkins connected with King Dixon for three touchdown passes in the Clemson game, propelling Carolina to a 24–7 win, one of the Gamecocks' finest victories in a long and storied rivalry. It was the Tigers' only regular-season loss on their way to an ACC championship and national title matchup with eventual champion LSU (coached by Paul Dietzel). The Gamecocks ranked fifteenth in the 1958 year-end poll.

On the strength of their 1958 performance, the 1959 team appeared in the AP preseason poll for the first time in program history at number 14, before climbing to 11. It was the high-water mark for the Gamecocks that season and for years to come. They lost their next two games, at UNC and in Columbia to Clemson in the final Big Thursday game. Griffin, *Encyclopedia of Gamecock Football.*

6. Gamecock great Bobby Bryant returned a Wolfpack punt ninety-eight yards for a touchdown in that 1966 game, which Carolina won 31–21. Bryant went on to play fourteen seasons in the Minnesota Vikings defensive secondary, a member of the Vikings' legendary "Purple People Eater" defense. Price, *'84 Gamecocks,* 118.

7. Carolina's first nationwide television appearance had been on November 1, 1980, when the Gamecocks' George Rogers squared off with the Bulldogs' freshman phenom Hershel Walker in Athens. The second time had been that same season, versus Pittsburgh in the Gator Bowl. The Gamecocks' other televised games, including the "pulled plug" game versus Pittsburgh in Columbia in 1981, had been regional telecasts. Before CBS jumped into the college football mix and ESPN and Atlanta's WTBS began offering national broadcasts via cable, ABC was the college football broadcasting behemoth. Price, *'84 Gamecocks,* 131.

8. Brown broke the previous program record for longest kickoff return, ninety-eight yards, set by King Dixon in the Gamecocks' legendary 27–21 upset of Texas in Austin on October 5, 1957. Tom Zipperly had tied Dixon's mark in an October 28, 1972, matchup versus NC State in Raleigh.

9. The Gamecocks returned to the Gator Bowl for a fourth time in 1987, a 30–13 loss to future SEC rival LSU. That contest capped a 0–8 start in bowl contests for the Carolina program, with four of those losses coming at Jacksonville's Gator Bowl. South Carolina has fared better in the years since, winning their first bowl game in the 1995 Carquest Bowl (following the 1994 season), a thrilling 24–21 victory over West Virginia, then of the Big East. They have won ten of seventeen bowl games starting with the 1995 matchup. The Gamecocks returned to the Gator Bowl in 2022, resulting in a hard fought 45–38 loss to Notre Dame.

10: The Backside of the Storm

1. Darmody was the final link to the McGuire era, having played as a freshman during McGuire's final season, 1979–80. Foster says he was "unofficially" part of that team as well, though he was not on scholarship and did not appear on the roster. His name did appear in a 1979 *Daily Gamecock* article in which team members signed their names in protest over the handling of McGuire's departure, lending credence to his story. He says coaches wanted to keep him close to the program while he put his academic affairs in order, though "going to school and not playing basketball was not my thing," and he soon left campus. He officially joined the program under first-year coach Bill Foster in 1980–81.

2. The Mountaineers were led by second-year head coach Sparky Woods. The thirty-two-year-old coach would become a very familiar name to Gamecock fans in a few years' time.

3. Mackie, a freshman on the 1987 squad, continued a string of steady and consistent placekickers in the Gamecock program. He replaced Scott Hagler, who had previously succeeded Mark Fleetwood. All three are still listed among the program's top ten all-time scorers. Mackie's 330 career points shattered George Rogers's career record of 202. His record stood until 2016, when it was broken by placekicker Elliott Fry (359). Fry's record was later broken by placekicker Parker White (368) in 2021. The Gamecocks' top four scoring leaders are all placekickers: White, Fry, Mackie, and Ryan Succop (251).

4. Payne went on to lead East Carolina, Oregon State, and USC Upstate at three different stops after leaving Felton's staff following the 1990–91 season. Smith went on to head coaching stops at Tulsa and Georgia before winning a national championship during his first season at the University of Kentucky (1997–98).

5. Dave Odom and Frank Martin each surpassed Felton's win total during their first five seasons, with one hundred and ninety-six wins, respectively.

6. Clark was later an assistant under Frank Martin at South Carolina between 2013 and 2020.

7. Carolina did not begin SEC participation in football until the 1992 season.

11: A New World Order

1. Wake Forest, Davidson, Richmond, and William and Mary joined the Southern Conference in 1936 to bolster membership following the departure of the SEC schools. Meanwhile, Sewanee departed the SEC in 1940 in a move to deemphasize athletics. Georgia Tech departed in 1964 and Tulane left in 1966; the SEC had thus long been stable at ten member schools at the dawn of the 1990s.

2. In 1960 the ACC implemented a minimum 750 SAT score for athletes, which it raised to 800 in 1964. This requirement, which was higher than the NCAA's minimum requirements, was at the crux of South Carolina's eventual departure in 1971.

The requirement was struck down by a federal court in August 1971, over a year after South Carolina's departure.

3. The SEC took a wait-and-see approach to South Carolina, initially contacting only Arkansas, Miami, and FSU to discuss expansion to twelve or possibly more if the University of Texas and Texas A&M could be persuaded to leave the Southwest Conference. Though Arkansas did not represent a lucrative television market, it was considered a linchpin for further movement within the Southwest Conference, namely the two Texas schools.

4. The NCAA imposed the "death penalty," or cancellation of the entire 1987 season, on the SMU football program because of repeated violations in the late 1970s and early 1980s. SMU was also unable to host home games during the 1988 season as part of the penalty, and the school ultimately forfeited that season. These penalties devastated the SMU program, as it only fielded one winning team over the next two decades. It would be more than three decades before SMU reappeared in a top twenty-five poll during the 2019 season.

5. Washburn and Kephart, who were assistants at USC from 1982 until 1988, were sentenced to three months in a halfway house and three-year probationary terms. Kurucz, who was an assistant from 1982 until 1986, received the harshest sentence for his role, six months in a halfway house and a three-year probation. Associated Press, August 11, 1989.

6. *Sports Illustrated* writer Rick Telander, who cowrote the Chaikin article in October 1988, expressed dismay over the NCAA's decision in a July 27, 1990, interview with David Newton of the *State*. "Really, for the life of me, I can't figure it out," he said. "If that doesn't merit some kind of public embarrassment, it's hard to say what big-time college football is all about."

7. In a September 26, 1990, interview with former FSU president Bernard Sliger in the *Orlando Sentinel,* columnist Larry Guest wrote that had the SEC pursued FSU more definitively early in the process, FSU would have joined. When Sliger's close personal friend ACC commissioner Gene Corrigan made it clear that FSU was the ACC's sole target for expansion, the FSU faculty solidly aligned behind that conference and its higher academic profile. Sliger noted that head football coach Bobby Bowden was not vocal about his conference preference.

8. When pressed for details about the meeting, including the menu for lunch, an upbeat and indulgent Smith revealed that lunch included gazpacho, salad, salmon with wild rice . . . squash . . . and for dessert, peanut butter pie. David Newton, "SEC Talks Make USC Optimistic," *Columbia State*, September 21, 1990.

9. The USC–Virginia Tech series spans twenty games, between 1905 and 1991, with Carolina holding a 11–7–2 advantage. Nine of the matchups were played during the independent era, the final matchup resulting in a 28–21 Gamecock win on September 21, 1991. The Gamecocks and Hokies have not met since South Carolina began SEC play in 1992.

10. Dingle's four rushing touchdowns versus the Hokies set a USC record, which he held until Kevin Harris's five rushing touchdowns versus Ole Miss on November 14, 2020.

11. The SEC never did add men's soccer. USC's Berson built Gamecock soccer from its former club team status, starting varsity competition in 1978, and developed a highly competitive program. The Gamecocks went on to a second-place national finish in 1993, losing 1–0 in the College Cup final to Virginia. Berson's Gamecocks ultimately joined Conference USA for men's soccer, where it competes with Kentucky, the only other SEC school boasting varsity men's soccer. In thirty-eight seasons at the helm, Berson compiled a 500–256–76 (.646) record at USC, making him the second winningest coach in Division I history behind Indiana's Jerry Yeagley and his 544 wins. Berson's overall total of 511 wins includes a one-season stint at the Citadel in 1977.

The SEC does offer a championship in women's soccer, and South Carolina first fielded a team in 1995 under head coach Sue Kelly. Since 2001 head coach Shelly Smith has led USC women's soccer to five SEC championships.

12. South Carolina's 1969–70 basketball squad is one of only eight teams in ACC history to go undefeated in regular-season conference play. Frank McGuire was also responsible for the first team to accomplish that milestone, with his NCAA champion 1957 UNC team. Other undefeated ACC squads include UNC ('57, '84, '87), NC State ('73, '74), and Duke ('63, '99).

Epilogue

1. Notes on USC's championship history: gamecocksonline.com/history/.

2. Equestrian championships are sanctioned by the National Collegiate Equestrian Association.

3. The SEC abandoned divisional alignment in basketball beginning with the 2011–12 season.

4. The corporate sponsor for Omaha's College World Series venue changed in 2021, and it is now known as Charles Schwab Field.

5. The 2020 Summer Olympic Games were held in 2021 due to a postponement over COVID-19.

6. In 2022 the SEC announced nearly $55 million in distributions per conference member, a record for the conference.

7. Nicole Auerbach, "Will the Power 5 Become the Power 2?," *The Athletic*, May 29, 2022, https://theathletic.com/3215360/2022/03/29/.

8. The super conference concept is emergent and loosely defined.

SOURCES

1: Storms in The Southland

Description of 1971 ACC championship game: Don Barton and Bob Fulton, *Frank McGuire: The Life and Times of a Basketball Legend* (Columbia, SC: Summerhouse, 1995), 109–10; Bob Cole, *Columbia State*, March 14, 1971; J. Samuel Walker, *ACC Basketball: The Story of the Rivalries, Traditions, and Scandals of the First Two Decades of the Atlantic Coast Conference* (Chapel Hill: University of North Carolina Press, 2014), 274–75.

Philip Grose, "Associate AD, Cage Coach—It's Official Now: Frank McGuire Accepts Dual USC Athletics Job," *Columbia State*, March 13, 1964.

"Cage coaches": Robert W. Peterson, "When the Court Was a Cage," *Sports Illustrated*, November 11, 1991, https://vault.si.com/vault/1991/11/11/.

McGuire's departure from UNC: Walker, *ACC Basketball*, 132–33, 190–92.

USC Basketball, 1964–65 season: Barton and Fulton, *Frank McGuire*, 84.

Grosso controversy: Barton and Fulton, *Frank McGuire*, 84–85; Walker, *ACC Basketball*, 194, 196–97.

Joe Whitlock, "Paul Dietzel Signs Ten-Year Contract; 'New Era in USC Athletics Begins,'" *Columbia State*, April 7, 1966.

Jeff Denberg, "Violation of ACC Regulations Takes Away Gamecocks' Only Football Championship," *Columbia State*, July 30, 1966.

Dietzel quote about 1965 season: Paul Dietzel, *Call Me a Coach: A Life in College Football* (Baton Rouge: Louisiana State University Press, 2008), 143.

1.6 GPA and 800 admission rules: Walker, *ACC Basketball*, 310–13.

Race and the 800 rule: Walker, *ACC Basketball*, 314–15.

Integration at USC: Henry H. Lesesne, *History of the University of South Carolina, 1940–2000* (Columbia: University of South Carolina Press, 2001); "Gamecocks Celebrate First African-American Student-Athletes," *Gamecocks Online*, November 18, 2013.

USC Board of Trustees statement regarding withdrawal from the ACC: *Columbia Record*, March 30, 1971.

2: Build It, and They Will Come

Ron Morris, "Gamecock Whodunnit? Was Coach Frank McGuire Involved in the 1968 Field House Fire?" *Columbia State*, March 26, 2015.

Conditions at Carolina Field House: Walker, *ACC Basketball*, 189.

Jay A. Gross, "USC Coliseum Sees First Game," *Columbia State*, December 1, 1968.

Elizabeth White, "Gamecock Roost Is the New Home of USC Athletics," *Columbia State*, April 17, 1969.

"USC Outlines $112 Million Expansion Plan," *Columbia Record*, December 8, 1969.

Carolina Stadium history: Lesesne, *History of the University of South Carolina*, 66–67.

Dot Tringali, "Stadium Naming to Be Decided," *Columbia Record*, January 4, 1971.

Kent Krell, "Cost of Athletics Doubles in Decade," *Columbia State*, June 13, 1971.

3: Into the Wilderness

Don Barton, *The Carolina-Clemson Game (1896–1966)*. Columbia: State Printing, 1967.

Charlie Senn, "Terps Nip Carolina," *Gamecock*, May 17, 1971.

Teddy Heffner, "USC Eliminates Virginia in ACC," *Columbia State*, May 10, 1971.

Herman Helms, "Dick Harris Keys Upset with Return and Blocked Punt," *Columbia State*, September 12, 1971.

Herman Helms, "Shining Hour for Defense, Dietzel," *Columbia State*, September 13, 1971.

Bob Spear, "Dietzel Says Gamecocks 'Had Almost No Offense,'" *Columbia State*, September 19, 1971.

Dan Klores, *Roundball Culture: South Carolina Basketball* (Huntsville, AL: AM, 1980).

Bob Cole, "USC Tackles Auburn in Opener of 'Most Challenging Schedule,'" *Columbia State*, December 1, 1971.

Bob Cole, "3rd-Rated Gamecocks Nudge Virginia Tech," *Columbia State*, December 19, 1971.

USC basketball media guides (1971–72, 1979–80).

USC football media guides (1971, 1972).

Curry Kirkpatrick, "You Know Me, Al' 'Right, Frank, and I Hate to Do It," *Sports Illustrated*, January 17, 1971.

It Was a Very Good Year, documentary film, 1972–73, USC Libraries Digital Collection.

David Caraviello, "Gamecocks vs. Marquette: NCAA Matchup Rekindles Memories of Super '70's Series with Al and Frank McGuire," *Charleston Post and Courier*, March 16, 2017.

Bob Cole, "Gamecocks Rally behind Joyce, Nudge Indiana," *Columbia State*, January 10, 1972.

Herman Helms, "New Coach Entitled to Fair Chance," *Columbia State*, December 15, 1974.

"Celebrities, Coaches to Honor McGuire," *Columbia State*, March 22, 1977.

Herman Helms, "Memories of Bones," *Columbia State*, March 27, 1977.

Bob Cole, "USC Trustees Name Arena for McGuire," *Columbia State*, April 21, 1977.

Dwane Morrison at Georgia Tech: "Dwane Morrison," *Wikipedia*, https://en .wikipedia.org/wiki/Dwane_Morrison (accessed March 5, 2023).

"Former USC Athletics Director Mike McGee Dies," *Columbia State*, August 16, 2019.

Jack Guenther, "56,000 Fans Stunned as OSC Whips Duke Devils in Rose Bowl," *Eugene (OR) Register-Guard*, January 2, 1942.

4: Legends, Logos, Mascots, and Traditions

Dan Lackey, "The Evolution of a Mascot," *Columbia State Magazine*, August 31, 1986.

Bob Gillespie, "Drawn to Sports," *Columbia State*, August 26, 2007.

"Block C Logo—New Look at USC," *Columbia Record*, April 11, 1975.

"Logo for the Birds," editorial, *Columbia State*, October 15, 1983.

First mention of Chicken Curse: Doug Nye, "The Legendary 'Chicken Curse,'" *Columbia State*, October 28, 1977.

Doug Nye, "Dixon Knows Power of Chicken Curse," *Columbia State*, August 26, 1990.

Dave Moniz, "USC Fans Seek Black Magic Cure to Chicken Curse," *Columbia State*, August 15, 1992.

Becky Lafitte, "The Birth of Big Spur," *Columbia State*, November 11, 1979.

Jeff Vrabel, "Lions and Tigers and Bears (and Zips and Banana Slugs and Purple Cows)—Oh My!" *NCAA Champion Magazine*, summer 2017, http://s3.amazonaws .com/static.ncaa.org/static/.

Chris Horn, "The Evolution of Cocky," *Remembering the Days—A UofSC Podcast*, August 26, 2020.

Kelly Hembrick, "Routh Enjoys Role as Carolina Mascot," *Gamecock*, January 27, 1982.

"Mr. Popularity—Gamecock Mascot, Cocky, Crowd-Pleaser in Omaha," *Columbia State*, June 8, 1982.

Sharon Kelly, "Gamecock Fans Put the Spurs to New Mascot," *Columbia Record*, November 25, 1980.

"History and Biography of Cocky" (2014). http://getcocky.ad.sc.edu/Pages/history .php.

Andy Demetra, "Did Paul Dietzel Hide His Initials in Gamecock Logo?," *Inside the Chart—Spurs & Feathers*, October 2, 2013.

Ron Wenzell, "Bill Smith, Designer of USC New Football Uniforms," *Columbia State*, March 20, 1983.

Bob Gillespie, "Woods Goes with Garnet," *Columbia State*, March 20, 1989.

Jessica Ruffin, "May the Ghost Be with You: Legend of the Talladega Jinx," NASCAR. com, October 31, 2017. https://www.nascar.com/news-media/2017/10/31/legend-of -the-talladega-jinx-halloween.

"Carolina Fight Song (aka Old Fight Song), Sheet Music." USC Libraries Digital Collections. https://digital.tcl.sc.edu/digital/collection/mus/id/625/rec/1 (accessed March 14, 2023).

"*Also sprach Zarathustra.*" Wikipedia. https://en.wikipedia.org/wiki/Also_sprach _Zarathustra (accessed March 14, 2023).

David Cheal, "Also Sprach Zarathustra—A Fanfare That Has Echoed Down through the Years," *Financial Times,* September 28, 2020.

Tommy Suggs, "A Gamecock for a Lifetime," *Gamecocks Online,* August 25, 2014. https://gamecocksonline.com/news/2014/08/25/tommy-suggs-a-gamecock -for-a-lifetime/.

Kristi Dosh, "Significant Growth in College Apparel," *ESPN.com,* September 13, 2013.

Patrick Flynn, "Nike Marketing Strategy: A Company to Imitate," honors thesis, University at Albany, State University of New York, May 2015.

Mike Livingston and Mike Lewis, "Swaying Has Fans Worried," *Columbia State,* October 7, 1986.

Michael Lewis, "Bad Vibrations—Harmonic Resonance Makes Some Stadiums Sway," *Columbia State,* October 7, 1986.

Scott Johnson, "Extra Study of Stadium Encouraged," *Columbia State,* October 22, 1986.

Michael Lewis, "Lookout—Fans Wanting to Sway May Be Taken Away," *Columbia State,* November 15, 1986.

Bill Robinson, "USC to Expand Stadium's Use—Board Members Allocate Funds to Shore up Wobbly Upper Deck," *Columbia State,* December 8, 1989.

Cory Nightingale, "Those Brilliant, Garnet Cockabooses Are South Carolina's Tailgating Institution," Saturdays Down South.com, 2016. https://www.saturday downsouth.com/south-Carolina-football/cockabooses-give-south-Carolina-unique -gameday-tradition/.

"South Carolina Brawl Fosters Louisville Win," *Washington Post,* February 21, 1988.

Tom Fladung, "Cockaboose Railroad," *Columbia State,* March 28, 1990.

Bob Gillespie, "Nothing Like a Cockaboose," *Columbia State,* March 14, 2015.

5: A National Power Emerges

Buddy Horres, "Richardson, USC Baseball—Living Legends," *Gamecock,* February 25, 1982.

Sarge Frye biography and history of Sarge Frye Field: 1993 USC baseball media guide, 82.

Jack Powers biography: 1971 USC football media guide.

First box score: *Columbia State,* April 9, 1892.

Jeff Wilkinson, "The Other Ballpark Debates: City's History Repeats Itself," *Columbia State*, April 10, 2014.

John Hammond Moore, *Columbia and Richland County: A South Carolina Community, 1740–1990* (Columbia: University of South Carolina Press, 1993).

Mark Bryant, *Baseball in Columbia* (Columbia: Arcadia, 2004).

"History of Elmwood Park." historicelmwoodpark.org/history/ (accessed March 14, 2023).

Bobby Richardson, telephone interview with author, June 23, 2021.

June Raines, telephone interview with author, January 11, 2022.

Noah Watson, "First Black Athletes at USC Laid Groundwork for Today's Athletics Department," *Gamecock*, April 25, 2021.

2022 USC baseball media guide. https://s3.amazonaws.com/gamecocksonline.com /documents/2021/12/13/2022bsbrecordbook.pdf.

6: Pullets, Chicks, and Lady Gamecocks

Richard C. Bell, "A History of Women in Sport Prior to Title IX," *Sport Journal* 20, March 14, 2008, https://thesportjournal.org/article/a-history-of-women-in-sport -prior-to-title-ix/.

Greg Hadley, "From Chicks to Champions: How South Carolina Women's Basketball Got Its Start," *Columbia State*, December 9, 2017.

South Carolina women's basketball history: "Women's Basketball," *Gamecocks Online*, April 18, 2002, https://gamecocksonline.com/news/2002/04/18/south-carolina -women-s-basketball-history/.

"Gamecocks Tab Parsons," *Columbia State*, April 10, 1977.

Gene Able, "Mason Quits, Suggest Violations," *Columbia State*, January 21, 1981.

Bob Cole, "Magazine: Lesbian Affair Led to Parsons's Dismissal," *Columbia State*, February 3, 1982.

Margaret O'Shea, "Story about Parsons Private, Witness Says," *Columbia State*, May 16, 1984.

Ben Williams, "1984 The Pam Parsons Scandal," My Past Gay Musings and Stories, July 23, 2013, http://benwilliamswritings.blogspot.com/2013/07/1984-pam-parson -scandal-21-march-2005.html.

Nancy Wilson, telephone interview with author, January 11, 2022.

Kristina Buck, telephone interview with author, August 11, 2020.

Marsi McAlister, telephone interview with author, August 3, 2020.

Margaret O'Shea, "Witness Says Parsons Admitted Love Affair," *Columbia State*, May 19, 1984.

Margaret O'Shea, "Lieber Stands behind Parsons Story," *Columbia State*, May 23, 1984.

Mike Lough, "Rumors, Allegations Fly in Parsons Story," *Gamecock*, February 4, 1982.

Mike Lough, "A Few Specially-Treated Players Found Kelly's Fairness, Well, Unfair," *Gamecock,* February 19, 1982.

Jill Lieber, "Stormy Weather in South Carolina," *Sports Illustrated,* February 8, 1982.

Margaret O'Shea, "Just Friends or Lesbian Lovers," *Columbia State,* May 27, 1984.

Michelle Burchette, "Internal Conflicts Hit Gamecocks," *Gamecock,* January 16, 1981.

"Mason Leaves Gamecocks," *Gamecock,* January 21, 1981.

Mike Lough, "Opinion Strong Concerning Resignation," *Gamecock,* January 20, 1982.

Mike Lough, "Roster Dwindles to Seven," *Gamecock,* January 25, 1982.

Mike Lough, "Returning Players, Recruits Solidify Women's Team," *Gamecock,* October 12, 1981.

Mike Lough, "Women's Team Young but Very Talented," *Gamecock,* November 19, 1981.

Tracy Mixon, "College of Charleston Coach Joins USC," *Gamecock,* April 2, 1984.

Liz Chandler, "Coach Has Left a Sad Legacy," *Charlotte Observer,* April 14, 1996.

Parson's appearance at 1998 House Committee Hearing: William J. Clinton Impeachment Trial. CSPAN. December 1, 1998, https://www.c-span.org/video/.

"Embattled Terry Kelly Quits USC," *Columbia Record,* March 9, 1984.

Marsi McAlister, telephone interview with author, August 3, 2020.

Nancy Wilson, telephone interview with author, January 11, 2022.

7: Any Port in a Storm

Richard Chesley, "Metro History: Short, Successful," *Columbia State,* November 20, 1983.

Alex Royals, "The Best Conference That Never Was," forgotten5.com (site inactive April 19, 2023), August 28, 2017.

Herman Helms, "Metro 7 Would Help USC," *Columbia State,* August 5, 1979.

Randy Laney, "USC Won't Seek Reaffiliation Now," *Columbia State,* January 23, 1976.

Bob Cole, "ACC Heads to Unveil Expansion Guidelines," *Columbia State,* May 19, 1976.

Dysfunction within the athletics department: Lesesne, *A History of the University of South Carolina,* 266–67.

USC's move from three athletics directors to two: Lesesne, *A History of the University of South Carolina,* 252–53.

Herman Helms, "Right Decision for Carolina," *Columbia State,* January 1, 1982.

"Holtz Not Leaving Arkansas," *Columbia State,* December 15, 1981.

Bob Cole, "USC Fires Coach Jim Carlen," *Columbia State,* December 13, 1981.

Herman Helms, "Late Season Collapse a Carlen Trademark," *Columbia State,* December 7, 1981.

John Feinstein, *Forever's Team* (New York: Villiard Books, 1990), 219–26, 361–66.

8: Good Times, Bad Times

Jimmy Foster, telephone interviews with author, November 19 and 24, 2020.

Will Vandervort, "Tigers Wear Orange Pants for the First Time," *Clemson Insider,* May 9, 2020.

"Division I Men's Basketball Records," NCAA.org. http://fs.ncaa.org/Docs/stats/m _basketball_RB/2021/D1.pdf (accessed March 14, 2023).

"List of Division I Men's Basketball Scoring Leaders," Wikiwand. https:// www.wikiwand.com/en/List_of_NCAA_Division_I_men%27s_basketball_season _scoring_leaders#/References.

"Heisman Trophy Winners List," Heisman.com. https://www.heisman.com/heisman -winners/ (accessed March 14, 2023).

Sam Goldaper, "Frank McGuire Is Given Garden Post," *New York Times,* February 28, 1980.

Seth Emerson, "Why Does Georgia Only Claim Two National Titles When It Could Have More?" *The Athletic,* March 30, 2020.

Bob Gillespie, "Richard Bell, One-and-Done as USC Coach: How 1982 Shaped Him, Players, Program," *Columbia State,* July 25, 2020.

Don Barton, *They Wore Garnet and Black: Inside Carolina's Quest for Gridiron Glory* (Columbia: Spur, 1985).

Doug Nye, "Race for Heisman," *Columbia Record,* October 1, 1980.

Herman Helms, "Georgia Holds off USC for 13–10 Win," *Columbia State,* November 2, 1980.

Herman Helms, "Rogers Receives Walker's Vote," *Columbia State,* November 2, 1980.

Herman Helms, "Harper-Smith Aerial Act Saves Gamecocks," *Columbia State,* November 16, 1980.

Herman Helms, "Underwood's Thefts Ignite Tigers, Trigger Clemson by Gamecocks 27–6," *Columbia State,* November 23, 1980.

Herman Helms, "Pros Eying Zam," *Columbia State,* February 1, 1981.

Bob Gillespie, "Rebirth," *Columbia Record,* February 3, 1981.

Bob Cole, "USC Wallops Eagles, Eyes Tournaments," *Columbia State,* February 24, 1981.

"All District Team Named, Fredrick, Nance Chosen," *Columbia State,* March 3, 1981.

Bob Gillespie, "Foster, Gamecocks Try to Forget Disappointment," *Columbia State,* March 10, 1981.

Doug Nye, "No Bid for USC," *Columbia Record,* March 9, 1981.

"Rogers on the Record," *Columbia Record,* September 4, 1980.

Herman Helms, "Rogers Strengthens Bid," *Columbia State,* September 22, 1980.

Bob Spear, "Defense Told Tale," *Columbia State,* September 22, 1980.

Herman Helms, "Henderson, Finney Defensive Gems Trigger USC Past Michigan 17–14," *Columbia State,* September 28, 1980.

"USC, Clemson Playing for Pride," *Columbia State,* November 22, 1980.

Dave Monitz, "Rogers Gets a Hero's Welcome," *Columbia Record,* December 2, 1980.

Will Lester, "USC Honors Rogers," *Columbia State,* December 16, 1980.

Katherine King, "Rogers to Be Depicted on Mural," *Columbia Record,* March 7, 1981.

Bob Cole, "USC Fires Coach Jim Carlen," *Columbia State,* December 13, 1980.

Doug Nye, "Carlen Could Never Conquer Himself," *Columbia Record,* December 14, 1981.

"Bell Throws Hat into Ring," *Columbia Record,* December 16, 1981.

Herman Helms, "USC to Take More Sensible Approach," *Columbia State,* December 20, 1981.

Herman Helms, "Bell Will Be Named USC Coach," *Columbia State,* January 9, 1982.

Bob Spear, "Confident Bell Takes Charge of Gamecocks," *Columbia State,* January 10, 1982.

Herman Helms, "Bell's Debut Pleasant; USC Routs Pacific," *Columbia State,* September 5, 1982.

Herman Helms, "Furman Erupts, Ambushes Gamecocks," *Columbia State,* October 17, 1982.

Bob Gillespie, "Beaten, but Not Bowed," *Columbia State,* November 21, 1982.

Bill Elchenberger, "Marcum: USC Won't Pay Remainder of Bell's pact," *Columbia Record,* December 2, 1982

Bob Gillespie, "USC Players' Reaction to New Coach Was Favorable," *Columbia Record,* December 6, 1980.

"Bell Third Former Coach to Sue USC This Year," *Columbia Record,* May 24, 1983.

Herman Helms, "USC Batters 3rd-Ranked UNC 31–13," *Columbia State,* October 24, 1981.

Herman Helms, "Carlen's Words Differ with His Actions," *Columbia State,* October 27, 1981.

Bob Spear, "Bowl Visions Dim as USC Falters 23–21," *Columbia State,* November 8, 1981.

Ernie Trubiano, "Air Woes," *Columbia State,* November 22, 1981.

Herman Helms, "Late Season Collapse a Carlen Trademark," *Columbia State,* December 7, 1981.

Bob Spear, "Hawaii Pounds 'Generous' Gamecocks," *Columbia State,* December 7, 1981.

9: The Man in Black

Tom Price, *The '84 Gamecocks: Fire Ants and Black Magic* (Columbia: University of South Carolina Press, 1985).

Bob Gillespie, "Evans' Return to USC Brings Mixed Feelings," *Columbia Record,* September 2, 1983.

Herman Helms, "Gamecocks Rip Southern Cal 38–14," *Columbia State,* October 2, 1983.

Ernie Trubiano, "Two USC's Swap Roles," *Columbia State,* October 2, 1983.

Bob Cole, "Garnet-Clad USC Tops State," *Columbia State,* October 30, 1983.

YouTube. "Going for It All (1984)." USC recruiting film featuring Pat Summerall. https://www.youtube.com/watch?v=IXSqiWCnCvU.

Herman Helms, "Late Burst Halts Gamecocks' Bid," *Columbia State,* November 6, 1983.

Bob Cole, "Gamecocks Scuttle Navy 31–7," *Columbia State,* November 13, 1983.

Harold Martin, "Another Chapter, Same Verse," *Columbia State,* November 20, 1983.

"Rugs Gone, Paving the Way for Real Grass at stadium," *Columbia State,* December 6, 1983.

Bob Gillespie, "History Runs Deep at Williams-Brice Stadium," *Columbia State,* April 10, 2015.

Herman Helms, "Gamecocks Shock #10 Georgia 17–10," *Columbia State,* September 30, 1984.

Doug Nye, "A Big, Big Victory for Morrison and USC," *Columbia Record,* October 1, 1984.

Bob Gillespie, "Stopping Third-and-Short Plays Added Up to Gamecock Victory," *Columbia Record,* October 1, 1984.

Bob Gillespie, "USC's 'Death Blow' Levels KSU," *Columbia Record,* October 8, 1984.

Jack McCallum, "Black Day for Notre Dame," *Sports Illustrated,* October 19, 1984.

Teddy Heffner, "Fruitful Trip: Morrison Convinced Kent Hagood to Return to Carolina," *Columbia State,* November 2, 1984.

Bob Gillespie, "Gamecocks Escape with Dream Intact," *Columbia Record,* November 5, 1984.

Doug Nye, "USC's Joe Morrison Unaffected by Success," *Columbia Record,* November 7, 1984.

Herman Helms, "Disappointed Florida State Praises USC," *Columbia State*, November 11, 1984.

Andrew Miller, "Loss to Navy in 1984 Still Bothers Former USC Football Players," *Charleston Post and Courier,* September 15, 2011.

Bob Gillespie, "Gamecock Offense 'Didn't Do the Job,'" *Columbia Record,* November 19, 1984.

Herman Helms, "Gamecocks Overhaul Clemson 22–21," *Columbia State,* November 25, 1984.

10: The Backside of the Storm

Josh Kendall, "What if Joe Morrison's Story Had a Different Ending?" *The Athletic,* July 7, 2020.

John Chandler Griffin, *The Encyclopedia of Gamecock Football, 1892–1994* (Lancaster, SC: Palmetto, 1995).

USC AP Poll history: Sports Reference.com. https://www.sports-reference.com/cfb /schools.

Jimmy Foster, telephone interviews with author, November 19 and 24, 2020.

Joe Morrison obituary, *New York Times,* February 6, 1989.

Teddy Heffner, "Heart Attack Kills USC's Morrison," *Columbia State,* February 6, 1989.

Bertram Rantin, "Roost Engulfed by Silence, Tears," *Columbia State,* February 6, 1989.

Bob Gillespie, "He Seemed like His Usual Self," *Columbia State,* February 9, 1989.

Bob Gillespie, "USC Routs Southern Miss," *Columbia State,* February 7, 1989.

Bob Gillespie, "Morrison's Legacy Looms 20 Years after Death," *Columbia State,* February 8, 2009.

Teddy Heffner, "Ellis' Memory of Morrison Holds Little about Football," *Columbia State,* February 7, 1989.

Salley McInerney, "'Coach Joe' Mourned by Friends from All Walks of Life," *Columbia State,* February 7, 1989.

"Morrison Was OK Moments before Collapse," *Columbia State,* February 7, 1989.

"Morrison Endeared Many with His Laid-Back Low-Key Style," *Columbia State,* February 7, 1989.

Bob Cole, "Friends, Fans Mourn Coach Joe," *Columbia State,* February 11, 1989.

Bob Gillespie, "Dunn Throws Hat into Coaching Ring," *Columbia State,* February 14, 1989.

Herman Helms, "USC Coaching Job Is Sheridan's to Take or Turn Down," *Columbia State,* February 14, 1989.

Herman Helms, "Sheridan No Longer in Picture at USC," *Columbia State,* February 17, 1989.

Herman Helms, "With Sheridan out, Satterfield, DeBerry Next on USC List," *Columbia State,* February 17, 1989.

Bob Cole, "Woods Sets Three Goals for Gamecocks," *Columbia State,* February 22, 1989.

Herman Helms, "Age One of Reasons USC Picked Woods," *Columbia State,* February 21, 1989.

Bob Gillespie, "Bestwick to Be New USC AD," *Columbia Record,* March 30, 1988.

Bob Cole, "Bestwick Replaced," *Columbia State,* October 4, 1988.

Bob Cole, "Overwork Caught Up with Bestwick," *Columbia State,* October 5, 1988.

Rick Scoppe, "Athletics Director Dixon 'Sick and Tired of Turmoil,'" *Columbia State,* October 26, 1988.

Maureen Shurr, "Dixon Gets Post at USC," *Columbia State,* October 28, 1988.

Bob Gillespie, "Bread-and-Butter Play Turned Sour," *Columbia State,* October 5, 1986.

Doug Nye, "Pitt Says Gamecocks Smaller, Weaker in '85," *Columbia Record,* October 5, 1985.

Teddy Heffner, "Georgia Tech Wrecks USC's Dream Season," *Columbia State,* October 16, 1988.

Herman Helms, "Saturday's Shameful Performance Worst of All in Gamecock History," *Columbia State*, October 16, 1988.

Bob Gillespie and Teddy Heffner, "Ex-Player Says USC Coaches New Steroids Used," *Columbia State*, October 19, 1988.

Tommy Chaikin and Rick Telander, "The Nightmare of Steroids," *Sports Illustrated*, October 24, 1988.

Bob Cole, "Grand Jury to Study Ex-USC Player's Drug Claims," *Columbia State*, October 20, 1988.

Pete Iacobelli, "USC Endured Steroid 'Nightmare,'" *Go Upstate*, August 27, 2005.

Herman Helms, "South Carolina Gives Morrison Special Win," *Columbia State*, October 30, 1989.

David Newton, "Ellis Immediately 'Knew It Was Serious,'" *Columbia State*, October 29, 1989.

David Newton, "Gamecocks Lose QB for Season in 20–10 Defeat," *Columbia State*, October 29, 1989.

David Cloninger, "Ex-Gamecock Football Coach Sparky Woods, Now at UNC, Reflects on Tumultuous Years at USC," *Charleston Post and Courier*, August 26, 2019.

Herman Helms, "Happy Young Coach Thinks of Others," *Columbia State*, March 30, 1986.

Bob Gillespie, "Gamecocks Welcome Felton Home," *Columbia Record*, March 25, 1986.

David Newton, "Felton Surprised by Firing," *Columbia State*, May 14, 1991.

David Newton, "USC to Discuss Basketball Job with Vanderbilt's Fogler," *Columbia State*, June 4, 1991.

Bob Gillespie, "USC Taking a Look at Two 52-Year-Old Coaches," *Columbia State*, June 26, 1991.

David Newton, "Rutgers' Wenzel Decides to Turn Down Gamecocks," *Columbia State*, July 9, 1991.

Bob Cole, "USC Tosses the Ball to Newton," *Columbia State*, July 11, 1991.

11: A New World Order

"30 Years Ago: How May 1990 Reshaped the SEC," SECsports.com, May 2020, https://www.secsports.com/.

"SEC Is Strong Despite Getting Less than It Bargained For," *Los Angeles Times*, October 7, 1990.

Matthew Gailani, "SEC: The Creation and Expansion of the Southeastern Conference," Tennessee State Museum blog, August 23, 2021, https://tnmuseum.org/.

Bret Weisband, "A Brief History of the Southeastern Conference," Saturday Down South, 2015, https://www.saturdaydownsouth.com/sec-football/.

Bob Gillespie, "SEC Keeps an Eye on Metro's Moves," *Columbia State*, May 6, 1990.

Bob Spear, "Metro Football Idea Offers USC Too Little," *Columbia State,* May 9, 1990.

Bob Gillespie, "USC's Athletic Future," *Columbia State,* May 20, 1990.

Doug Nye, "Metro Football on TV Might Lack Dollars to Make Sense," *Columbia State,* May 21, 1990.

Bob Cole, "ACC: League Not Interested in Expansion," *Columbia State,* May 22, 1990.

Bob Cole, "Curry Discounts Immediacy of Southeastern Expansion," *Columbia State,* June 2, 1990.

Bob Gillespie, "USC Concerned with NCAA, Marcum," *Columbia State,* June 22, 1990.

Bob Gillespie, "NCAA Hands Down Its Decision," *Columbia State,* July 26, 1990.

David Newton, "SI's Telander Dismayed by Decision," *Columbia State,* July 27, 1990.

David Newton, "USC Receives SEC's 'Expression of Interest," *Columbia State,* July 14, 1990.

Bill Robinson, "Bestwick Gets Settlement, New Job," *Columbia State,* September 5, 1990.

David Newton, "USC President Smith Quote about Guarded Optimism," *Columbia State,* September 8, 1990.

David Newton, "ACC Invites Florida State: USC Hopes for SEC Bid," *Columbia State,* September 14, 1990.

David Newton, "USC May Hold Edge for SEC's Purposes," *Columbia State,* September 15, 1990.

David Newton, "SEC Talks Make USC Optimistic," *Columbia State,* September 21, 1990.

Amanda Mays, "USC Coaches Hail Move, Cite Challenges of the SEC," *Columbia State,* September 26, 1990.

Larry Guest, "SEC's Offer Year Too Late," *Orlando Sentinel,* September 26, 1990.

INDEX

ABOUT THE AUTHOR

ALAN PIERCY is a freelance writer who currently resides in Raleigh, North Carolina. Piercy is a Columbia, South Carolina, native; a 1995 graduate of the University of South Carolina; and lifelong Gamecock fan. He hosts a collection of his general interest writings online at *Yellow Dog Journal,* and his *South by Southeast: A Gamecock History* online newsletter features stories spanning decades of Gamecock athletics.